The Hidden Power of Illustrator CS:
Web Graphics Techniques

The Hidden Power™ of Illustrator® CS:
Web Graphics Techniques

STEVE KURTH

SAN FRANCISCO | LONDON

Associate Publisher: Dan Brodnitz
Acquisitions Editor: Bonnie Bills
Developmental Editor: Jim Compton
Production Editor: Erica Yee
Technical Editor: Matt LeClair
Copyeditor: Liz Welch
Compositor: Maureen Forys, Happenstance-Type-O-Rama
Proofreader: Emily Hsuan, Amy Rasmussen, Nancy Riddiough
Indexer: Ted Laux
Book Designer: Caryl Gorska, Gorska Design
Cover Designer: Ingalls + Associates
Cover Illustrator/Photographer: Øivind Sandum

Copyright © 2004 SYBEX Inc., 1151 Marina Village Parkway, Alameda, CA 94501. World rights reserved. No part of this publication may be stored in a retrieval system, transmitted, or reproduced in any way, including but not limited to photocopy, photograph, magnetic, or other record, without the prior agreement and written permission of the publisher.

Library of Congress Card Number: 2003107708

ISBN: 0-7821-4158-7

SYBEX and the SYBEX logo are either registered trademarks or trademarks of SYBEX Inc. in the United States and/or other countries.

TRADEMARKS: SYBEX has attempted throughout this book to distinguish proprietary trademarks from descriptive terms by following the capitalization style used by the manufacturer.

The author and publisher have made their best efforts to prepare this book, and the content is based upon final release software whenever possible. Portions of the manuscript may be based upon pre-release versions supplied by software manufacturer(s). The author and the publisher make no representation or warranties of any kind with regard to the completeness or accuracy of the contents herein and accept no liability of any kind including but not limited to performance, merchantability, fitness for any particular purpose, or any losses or damages of any kind caused or alleged to be caused directly or indirectly from this book.

Manufactured in the United States of America

10 9 8 7 6 5 4 3 2 1

Dear Reader,

Thank you for choosing *The Hidden Power of Illustrator CS*. This book is part of a new wave of Sybex graphics books, all written by outstanding authors—artists and teachers who really know their stuff and have a clear vision of the audience they're writing for.

Founded in 1976, Sybex is the oldest independent computer book publisher. More than twenty-five years later, we're committed to producing a full line of exceptional graphics books. With each title, we're working hard to set a new standard for the industry. From the paper we print on, to the writers and photographers we work with, our goal is to bring you the best graphics books available.

I hope you see all that is reflected in these pages. I'd be very interested to hear your comments and get your feedback on how we're doing. To let us know what you think about this, or any other Sybex book, please visit us at www.sybex.com. Once there, go to the product page, click on Submit a Review, and fill out the questionnaire. Your input is greatly appreciated.

Please also visit www.sybex.com to learn more about the rest of our growing graphics line.

Best regards,
Dan Brodnitz
Associate Publisher
Sybex Inc.

Software License Agreement: Terms and Conditions

The media and/or any online materials accompanying this book that are available now or in the future contain programs and/or text files (the "Software") to be used in connection with the book. SYBEX hereby grants to you a license to use the Software, subject to the terms that follow. Your purchase, acceptance, or use of the Software will constitute your acceptance of such terms. ■ The Software compilation is the property of SYBEX unless otherwise indicated and is protected by copyright to SYBEX or other copyright owner(s) as indicated in the media files (the "Owner(s)"). You are hereby granted a single-user license to use the Software for your personal, noncommercial use only. You may not reproduce, sell, distribute, publish, circulate, or commercially exploit the Software, or any portion thereof, without the written consent of SYBEX and the specific copyright owner(s) of any component software included on this media. ■ In the event that the Software or components include specific license requirements or end-user agreements, statements of condition, disclaimers, limitations, or warranties ("End-User License"), those End-User Licenses supersede the terms and conditions herein as to that particular Software component. Your purchase, acceptance, or use of the Software will constitute your acceptance of such End-User Licenses. ■ By purchase, use, or acceptance of the Software, you further agree to comply with all export laws and regulations of the United States as such laws and regulations may exist from time to time.

Reusable Code in This Book The author(s) created reusable code in this publication expressly for reuse by readers. SYBEX grants readers limited permission to reuse the code found in this publication or available for download from our website as long as the author(s) are attributed in any application containing the reusable code and the code itself is never distributed, posted online by electronic transmission, sold, or commercially exploited as a stand-alone product.

Software Support Components of the supplemental Software and any offers associated with them may be supported by the specific Owner(s) of that material, but they are not supported by SYBEX. Information regarding any available support may be obtained from the Owner(s) using the information provided in the appropriate read.me files or listed elsewhere on the media. ■ Should the manufacturer(s) or other Owner(s) cease to offer support or decline to honor any offer, SYBEX bears no responsibility. This notice concerning support for the Software is provided for your information only. SYBEX is not the agent or principal of the Owner(s), and SYBEX is in no way responsible for providing any support for the Software, nor is it liable or responsible for any support provided, or not provided, by the Owner(s).

Warranty SYBEX warrants the enclosed media to be free of physical defects for a period of ninety (90) days after purchase. The Software is not available from SYBEX in any other form or media than that enclosed herein or posted to http://www.sybex.com. If you discover a defect in the media during this warranty period, you may obtain a replacement of identical format at no charge by sending the defective media, postage prepaid, with proof of purchase to:

SYBEX Inc.
Product Support Department
1151 Marina Village Parkway
Alameda, CA 94501
Web: http://www.sybex.com

Disclaimer SYBEX makes no warranty or representation, either expressed or implied, with respect to the Software or its contents, quality, performance, merchantability, or fitness for a particular purpose. In no event will SYBEX, its distributors, or dealers be liable to you or any other party for direct, indirect, special, incidental, consequential, or other damages arising out of the use of or inability to use the Software or its contents even if advised of the possibility of such damage. In the event that the Software includes an online update feature, SYBEX further disclaims any obligation to provide this feature for any specific duration other than the initial posting. ■ The exclusion of implied warranties is not permitted by some states. Therefore, the above exclusion may not apply to you. This warranty provides you with specific legal rights; there may be other rights that you may have that vary from state to state. The pricing of the book with the Software by SYBEX reflects the allocation of risk and limitations on liability contained in this agreement of Terms and Conditions.

Shareware Distribution This Software may contain various programs that are distributed as shareware. Copyright laws apply to both shareware and ordinary commercial software, and the copyright Owner(s) retains all rights. If you try a shareware program and continue using it, you are expected to register it. Individual programs differ on details of trial periods, registration, and payment. Please observe the requirements stated in appropriate files.

Copy Protection The Software in whole or in part may or may not be copy-protected or encrypted. However, in all cases, reselling or redistributing these files without authorization is expressly forbidden except as specifically provided for by the Owner(s) therein.

About the Author

Steve Kurth is the author of the *Illustrator 10 Shop Manual* and coauthor of *Digital Prepress Complete*, as well as the technical editor for several other publications. Steve has created and led a robust series of hands-on and self-paced training courses in the digital graphic arts for such clients as Verizon , L. L. Bean, and Hasbro. Steve is also a freelance illustrator. He makes his home in Portland, Maine. Find him on the Web at http://www.illustratoranswers.com.

Acknowledgements

My deep thanks to Bonnie Bills, Jim Compton, Liz Welch, and Erica Yee of Sybex. Bonnie, thanks for the vision. Jim, thanks for the tireless work. Thanks also to Matt LeClair for his excellent tech editing and advice, and Java Imhoff for his input. Matt, we nailed another one. As always, thanks to Neil Salkind and the fine folks at Studio B. I would also like to tip my pen to Donnie O'Quinn, Tim Plumer, Randy Hagan, Greg Heald, Chris Fournier, Mordy Golding, and Todd Macadangdang. ■ On a personal note, I would like to say hey to Michelle, Beth, Joel, Dad, Katy, and Matt. Mom, I wrote this with you in mind. Thanks, everybody.

CONTENTS AT A GLANCE

Foreword ▪ ix

Introduction ▪ xv

Chapter 1 ▪ Core Terms and Concepts 1

Chapter 2 ▪ Essential Illustrator Tools and Techniques 23

Chapter 3 ▪ Save For Web Reference 69

Chapter 4 ▪ Gathering the Required Information 103

Chapter 5 ▪ Preparing the Work Environment 129

Chapter 6 ▪ Creating Single Graphics 169

Chapter 7 ▪ Optimizing Spot Illustrations 223

Chapter 8 ▪ Creating Complete Pages 241

Chapter 9 ▪ Creating Animations 267

Chapter 10 ▪ Creating Scalable Vector Graphics (SVG) 293

Index ▪ 315

Contents

Foreword	ix
Introduction	xv
Chapter 1 ▪ Core Terms and Concepts	**1**
Web Terms and Concepts	2
Illustrator in a Web Workflow	18
Chapter 2 ▪ Essential Illustrator Tools and Techniques	**23**
Document Features	24
Object Classes	25
Understanding Color Controls	39
Using the Direct Selection Tool	49
Duplicating and Aligning	52
Exploring Basic Text	53
Transformation Essentials	55
Layers	61
Chapter 3 ▪ Save For Web Reference	**69**
The Save For Web Dialog Box	70
GIF Optimization Controls	84
JPEG Optimization Controls	89
SWF Optimization Controls	92
Save For Web SVG Optimization Controls	95
Additional SVG Options via Save	98
Color Table Controls	98
Image Size Controls	100
Exporting to CSS Layers	101

Chapter 4 ▪ Gathering the Required Information   **103**

    Figuring Pixel Dimensions   104

    Understanding HTML Background Colors   112

Chapter 5 ▪ Preparing the Work Environment   **129**

    Choosing Typical Web Preferences   130

    Creating a New Document   145

    Setting Preview Models   149

    Saving and Editing Views   151

    Preparing Reusable Color Palettes   153

    Adjusting Illustrator's Defaults   161

    Customizing Shortcuts   163

    Creating Browser Templates   164

Chapter 6 ▪ Creating Single Graphics   **169**

    Streamlining Your Work with the Graphic Styles and Appearance Palettes   170

    Creating Typical Appearances   179

    Building Common Buttons   185

    Symbols and Icons   209

    Producing Background Images   217

Chapter 7 ▪ Optimizing Spot Illustrations   **223**

    Optimizing Sections of a File   224

    Basic Optimization Steps   230

    Automation   238

Chapter 8 ▪ Creating Complete Pages   **241**

    HTML Page Layout in Illustrator   242

    Slicing   243

    CSS Layers   253

    Building Links   253

    Building a Common Layout   261

Chapter 9 ■ Creating Animations	**267**
Creating Simple Animation in Illustrator	268
Export for Animation	285
Chapter 10 ■ Creating Scalable Vector Graphics (SVG)	**293**
SVG Basics	294
Creating SVG Files	298
Adding Interactivity to SVG Files	306
Applying SVG Filters	311
Index	315

Foreword

"I'll need to see some ID…"

For my 28th birthday a couple of my buddies took me out to see the New York Mets play (dismally) against the Atlanta Braves. When the beer man came by, we asked for a couple of cold ones. He looked at me and said, "I'll need to see some ID," which totally surprised me. As I fumbled through my wallet, full of photos of my kids, trying to find my driver's license, I realized that getting "carded" can be quite a compliment.

Adobe Illustrator was introduced to the design world nearly 10 years before most people knew what a website was. Quickly setting the standard for vector graphics, Illustrator became a household name for anyone doing print-based designs. When the Web began to demand high-quality graphics, designers moved to pixel-based design applications, such as Photoshop, to create their Web designs. Afterall, where do vector graphics fit on the web?

Almost without notice, Illustrator has evolved to embrace newer technologies and has added pixel-based effects, all-the-while preserving the benefits of working with editable and scalable vector graphics. The result is an enhanced Illustrator that is the perfect tool for web design, making it easy to repurpose graphics for print, when necessary. In fact, if you look at Illustrator today, you might "card" it thinking it's a new web graphics tool—and that's quite a compliment to Illustrator, considering it's still the industry-standard vector graphics application.

The Hidden Power of Illustrator CS: Web Graphics Techniques will turn a few heads as people begin to realize Illustrator is a powerful tool for Web design. I'm not suggesting it as a replacement to other Web design tools (such as Photoshop or Flash) but rather as a complement to them. Those who use Illustrator in their Web design workflow already share an advantage over anyone else in their field. By reading this book, you will have gained that advantage as well.

So the next time a friend asks you why you're so successful and smart as a Web designer, smile and proudly display your "card"—Adobe Illustrator.

—Mordy Golding
  Adobe Illustrator Product Manager
  Adobe Systems Incorporated

Introduction

I've trained digital graphic arts professionals for almost 10 years. Many of them had Illustrator on their desks but never did a thing with it. They would often concoct elaborate, inefficient Photoshop workarounds to avoid basic tasks in Illustrator. Most would either say that Illustrator confused and frightened them, or that they could simply "do more" in Photoshop. The fact is that Illustrator is one of the most misunderstood and underutilized applications on the planet.

Back in the day, people used Illustrator as a complement to Photoshop—they would mostly use it to perform some functions that Photoshop didn't have. Today, the tool is as strong as Photoshop and even handles some functions better. There are still some areas that require a little extra practice to master, but that's true with most things.

In particular, as Illustrator has grown into its own, it has become a full-fledged web graphics tool. Again, many users fail to take advantage of this, but Illustrator offers robust web creation tools that Photoshop lacks. Further, Illustrator has web-authoring tools that you won't find in any other professional-grade application. These capabilities are the focus of *The Hidden Power of Illustrator CS: Web Graphics Techniques*. If you need to create Illustrator art for the Web—logos, buttons, or other graphics; whole page designs; or animations—this is the book for you.

The Goal of This Book

The goal of this book is to take apart the process of creating web art in Illustrator. We look at more than just the tools—we also delve into the thought process behind them and their common uses in a practical environment. We break down individual topics and focus on what you should know about them. We explain the purpose of each technique and how you can benefit from it. Common tasks, problems, and solutions are highlighted with specific examples.

This isn't a survey book about every facet of Illustrator. Its goal is to teach you the process of using Illustrator to create art specifically tailored for the requirements of the Web. You will get the most out of this book if you have at least some Illustrator experience. Ideally, you'll have the basic Illustrator graphic skills to draw or generate any piece of art you intend to use in a web design.

How This Book Is Organized

The Hidden Power of Illustrator CS: Web Graphics Techniques brings together reference materials, practical advice, and tutorials. The focus of our tutorials is to illustrate the realistic manner in which you'd typically use Illustrator tools. The intention is not to show you how to create a specific piece of art, but to show how complex art is built from simple objects and to demonstrate how techniques come together. After going over the specifics of a project, you should be able to see the general themes of the technique and apply them to your projects.

The reference materials provide supporting details for the discussion. Designers, artists, and production folks in different environments will have different needs for the tools. We describe the most common settings and uses, but we've provided general reference material to assist users with out-of-the-ordinary situations as well.

The book consists of 10 chapters:

Chapter 1: Core Terms and Concepts In this chapter, you'll learn the basic vocabulary, key concepts, and issues involved in a web workflow. This chapter primarily targets traditional print designers and others new to web authoring.

Chapter 2: Essential Tools and Techniques Here, you'll learn common Illustrator techniques and get a refresher on the interface. Although this chapter primarily targets newcomers as well, experienced users may also find this material useful.

Chapter 3: Save For Web Reference The sprawling Save For Web dialog box is the core of Illustrator's web support, and this chapter explains every button and switch in this complex interface. Armed with this reference, you'll be ready to tackle the tutorials on optimizing graphics that follow in later chapters.

Chapter 4: Gathering the Required Information To create Illustrator graphics for use in a webpage, you need certain information, such as the size available for your graphic and the background color that will surround it. This chapter shows you how to find that information using authoring tools such as Dreamweaver and GoLive, and in existing webpages.

Chapter 5: Preparing the Work Environment Here, you'll see how to set up Illustrator files for web work. You'll learn about document resources—how to prepare them and how to manage them for use with different jobs.

Chapter 6: Creating Single Graphics In this chapter, you'll see step by step how common graphics are created. From these carefully chosen examples, you should begin to see how to create your own custom shapes and objects.

Chapter 7: Optimizing Spot Illustrations This chapter focuses on the process of optimizing individual graphics for the Web. Here, you'll learn how to pick file formats, evaluate details, and assess file sizes.

Chapter 8: Creating Complete Pages In this chapter, you'll find out how to build complete HTML pages in Illustrator. You'll learn to set up and separate your files for both table and Cascading Style Sheets (CSS) output.

Chapter 9: Creating Animations This chapter shows you how to use Illustrator to set up and generate sequential animations. We explain in detail how to create and finish both SWF and GIF files.

Chapter 10: Creating SVG This chapter focuses on the SVG file format. Here, you'll learn how to create and save SVG files. We examine editing SVG in a text editor as well as creating basic interactions.

Going Further

Additional materials on this topic are available to you through this book's page on the Sybex website (http://www.sybex.com). Materials are also available at http://www.illustratoranswers.com. Throughout this book, you will see icons referring to resources that can be downloaded. Check the Sybex website for revisions and expanded, bonus materials too lengthy to include in this book.

CHAPTER 1

Core Terms and Concepts

Any Illustrator user who plans to make graphics for the Web needs to be aware of some basic ideas and options. For example, you must take into account how you control the space for a graphic in an HTML document, what file formats are available to you, and how download time affects the site visitor's experience. Within Illustrator itself, you can choose among various ways of putting graphics into a web page. Which workflow you use will affect the choices you make as you create graphics. We'll refer to these issues throughout the book. If you already have a clear sense of them, consider skipping ahead to Chapter 2, "Essential Illustrator Tools and Techniques."

This chapter covers the following topics:

Graphic space in HTML

File formats

Transfer times

Color issues

Using Illustrator in a web workflow

Web Terms and Concepts

This section introduces the core issues involved in working with graphics in HTML pages: how graphics can be placed on a page, the various web file formats, download times, and the "web-safe" color limitations.

Graphic Space in HTML

Users of Illustrator are accustomed to being able to place objects exactly where they want them. If you want an object in a specific position on a page, you just put it there. This is not how things work in HTML. HTML was designed to transfer text data; it was never intended to do the work it is doing now, and that includes handling robust page design. Objects flow in HTML as in a text document. Things start in the upper left and flow to the right and down. Graphics appear inline, as though they were characters in a word. This means that to place objects in specific locations, you'll need to work around HTML with one of four basic workflows (listed here in order of preference).

Tables

What they are: *A basic HTML workaround for controlling graphic space.*

What you should know: *The majority of web pages use tables because they are widely understood by web browsers. They are a bit clunky compared with CSS layers (see the next section, "Cascading Style Sheets (CSS)").*

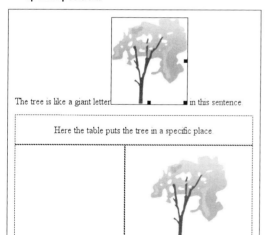

Figure 1.1

By default, objects in an HTML page flow like text. Tables enable you to set items in a specific position.

The most common way to control graphic space is by using a table. These tables are similar to the ones you'd create in a word processor or spreadsheet. You divide a rectangular area into boxes. Each box, or *cell*, can contain text, graphics, or even other tables. You can make the table large enough to cover an entire page. The contents of each cell are expanded, contracted, or combined with other cells to push and pull items into the position you desire. By nesting tables together and adjusting the amount of area cells take up, you can place items where you want them to be. Figure 1.1 shows the difference between simply placing an image on a page and placing it within a table.

Tables are useful and common, but they have limitations. Objects can't be on top of other objects, and they may not appear the same in different browsers. These issues aren't showstoppers, but you need to be aware of them. Illustrator can generate tables for you automatically. For more information, see Chapter 8, "Creating Complete Pages."

Cascading Style Sheets (CSS)

What they are: These style sheets form a modern structure for describing graphic space using x- and y-coordinates.

What you should know: CSS is understood only by 4.0 or later web browsers; they feature richer design opportunities than tables.

Cascading Style Sheets (CSS) create a model for defining graphic space that is understood by 4.0 and later browsers. This means site visitors must have Netscape 4 or Internet Explorer 4 or later to view pages that use CSS. Other contemporary browsers, such as Safari, Camino, and Phoenix, also recognize CSS. Current statistics place the number of users with pre-4.0 browsers at less than 1 percent. This number is still a concern for conservative designers and those responsible for sites that reach broad audiences.

This is not an insurmountable problem. Often, sites designers create two versions of websites: one for those with modern browsers, and one for those without. When users load the site's home page, they are sent to the version of the site that's appropriate for their browser.

Why would you go to these lengths? Because style sheets enable you to do things you can't with standard HTML. Namely, you can position objects where you want them, make objects overlap each other, show and hide the items with scripting, and animate objects. Most of the drop-down menus that you see in web pages (like the one shown in Figure 1.2) are created using CSS. As time passes, this model will likely surpass tables as the de facto choice for web page creation. Like any technology, CSS can be misused to create visual noise and incompatible web pages, but it is very promising.

CSSs are commonly referred to as *layers*, or *floating boxes*. They can be used in conjunction with tables or in lieu of them. Illustrator can generate them for you; you'll learn more about working with Cascading Style Sheets in Chapter 8.

Figure 1.2

Drop-down menus illustrate the way CSS objects can overlap other contents.

Frames

What they are: Frames use different HTML pages to break up graphic space; this is a mostly passé model.

What you should know: Frames are often used to separate navigation items from page content. They are used less and less frequently as other technologies obviate their need.

Frames are HTML documents that contain other HTML documents. This breaks space up into rectangular space, as shown in Figure 1.3. Often, users set up common items in a single document, creating links that load in another frame. This doesn't exactly solve the positioning issue, but it can be used to block out documents. Because frame documents can contain other frame documents, you could conceivably nest enough of them together to position objects exactly. And, of course, framed documents can use layers or CSS.

Frames have other problems, though. Their structure prevents them from being indexed properly, making it harder for users to find your page. In addition, they can't be understood by screen readers. When the visually impaired experience a web page, it is read to them by screen-reader software. Frame documents contain only references to other HTML pages, so there is no text to read. This flummoxes the software, rendering the page unusable to a portion of your potential audience.

Illustrator doesn't make frames. Likely you shouldn't either.

Figure 1.3
A frame document and its component pages

PDF Files

What they are: *Files that will appear exactly as you designed them in Illustrator. They can be used instead of HTML or as part of a page.*

What you should know: *PDFs require a plug-in in order for them to be viewed in a browser. This can cause hiccups in the user experience.*

PDF files can appear in a browser exactly as you designed them in Illustrator (Figure 1.4). Given this, they could be used to set up entire pages, complete with the font of your choice. That is seldom the case, however. Instead, PDFs are used almost exclusively for downloadable versions of print documents.

Some people feel that requiring a plug-in has prevented PDF files from being more widely used as web content. The truth is more likely that the viewing experience is just different enough to irritate users. You have to wait for the plug-in to load, the Acrobat interface loads by default, and you need a special tool to select text. Until Acrobat 5, PDF files also couldn't be understood by screen-reading software. So while it's possible to use PDFs to design graphic space, it's rarely done. The reasons in this case concern individual preference more than technical limits.

File Formats

When you save art, you need to assign a format to it. The format encodes the picture in a specific way. This may alter the way the file appears and may change what you can and can't do to the file later.

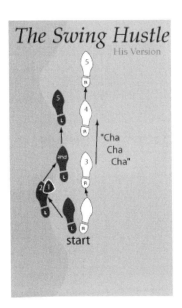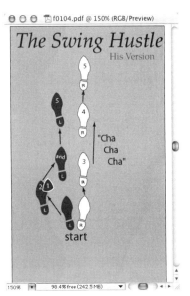

Figure 1.4

A PDF file (left) in Illustrator and then (right) used in a web page.

You should consider two major aspects: the way graphic space is described and how color is handled. Let's look at the most basic difference first—pixels, which are often also called "bitmap" or "raster" art, and vectors.

Pixel-Based (Bitmapped) vs. Vector Graphics

Web graphics may be either pixel-based (bitmapped) or vector based. Illustrator is one of the few applications that can create both. Pixel graphics are the most popular online choice. Pixels are tiny, colored squares. The file is composed of a grid of these squares. Together they create the appearance of the image. The larger an image is, the more pixels are required to describe it and the larger the file size is. Pixel images are optimized to a specific physical size and, once optimized, work best at that size. HTML tags can change the size at which the image is displayed, but this usually results in poorer image quality or inefficiency (Figure 1.5). Additionally, the requirements for displaying pixel images are different than those for printing them. This means that viewers will be able to see your images clearly, but will not get great results if they attempt to print the images.

Pixels can be saved into several file formats, and each has its own set of requirements (which we discuss in the sections that follow). Several of these formats are extremely popular online because web browsers understand them right out of the box. The HTML tags used with pixel images enable you to add links and image maps to graphics, increasing their functionality.

Vector is the model Illustrator uses to describe graphics by default. When you are working in Illustrator, you are most commonly creating vector art right on the page. As you may know, vectors create art with a connect-the-dots model. Points in space are identified and lines are drawn between them to create shapes (Figure 1.6).

Vector graphics are great because they can be sized up and down without affecting edge definition or detail. Edges in these graphics are sharp, and type can even be retained so that it may be copied or searched. Normally, when you make raster art, text becomes a picture of the characters. It's locked in that format and you can't highlight the word to

Figure 1.5
Pixel graphics scaled up (left) suffer detail loss. Vector graphics (right) do not.

select its content. With Scalable Vector Graphics (SVG), you can. You can select text, or even assign it to a different font on the fly. These graphics may even be printed at high resolution. Vector graphics may contain links, animation, and additional functionality, but these features must be added in the application that authors the graphics, rather than in the HTML that surrounds them.

Several vector file formats can be understood online by web browsers. The Shock Wave Flash (SWF) and SVG are the two most commonly used. Unfortunately, browsers don't have the ability to display these graphics out of the box and require a plug-in to view them. The plug-ins are free, and modern browsers come with the Flash plug-in already installed. A recent study by Macromedia (creators of the SWF format) indicated that over 92 percent of current web surfers have the Flash plug-in installed. Still, many designers are concerned that requiring users to download a missing plug-in will drive them away from their site. In addition, the SVG plug-in doesn't have anywhere near the penetration that Flash does.

When deciding whether to use pixels or vectors, take the plug-in into account. Consider your audience: the more technically sophisticated they are, the more likely they are to already have the plug-ins required. You may be developing for CD or intranet distribution, where you can control the environment the page is viewed in. You should also consider whether you intend to author entire pages in vectors or integrate them with HTML items and pixel graphics. Often, designers will isolate the use of vector graphics to self-contained vector pages that open as separate windows or offer complete alternate websites for non-vector-enabled websites. You may simply decide that the advantages of vector graphics outweigh the risk of inconvenience and proceed.

Figure 1.6

Vector graphics describe space with points and lines instead of pixels.

Color

Different file formats support different color models. This means that the act of saving to a particular format switches the color in the image to the model the format understands. This is mostly an issue when saving pixel graphics. Each pixel must be set to a specific color. The act of changing each pixel may alter the appearance of the image overall.

Colors are measured in terms of the amount of memory assigned to each pixel. The more memory that is allotted, the larger the number of colors that can be used. Memory is measured in bits. Bits are computer units that are typically grouped in sets of eight (the byte). An 8-bit image can support up to 256 color choices. Grayscale art uses this model of color. Twenty-four-bit color uses three *bit channels*, or color components. The famous *RGB* (Red, Green Blue) color space uses this model.

How pixels are assigned each color is also an issue worth discussing. In an 8-bit format, each pixel is assigned to one of the 256 colors available in the document. In practice, you'll have some power over which specific colors are used. In full RGB color, you won't be choosing specific color sets, but you will still have to make choices. Files are smaller, and transfer over the Internet faster, if pixels are similar to each other. To make files smaller, pixel values are changed in the course of saving them. You will have to balance between speed and quality of your image. Further, as you save over a web graphic again and again, the degradation keeps adding up. This is not a function of bit depth, but it's good to be aware of that up front.

Formats

In this section, we'll examine each of the popular file formats.

GIF

> What it is: *An 8-bit pixel based file that supports animation and transparency.*
> What you should know: *Graphics Interchange Format (GIF) is likely the most common file format you will be saving from Illustrator. The GIF was originally developed by CompuServ (an early AOL-style online service).*

GIFs are typically used for logos, buttons, and art with areas of flat color. It's a common format for Illustrator to create because the strengths of the format often dovetail with the kinds of images created in Illustrator. GIFs are also commonly used as *spacer graphics*— placeholder objects that help control graphic space inside a table (see the earlier section "Tables"). Illustrator may produce these automatically as it generates HTML, but it is rarely done manually.

GIFs use an 8-bit color model. This means that each pixel must be assigned one of 256 possible colors. You need not use all 256 colors. In fact, using fewer colors reduces the overall file size. The set of possible colors that each pixel can call from is called a *color table*. You can define color tables for different graphics to help optimize image quality. Still, reducing the colors in a file down to this number may seriously hurt the appearance of the art, as you can see in the bottom two images in Figure 1.7. Understanding the process of defining and applying color tables is a major part of creating GIFs.

Because GIFs use a limited number of colors, they tend to be best suited for graphics that have large areas of flat color rather than ones with a lot of color changes, like photographs. Illustrator files often consist of solid areas of color, making GIFs a common choice for their optimization. The presence of gradients, gradient meshes, feathers, drop shadows, or raster art in an image may result in a file better served as a JPEG, though, as you can see in Figure 1.8. You should certainly consider all options as you optimize files.

GIFs support both sequential animation and transparency. Many of the animated banner ads that you see on the Web today are GIFs. You can't produce animated GIFs directly out of Illustrator, but you can set up objects to be animated in another application. In fact, Illustrator is often an excellent choice for setting up animation because of such features as blends and brushes. For more information, see Chapter 9, "Creating Animations."

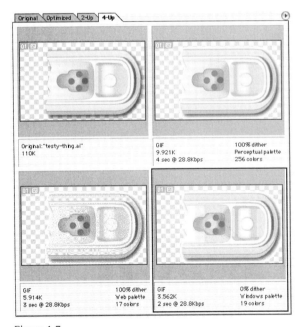

Figure 1.7

The same graphic optimized with different color tables appears very different.

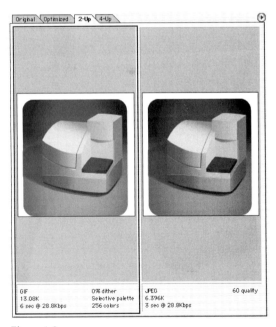

Figure 1.8

Although the image has areas of solid color, it is too large when optimized as a GIF (left) because of the gradients. Optimized as a JPEG (right), it reduces in size.

Illustrator supports one hundred levels of opacity. GIFs support one. Pixels in the GIF format must be either opaque or transparent. You won't be able to make pixels semitransparent and build them atop other images in a web page; Figure 1.9 shows what happens when you try. Nonetheless, this is a fine feature and enables you to create objects with negative space. This is often used to display background images behind art (Figure 1.10) or to give the appearance of a non-square image.

GIFs may be *interlaced*, which means they load in stages. As shown in Figure 1.11, they start as blocky images and resolve themselves over time. Users are given a sense of the item at first, but it may take a few passes to see what it really is. This is intended to make the loading of pages quicker. It does reduce the load time overall but can be frustrating when used on important or large images. In addition, this approach increases the file's size slightly. For this reason, interlacing is usually reserved for nonessential graphics.

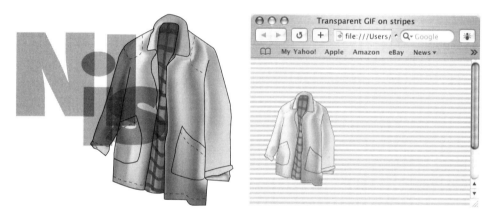

Figure 1.9

Partially transparent objects in Illustrator (left) are flattened in the optimized GIF (right). This results in images that appear correct relative to one another but do not continue to be transparent against other graphics on a page.

Figure 1.10

A transparent GIF by itself (left) and used in a web page with a background image (right)

JPEG

What it is: *The file format most commonly used online for photos and art with continuous tone.*

What you should know: *The Joint Photographic Experts Group (JPEG) format is used for both print and web.*

Assuming that all JPEGs are web-ready is a mistake. The format supports multiple color models (including both RGB and CMYK) and high resolution. CMYK images can't be viewed in web browsers, and images are displayed at screen resolution, making high-resolution images gigantic. You can avoid both of these issues if you are making JPEGs from Illustrator by choosing File → Save For Web. Do not confuse this command with the File → Export method for making JPEGs, which you'd use to create print graphics.

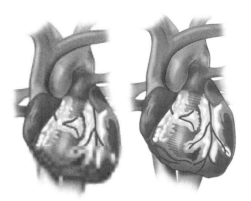

Figure 1.11

An interlaced graphic loads in several passes, appearing blocky at first (left) and then becoming clearer until finishing (right).

LOSSY AND LOSSLESS COMPRESSION

All compression algorithms are defined as either *lossy* (like JPEG) or *lossless (like GIF)*. As the name implies, lossy compression methods actually lose some information; that is, they discard pixel data that the algorithm determines to be redundant, often by changing pixel values if they differ only slightly from neighboring pixels. Color values are lost, not resolution. This displays itself as ugly artifacting in some JPEGs. The effect is cumulative. That is, each time you open and save a JPEG the compression is applied again, further degrading the image. In this sense JPEG is often used as a verb as in "that file has been JPEGed too much".

Lossless compression methods achieve their compression without discarding any color data. The most common web example of lossless compression is GIF. GIFs can only hold up to 256 colors, so in that sense, color from your image may be "lost" as you save for web, but the effect is not cumulative each time you re-save the optimized graphic. In that sense the compression is "lossless".

What you should take away from this is that you should always save your Illustrator files along with the web graphics. Having the source graphic enables you to create a fresh version of the art. If you must edit a web graphic, be aware that repeatedly saving JPEGs will eventually wreck them. For full details on compression, see Chapter 3.

JPEGs use 24-bit color (RGB). Images are simply RGB; no color tables are needed. JPEGs are well suited for photographs and images with continuous tones. When you are creating graphics in Illustrator that have a lot of gradients, meshes, or soft-edge effects (such as Gaussian Blur), you should consider JPEGs.

JPEGs use a *lossy* compression model. When making JPEGs, there is a direct connection between the amount of compression and the amount of damage done to an image (Figure 1.12). In photos, you may not notice this damage, especially at higher settings. In solid images, though, it often results in noticeable artifacts about the edges. You can mitigate this effect somewhat, but you may end up with unrecoverable files.

JPEGs do not support transparency or animation. The only special feature they support is interlacing. Interlaced JPEGs are called *progressive* JPEGS. As with interlaced GIFs, progressive JPEGs load in a series of passes, each one more greatly resolving image detail. Very old browsers may not support progressive JPEGs. Unsupported graphics display as an empty box with an "X." For more information, see Chapter 7, "Optimizing Spot Illustrations."

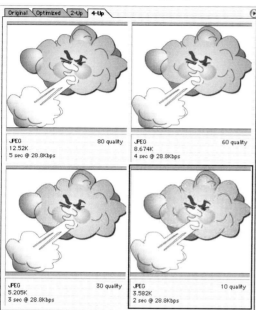

Figure 1.12
JPEGs often produce ugly artifacts near edges. Here we see the same image with progressively stronger compression. As the compression increases, the defects become more pronounced.

PNG

What it is: *An alternate to both GIF and JPEG.*

What you should know: *The Portable Network Graphic (PNG) is a promising format that is not fully supported by all browsers. For this reason, most users avoid the format unless they are working in a completely controlled viewing environment, such as a CD or intranet delivery. It's unfortunate that the format is not widely accepted, because it has distinct advantages.*

PNG has been the "format to watch" for several years now. Delightfully, it supports full transparency, rather than the one level of transparency GIFs use. Combined with CSS layers, PNGs could make web design more like traditional page design. The problem is the way that transparency is handled. Internet Explorer versions 5 through 6 for Windows (the most dominant browser on the market) renders only one level of transparency. This makes your nice soft drop shadows look fine on the Mac and in Netscape but lousy on the PC. Although this is no different than GIFs, it is highly frustrating and can lead to complications. Many users avoid the PNG format principally out of old habits or latent distrustfulness. You can check in on the PNG format to see the current level of browser support at www.libpng.org/pub/png/pngstatus.html.

Illustrator can write two PNG formats: PNG-8 and PNG-24. The "8" and "24" refer to the bit depth of the graphics created. For simplicity, you can think of the 8 and 24 versions of the formats as alternatives to GIF and JPEG, respectively.

The PNG-8 format uses a color table just as GIFs do. PNG-24 supports full (RGB) color. For more information, see Chapter 7.

Both PNG formats support transparency. The PNG-8 version features the same transparency as GIF files. PNG-24, however, features a full 256 levels of transparency, as illustrated in Figure 1.13. This means web graphics can have the same transparency as the source Illustrator objects, even against other objects in a page. Combined with CSS floating boxes, this is a potent combination.

Both PNG formats may be interlaced. PNGs do not support animation.

SWF

What it is: An online vector file format commonly used for animation, logos, and interactivity. What you should know: The ShockWave Flash (SWF) format was developed by Macromedia. It is commonly generated by Macromedia's Flash and has reasonably high browser penetration. Illustrator can make these files for you, but it can't add the interactivity or animation. For this reason, SWF files are usually either spot logos or text illustrations or are continued in Flash or LiveMotion (Adobe's SWF animation application).

SWF files support full RGB color and can contain both raster and vector art. In fact, some art may be converted to pixels in the saving process. This is one of the things to watch for when you're creating these files, because some Illustrator techniques will create art that converts to pixels automatically. Including pixels will dramatically increase the file's size. For information on anticipating and mitigating this, see Chapter 9. Because SWF files are vector based, they are scalable. This means that you can use the same file at different sizes on the same page without the edges becoming fuzzy (see Figure 1.14).

As we mentioned earlier, SWF files can contain interactivity as well as animation. Because of this, you can create entire websites as SWF files. This approach completely bypasses the problems associated with HTML graphic space. When SWF files were first introduced, a spate of websites appeared that were created in Flash, and this technique was briefly fashionable. Things were flying all over web pages, often for no particular reason. Today, sites still use SWF files, but designers are integrating it in ways that make the site seem more natural and less intrusive to the experience.

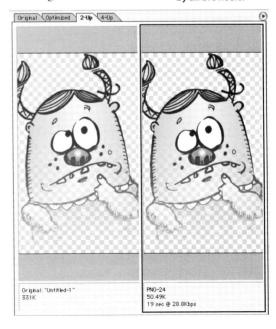

Figure 1.13
PNG-24 supports full transparency. Unfortunately, it is not fully accepted by all browsers.

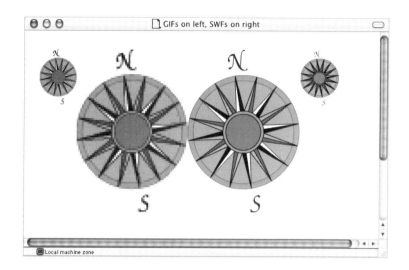

Figure 1.14

The same (SWF) logo used at different sizes in a web page shows none of the degradation its pixel counterpart does.

SWF files are handled differently than standard graphics in HTML. Macromedia has ownership of the file format and produces separate software (a plug-in) that the browser uses to interpret the files. This strategy enables Macromedia to update its software independently of the browser, but it does create some differences in how the art is handled. HTML tags have attributes. *Attributes* specify such factors as the thickness of a table's border and the color of text. They also enable you to use graphics as links. The HTML tag that is used for standard graphics (`img`) isn't the one used for SWF files (`object`). What this really means is that if you want SWF files to act as links, you'll need to build that into the file and can't add it later in the HTML.

Illustrator is well suited to preparing SWF files and has tools designed for that purpose. But there are specific do's and don'ts related to creating these sorts of files. For a more in-depth discussion, see Chapters 7 and 9.

SVG

What it is: *An online vector file format intended to compete with SWF.*
What you should know: *Scalable Vector Graphics (SVG) is an open-source format that could either be a next big thing or a footnote. Learn more in Chapter 10, " Creating Scalable Vector Graphics (SVG)."*

In many ways, SVG can be compared to SWF, the other online option for vector graphics. Both offer interaction, sophisticated scripting, and animation, and both require plug-ins. SVG has some color- and text-handling advantages over SWF, though. Notably, text in an SVG file can remain live, meaning it can be searched, and copied and pasted as type (see Figure 1.15). SWF files convert text to outline vector shapes. This is a major difference.

Retaining text enables developers to format text on the fly inside an existing file and produces a file that can be read by screen-reading software, providing greater accessibility and compliance to federal laws. Also, SVG is an open format and you don't have to pay royalties to Macromedia (the inventors of SWF).

SVG is based on Extensible Stylesheet Language (XML), and browsers will soon be written to accommodate it without requiring plug-ins. Currently, though, it is not widely adopted and has some limitations on some systems with some browsers. For a full discussion of these issues, see Chapter 10.

Two file formats are associated with Scalable Vector Graphics: SVG and Compressed SVG (SVGZ). The Compressed version can be up to 80 percent smaller than the regular version, but it cannot be edited by a text editor. Both formats use the same dialog boxes when saving.

Figure 1.15

An SVG graphic used in a layout may contain live type.

Transfer Times

In most cases, web graphics are transmitted over the World Wide Web. They also see use in intranet models and CD workflows, though, so it's wise to make a distinction. When your art is going to be transmitted over the Internet, you need to factor in the amount of time it will take to download. Slowly loading pages turn users away and is a mark of poor craft. Further, some service providers charge for web hosting based on the amount of data transferred. Seemingly small file size differences are multiplied over the amount of times the file is served. In popular sites, this can translate to a substantial amount of money.

This book devotes an entire chapter (7) to the specifics of optimizing graphics. But for now, be aware that for standard (pixel) graphics, the bigger the art is and the more color it has, the larger the file size will be.

Different web page audiences fall into different demographic groups. This means they may have access to different web technology and will see images and text at different rates. Time, then, is less useful a measure than file size. Although there is room to wiggle on this, try to keep within the following guidelines. Ads and graphics should be no larger than 15k. Buttons and icons should be no larger than 5k. The entire page (including all the graphics) shouldn't be larger than 50 or 60k.

Many designers chafe under file size restrictions. They argue that as newer computers come out, the issue of file size is not as pressing. They feel justified in designing graphics-rich pages with all of the bells and whistles. Remember that the computer the audience has is only half the issue. Web pages are only as fast as the servers that are transmitting them. I've spent the last year traveling across the country in major metropolitan areas. I have a cable modem at home but use dial-up on the road. Although I have a 56K modem in my laptop, I frequently am unable to connect any faster than 28.8K. This is the case in many cities I visit.

To give you a sense of what these numbers translate to, consider the pipeline that graphics are traveling down. In the next sections, we discuss the technology models your audience will use to see your pages

Modem

Modems use telephone lines to transmit and receive digital data. Speed can be measured several ways, but is usually done in kilobits per second (kbps). Note this is *bits*, not bytes. A byte is eight times as large as a bit. File sizes are measured in kilobytes (k), transfer speed in kilobits (kbps). Most new computers come with 56K modems. This means they are capable of receiving 56,000 bits per second. A slower modem could be transmitting, though, reducing the transfer time. At 56.6kbps, 5k of data transmits in about 2 seconds. At 28.8kbps, it takes about 3 seconds. This means that 15k of data takes around 4 seconds to transmit at 56.6kbps and about 6 at 28.8kbps. Also, 50k takes about 10 seconds to load at 56kbps and about 20 seconds at 28.8kbps. Increasing a page's size to 70k from 50 adds between 4 and 6 seconds to the download time. Sneak up to 80k and it takes a full 30 seconds to load a page at 28.8kbps.

DSL

Digital Subscriber Line (DSL) uses your standard phone line with a special modem. The service is not available in every location. DSL uses part of the phone line, but unlike modems, it doesn't have to tie the phone up so that you can't use it. DSL is typically 3 to 5 times faster than standard phone lines and is one of the two options usually referred to as *broadband*.

There are several types of DSL. Consumers usually get ADSL. The "A" stands for asynchronous, which means the transfer times are different for uploading and downloading. Most ADSL connections let you download at up to 1.5 megabits per second (mbps). (A megabit is a thousand kilobits.) This is great for large downloads. Uploading is slower, typically 128 to 256kbps. The rates will vary, though, depending on your service. You may also be able to get Symmetric DSL (SDSL), which sends data back and forth at the same pace. This is usually 256K to 768K.

A 15k file could download at 1.5mbps in one second. In fact, you could download an 80K file in a second at that pace. At 128 or 256kbps, the 15K file would take 2 seconds. A 5k file transmits in less than a second using any of those options.

Cable

Cable modems transfer data through the cable that brings you cable television. As with DSL, it's much faster than standard cable and the upload times are slower than the download times. Cable can potentially run faster than DSL, but the speed depends on the number of users in your area accessing the service at the same time. Users don't notice this most of the time for day-to-day surfing. The top speed for cable connection is usually 2mbps (although some areas offer 3mbps). Downloads typically clock in around 128 to 384kbps.

As with DSL, our 15k and 5kB files transfer in less than a second. At the top speed of 2mbps, you can download a 100k file in a single second. That would take 40 seconds with a 28.8kbps modem.

Color Issues

Several color terms and concepts are thrown around frequently, and they bear a little discussion here. As with most web issues, you'll need to weigh their importance to your situation and decide what, if anything, to do about them. We'll help you with those decisions in Chapter 7.

Color Naming

In HTML, color is identified either by name or by using hexadecimal notation. You'll see this in the code used to describe text, borders, and the background colors of tables, cells, and layers. Hexadecimal (or *hex*) is the more common model of the two. A finite number of named colors exist, and this model is not used by Illustrator or Photoshop. Illustrator does use hex color values, and it's common to copy and paste the color code between applications.

Basically, hexadecimal is just a way of writing down RGB values with fewer digits. Hex uses base 16 instead of base 10 numbers. This means instead of going from 0 to 9 (base 10), numbers go from 0 to F. In this system, A represents 10, B represents 11, and so on, up to F (15).

To make larger values, numbers are set right to left. In base 10, the second number to the left represents the number of tens. In base 16, it equals the number of 16's. So the number 11 in hex equals 17 (one 16 and one 1). The number F0 equals 240 (fifteen 16's and no 1s).

RGB colors are described in the amount of red, green, and blue light a color is made of. In base 10, the lighting values are measured on a scale of 0 (no light) to 255 (pure bright light). Web colors are rendered in hex with two digits for each color component. The first two are the red component;, then the green and the two on the right are the amount of blue light. For example, the color CC0000 is CC red, 00 green, and 00 blue. This translates to 194 red and no green or blue.

Cascading Style Sheets often identify colors by name. In HTML 4, using style sheets this way is preferable to using color attributes in tags. There are 16 preset colors: Aqua, Black, Blue, Fuchsia, Gray, Green, Lime, Maroon, Navy, Olive, Purple, Red, Silver, Teal, White, and Yellow.

Web-Safe Color

The concept of web-safe color is a controversial one. Here is the basic idea: Different monitors, because of differences in their mechanics, can display different sets of colors. All Macintosh monitors can display, at a bare minimum, 256 specific colors. The same is true for PC monitors, but the sets of colors each can display are not the same. Of those 256, the two sets have 216 colors in common.

These colors are the ones that can be displayed with certainty on every monitor in use today. Collectively, they make up the *web-safe color set*. If a monitor can't display a specific color, it may try to approximate it by *dithering*. Dithering is when pixels of different colors are put next to each other to trick the eye into seeing some other color. This generally isn't a desirable situation—it often looks bad. The safest way to avoid dithering is to use colors you know can be displayed on every monitor. Using these colors doesn't guarantee color veracity. Web-safe colors don't display the same on every monitor—they just don't dither. Further, JPEGs don't use web-safe color. This is only an issue for solid colors, such as HTML text and background colors and GIF files.

Recent studies show that most (over 90 percent) web users have monitors that can display more than 256 colors. Unfortunately, many Windows systems set the default color display to 8 bit, effectively creating low-end monitors from high-end ones. Also, AOL has a feature that compresses art on the fly, limiting the number of colors in the image to 256. Most AOL users have this turned on by default and are unaware of the option. AOL users currently represent about 5 to 6 percent of the web audience.

Hence, the real question is, are there enough AOL and Windows users out there to justify restricting yourself to the (ugly) web-safe color palette? While there is a growing number of artists who feel the answer is no, the issue remains controversial. Better monitors alone have not solved the web-safe problem.

Web colors have hex colors that are stepped in units of 33. Each RGB color must be the 00, 33, 66, 99, CC, or FF hex value in order for the color to be web safe. You can use this to spot a web-safe color at a glance. For example, the color 003CFF is not web safe because the G component (the second set of digits), 3C, is not divisible by 33.

Illustrator in a Web Workflow

This short section is intended to help you place Illustrator into context in a web workflow. What role will Illustrator play as web content is devised, designed, and implemented? Several tools are available, and Illustrator can wear different hats in terms of its use in graphics creation. You may or may not yet have a clear sense of what you want from the application. Here we'll look at typical web workflows and the role Illustrator may play inside them. We'll also examine the role of other common applications, such as Photoshop and Dreamweaver, and when not to use Illustrator.

Design and Implementation

The first thing to be aware of is that there are two overall functions to creating a website:

- The design of the graphics
- The actual creation of the pages

You can think of these functions as *design*, the shaping of the appearance of a graphic or page, and *implementation*, the construction of the code that delivers it to people's homes. These are two different disciplines with different concerns. Although you may be responsible for both of these things, in many environments the people who design web pages are not the people who actually prepare them. In many large companies, the design department prepares graphics and web pages that the IT department then picks up and adjusts for form and correctness.

The reason this happens is because the IT department has to support the site and is typically responsible for fixing errors. In a complex site with e-commerce and databases, this can be a complicated task. We're taking the time to mention this, because some workflows may not be supported in some environments. Just because a tool exists does not mean its use is permitted or endorsed. The options for Illustrator's use may be limited by your environment. Remember this as you consider your options.

Basic Goals

First, you have to decide what you want to do. Illustrator can generate individual web graphics, graphics that will be converted to web graphics by another application, and complete web pages. Which you choose depends on the particulars of your work environment and what other tools are at your disposal.

Generating Complete Pages

What it is: *Creating HTML as well as graphics when using the File → Save For Web command.*

What you should know: *You can generate complete pages quickly, but they can be hard to edit later and lack some common features.*

Illustrator can generate complete, single HTML pages. When this happens, graphic space is divided using either tables or CSS. Different graphics are generated to represent each part of the page. Parts of the page can be designated as non-image areas. This enables you to fill in the areas later with HTML objects, such as tables and text. You can even convert existing text to tagged HTML type. Basic interactivity in the form of links and image maps can be created as well. For information on doing this, see Chapter 8, "Creating Complete Pages."

Illustrator is typically not the end of the web page production cycle, however. It doesn't have a rich set of production tools and usually requires additional code massaging to make its pages ready for posting. This isn't a flaw. Illustrator is a graphics creation tool, not an HTML editor. Adobe expects that you will adjust the HTML either manually or in a visual editor, such as GoLive or Dreamweaver.

Editing the pages Illustrator creates can be challenging as well. Notably, you may find the tables it constructs difficult to modify. As users add and subtract cells, the table structure may become confused. It usually takes so much tweaking that it makes more sense to go back to Illustrator and regenerate the page from there.

If you are a GoLive user, generating complete pages also locks you out of a SmartObject workflow (see the next section). For these reasons, Illustrator users typically create complete pages only to comp out a design or to create smaller HTML parts that are then assembled elsewhere. For example, a user may create a navigation interface in Illustrator, save the document as an HTML page, and then place that code in the cell of a table in another document (see Figure 1.16). For instructions, see Chapter 8.

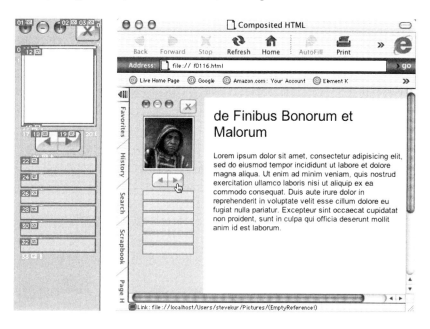

Figure 1.16

Illustrator art is saved as HTML to create a complex table (left). The table is then added to an existing layout (right).

Converting Graphics

> What it is: *Creating files that will be converted to web graphics by another application, typically Photoshop, ImageReady, Flash, or GoLive. These are usually either native Illustrator files or Photoshop documents.*
>
> What you should know: *Graphics are typically optimized for the web in other applications to fit into specific workflows, because of user familiarity with other applications or to take advantage of features in other applications.*

Although Illustrator supports a wide array of file formats and web optimization tools, some users prefer to create web art elsewhere. The most compelling reason to do this is that you want to do something you can't do in Illustrator.

A common example is creating animated GIFs and SmartObjects. *SmartObjects* are a workflow device Adobe GoLive uses. The idea is to connect a high-resolution graphic to a web version. This happens when the user places an Illustrator file into a GoLive document. Also, when Illustrator writes HTML it can produce SmartObjects automatically. GoLive walks you through converting the file to a web graphic and then manages the connection. As you make changes to the high-resolution version, the corresponding web graphic is updated automatically. Likewise, you can re-optimize the web version from the high-res version.

GoLive does this by including an extra snippet of code in the HTML. The code is small and can be automatically stripped out when the file is uploaded. Nonetheless, this feature makes some IT departments nervous. They are concerned that GoLive will further rewrite the code they so lovingly created. You should discuss the issue with them and alert them to GoLive's HTML writing preferences. You will also want to be careful about sizing and bounding box issues when using this sort of file.

Animated GIFs are often generated in Photoshop's sister application, ImageReady (free with Photoshop). Users set up an animated GIF by creating a layered Illustrator file and then exporting it to the Photoshop native format. For instructions on this, see Chapter 9.

A third scenario in which you'd want to save graphics for optimization elsewhere is when you are batch-optimizing graphics in an automated workflow. Here, you're optimizing a series of files automatically using a script or an action.

Creating Single Graphics

> What it is: *Manually optimizing files for use online, typically through File→ Save For Web but possibly by File → Export.*
>
> What you should know: *You should be aware of a couple of issues involving bounding boxes and edges.*

This workflow is the most common. Here, you're creating vector art in Illustrator and then converting them to web graphics. This is a broad topic, and much of Chapters 3 through 7 is devoted to this workflow. Read on.

CHAPTER 2

Essential Illustrator Tools and Techniques

Now that we've defined basic terms, let's review several fundamental Illustrator concepts. Not necessarily web-specific issues, these techniques represent basic building blocks that are required for any art creation.

This chapter is not intended to provide a basic Illustrator how-to. We describe these tools and techniques so you can use them to speed the web graphics creation proces.

This chapter covers the following topics:

Document features

Object classes

Understanding color controls

Using the Direct Selection tool

Duplicating and aligning

Basic text

Transformation essentials

Layers

Document Features

Illustrator divides the workspace into three areas: the Pasteboard, Page Tiling, and the Artboard (see Figure 2.1). In this section, we'll look at each of these features.

The Artboard

> **What it is:** *The solid rectangle that defines the boundaries of an Illustrator file.*
> **What you should know:** *The Artboard does not establish "page" boundaries per se. It is used to set the size of HTML tables, PDF files and web graphics.*

Most users are familiar with the basic arrangement of Illustrator documents. And yet most users still don't understand the Artboard. It's mildly complicated and usually confused with Page Tiling.

The Artboard plays a key role in web graphics creation. You'll use it to set the final size of your art. This size will likely vary from the actual size of your art, so you'll need to take care. You'll find information about determining and setting Artboard sizes in Chapters 4 ("Gathering the Required Information") and 5 ("Preparing the Work Environment").

The Artboard also represents the area that's sized when you choose View → Fit In Window. This is useful in and of itself. By sizing the Artboard to fit your work, you'll save time zooming in and out. Instead, you'll toggle between View → Fit In Window (⌘/Control+0) and View → Actual Size Window (⌘/Control+1).

The Pasteboard

> **What it is:** *The total area available for objects in a document*
> **What you should know:** *Objects on the pasteboard are included in web graphics by default, even if they are not on the page.*

The *Pasteboard* is the entire working area in the document. Objects can be located anywhere on the Pasteboard and still be included when the file is saved. Technically, parts of objects can also exist outside the Pasteboard, but it's so large that only in extreme cases would that be true.

Some artists want to use the Pasteboard as a "scratch" space for objects that aren't necessarily in the final design. This is fine, but be aware that objects outside the Artboard aren't excluded from web documents by default. You'll see how to work around this in chapter 7.

You can't change the size of the Pasteboard. This is actually an advantage. It enables you to copy and paste objects into the same position in different documents. When you use Edit→ Paste in Front or Edit→ Paste in Back, copied objects are pasted into the same X and Y position they were copied from. Because pasteboards in different documents are the same size, you can paste an object into the same relative position in a different document. This is handy for repeating art but also for working on tricky objects. For example, you can cut complex art from one document, and then paste it in front in a second document. After working on the art in the blank document, you then repeat the cut and paste in front to return it to the original document.

Page Tiling

What it is: *A dotted line indicating the printable area of a document.*
What you should know: *The area is based on the currently selected printer's capabilities. It does not affect how art is saved or imaged for the web.*

The Page Tiling represents the part of the document that images if you print directly out of Illustrator. The capabilities of the printer you're connected to sets these options. That is, you'll see a different imageable area if you select a different printer for your system. It doesn't play a large role in print workflows, and has an even smaller role in a web workflow. We won't discuss it here other than to say that you'll usually want to hide it (View → Hide Page Tiling). For instructions on permanently hiding the Page Tiling, see Chapter 5.

Object Classes

Objects in Illustrator fall into specific classes. Each class has its own attributes. Some objects are limited in the things that you can do with them, so it's good to have a sense of what they are. By default, objects are identified by class in the Layers palette. Each object is named by its class (within angle brackets). For example, every new path is named *<path>*, each guide is named *<guide>*. Thus, you can use the Layers palette to make plain the class of each object in the document. This can be a lifesaver in complex documents where the nature of items may not be immediately clear. In this section, we'll look at each of Illustrator's classes.

In many instances, items are combined to create an object. For example, several paths can be combined to create a compound path, a group, or a blend. This concept can be confusing, since paths are objects as well. One way to recognize

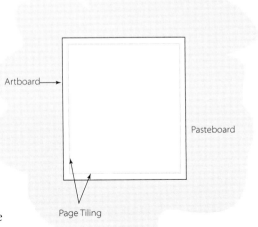

Figure 2.1
The three areas of an Illustrator document

the difference involves the way they are selected. The Selection tool acts on objects and selects them with one click. The Direct Selection tool selects parts of an object, and it may require several clicks to completely select that object. So, a group, which may consist of many items, is an object because the Selection tool can activate it with one click.

Paths

What they are: *The basic connect-the-dots shapes that all of Illustrator's tools create initially.*

What you should know: *Many of the objects that we will discuss have special ways of handling paths. Paths are made of vectors and are converted to pixels when you save to all web formats except SWF, SVG, and PDF.*

Paths are the most common kind of object in Illustrator. As you apply commands to paths, they may change to become other kinds of objects.

Path objects are defined with segments and points. *Points* are markers that record a position in space; *segments* are the lines that connect the points. Neither the segments nor the points have any inherent visual attributes and serve only to record the position and boundaries of an object. An object can have only a single point to be considered a path, but in practice most objects consist of a series of points and segments (see Figure 2.2).

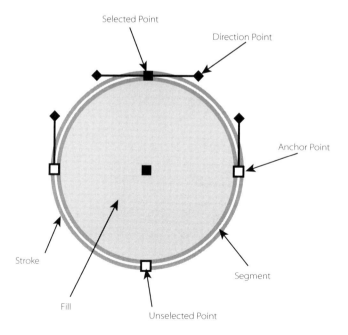

Figure 2.2
The components of a path

Groups

What they are: *One or more objects collected as a unit through the command Object → Group.*

What you should know: *Items in a group are all next to each other in the stacking order. Groups can be moved, styled, and deleted as a single unit. Illustrator includes special tools for selecting grouped items. Some commands create groups automatically.*

Groups are a handy way to connect objects that have a logical association. You can select grouped items with a single click of the Selection tool. The objects in a group retain their relative positions when being moved

As you work on an illustration, you may find it useful to group objects that should be connected. For example, you might group an imported photograph with the caption you've placed under it. This enables you to select and position both items at the same time.

Groups can support special styling that applies to all the members of the group. This is in addition to the individual styling group members may have. That is, a group can have a fill and stroke in addition to the fill and stroke of the members of the group. This behavior is used extensively in the techniques described in this book. You will find more information about groups, layers, appearance, and styles in Chapter 6, "Creating Single Graphics."

Items that are grouped must be next to one another in the stacking order. That is, you can't have objects that aren't in the group *between* group members. If objects aren't next to each other when you create the group, Illustrator repositions the items underneath the topmost item. This arrangement is evident in the Layers palette, where groups appear as a expandable nest (see Figure 2.3).

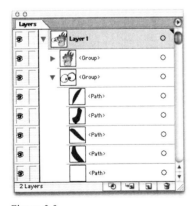

Figure 2.3
A group in the Layers palette

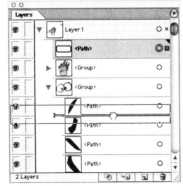

Figure 2.4
Here we're adding items to a group. Note the bar indicating the position the item will occupy when we release the mouse.

You can manually add items to, or delete them from, a group by dragging them in or out of the set in the Layers palette (see Figure 2.4). This approach can be a handy way to modify the contents of a group without ungrouping and regrouping.

Groups may be created automatically when you issue certain commands. For example, when you turn type into outlines a group is created automatically. In addition, Illustrator automatically creates groups when you:

- Create multiple objects with a pathfinder
- Use the Object → Expand or Object → Expand Appearance commands
- Expand a blend (Object → Blend → Expand)
- Make a clipping mask (Object → Clipping Mask → Make)
- Flatten transparency (Object → Flatten Transparency)

Clipping Mask

What it is: *A path that defines the visible areas of other objects.*

What you should know: *Clipping masks can affect either a chosen set of objects or a complete layer. When they affect a specific set, the objects involved are grouped to the clipping mask.*

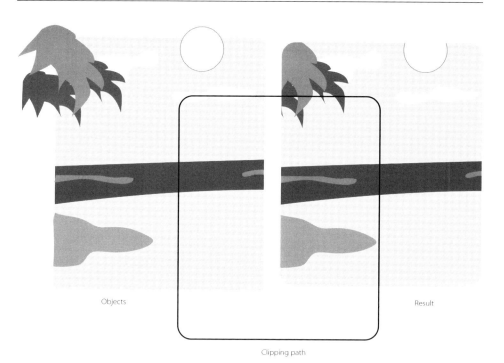

Figure 2.5

An object, its clipping path, and the clipped object

Clipping masks crop items by defining the area that is visible (see Figure 2.5). Users skilled in page layout applications will find the experience similar to using picture boxes in QuarkXPress and frames in Adobe's PageMaker and InDesign. The clipped items remain independent objects and may be styled or modified at any time. Illustrator is a little inconsistent with names here. The command named Clipping Mask produces an object named Clipping Path in the Layers palette. In our discussion, Clipping Path refers to the actual object that defines the visible area.

Illustrator contains two types of clipping masks: clipping groups and layer masks. Both behave the same, but layer masks affect the entire contents of a layer, while clipping groups affect only specific objects. In both cases, the object that does the clipping must be a path, a type object, a compound shape, or a group of those kinds of objects, and it must be on top of the objects that will be clipped. Those objects may be of any type.

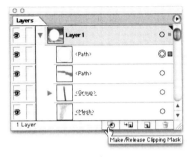

Figure 2.6
Making a layer mask

You make a clipping group by selecting the items to be clipped and choosing Object → Clipping Group → Make or by pressing ⌘+7/Ctrl+7. The top object becomes a mask for the others and is set to a fill and stroke of None. You create a layer mask by clicking the name of the layer in the Layers palette and then choosing Make Clipping Mask from the Layers palette menu (see Figure 2.6). The top object becomes a mask for the other objects in the layer. Additional objects added to the layer are clipped automatically. Once established, clipping masks no longer need to be the topmost object; you can put other things on top of them and they will be clipped as well.

When using masks, keep in mind the difference between the visible area in the document and the bounding box. Illustrator includes clipped parts of objects when determining how large to make a web graphic. You can work around this behavior by sizing the Artboard correctly. Some workflows, such as using SmartObjects in GoLive, don't offer you this option, however. In those cases, you'll need to know how to simplify masks. For more information, see Chapter 7, "Optimizing Spot Illustrations."

Images

What they are: *Pixel-based art. Images can be opened, imported, or created directly in Illustrator.*

What you should know: *Images have resolution. This means you have to handle them with care. Illustrator has limited tools for handling images.*

Illustrator calls anything made out of pixels an *image*. You'll recognize images because individual parts of these objects aren't described with paths. They appear as a single rectangle or a rectangle with crossed diagonal lines (see Figure 2.7). Images can come from Illustrator itself, such as items you create by issuing the command Object → Rasterize.

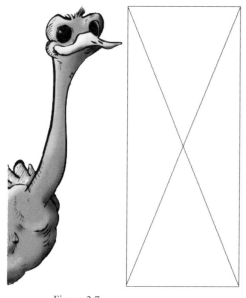

Figure 2.7
An image object in preview and artwork modes

Images may also be created by issuing the commands Object → Flatten Transparency or Object → Expand Appearance. It's not uncommon for images that are pasted or created as a result of one of the Expand commands to be masked. This can cause confusion when you're selecting and moving images, so be certain you know what you've got.

More commonly, images are created in other applications. Illustrator has no direct image-acquisition function. You can't scan into Illustrator the way you can in Photoshop. You can open (File → Open) pixel files, place them (File → Place), and paste them (Edit → Paste). Images you open or paste will be completely contained within the document or embedded. If you place an image, you may embed it or link it. *Linking* imports a preview of the file and creates a connection to the source file. In this way, you can change the graphic in the application it was created in and it will automatically update in Illustrator. You link images by checking the Link option in the Place dialog box (see Figure 2.8).

Because linked images are not part of the Illustrator file, they are not available for some commands. Most notably, some of the filters will not work with them. In general, you should link images only if you want to continue editing them in their source application or if you don't intend to keep them around. This is typically when you're tracing an image or using it for sizing reference.

As we explained earlier, images consist of pixels. This means you should be careful about scaling them up. If you are working with existing web graphics, you shouldn't scale them at all. The edges will decay and the detail will look poor. There is very little wiggle room on this. You can scale them down, but sizing them up invariably causes problems. Images with higher resolutions can be scaled up before edges start to suffer. Use Table 2.1 as a reference.

Table 2.1
A Guide to Scaling Images

ORIGINAL RESOLUTION	MAXIMUM SCALING
300 ppi	400%
200	275%
150	200%
100	130%

Symbols

What they are: Objects consisting of other items that are used in SWF and SVG workflows.

What you should know: Symbols are connected to their definitions, enabling you to modify and replace them in special ways.

Symbols are used to reduce document size and to prepare a document for converting it to a SWF or SVG file. Any kind of object or series of objects can be converted to a symbol (via the Symbols palette) and then placed back into the document. You do this by dragging objects directly into the Symbols palette or selecting items and clicking the New Symbol button in the Symbols palette (see Figure 2.9).

Symbols are inserted into a document either individually or as part of a symbol set. Different symbols can reside in the same set. You insert symbols into a document either by clicking the desired symbol in the Symbols palette and clicking the Place Symbol Instance button or by using the Symbol Sprayer tool.

Because the Symbol Sprayer is typically only used to create an artistic effect, we won't discuss it in depth here. Individual symbol instances are quite useful, however. Because they are connected to their definitions in the Symbols palette, you can adjust a complete layout by switching the definitions of symbols. For example, by setting up a web page using symbols, you can then create a new version of the same page by switching out the symbols. This approach is faster and easier than creating a new page from scratch. We discuss this technique in detail in Chapter 8.

Keep in mind that you can't edit the individual parts of a symbol when it is in the document. For example, you can't edit the text inside a placed symbol. Symbols are based on a rectangle that describes the bounding box of the items contained within the symbol. You also can't transform them in a way that would alter that rectangle. For example, you can't twirl them, use the liquify tools on them, or edit their anchor points with the Direct Selection tool. However, you

Figure 2.8

The Link option in the Place dialog box

can scale, reflect, rotate, and shear them as well as transform the contents of instances and symbol sets using the symbolism tools.

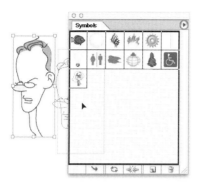

Figure 2.9

Creating a new symbol

Symbols are useful for their special handling options, but are more essential for preparing SWF and SVG output. Flash (the program most commonly used to create and edit SWF files) uses symbols as well. If you use symbols in an Illustrator file, output it as SWF file, and then import the SWF into Flash, the symbols will carry over. This is a major timesaver and will greatly improve the organization of your objects. For more details on this, see Chapter 9, "Creating Animations."

Compound Paths

What they are: *Path objects combined to create a single item. Where the paths overlap each other, there is negative space.*

What you should know: *In addition to being created manually, compound paths are produced automatically when you turn type into outlines and, in some cases, when you expand compound shapes. Sometimes, compound paths don't work quite right and require editing.*

Compound paths are the predecessor of the compound shape (see section "Compound Shapes"). They consist of paths, usually more than one, although a single path can be converted to one. When compound paths consist of more than one shape, the area the paths have in common is set to *negative space*. Negative space is the donut hole in the donut. You can see through to any objects behind it (see Figure 2.10). This is not a permanent arrangement, and can be reversed or edited.

Compound paths are single objects; all the paths that comprise it share the same fill and stroke attributes. The shapes are independent, though, and can be moved, edited, or scaled as needed. You'll select the individual parts of the compound path using the Direct Selection and the Group Selection tools.

To create a compound path manually, select the paths you want to convert and choose Object → Compound Path → Make. The paths are converted to a compound path, which is given the fill and stroke attributes of the top path. You can reverse the arrangement later by choosing choose Object → Compound Path → Release. When you release a compound path, the objects go back to being regular paths, but they don't get their old printing attributes back. Instead, they keep the attributes of the compound path.

Figure 2.10
We begin with two shapes (left) and convert them to a compound path. The common area becomes see-through.

Compound paths are commonly used when type is converted to outlines (Type → Convert To Outlines) or expanded (Object → Expand). You do this by first selecting the text object with one of the selection tools. Artists often use this technique when they want to use letter forms as art. Most users are familiar with this process. When type is expanded, Illustrator converts each letter to a compound path and groups them all together.

Compound Shapes

> What they are: *A single object composed of other objects, such as paths, blends, envelopes, compound paths, symbol sets, text objects, and other compound shapes. Each item in the compound shape has an editable mode that determines how it affects the overall shape of the object. Most commonly, objects add to or subtract from a shape.*
> What you should know: *Compound shapes provide added flexibility when you're designing and you can integrate them with Photoshop.*

Compound shapes are similar to compound paths, but they offer more functionality. Compound paths have one interaction mode: the places where objects overlap is set to negative space. Compound shapes have four interaction modes and can support different modes within the same object.

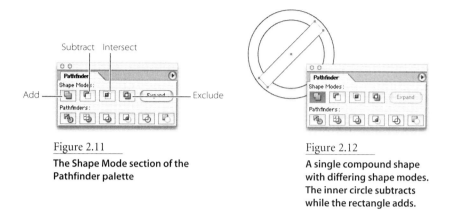

Figure 2.11
The Shape Mode section of the Pathfinder palette

Figure 2.12
A single compound shape with differing shape modes. The inner circle subtracts while the rectangle adds.

You create compound shapes using the Pathfinder palette. To create one, select the desired items and click one of the Shape Mode buttons in the palette (see Figure 2.11) or choose Make Compound Shape from the Pathfinder palette menu.

Each item in a compound shape has a shape mode. The overall appearance of the object is determined by the interaction of the individual objects and their modes. The component items' modes remain independently editable. This enables you to have different shape modes within the same object. In Figure 2.12, the bar is switched from Subtract (as is the inner circle) to Add. This creates the complete effect within the single object.

When you make a compound shape, the top component item's fill and stroke are applied to all the items. If the object has more than one fill or stroke, all of them are applied. Although transparency is carried over to the compound shape, effects are not. Effects and styles can be applied or moved to the compound shape after you create it. If you change your mind, you can turn the components back into individual shapes (by releasing them) or convert them into a simple path shape without component objects (by expanding them). Component objects return to their original attributes in the event that the compound shape is released.

Figure 2.13
A compound shape reveals its components in the Layers palette.

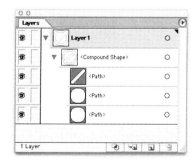

The Layers palette displays the items in a compound shape (see Figure 2.13). You can inspect, add, and remove component objects there.

Guides

What they are: *Nonprinting vector shapes intended to help you lay out art.*
What you should know: *Guides can be created by dragging them out of a document's rulers. You can also convert path objects into guides.*

Guides are essentially special paths with a fill and stroke of None. Illustrator handles them in a special way, enabling you to align objects precisely to them. When you choose View → Snap To Point, Illustrator displays a special cursor that indicates the mouse is on top of a guide (see Figure 2.14). Users make guides by either dragging them out of a ruler or by selecting a path and choosing View → Guides → Make Guides.

In a web workflow, guides are sometimes used to create slices. *Slices* define the cells in an HTML table when you're using the Save For Web command. Users first set the Artboard to the size of the table they wish to create and then position guides to divide the Artboard into rectangles (see Figure 2.15). After choosing Object → Slice → Clip To Artboard, you can choose Object → Slice→ Create From Guides. This creates slice objects that make up the rectangles described by the intersection of the guides and the Artboard. This workflow is not typical but can be handy when you need a table with exact dimensions.

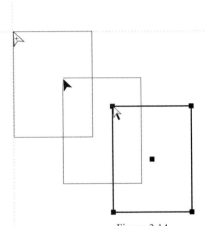

Figure 2.14
Aligning an object to a guide. Note the cursor changes when the mouse is aligned.

Meshes

What they are: *Objects with special fills that can blend color in multiple directions. They are often used to describe three-dimensional shapes and can be handy for creating realistic color modulation.*
What you should know: *Meshes can't have strokes. They become raster art when you're saving SWF and SVG files.*

Meshes break an object's fill up into a chicken-wire array of points. The segments between the points are controlled by direction points, with up to four on each anchor. Each point can also support its own color. Values are blended between anchor points in all directions, based on the curve of the segments (see Figure 2.16). As you reposition the points and segments, the colors are updated to match.

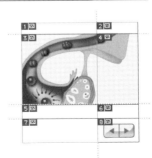

Figure 2.15
Guides are positioned to break up the document and then converted to slices.

Figure 2.16
Color is blended between the mesh points, creating a rounded appearance.

You create a mesh in one of three ways:

- By selecting an object and choosing Object → Create Gradient Mesh
- By clicking on a valid shape with the Mesh tool
- By selecting an object with a gradient and choosing Object → Expand and selecting the Expand Gradient To Gradient Mesh option

The first method is used to create an evenly spaced mesh with regular color changes. The second is used to create a customized blend, and you can use the third method to base a mesh on a preexisting gradient.

Meshes are most commonly used in web graphics to create customized buttons. The glowing aqua-style buttons in the Mac OS could be created in this way. We provide instructions for creating these types of buttons in Chapter 6.

Envelopes

What they are: *Objects distorted via a mesh. Objects in the envelope are pulled and distorted based on the points and segments in a mesh but remain independently editable.*

What you should know: *Envelopes are commonly used to create warped text effects, but can be used on almost every type of object.*

Envelopes use the same interface and tools that meshes do. They differ from meshes in that the curves used describe the way the object is reshaped rather than the way color is blended (see Figure 2.17).

Envelopes are created from a prebuilt shape (Object → Mesh → Create From Warp), an existing path (Object → Mesh → Create From Top Object), or a mesh (Object → Mesh → Create From Mesh). You can't use an existing mesh; you must create the mesh shape from scratch. Often the Warp option is used to create text effects. You see these effects used for banners and logos. Top Object envelopes are typically used when you want to bend an object around a specific shape, such as to wrap it around a pen (see Figure 2.18). Mesh envelopes can be used to create a custom distortion.

In practice, there is no distinction among the types of meshes. You can edit and treat them all the same. The only real distinction is the manner in which they are initially created.

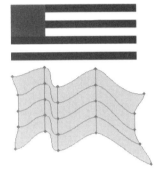

Figure 2.17
Objects, the envelope form, and the resulting object

Slices

What they are: Rectangular paths that mark where cells are created in an HTML table.
What you should know: Slices can be made to a specific size; you can also create them so that they update automatically as specific items change. Because tables are rectangular, Illustrator may need to create its own slices to fill up space.

Slices represent the areas where table cells are made when you issue the File → Save For Web command and select the Tables option. Graphic space is usually described with CSS layers, tables, or both. (We discussed this topic in Chapter 1, "Core Terms and Concepts.")

Slices mark the size and location of each table cell. When you save for the Web, the cell is filled with a graphic by default. Illustrator breaks up the objects along the slice lines, putting them back together in the web page (see Figure 2.19).

You'll use slices only when creating HTML files. You can read more about them in Chapter 8.

Figure 2.18
A typical warp and top object envelope

Figure 2.19

A sliced graphic and the resulting web graphics

Graphs

> What they are: *Objects created by using any of the graphing tools—the familiar bar charts and line graphs used to express numerical data.*
>
> What you should know: *Graphs are connected to the data they describe, which means they update automatically as information changes. They are a special kind of object and aren't available for a lot of techniques other than graphing.*

You create *graphs* by using the graphing tool suite. Simply click and drag with any of the tools to define the area that the graph data occupies. From there, you enter or import your numeric data and adjust the graph to suit your tastes.

Graphs feature their own toolset, selection techniques, and special ways of being styled in Illustrator. They are not well integrated with the other tools. For example, graphs are one of the few object classes that can't be converted to a symbol. Nor can graphs be used as brushes or masks or anything other than a graph. You can convert a graph into paths and text by choosing Object → Ungroup, but this makes them uneditable as graphs. You can't go back and update the graph information automatically.

Blends

> What they are: *Paths converted to blends using the Blend tool or the command Object → Blend → Make.*
>
> What you should know: *Blends create automatic intermediate shapes between path objects, blending their color, size, and position. The effect is similar to a "tween" in Flash. As you edit the shapes that are blended, the intermediate objects update automatically.*

Blends are a handy way to create a series of objects that meld the attributes of other objects. You start with paths or groups of paths (you need at least two, but it could be more) and then convert them to a blend with the command Object → Blend → Make (see Figure 2.20). You could also use the Blend tool, but this is a less common approach. The Blend tool bases the appearance of the intermediate objects in a blend on the anchor points clicked when creating the blend. The result is often twisted or inverted objects. After you create a blend, you can add new shapes to it by selecting additional objects and repeating the command.

Blends are used a lot for creating custom borders and effects. They also have a special use in animation; objects created in a blend can be used as frames in sequential animations. This makes it easy to bend or alter a shape that would otherwise be difficult to redraw (see Figure 2.21). For more on this special use of blends, see Chapter 9.

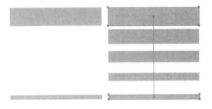

Figure 2.20
Objects before and after blending. Note that the shapes in between do not have vector outlines when highlighted.

Understanding Color Controls

To build web graphics, you must be able to use color. In this section, we examine the essential tools and techniques for coloring objects in Illustrator: fills and strokes, the Color palette, the Tools palette color controls, swatches, and swatch libraries. We also discuss quick tips and essential setup tools.

Fills and Strokes

What they are: The basic color attributes of all vector art. The fill is placed within a shape; strokes are used along the path itself.

What you should know: You can set the fill and stroke a number of ways. Also, be aware that objects can have more than one of each type.

Figure 2.21
These objects will become frames in an animation. Note how the first and last objects generate all of the objects in between.

Fill and *stroke* are key ideas in Illustrator. Fill describes the area inside a path shape. It can be a solid color, a gradient, or a pattern (see Figure 2.22). Gradients, which blend colors together, run in a straight line or a circle. You specify them using the Gradient palette. Patterns are predefined designs that fill up a path, like wallpaper. You can use existing ones or create your own.

The *stroke* is the area along the path. You can think of it as a border for the shape. By default, it is in front of the fill. Half of the stroke is on one side of the path and half on the other. You can't change this. This sometimes creates hiccups when creating borders for small (text) objects and understanding the actual size of objects. Chapter Six provides techniques for handling these issues. Strokes can have color or patterns, but not gradients (see Figure 2.23). On the other hand, you can set the width of a stroke, make it dashed, or apply a brush to it.

To set the fill and stroke attributes, you need, at a minimum, either the Tool palette or the Color palette. You may also use the Swatches, Gradient, and Stroke palettes. To add more than one fill or stroke, you use the Appearance palette.

When you set these attributes, you are setting the *current* fill or stroke. The current fill or stroke applies to any item you've selected or to the next object you create. For example, if you set the fill to black and you have an object selected, that object will get the black fill. If nothing is selected on the page, the next item you create receives the black fill. Keep in mind that some objects, like text, mesh points, and graphs, have automatic default values that override the current setting.

Figure 2.22
Various fills

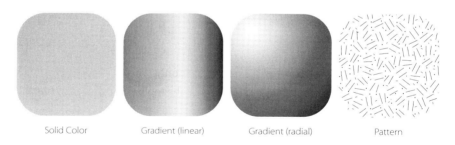

Figure 2.23
Various stroke options

The Tool Palette Color Controls

What it is: Controls contained in a section at the bottom of the Tool palette.
What you should know: You can select the current fill and stroke here for editing in other palettes, open some palettes, and set common attributes.

Near the bottom of the Tool palette you'll see a section devoted to object attributes (see Figure 2.24). In this section, we'll look at these attributes.

Fill and Stroke Swatches

The solid box represents the fill, and the outlined box represents the stroke. You can change only one attribute (the fill or the stroke) at a time. The attribute that's in front (the active attribute) is the one you can change. If you want to set the other item, click on it to activate it. You can also use the keyboard shortcut X to do this.

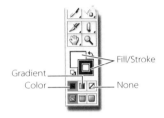

Figure 2.24
The bottom section of the Tool palette

An icon on the toolbar displays the current fill or stroke. That is, if the fill is a pattern, you'll see a small thumbnail of the pattern in the toolbar. If more than one item is selected and they have different attributes, Illustrator displays question marks in the icons. You can set solid color fills by double-clicking on either swatch to open the Color Picker dialog box. Using the Color Picker is not the most efficient way to set color, though, and you should avoid this approach if you can. We'll discuss other options in the sections that follow.

You can color objects by dragging the fill or stroke swatch directly onto them. This is usually done with objects you have not yet selected. You can drag either the fill or stroke swatch onto items, but you can set the active characteristic only. That is, if you drag the fill swatch onto an item but the stroke attribute is forward in the toolbar, you'll apply the fill color to the stroke of the item. The exception to this is when you're dragging gradient fills—gradients are always applied to fills.

SWAPPING FILL AND STROKE

You click the icon shown in Figure 2.25 to switch the active fill and stroke attributes. For example, if your object has a black fill and a white stroke, you'll get a white fill and a black stroke. This technique is often used in conjunction with the default fill and stroke shortcut to style an object quickly. The keyboard shortcut is Shift+X.

Figure 2.25
Swapping the fill and stroke

DEFAULT FILL AND STROKE

Click the icon shown in Figure 2.26 to set the active fill and stroke to the default style in the Style palette. Unless you've changed it, the default style is a white fill with a one-point black stroke. In the Style palette, Illustrator indicates the default style with a corresponding icon. The keyboard shortcut for this command is D. Using this in conjunction with the other color keyboard shortcuts can speed common fill and stroke combinations. For example, to set a black fill and no stroke, press D for the default values, and press Shift+X to swap the fill and stroke. If the fill is active, press X to bring the stroke forward, and then press / to set the stroke to None.

Figure 2.26
Setting the default fill and stroke

Click here to set the current fill and stroke as the default.

Color, Gradient, and None

Click the Color button to display the Color palette and set the active color to the one you used previously in the Color palette. The Gradient button does the same thing except that it shows the Gradient palette. It also activates the fill attribute automatically. The None button sets the current attribute to nothing. Empty attributes are invisible. The shortcuts are next to each other on the keyboard: press < for Fill, press > for Gradient, and press / for None.

The Color Palette

> *What it is:* A palette that you'll use to set color values using numeric inputs.
> *What you should know:* In addition to setting fill and stroke colors, you can use this palette to define gradient sliders and gradient mesh node colors.

You'll use the Color palette a lot in Illustrator. For example, it lets you define colors, either for the fill or stroke, or for a color component of a gradient or gradient mesh. The colors mixed here can be applied to existing items or saved as swatches for later use.

The fill and stroke icons in the Color palette are synced with the swatches in the Tool palette. As you activate attributes in one palette, they go forward in the other as well. They behave the same way in all respects. You can click one to activate it, double-click to open the Color Picker, and click-drag onto objects to style them.

You can build color using any of the five color models. You choose the model from the palette's flyaway menu or by Shift-clicking on the spectrum at the base of the palette to cycle through the options. For web graphics, it doesn't make much difference which color mode you use as long as the document is in RGB.

The Web Safe RGB color model represents a full RGB spectrum using hexadecimal values. (For information on hex, see Chapter 1.) This is different from displaying only the 216 web-safe colors we discussed in Chapter 1.

Each color component slider is bracketed with six stops, which the slider will snap to as you drag. These brackets represent the truly web-safe combinations. When your cursor is snapped onto one of those combinations for all three color sliders, the color is web safe. If a color isn't web safe (which is most of the time), Illustrator displays the In Web Color button (see Figure 2.27). Click this button to correct a color to its nearest web-safe equivalent.

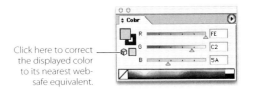

Click here to correct the displayed color to its nearest web-safe equivalent.

Figure 2.27
The Web Safe RGB model with the In Web Color button

If you're pasting hex numbers from another application, you'll probably want to use the Color Picker. The problem is that you can't paste a complete six-digit hex number into the fields in the Color palette. You could memorize the number and type it in manually, but it's easier to double-click a swatch and use the Picker. At the bottom of the Color Picker you'll see the # field. This is where you'll paste the hex number.

Don't be afraid to mix color models in the palette. Just consider the models different ways of describing the same color, and keep in mind that some slider sets are better suited for specific tasks. For example, to make a tint of a color, you could switch to the HSB model and drag the B slider left (to darken) or right (to lighten) a color. The CMYK sliders enable you to add black to a color, creating a shadow version of the color.

The Swatches Palette

What it is: *A palette you'll use to manage and apply colors, gradients, and patterns.*
What you should know: *Although not strictly necessary in all cases, it's a good practice to store colors as swatches. Using swatches increases consistency and makes it easier to edit files later.*

Use the Swatches palette to store the colors you use in the document. To save a color as a swatch, drag a color swatch from the Tool or Color palette directly onto the Swatches palette (see Figure 2.28). To save the active color as a swatch, you can also click the New Swatch button at the base of the palette. Be careful not to drag objects onto the palette, because this creates a new pattern swatch. There's nothing wrong with that; it's just a different technique. You can save gradients as swatches by dragging the swatch from the Gradient palette or clicking the New Swatch button when a gradient fill is active.

You click a swatch in the palette to set it to the active attribute. That is, if the fill attribute is forward in the Color palette, click on a swatch in the Swatches palette to make the fill that color. Alternately, you can drag a swatch directly onto objects to color them.

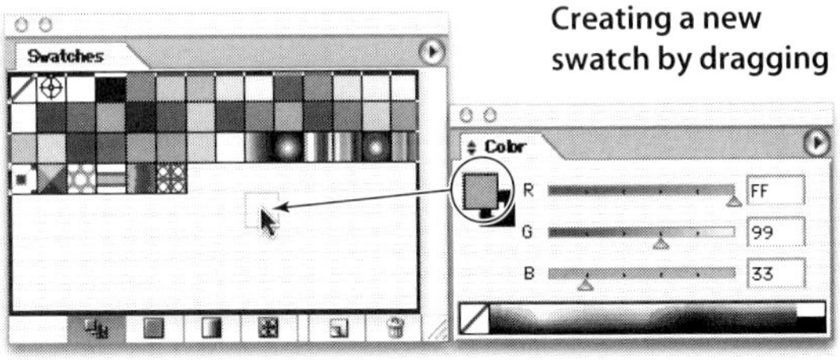

Figure 2.28
Creating a new swatch by dragging

You can set a swatch's options (including its name) by double-clicking on the swatch. This opens the Swatch Options dialog box. Gradient and pattern swatches have no option except their names, but color swatches have several. Most importantly, you can adjust the color build of the swatch. But be aware that if you do this, objects that were styled using the swatch are not automatically updated. By default, there is no connection between a (non-global) swatch's color definition and the objects that have been styled using the swatch. Standard swatches are strictly storage locations for color values.

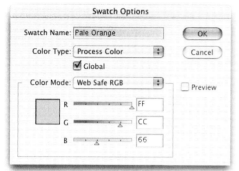

Figure 2.29
The Global checkbox in the Swatch Options dialog box

Swatches that are saved using the Global option (as spot colors are) are connected to the objects that use them. To set this up, create a new swatch and then double-click it. In the Swatch Options dialog box, click the Global option (see Figure 2.29). After you apply the swatch to objects, they will update as the swatch changes. This is a great way to streamline large changes in a document. Applying global swatches to objects rather than unique color mixes allows you to switch all of the colors at once. This works for gradients, patterns, and symbols that use the swatch as well. When a global swatch is active, the Color palette displays a tint slider, enabling you to style objects with percentages of the color. The tint percentages are retained when the swatch color is changed. In Chapter 6, we'll use the concept of the global swatch to create buttons that can be easily reused with various color schemes.

The swatches that you create are part of the current document and are not automatically available in other documents.

Libraries

What they are: *Documents that you'll load as palettes to use the brushes, styles, swatches, or symbols contained within them.*

What you should know: *Illustrator ships with a set of prebuilt libraries, including PANTONE colors and the web-safe set.*

Libraries are Illustrator native or EPS files that you load as palettes. Illustrator reads the document and displays some of its contents as a library. The program offers libraries for brushes, styles, swatches, and symbols. You'll find them all at the bottom of the Window menu. To open one, choose it from the appropriate menu. For example, to load the default brushes as a library, choose Window → Brush Libraries → Default_RGB.

You can load your documents as libraries by choosing Other Library from any library submenu. For example, if you want to get at the swatches you created in a previous document, choose Window → Swatch Libraries → Other Library. In the resulting dialog box, navigate to the file you've saved. This is another good reason to use swatches: Only the swatches in the document are opened as a library and not every color used in the document.

Libraries resemble palettes in appearance. The key difference is that you can't edit the contents of a library. Therefore, the palette offers no buttons at its base and instead displays a pencil with a line through it, indicating that the contents are not editable. To use the contents of a library, click on an item within the library.

To learn more about setting up libraries and customizing default settings, see Chapter 5, "Preparing the Work Environment."

The Stroke Palette

> What it is: *The palette you'll use to set the width and style of strokes.*
> What you should know: *This palette is often docked to the Color palette to keep it handy.*

The Stroke palette sets the active width of the stroke. Like the active color, the active width sets the size of the stroke of the current selection (if there is one) and of the next object you create. The Stroke palette sets only the width and basic style of the stroke and not its color.

You use the Weight field to set the width of the stroke. You can use the up and down arrows to the left of the field, dial in a number directly, or choose one of the preset values from the menu to the right of the field.

Strokes can be dashed or straight. To make more complicated strokes, you'll need to use brushes. To make a dashed stroke, check the Dash option in the bottom left of the palette. This section of the palette is hidden by default. If it's hidden, choose Show Options from the Stroke palette menu. When using the Dash option, you can set up to three pairs of dash and gap widths. You don't need to set anything other than the first dash value. If you don't set a gap value, the dash value will be used.

Strokes also have caps and joins. *Caps* are the ends of strokes and dashes; *joins* are the corners. Caps can be flat, round, or projecting. Round caps end with semicircles, and projecting caps end with squares that rise beyond the end of the item. Commonly, round caps are used to make round dashed lines. If you set the dash width to 0 and the gap width wide enough when using round caps, the line appears as a circle.

Joins can be miter, round, or beveled. Miter joins are sharp corners that project, round corners have curved turns, and beveled corners flatten the edges. Miter joins also have a miter limit. Because miter corners project, stroke weight is often larger at the corners of paths than in flat areas. The tighter the angle of a join, the wider the stroke will be at the corners. Miter Limit sets the maximum stroke weight for the path as a multiple of the stroke's weight. For example, a path with a 1-point stroke and a miter limit of 4 can have corners up to 4 points in width. If the angle of the corner is so tight that it would result in a stoke larger than 4 points, the corner will be beveled. To keep corners mitered, increase the miter limit. Figure 2.30 shows the stroke options.

The Transparency Palette

What it is: The palette you'll use to set the opacity and blend mode of items.
What you should know: Although Illustrator graphics support a full range of transparency, most web graphics do not. They will look the same, but they won't be transparent against other objects in the web page.

The Transparency palette enables you to set the opacity and blend mode of objects and to make opacity masks. Opacity is the light-stopping power of an object. The more opaque something is, the less you can see through it. By default, if you create an object with an opacity of 100 percent, you won't be able to see anything behind it. At 0 percent opacity, the object is invisible. At levels in between, you see more or less of the other objects. This feature also has

the effect of lightening or darkening colors based on the objects beneath them. Against white, objects lighten overall. To set the opacity of an item, select it and then enter a number in the Opacity field or click the arrow to the right of the field to use the slider.

A blend modes is a special type of transparency that mixes colors that cross each other. Unlike opacity—where objects are lightened when they are on a blank area of the page— other objects must be involved to change an object's colors. When you apply a blend mode to an object or attribute, the colors of an object change based on the color in the

Figure 2.30
Stroke options

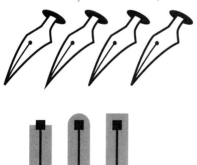

object, the object below it, and the blend mode applied. As you adjust the colors in the objects, the effect is updated automatically.

Blend modes are based on complex math that often makes them seem obscure and difficult to anticipate. While many users report a hit-or-miss strategy of trying different modes until they find an effect that pleases them, it is important to remember that each mode was created as a production aid. When used correctly, blend modes are often part of a more focused technique, as in Figure 2.31. Several are discussed in context in Chapter 6.

Opacity masks map the transparency of an object to the tone of other objects. The darker the masking objects are, the less opaque the masked items are, as in Figure 2.32. This is often used to create ghosting effects and to blend objects together. The process is somewhat complex, space prohibits a full discussion here.

Appearance Palette

What it is: A palette that gives complete details on the attributes that affect a selection. *What you should know:* This palette is useful for complex effects and its use is connected to the Style palette.

The Appearance palette lists everything that affects an object's display. It shows its fill and stroke, any effects or transparency in use, and the attributes that an object inherits from its layer or group. The items are listed from the top to the bottom in the palette. That is, objects at the top of this palette are on top of items in the selection.

Figure 2.31

The effects of the Normal, Overlay and Color Burn modes applied to the text (see color insert).

The object class appears in bold at the top of the palette. Attributes within the class are listed below it. Items that affect an object from layers or groups are listed at the top. For example, with a basic shape, the fill and stroke would be under the word *Path*. Clicking on an attribute activates it, enabling you to edit it with the Color or Swatches palette. It also targets the attribute for opacity or effects. That is, if you click on the fill attribute in the Appearance palette and reduce the opacity, only the fill will be affected and not the stroke (see Figure 2.33). When an attribute has an effect or transparency applied to it, it will have an upside-down triangle next to it, with the special features listed below it.

Figure 2.32
Note the thumbnails of the original art and the opacity mask in the Transparency palette. The dark areas in the mask are transparent, the lighter areas are opaque.

Whenever objects have a special appearance, such as an additional fill, an effect, or a brush stroke, the target circle next to the object in the Layers palette displays a gradient. Normally, the circle is clear. The gradient circle icon indicates that the art has a special appearance. This partially explains the icons at the base of the palette. The first button from the left features either three gradient circles or a gradient circle followed by two plain circles. This button determines whether the next object created has the same special features as the current one or if they are discarded. When the three gradients are showing, it means that the special appearance will be applied to the next object you create.

At the other setting (a gradient circle followed by two plain circles), the extra features are discarded, leaving a plain object with a single fill and stroke. This setting is often a source of confusion. Often users use an effect such as a drop shadow on an object and then find that all the objects they create have drop shadows. If you're going to start using such effects, be certain you have this option set the way you want it.

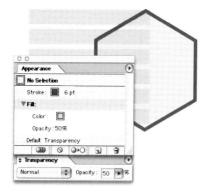

Figure 2.33
Here the fill is targeted in the Appearance palette. After we set the opacity to 50 percent, the stroke remains opaque.

The button with the gradient pointing to the plain circle strips all transparency, extra fills and strokes, and effects from the selection. Use this button to quickly get rid of anything other than the basic characteristics of an item.

The Duplicate Selected Item button copies any item in the Appearance palette. You can use this button after highlighting a fill or stroke to create additional attributes to the path. Any effects or transparency the item has are duplicated as well. The Appearance palette menu also provides commands that let you add new fills and strokes.

Appearance can be useful for creating common effects that might normally require multiple objects. For examples of these techniques, see Chapter 6.

Styles

What they are: A tool for recording, applying and managing the contents of the Appearance palette.
What you should know: Styles aren't just for fancy effects-driven techniques; they can streamline everyday styling by saving common fill-stroke combinations.

A style is a set of object attributes. It is typically a fill and stroke combination, but it may also include a series of effects. The default styles all use effects. This creates the impression that styles are useful only for high stylization, but that's not the case. Simple styles can record the most commonly used object appearances to save you the time of applying each fill and stroke setting manually. Further, styles are linked to objects, which means they are updated automatically as you make changes to the style. For example, if you used styles to set a series of buttons to red fills and black strokes, you could change them all to blue fills by changing the definition of the style.

To create a style, first check the Appearance palette. The contents of this palette are saved as a style. Be sure the palette doesn't contain any settings you don't expect. Also check the strokes used. Stroke weight and options are recorded in a style but they are not displayed in the Appearance palette. Next, click the New Style button in the Style palette. Alternately, drag the swatch at the top of the Appearance palette directly onto the Swatches palette.

When a selected item uses a style, the Appearance palette displays the style's name next to the object's class. You can still edit the appearance of the item, but if you do, you sever the connection to the style. If you choose, you can also reset the style based on the changes you made. To do this, choose Redefine Style from the Appearance palette menu. This updates all of the objects that use the style automatically.

Using the Direct Selection Tool

The Direct Selection tool ( ) is the most important tool in Illustrator.

You'll probably make most of your selections with it because it offers you complete access to all items in a document. You can select all of an item or just the specific point you want to tweak. But Direct Selection is a complex tool that requires attention to detail.

This section explains how to use the Direct Selection tool efficiently. You can use this tool to accomplish all of the selection functions of the Selection tool, even in complex selections and different view modes.

Basic Selecting

What you're doing: *Selecting items with the Direct Selection tool.*
Why you're doing it: *It's more convenient to stick with a single tool for your selecting rather than switching all the time.*

The Direct Selection tool is a little tricky to master. It behaves differently in different view modes. Sometimes it's difficult to see what you have selected until you try to move the object. Also, some techniques, such as Snap To Point, require that you first select and then move the object. When you're first learning to select with this tool, consider selecting and moving as two different behaviors. Try to avoid click-dragging quickly or going click-crazy. When using the Direct Selection tool, these behaviors simply lead to frustration.

First let's see what Use Area Select does. Use Area Select is a preference (Edit → Preferences → General) that is enabled by default. When this option is activated, you can select an entire filled path by clicking on its interior when the document is in preview mode. If the object has a fill of None, this doesn't work. It also doesn't work when the document or layer is in outline mode.

When Use Area Select is on and the Direct Selection Tool is over a fill, the cursor display adds a black box. Be careful that you are actually *inside* the fill area. When you are directly on the path but not on an anchor point, the cursor will also display the black box. When you see the black box, click to select the entire shape. If you are in outline mode and you want to select an entire path with the Direct Selection tool (by clicking Option/Alt), click directly on the path to select all of it. After doing this, be sure to release Option/Alt before moving on to other activities.

To select a specific anchor point, position the Direct Selection tool directly on top of it. When you're over an anchor point, the cursor will display a white box. When you see this white box, click to select the point.

When anchor points are selected, they appear solid in the color of the layer they are on. Unselected points appear hollow, or white. When segments are selected but not anchor points, you will see the direction handles for the segment (if there are any), but the anchor points will be hollow.

To select a segment, position your cursor over it and click. You will need to place the tip of the Direct Selection tool precisely on the path. If you are too far on the inside of a filled path in preview mode, you may select the whole path inadvertently. The effect you get when moving a segment depends on whether the path is curved. If the segment is affected by direction points, dragging the segment adjusts its curve but the anchor points remain in their position. If it's a straight segment, dragging will reposition the segment and the anchors.

When you click-drag with the Direct Selection tool, a guide follows the motion of your cursor, creating a rectangle. Any segment or anchor point within the rectangle is selected when you release the mouse.

Complex Selecting

What you're doing: *Selecting complex objects or multiple anchor points.*
Why you're doing it: *It's more convenient to stick with a single tool for your selecting needs rather than switching all the time.*

The Direct Selection tool is connected to the Group Selection tool. When using either tool, holding down Option/Alt will temporarily switch you to the other. Most users start with the more versatile Direct Selection tool and then switch to the Group Selection tool as the need arises. The Group Selection tool selects all of the anchor points on a path with a single click. Clicking again on the same path selects all objects grouped to that path. If items are then added to the group, additional clicks select those items as well. The same technique works for items that are associated but not necessarily grouped. Shapes in compound paths, compound shapes, and enveloped objects are affected this way.

The second important idea is that Shift-clicking toggles the selection state of an item when you're using the arrow-style selection tools. This is not the case with the lasso-style selection tools or the Magic Wand, where Shift adds to a selection and Option/Alt subtracts from a selection. This works for dragging as well as clicking and, in conjunction with Option/Alt, switching to the Group Selection tool. So, if you wanted to completely select all but one of a series of objects with the Direct Selection tool, you could hold down Option/Alt and drag a marquee around all the objects and then hold down Shift+Option/Shift+Alt and click on the offending object.

When you convert text to outlines, you create a group of compound paths. If you're attempting to select some but not all of the letters, your best bet is to do it in preview mode so that you can take advantage of the Use Area Select preference. From there, you can Shift-click on the items you want to select. If you want to do this in outline mode, or if your text does not have fills, you'll need to use modifiers unless you want to ungroup. If the letters you want to select have counters, it will be more difficult. With the Direct Selection tool, hold down Option/Alt and click on the edge of a path. If the letter has a counter (like a *b* or an *e*) click a second time to select that as well. Position your cursor on another path and, while holding down Shift+Option/Shift+Alt, click to select that path as well. If the second shape has a counter, release the Shift key, hold down Option/Alt, and click the counter. This will add the counter without deselecting the other objects. Repeat as necessary.

If you've spent a long time selecting, you should save the selection (Select → Save Selection). This saves the selected state of specific anchor points and objects. After choosing the command, you will be prompted to name the selection. Give it a name that will make sense to you a year from now. Once named, saved selections appear at the bottom of the Selection menu.

Duplicating and Aligning

This section describes how to use the Direct Selection tool to duplicate and align objects. We also explain the importance of Snap To Point and Area Select.

Duplicating

What you're doing: *Creating copies of items by dragging them.*
Why you're doing it: *It's faster to duplicate items exactly where you want them rather than copying, pasting, and repositioning.*

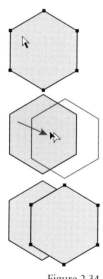

Figure 2.34

After selecting the object, start to move it and then add the Option/Alt key to create a copy. Keep pressing the modifier key until you release the mouse.

Duplicating is a keyboard shortcut that works with most selection and transformation tools in Illustrator (key exception: the Free Transform tool). Any time you press down the Option/Alt key as you drag an object with a selection or transformation tool, you move or transform a duplicate of it. This is true when you drag objects around the page with the Direct Selection tool (see Figure 2.34) or gradient sliders in the Gradient palette. It's important to note that you should add your modifier key after you start dragging. With most tools, adding it before you start creates a different effect. .

Using this method to duplicate items is different than copying and pasting in two ways. First, the duplicated item is directly in front of the original object in the stacking order. Pasted objects are at the top of all objects by default. Often this means that duplicated objects require less repositioning both forward and backward. Second, a duplicate retains any group affiliation that the original object had. For example, if you Option/Alt+drag an object in a compound shape, the duplicated item will retain the compound shape (see Figure 2.35). This may be exactly what you want, but if it isn't, you should consider copying and pasting instead.

Option/Alt+dragging objects is often followed up by choosing Object → Transform → Transform Again. This keystroke repeats the pervious transformation, including the copying aspect. So if you want to make a series of evenly spaced buttons, it makes sense to drag-duplicate one the distance you require and then create the others using the Transform Again command.

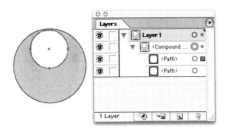

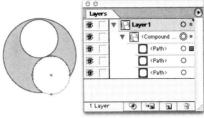

Figure 2.35

Option/Alt+dragging a member of a group (left) creates a duplicate in the same group (right).

Snap To Point

What you're doing: *Aligning anchor points in different paths to create perfect fits when positioning objects.*

Why you're doing it: *To accurately position items in ways unavailable in the Align palette.*

The command View → Snap To Point changes the display of cursors when the mouse is on top of anchor points or guides. The anchor points must be unlocked and visible for this to work. You can use this technique to line up objects accurately.

The key to this technique is to select first and then position the Direct Selection tool accurately before dragging directly onto another anchor point. This is usually done with the Direct Selection tool because the Selection tool's bounding box often interferes with cursor positioning.

To set this up, first get your selection correct. Next, position the cursor directly on top of an anchor point. You'll know your mouse is there when the cursor displays a white box. Next, click and drag to another anchor point. Again, the cursor will change when you are over the point—this time, it turns from black to white (see Figure 2.36). To move a duplicate, press down Option/Alt after you start the drag.

Figure 2.36

Snap To Point cursors: when over an anchor point; while dragging; when over another point; when over a point with a duplicate.

Exploring Basic Text

This section highlights the three kinds of text in Illustrator and explains why certain types create problems for web graphics. We also tackle the vital concept of the bounding box.

Space prohibits a full discussion of character and paragraph options. Instead, we'll focus on the most essential issues.

Type

> What it is: *The three models and two orientations for type flow.*
> What you should know: *Illustrator offers six type tools; you can get away with just using one.*

Illustrator allows you to create three models of type as graphics: point, area, and path.

Also, type can flow in two directions: horizontal and vertical. This yields six different models for text, and there is a tool for each one of them. With a little practice, though, you can use the basic Type tool to create all six kinds. For web graphics, though, you'll most commonly be creating horizontal point type.

Type Orientation

Type runs either horizontally or vertically. Vertical type is associated with Asian languages and, as such, breaks left to right instead of right to left. You can't reverse this and will need to plan ahead. As you create type, you can use the horizontal or vertical versions of the tools (the vertical versions have down arrows on the icons), but this can slow you down. Instead, Shift-click when using the horizontal type tool to switch to vertical as you create the text. Another common method is to create the type horizontally first and then switch to a selection tool. Choose Type → Type Orientation → Vertical to switch the direction.

Point Type

Point type is created when you click in the document with the Type tool. Don't click-drag—just click. This type has a single anchor point, and the text orients itself about this anchor point. Point type is best suited for text consisting of only a line or two and is therefore best for most web graphics. If you have more than a line or two to say, you should consider making HTML text instead of a graphic. Once you've clicked, type in the text you want. To break to the next line, you'll need to press Return or Shift+Return.

Area Type

Area type is created when you click-drag with the Type tool or click with the hot point of the Type tool on a closed path. The *hot point* is the horizontal bar toward the base of the Type tool icon (see Figure 2.37). When that part of the icon touches a closed path, the normally rectangular dotted line around the icon becomes rounded, indicating it has switched to the Area Type tool. If the hot point crosses an open path, it switches to the Path Type tool. If this happens, you can toggle back to the Area Type tool by holding down Option/Alt. When you click on a path this way, it loses its fill and stroke and becomes a pure bounding box for text. You will be hard-pressed to change it back, so be careful before you do.

Area type wraps when it hits the boundaries of its container and is best suited for paragraphs. Since there aren't a lot of paragraphs in web graphics, we'll move on to the more common path type.

Figure 2.37

The hot point in the Type tool icon

When this point touches a path, the Type tool switches to the Area or Path Type tool.

Path Type

Path type is created when you click on an existing path with the Path Type tool or with the Type tool positioned with the hot point directly on a path. If the path is closed (such as a circle), hold down Option/Alt before you click to create the path type. Once you click, the path loses its fill and stroke and becomes a baseline for type. Switch to the Direct Selection tool and you'll see an I-beam in the spot you clicked on the path. Click-drag the I-beam to reposition the text about the path. Remember that you can still use paragraph alignment on path type. It often makes sense to position the I-beam on an anchor point and center the text about that.

Path and area type typically have a bounding area larger than the actual characters. The (invisible) containers for the text are counted when Illustrator calculates how large to make the web graphic. This usually results in a too-large graphic upon export. Your options in this case are to expand the type or to plan for this by building your Artboard correctly. Of the two, the Artboard is the better solution because it allows you to change your mind by leaving it as text. For information on setting up the Artboard, see Chapter 5.

Transformation Essentials

This section covers key uses of the basic transformation tools. It is intended for quick review of these often-misunderstood tools.

Core Transform Tools

What you're doing: *Transforming objects using a family of similar tools.*
Why you're doing it: *The tools provide a high degree of flexibility.*

The Reflect, Rotate, Shear, and Scale tools all behave in the same way. If you learn one, you've learned them all. The tools are tricky in that they offer three distinct styles of transformation and that keyboard shortcuts must be timed correctly. While you're learning to use them, be careful about what you do and try to get in the habit of not clicking needlessly.

Point of Transformation

The *point of transformation* is a crosshair that appears whenever you select one of these tools. This is the location around which the action takes place. It is where objects rotate, scale toward, and reflect across. By default, the point of transformation is the center of the bounding box of the current selection—and it will stay there unless you move it. Moving it can be a great idea—it enables you to position things as you transform them—but be aware that you don't strictly need to do this.

To reset the point of transformation, click anywhere with one of the transform tools. Again, don't drag—just click. The crosshair is reset and the cursor switches to the transform arrowhead. If you have moved the point and want to move it again, either click-drag directly on the point of transformation or double-click elsewhere to reset it.

Numeric Transforming

You can transform a selected item numerically in several ways. The fastest method is to double-click on the Scale, Rotate, Reflect, or Shear tool to open the dialog box corresponding to the tool. This kind of transformation takes place about the center of the selection's bounding box. To transform numerically about a different point, select the items to transform and then, using Scale, Rotate, Reflect, or Shear, hold down Option/Alt and click where you want to set the point of transformation

Be aware that this kind of numeric transforming does not enable you to set objects to a specific size, but rather to a percentage of their current size. To set things to an exact pixel dimension, use the Transform palette.

Visual Transforming

You can click-drag with the transform tools to adjust an object visually. This method enables you to evaluate the changes on the fly. To do this, first decide if you want to move the point of transformation. As noted in the previous section, clicking in the document with the Scale, Rotate, Reflect, or Shear tool resets the point to transformation, so be careful. For best results when transforming, move your cursor away from the action before click-dragging. This will give you plenty of room to see what is happening in the document. If you start your drag too close to the objects, it will be harder to control the action. Consult Figures 2.38–2.41 to see cursor positioning, dragging, and shortcuts for performing common transformations.

TRANSFORMATION ESSENTIALS **57**

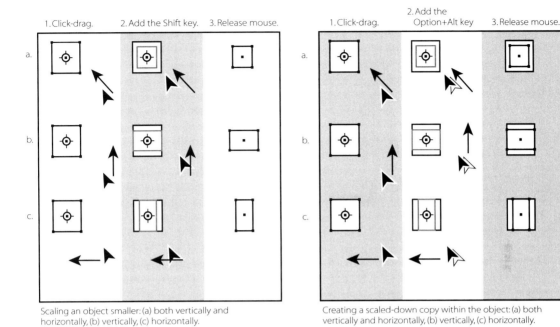

Figure 2.38
Scaling an object

Figure 2.39
Rotating an object

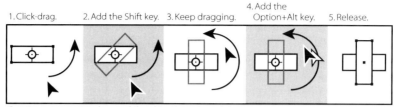

Creating a copy rotated around the object's center point.

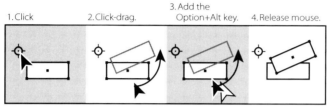

Creating a copy rotated around a point outside the object.

Figure 2.40
Reflecting an object

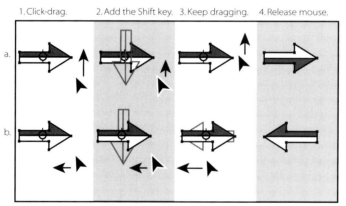

Reflecting an object around its center point: (a) vertically, (b) horizontally

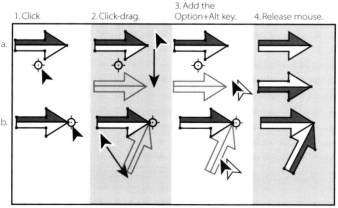

Reflecting an object around an external point to create a copy: (a) vertically, (b) diagonally.

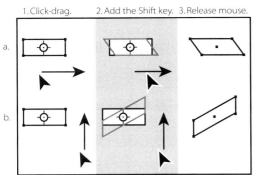
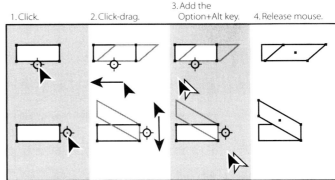

Figure 2.41
Shearing an object

Using the Transform Palette

What you're doing: *Transforming objects to a specific size.*
Why you're doing it: *You will often need objects to be a particular pixel size to fit in an HTML table cell.*

The core transform tools we've discussed are great, but they don't give you the ability to set objects to an exact size. That is, if you need a rectangle to be 100 pixels long, you can't do it with the Scale tool. The Transform palette is your best bet for making things a particular size (see Figure 2.42). It also features positioning, rotation and shearing, so it's a good tool to know about.

Reference Point

The Transform palette uses a point of transformation, just as the Scale, Shear, Rotate, and Reflect tools do. This is the point where the palette measures from, scales toward, rotates around, and so on. The point must be one of the nine points in the box in the palette. The box corresponds to the bounding box of the selection. Illustrator indicates the reference point with a larger black box. Simply click on a point to set it as the reference point. Keep your eye on the reference point as you transform items, particularly when positioning objects.

Use Preview Bounds

By default, the Transform palette measures the size of vector shapes and not the actual space they occupy. So if you have a 100-pixel-long object with a 2-pixel stroke, the actual size of the

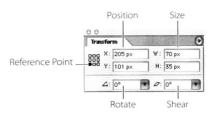

Figure 2.42
Features of the Transform palette

shape is 102 pixels but the palette will display only the 100 pixels the vector occupies. You can switch it so that it displays the actual size by choosing Edit → Preferences → General and checking the Use Preview Bounds option.

The problem with Use Preview Bounds is that it often leads to odd measurements. As you adjust the size of items, the width and height may not be what you type in. For example, if you dial in 100 pixels width and press Return, the palette may read 99.788. If you zoom in on the item and repeat the transformation, you may eventually set it, but having to do that is a hassle. It's better to anticipate the added size brought on by stroke weight and such when creating shapes. If you want a 100-pixel rectangle with a 2-pixel stroke, create a 98-pixel rectangle.

Constrain and Duplicate

To constrain the width and height when transforming, enter the value for one measurement and press ⌘/Control+Return, and your object will be scaled uniformly. To transform a copy, set your transformation and press Option/Alt+Return. Illustrator creates the copy of the object with the transformation. Use the two shortcuts together to uniformly transform copies: ⌘+Option+Return/Control+Alt+Return.

Compound Shapes

What you're doing: Combining shapes to create new custom shapes.
Why you're doing it: Compound shapes are a flexible, easy way to create custom objects. Plus, they can be shared with Photoshop.

You create compound shapes using the buttons in the top row of the Pathfinder palette. The idea is to simplify the process of making custom shapes by using paths to chop each other into pieces. For example, instead of using the Pen tool to draw a crescent-moon shape, you could knock one circle out of another. Each of the circles remain editable in the process, enabling you to adjust their size and position (see Figure 2.43).

Figure 2.43
Left, two shapes; middle, converted to a compound shape; right, after editing one of the shapes

Each object in a compound shape, except the bottom one, has a shape mode. The modes are adjustable as well. You can directly select a shape and switch it so that it adds to instead of subtracts from a shape. The real power of this method is that you can have a single shape with objects adding and subtracting from it to create exactly the shape you need. Once compounded, paths become a single object and all share common attributes.

There are four shape modes: add, subtract, intersect, and exclude. Add combines the shape to the overall path, and subtract removes it. Intersect retains only the item the shape and the other objects in the compound shape have in common. Exclude does the reverse; it removes the common areas (see Figure 2.44).

Compound shapes show up as a group in the Layers palette. There, you can inspect the individual items in it and even drag items into or out of the shape. To do this, you drag the items in the Layers palette rather than on the page. As groups can be ungrouped, compound shapes can be released or expanded. Releasing a compound path (choosing Release Compound from the Pathfinder palette menu) undoes the shape, returning objects to their standard state. Expanding (choosing Expand Compound from the Pathfinder palette menu or clicking the Expand button on the face of the palette) reduces the shapes to basic objects, leaving their appearance the same but removing your ability to edit it as compound shape. You can also expand compound shapes immediately upon creating them by Option/Alt+ clicking on the Shape Mode button. Expanding is sometimes required to continue specific techniques.

Layers

The Layers palette is important for all Illustrator users, but has special importance to web graphic creators. In general, layers make it easy to organize a document and enable advanced styling options. They clarify the organization of the document and offer access to all its parts. Web developers can also use layers to set up sequential animation and to set up web pages using Cascading Style Sheets (CSS).

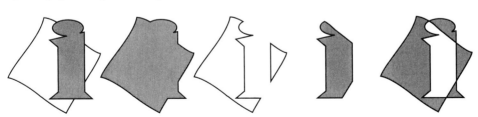

Figure 2.44

From left to right: the original objects, add, subtract, intersect, and exclude

Layers break the stacking order into sections. Each layer has a position relative to all the other layers. As objects are sent to the front or back, they go to the front or back of that layer. This behavior keeps logically connected objects together. The Layers palette enables you to reposition, select, and lock and hide items as well. For more details, see the next section.

Web users will want to use layers when designing complete pages. HTML can describe graphic space using tables or CSS. (We discuss CSS and tables in Chapter 1.) Layers are important because you can assign their content to layers in the HTML document. That way, you can establish graphic space as well as set up rollovers, drop-down menus, and pop-up ads. This process is described in Chapter 8, "Creating Complete Pages."

Layers also can be used as frames in sequential animation when you're saving SWF files. By moving repeating objects across several layers, you can create motion and fade animation directly in Illustrator. Additionally, breaking objects into layers makes it easy to convert an object to an animated GIF in ImageReady or Fireworks. For information on this, see Chapter 9.

Using the Layers Palette

What it is: The palette you'll use to organize a document into separate sections.
What you should know: The Layers palette makes it easy to handle complex documents and enables features like CSS and animation.

The following section describes how to use sections of the Layers palette based on Figure 2.45.

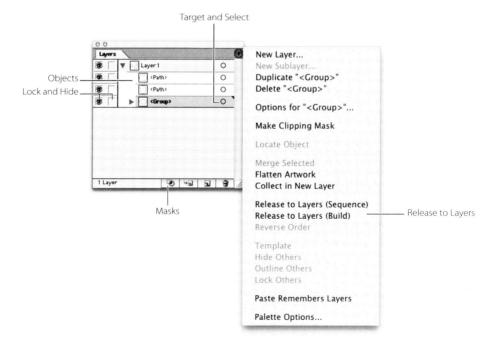

Figure 2.45
Components of the Layers palette

Objects

Each object in the document is accounted for in the Layers palette. Objects appear top to bottom in the palette based on their position in the stacking order. Items on top of each other are closer to the top of the Layers palette. You can reposition objects in the stacking order by dragging them around in the palette. Likewise, layers can be repositioned. As you drag, a black line indicates where the item will reside when you release the mouse. You can also drag items into layers or groups (indicated by black triangles). See Figure 2.46.

When an item is highlighted in the Layers palette, it is said to be *activated*. This indicates to Illustrator which item to use for commands from the Layers palette menu, such as Duplicate and Delete. It also is the point above which Illustrator creates new items, including new layers. Keep an eye on which item is activated in the Layers palette. Unless you are doing something specific, the layer itself should be active.

By default, each object is named by its class. Thus, paths are named *<path>* and guides are named *<guide>*. Objects that have component items, like groups and compound shapes, feature turn-down arrows next to them. These can be opened and closed by clicking on them to reveal the contents of the group.

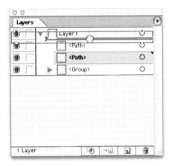

Figure 2.46
Left: dragging items to a new position in the stacking order. Right: dragging items into a group.

Target and Select

The right side of the Layers palette contains two related icons. When objects are selected on the page, a square of the layer's color appears in the column at the far right. Click in that location to select an item. Groups and layers can also be selected in this way. If only some members of a group or layer are selected, a smaller box will be displayed.

The best way to move objects between layers is to drag these selection icons between the layers (see Figure 2.47). If you're moving more than one object, be sure to drag the selection indicator next to the layer you're dragging from (as opposed to the indicator next to an object).

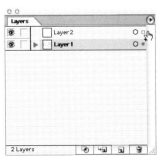

Figure 2.47
Moving items from one layer to another

The circle to the right of items in the Layers palette is the *target circle*. When an item has a special effect, such as a brush stroke, effect, or transparency, this circle displays a gradient. You can drag the gradient from one target circle to another to switch the effects to different items. As always, adding the Option/Alt key as you drag duplicates the appearance. Dragging the gradient circle onto the trash icon at the bottom of the Layers palette deletes the effects but keeps the object intact.

Layers and groups can have their own fills, strokes, effects, and transparency. To activate a layer to receive effects, you need to click in the target circle next to its name in the Layers palette. The result is not the same as selecting all of the items on the layer. This is confusing, because targeting the layer also selects all the items on the layer. Selecting all the items in a group does target the group, however, so you can do that with the Selection

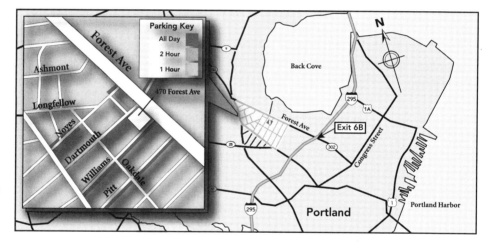
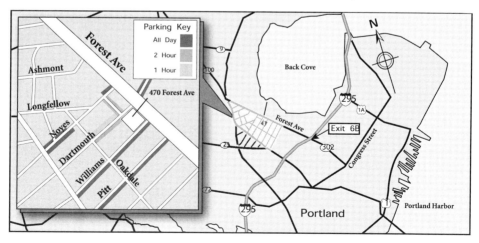

Figure 2.48
The difference between selecting all the items in a layer (top) and targeting a layer (bottom). When the layer is targeted, the contents of the layer are considered together and the shadow falls behind.

i didn't see the replacement image on the server. please advise.

tool. (You'll find examples of group and layer effects and their use in Chapter 6.) Figure 2.48 illustrates the difference. In the inset map, we obviously don't want a drop shadow on each individual street (obscuring the shading used for the parking key), which is the result of selecting all the items in the layer. Instead, targeting the layer gives the desired effect.

Lock and Hide

The two columns in the left of the Layers palette are for locking and hiding objects. The eye icon indicates the item's visibility. Click the eye to hide the item that corresponds to it. Hidden items can't be seen or selected. The next column is the lock column. Click in the empty square to lock the corresponding item. Locked items can be seen but not selected.

If you lock or hide an object that has subordinate items, such as items in a group, those objects will be locked or hidden as well. In this case, the subordinate objects will display a grayed lock or show icon. Both columns also share a keyboard shortcut. Option/Alt+click a layer's lock or hide icon to lock or hide all layers except the current one. If layers are locked or hidden, Option/Alt+click to unlock or show all the layers.

Masks

Masks are a common technique used to hide parts of an item. It's a versatile way of cropping items to a specific shape without actually altering the object's shape. The button at the left of the base of the Layers palette converts the top object in the layer to a cropping area. All of the other objects in the layer are hidden where they do not intersect the top object (see Figure 2.49). The top object is usually a path or type and the layer has to be activated (highlighted) in the palette.

Masks change the visible area of the document, but they do not change the bounding box Illustrator uses when using the Save For Web command. This invariably creates an issue best solved by planning ahead and sizing your Artboard correctly. For information, see Chapter 5.

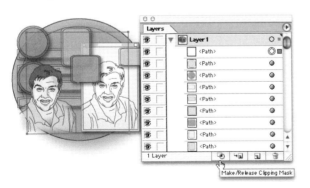  

Figure 2.49

Left: Making a clipping mask in the Layers palette. Right: the resulting mask.

Release To Layers

There are two Release To Layers commands in the Layers palette menu: a sequence version and a build version. Both do basically the same thing. Use Release To Layers (Sequence) to create a new sublayer for every item in a layer and distribute each object onto its own layer. When you execute this command, each object is placed on a discrete sublayer. The stacking order of the objects is reflected in the positions of the new layers. To use these layers as described earlier, the layers will need to become independent layers.

This model of releasing to layers works best when you are preparing an animation where things change or move. Note that the groups have been converted to layers (see Figure 2.50).

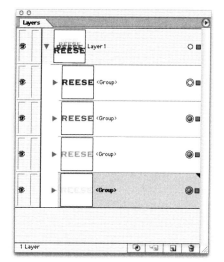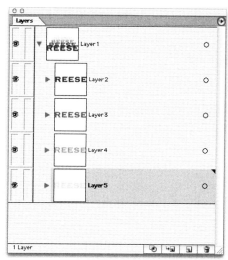

Figure 2.50
The original file and the result of releasing to a sequence.

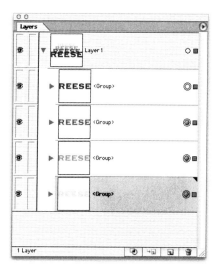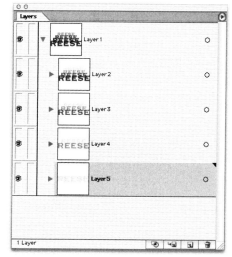

Figure 2.51
The original file and the result of releasing to a build

With Release To Layers (Build), the only difference is that the animation it is intended to prepare for adds items to each frame instead of replacing them. For example, a build animation might spell out a word by adding a letter each time, or reveal a logo one piece at a time (see Figure 2.51).

What this means in Illustrator is that each sublayer contains all of the objects before it plus one new object. The sublayer at the bottom contains only the last item. The next sublayer contains that item and the next one on top of it. This way, as frames in the animation progress, each object is retained. For more information, see Chapter 9.

CHAPTER 3

Save For Web Reference

This chapter summarizes all of the options in the Save For Web dialog box, Illustrator's main tool for making art ready for online use.

This chapter covers the following topics:

Elements of the Save For Web dialog box

Optimization controls for GIF images

Optimization controls for JPEG images

Optimization controls for SWF images

Optimization controls for SVG images

Color table controls

Exporting to CSS layers

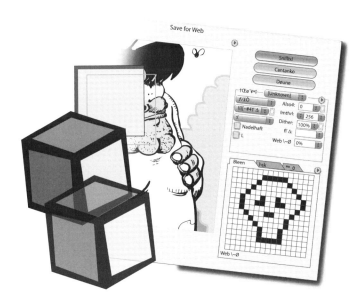

You'll find the Save For Web command in the File menu, and it's the best way to create most web graphics and HTML. (You have two other options for creating web graphics: you can save to the SVG and SVGZ formats, or you can export JPEG and SWF files. For more information, see Chapter 9, "Creating Animations," and Chapter 10, "Creating Scalable Vector Graphics (SVG).") Save For Web is so powerful that it's practically another application. It offers a preview, multiple options, transfer times, and slice controls. The dialog box gives you a broad range of choices and lets you establish settings that you can recall for later use. What's more, the dialog is virtually identical in other Adobe applications. Learning to use it here will pay off if you find yourself working in Photoshop or GoLive as well.

Another key component of Save For Web is the concept of slices. Illustrator can save an image as multiple files based on the slices produced by the Slice tool or Object → Slice command. When you export the image, it splits into a series of smaller files; the HTML code required to reassemble the image in a web browser is saved with the components. That way, you can save various parts of an image in different formats or with different settings. For example, you might save a logo as an SWF or a GIF while the photo underneath might become a JPEG.

Save For Web has its own preferences file. If the feature is behaving poorly, consider deleting this file. You'll find it in the same directory as Illustrator's preferences.

To learn how to use this dialog box in common workflows, see Chapter 7, "Optimizing Spot Illustrations."

The Save For Web Dialog Box

Figure 3.1 shows the Save For Web dialog box. In the following sections, we explain the controls and settings labeled in the figure. Then, in the second half of the chapter, we'll look at the controls that are specific to the GIF and JPEG file formats.

The View Tabs

What they are: *Tabs that control the preview images that display in the Save For Web dialog box.*

What you should know: *Most users prefer the 2-Up setting.*

Original

This option displays only the original image, with no applied compression. It represents the ideal version of the file. As you optimize a file, you'll refer to this version to evaluate the web version. You can use this option to get a clear idea of where you started with the image.

Optimized

This option displays a single compressed version of the image, based on the current settings of the dialog box.

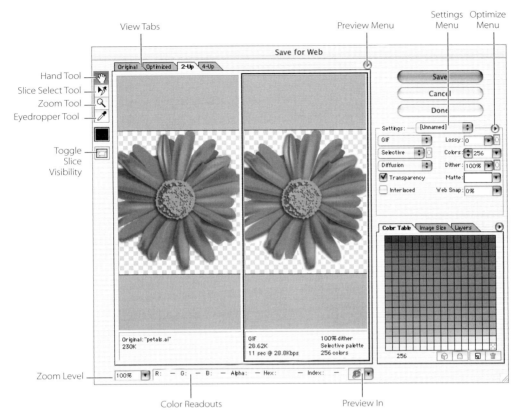

Figure 3.1

The Save For Web dialog box

2-Up

This option displays the original image, plus an optimized version (based on the current settings in the dialog box). As you manipulate the settings, the optimized version changes to reflect the new values. This way, you can compare the compressed image to the original.

Click on one of the panes to activate it. When the Original tab is highlighted, the optimization controls will reset themselves to Original. You can change this setting to create two optimized versions of the art. Do this by changing the Settings field to anything other than Original. This isn't common—typically, users leave the original alone so that they can compare the original to the optimized version.

4-Up

This option displays the original image, plus three compressed versions. One is based on the current settings, and the other two are automatically given settings that further reduce the quality and file size. This way, you can pinpoint the settings that give you the best balance between size and quality, and still compare them to the original.

Click a preview to specify the settings you want to apply when you click OK. A black border indicates the current preview. This option takes longer to load than others, but it is a good choice if you aren't positive which setting you want to use.

The Hand Tool

What it is: A tool that lets you reposition the part of the image you're previewing.
What you should know: You can use the tool only if the image is not completely visible.

Use this tool to scroll the images within the preview frames. You click-drag in the preview pane with the tool. The initial point in the preview is reset to the position in which you release the mouse. When you drag one preview, any others move as well. This way, you can continue to compare the same image areas.

As with its counterpart in the Tool palette, you can double-click on the Hand tool to set the view to fit in the window. Typically you wouldn't do this, because most optimization is done at a 100 percent view depth.

The Slice Select Tool

What it is: The tool you'll use to activate slices so that they can be optimized differently.
What you should know: You can't reposition slices with this tool, so be certain you have them positioned correctly before saving for the Web.

Click on a slice with this tool to select it. When you do, the slice's edge highlights and the Settings section updates to reflect the current slice's options. When the document contains multiple slices, select them by Shift-clicking on them or click-dragging over them. If slices with different settings are selected, the Settings section goes blank. If you apply a setting at that point, it will apply to all of the slices you've selected.

You can't change the size or position of the slices, but you are able to apply different compression settings to each one. Remember that a sliced image ultimately exists as a *series* of files; therefore, each one can receive different settings, and can even exist in a different file format. For example, you can draw a slice around an important image area, and then apply settings to it that retain the most detail. You can set the remaining slices to a much lower compression setting, producing an image that takes less time to display on screen.

Double-click a slice with this tool to access the Slice Options dialog box. Normally, you specify slice options by choosing Object → Slice → Slice Options. That command is linked to the options in this dialog box. That is, if you change a slice from Image to No Image, it will stay a no-image slice after you close the Save For Web dialog box.

Slice Options

What they are: *The options that determine whether each section of an HTML page is exported as text or graphics.*

What you should know: *Many times when you're creating an image you'll make image slices.*

Illustrator can make three kinds of slices: Image, No Image, and HTML Text. Set the kind of slice you want by choosing it from the Slice Type menu (see Figure 3.2).

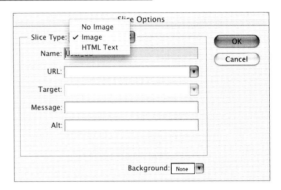

Figure 3.2

The Slice Type options

The Image type is designed for graphic information and is the default setting for all slices. No Image slices contain text. Graphic information in the slice is not exported when you're saving for the Web. You choose this option when you are making complete HTML pages and want to leave a spot to put something else, such as a table or other HTML content.

HTML Text slices write styled HTML into a cell based on the text in an object slice. This option is available to only type objects that have been made into object slices. HTML Text records the size, color, and styling, such as bold or italic, of the text in the slice, even if the text is styled differently from word to word. As the text in the slices changes, Illustrator updates the HTML text to match. The HTML produced is crude by modern standards and cannot include CSS styling.

Except for Background color, all of the remaining options in the Slice Options window depend on your choice of Slice Type.

BACKGROUND

Use this option to set the background color of the slice. This option sets a background color for the table cell in the HTML generated. You can select one of the colors from the list or choose a custom color from the Color Picker by clicking Other. The Eyedropper color is the last color picked in the Save For Web dialog box. This option is available for all slice types.

Figure 3.3

The options for Image slices

IMAGE SLICE CONTROLS

Figure 3.3 shows the options available when the Slice Type is Image. Let's look at each of the fields:

Name Use this field to name a slice. By default, slices are named sequentially across and down from top left to bottom right. Slice names are sometimes used by developers and coders in automated workflows, but aren't strictly required for day-to-day users.

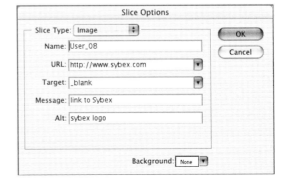

URL Enter a web address into this field to generate a link to another web page or choose one of the recent URLs from the pop-up menu at right of the field. The link will be written into the HTML generated when you execute the Save For Web command. The contents of the cell act as a button, linking viewers to the address entered in this field. This may be an absolute or relative URL.

Illustrator supports both local and absolute addressing in this field. That is, you can write the actual long URL, such as `http://www.illustratoranswers.com/default.html`, or if you know where the file you make will live on your website, you can write in a short relative address, such as `default.html`.

If you plan to use this option, be careful about adding image maps as well. Illustrator enables you to write link locations using the Attributes palette. These two models for linking can lead to confusion and bad code, so use one model or the other.

Target The Target field is used in conjunction with the URL field to set the page the URL link opens in. This option is commonly used in an HTML document that contains frames. Frames break an HTML document into a container of other HTML pages. They are fading from fashion as other techniques offer better options for controlling graphic space. Frames are given names in an HTML document to identify them, which allow you to link from one frame to another, as in pages with one frame for navigation and another for content. Enter the name of a specific frame in the Target field or use one of the defaults listed.

Another use for targets is to spawn new pages from links. Instead of having the link replace the current contents, you can call for the link in a new window, leaving the initial page open. This is a good choice when you're writing links to websites you don't have control over. The _blank target does this, creating a new webpage for the link but leaving the current page open. _self replaces the page with the referenced page in the same frame. This is the default action in most browsers. _parent loads the link into the frame that encases the current frame. _top replaces the entire frameset with the link.

Message Text entered in this field appears in the browser status bar. It provides details about the link, particularly when the URL itself is not descriptive. When you use this feature without completing the URL field, a null (#) link is generated in the HTML so that the message can be displayed.

Alt The Alt field supplies alternate text to the browsers. The text is displayed while images are loading and on browsers that are set to not display images. The information you supply in this field is important because it is utilized by the screen-reading software used by the visually impaired.

NO IMAGE OPTIONS

Figure 3.4 shows the options available when the Slice Type is No Image. The available options are as follows.

Text Displayed In Cell Use this field in the dialog box to enter text that appears in the cell. Typically, you enter placeholder text into the cell to be finished later. That is, you could leave a note to yourself indicating what you intend to do with that area and then fix it later.

You can also enter HTML text to set the basic look of text. Non-HTML text that is entered will still appear in the cell in the webpage but will not be styled. Text Object Slices (slices created from text objects) populates the cell with HTML that describes the text's size, color, and style. This option is similar to the HTML Text slice option except that it is not dynamic and will not update as text changes. However, unlike with HTML text, you can edit the text in this field and adjust it manually as needed. This only works if you select a type container and choose Object → Slice → Make. It is not sufficient to have text objects in the cell area.

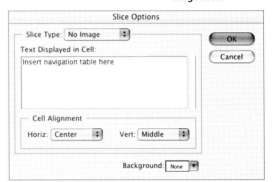

Figure 3.4
The options for No Image slices

Cell Alignment Use the Cell Alignment options to set the horizontal and vertical alignment of the text within the cell.

HTML TEXT OPTIONS

Figure 3.5 shows the options when you choose HTML Text as the Slice Type. The options in this dialog box are:

Text Displayed In Cell You cannot modify the contents of this field. To change the HTML text, you must edit the text in the object slice directly on the page. This option does not generate Cascading Style Sheets or record font information, and will not preserve the exact look and feel of the text.

Cell Alignment Again, use the Cell Alignment options to set the horizontal and vertical alignment of the text within the cell.

The Zoom Tool

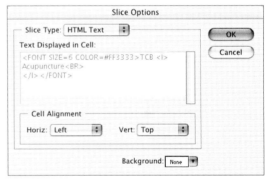

Figure 3.5
The options for HTML Text slices

What it is: *A tool for changing the view depth.*
What you should know: *In most cases you'll want to leave the depth at 100 percent.*

Use this tool to enlarge or reduce the images in the preview frames. When evaluating web images, it's best to do it at 100 percent view depth. Therefore, the tool is used infrequently, usually to investigate a part of the document that seems odd.

This tool works the same as Zoom tool in the Toolbox. You click to step in incrementally, click-drag to enlarge a specific part of the document, Option/Alt click to zoom back, and double-click on the tool itself to set the view depth to 100 percent. When you click one preview with the Zoom tool, the others respond in kind. This enables you to continue comparing the same image areas.

The Eyedropper Tool

What it is: A tool for sampling a color in your image.

What you should know: The samples are generally used to set the color the image is matted against.

Use this tool to sample color values from the image preview. You'll typically do this to set the matte color to a specific color in the image. Once you click with the tool in a preview pane, the color you sampled appears in the color swatch, located directly beneath the Eyedropper tool. Click the swatch to open the Color Picker, which lets you inspect or fine-tune the values of the color.

If you're making a web graphic that uses a color table (e.g., a GIF), the Eyedropper colors are highlighted in the color table. This gives you the opportunity to push the color to web-safe if you choose. Colors sampled with the Eyedropper can be added to the table by clicking the New Color icon.

Toggle Slices Visibility

What it is: An option that shows or hides slice boundaries.

What you should know: Hiding the slices is useful for seeing the image clearly.

Click this button to display or hide slices in the preview frames. By default, slices are visible. In a complex document, all the slice boundaries can be distracting as you assess an image. Use this button to hide them so you can make your evaluation. Click it again to turn them back on. Anytime you click in the image with the Slice Select tool, the slices are set to Visible.

Zoom Level

What it is: The size at which the image is being viewed (given as a percentage).

What you should know: Most of the time you're going to be at 100 percent.

This option enables you to choose a predefined zoom percentage from a pop-up menu. To zoom to a particular percentage, manually enter the desired value in the field. Unless you have a good reason to do otherwise, try to keep this at 100 percent. This setting shows you what you'll actually see in a web browser.

Color Readouts

What they are: Information about the color the cursor is over.

What you should know: These fields aren't used excessively, but can be handy in a pinch.

These items display the current RGB, hexadecimal, Alpha, and Index values of the preview color currently underneath the cursor. The Alpha value displays the opacity level of the pixel on a scale from 0 to 255 (0 is transparent and 255 is completely opaque). Only the Original image and PNG 24 images will display an Alpha value other than 0 or 255. The Index value is used for optimizing GIF and PNG 24 files. This value indicates the colors' position in the Color table.

Preview In

What it is: A chance to see the image in an actual web browser before you save the file.
What you should know: The preview also provides information about the file and the source HTML code, if any.

This option enables you to preview the current image in the web browser of your choice. When you click this button, your operating system launches the designated browser and opens the image in a new window. The image will open in a temporary HTML page containing the optimized output, the settings used to generate it, and the HTML connected to it (see Figure 3.6).

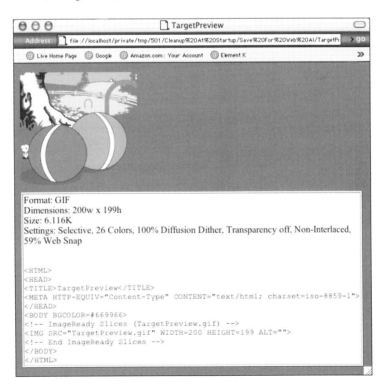

Figure 3.6

A previewed file. Note the administrative data below the image.

To set a different browser, choose an item in the Select Browser menu (to the button's immediate right). To add a new browser to the list, choose Other from the menu, and then direct Illustrator to the desired program.

The Settings Menu

What it is: Groups of prebuilt optimization settings.

What you should know: This menu makes it quick to select common choices, and you can add your own group to the list.

This pop-up menu displays a list of 14 predefined settings for creating GIF, JPG, or PNG images.

Choosing one of these predefined options sets a group of common choices for all of the settings fields. You're not committed to use all the options; however, many people use them as a starting point by choosing an option and then fine-tuning the values. It's also possible to add your own settings to the list. (For more information, see the next section.)

The Optimize Menu

What it is: Home to most of the administrative commands in this dialog box.

What you should know: One of the key commands, Edit Output Settings, is also available in the Save Output As dialog box. This gives you a backup chance to set your output settings if you fail to at first.

The options in the Optimize menu control how files are compressed, how HTML is generated, and how the optimization settings are applied.

Save Settings

Choose this command to save the current settings into a separate file, stored in Illustrator's Optimized folder (Adobe Illustrator CS → Presets → Save For Web Settings → Optimize). The settings are then available as in the Settings pop-up menu.

Delete Settings

Choose this command to delete selected custom setting sets from the Settings pop-up menu. You cannot delete default settings. This doesn't change the current values chosen; it just removes the collected settings file.

Optimize To File Size

Use this command when you want to compress a web graphic to a specific file size. Issuing the command opens the Optimize To File Size dialog box, which asks you how large a file you want to create. From there, you can fine-tune the level of quality by tweaking the remaining settings, but Illustrator does the work of changing the settings to generate a file of the desired size.

In the Optimize To File Size dialog box, you can specify that you want to use the current Save For Web settings, or you can let Illustrator choose GIF or JPG on the fly, based on which option produces the best results. Also, if the image contains multiple slices, you can use this dialog box to tell Illustrator to apply the size limitation to the currently selected slice, to each image slice, or to the total size of all slices combined.

Repopulate Views

Choose this command to draw new image previews, based on the settings of the currently selected frame. In the resulting dialog box, if you select the 4-Up setting, you'll see the following:

- The original image
- The preview that was selected when you chose the Repopulate Views command
- Two previews that result in smaller file sizes

Link Slices

Use this command to connect the Optimize settings of at least two selected slices. Linked slices are optimized using the same settings, so that as you change one slice's Optimize settings, the other's settings change as well. Linked slices are indicated with a figure-eight "link" icon in the slice (see Figure 3.7). Slices that Illustrator generates to fill in around the slices you made (known as *auto slices*) are linked automatically. That is, every slice that you didn't create yourself is optimized the same way.

Unlink Slices and Unlink All Slices

Unlink Slices breaks the connection between selected linked slices, enabling you to optimize them differently. Unlink All Slices breaks the connection between all linked slices, whether or not they are selected. To convert an auto slice (one that Illustrator has generated) into one that you can customize independently, use the Unlink Slices command.

Edit Output Settings

Use this command to open the Output Settings dialog box (Figure 3.8). You can also access this dialog box by clicking Output Settings in the Save Optimized As dialog box. The Output settings let you control how Illustrator writes HTML by establishing HTML generation conventions.

Figure 3.7
Linked slices

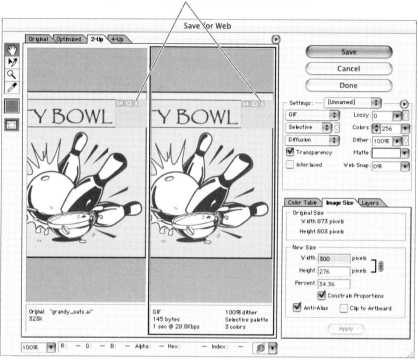

Output settings are akin to *preferences* for HTML generation. People who write and manage HTML documents for a living are particular about the flavor of HTML they see. Having pages written in a consistent fashion across a site makes it easy for them to read the content and to identify problems when they crop up. If someone else is involved in the care and feeding of your HTML, you should discuss these options with that person.

You can save your settings to a file that can be recalled later and even loaded onto different workstations. By moving the file to different computers, you can set up an entire workgroup quickly. You save and load the settings by using the buttons on the right side of the Output Settings dialog box. When you're using a saved set, its name will appear in the Settings menu. Otherwise, the menu will read *Custom*.

HTML OPTIONS

The HTML pane of the Output Settings dialog box contains four sections.

Formatting The Formatting section provides options for how code is written. These are preference aspects: capitalization, indenting, and such. The IT person in your group will be most interested in these settings.

Coding The Coding section has two important options we'd like to point out. First, Include Comments marks the tables that Illustrator writes with the comments

    <!-- ImageReady Slices
    <filename.html> -->

at the beginning and

    <!-- End ImageReady Slices -->

at the end of any tables and CSS code it creates. This text doesn't appear on the page; the <! tag marks notes or comments within the HTML. It helps to leave notes in the code so that you can quickly locate code later. This sets the code Illustrator creates out from the rest of the HTML, making it easier to copy and paste. You should probably leave this option enabled (as it is by default).

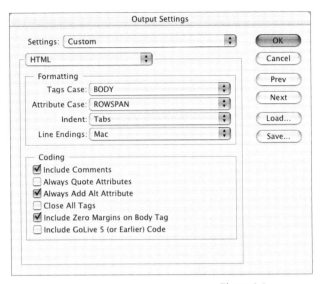

Figure 3.8
The Output Settings dialog box

The Include GoLive 5 (Or Earlier) Code option adds some code that can be handy if you're going to continue the page in Adobe GoLive. The most obvious difference is the automatic creation of SmartObjects. SmartObjects are a convenient option in GoLive that lets you connect a high-resolution object to a web-optimized one, making it easy to update graphics. When you select this option, each graphic gets an additional attribute tag:

    LIVESRC="SVGExport/filename-1.svg"

From this code you could deduce that the high-res version Illustrator creates are SVG files that live in a folder named SVGExport. Unless you are a GoLive user, you don't need or want this extra code. But if you are, the options are solid and, in fact, make it much easier to edit pages in GoLive. If when using GoLive you experience weird problems editing a page from Illustrator, check to make sure that this option is active.

Slice Output This section determines if Illustrator writes a table or CSS to describe slices and how it should do that. CSS writes layers, similar to Illustrator layers, into the HTML. The connected options set attribute options for the code. Each CSS layer is created using the tag DIV. It's called DIV because it *divides* an area. The DIV tag can also be assigned attributes. You can give it attributes that you can then use to reference the layers, typically with scripts. Your choices are By ID, By Class, and Inline.

Referencing by ID gives the layer a name. This name identifies the layer so that you can address it specifically with a script. For example:

    <div id="background">

Then, later in a script the layer could be addressed directly, as in

`document.background.someproperty=somevalue;`

When you reference by class, you include an attribute that links the layer to a style. You may define a style class either in the HTML file or in a style sheet document that will set the CSS parameters. By default Illustrator writes a class definition into the head of the HTML. Objects that are members of the class will use those settings. This approach lets you control objects from a central location.

Inline referencing doesn't add any special attributes. It produces the simplest documents, and you should use this option unless you plan to address the layers with scripts or perform other development work on the files.

If you are saving slices as a table, you'll have more options to contend with. The Empty Cell option in the Slices section of the dialog controls what happens to cells that are blank. Empty space in a table must be filled with either a one-pixel transparent GIF that Illustrator generates for you or a text code. If you're going to use a graphic, you apply the size for the cell either to the cell itself or to the spacer graphic. The tag for a cell, TD, uses the attributes W (width) and H (height). So, specifying GIF, TD W & H sets a spacer graphic and applies the size to the cell. Compare with GIF, IMG W&H, which applies the size to the graphic and lets the cell expand around it. This is the most flexible option. The text option (NoWrap, TD W&H) also applies the size directly to the cell. The `NoWrap` code forces text in the cell to stay on one line. Here, it acts as a placeholder to keep the cell from collapsing. The code is being deprecated in HTML 4. As HTML evolves, the consortium that makes recommendations about it occasionally attempts to leave some tags behind. This is done to encourage advancement in the language and to avoid problem or awkward tags. This "deprecated" code may work fine in most browsers, but should be avoided if you have a choice.

The TD W&H menu allows you to specify whether Illustrator should include the size attributes for each cell. Typically, you choose the Auto option. Illustrator adds enough W&H attributes to describe the table but reduces the code by leaving some out. Some users find it difficult at first to find where Illustrator has placed the attributes and prefer one of the absolute models (Always or Never).

The same options and reasoning applies to the inclusion of spacer cells. Most everyday users let Illustrator choose and be done with it.

BACKGROUND OPTIONS

You'll probably use the options here only infrequently. The main choice is whether the current document is intended as art or a background tile. If you set it to Background, the HTML will use the object as a background image. This is handy if you're setting up files for background images and want to see how they tile. You can enable this option and then use the Preview In option.

If the art is intended to be an image and you want a background file referenced in the HTML, you can dial that in here as well. If you know the directory for the file you want, type it in the Path field.or use the Browse button to navigate to another file. Images used as backgrounds will be placed in the same directory as page graphics.

SAVING FILE OPTIONS

These options control how files are named and placed. The first section features a lengthy naming convention recipe. Much of it doesn't apply to Illustrator graphics because you aren't generating rollovers. Most shops are very particular about filenaming, though, and you should check with your IT department to see what filenaming convention they prefer you to use. The Slices section of this dialog box features a similar section for naming slices.

The most important setting here is Put Images In Folder. When this option is activated, Illustrator writes all of the image files into a new folder (named `images` by default) and generates HTML that references that directory. If you move the images, the page won't work. If you're writing to a directory that already has an `images` folder, Illustrator uses that one rather than creating a new one. If you're saving files directly into an existing site, you should type the name of your graphics directory in this field. That way, you minimize any potential confusion.

The Preview Menu

The items in this menu enable you to control the display of the preview images.

Browser Dither

When a monitor can't display a color naturally, it simulates the color by adding randomly placed pixels of another color to a base object. Ideally, the colors would mix and your eye would be tricked into seeing the color. Instead, it just looks ugly and unprofessional. This option simulates how a graphic will display on an 8-bit color monitor. This way, you can anticipate the amount of dithering that will result. You should see the web-safe colors remain solid and all the non-safe ones dither (see Figure 3.9).

Browser Dither

Size/Download Time (9600 bps Modem)
Size/Download Time (14.4 Kbps Modem)
Size/Download Time (28.8 Kbps Modem)
✓ Size/Download Time (56.6 Kbps Modem/ISDN)
Size/Download Time (128 Kbps Dual ISDN)
Size/Download Time (256 Kbps Cable/DSL)
Size/Download Time (384 Kbps Cable/DSL)
Size/Download Time (512 Kbps Cable/DSL)
Size/Download Time (768 Kbps Cable/DSL)
Size/Download Time (1 Mbps Cable)
Size/Download Time (1.5 Mbps Cable/T1)
Size/Download Time (2 Mbps)

Size/Download Time

All of the additional options in the Preview menu determine the download rate used to display the transfer times listed at the bottom of each preview. You should choose a size/download time setting based on your anticipation of your target audience. If you don't have a specific group in mind, consider setting it to 56Kbps. This is a reasonably common connection speed on the high end of dial-up.

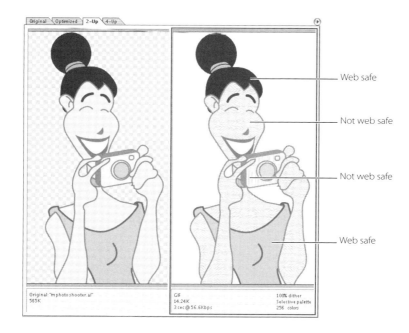

Figure 3.9
Previewing with the Browser Dither option. Note the web-safe colors don't dither.

GIF Optimization Controls

GIF files are well suited to images with areas of solid color. You'll be creating GIFs a lot of the time. These images support transparency and, although not in Illustrator, animation. It is common, though, to set up an animation in Illustrator and complete it in ImageReady. We'll discuss preparing a file for GIF animation in Chapter 9. Figure 3.10 shows the optimization settings available for a GIF image.

Lossy

What it is: *A slider that determines how much detail is retained in the file.*

What you should know: *Low values retain more detail, resulting in higher file sizes; higher values reduce the level of detail, resulting in a lower file size.*

The Lossy slider isn't used in Illustrator very much. It tends to wreck images too quickly without offsetting file size savings. The option to the right enables you to base the lossiness on an alpha channel. This is a holdover from Photoshop, which also uses this Save For Web interface. There are no alpha channels in Illustrator. Even if you open a Photoshop file with channels, you won't be able to use this option.

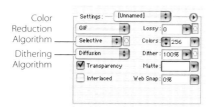

Figure 3.10
The GIF section of the Save For Web dialog box

The Color Reduction Algorithm

> *What it is:* The setting that establishes how Illustrator will pick the colors used in the GIF.
> *What you should know:* GIFs can't have more than 256 colors, but they don't have to be the same 256 from file to file. These settings determine how the colors are chosen.

```
Perceptual
• Selective
  Adaptive
  Web

  Custom

  Black & White
  custom
  Grayscale
  Mac OS
  Windows
```

Dynamic Options

The Perceptual, Selective, and Adaptive options use an algorithm to create a table based on the relationship between the image colors and the value entered in the Colors field. The table's values are regenerated any time you edit or re-optimize the image. *Perceptual* picks colors favoring ones the eye can see best. *Selective* picks colors the eye can see as well, but includes more web-safe colors in its set. *Adaptive* bases its picks on the colors that are actually in the image. Selective is the default choice, and it tends to work well. Some users prefer the Adaptive palette, especially when they believe the work will be seen by users with high-end monitors.

Fixed Options

The Web, Mac OS, Windows, Black & White, and Grayscale options are fixed, or use a predefined palette of colors. The set of available colors is always constant, but the actual table depends on the colors available in each particular image. These options don't see a lot of use. It might seem tempting to use the Web option, but this can actually result in larger files and we discourage you from choosing it.

The Custom Option

This option refers to a custom-designed or preexisting color table. For example, if you modify a color table or optimize an existing GIF, the table is considered Custom.

You can save color sets for use later on. Do this by choosing Save Color Table from the Color Table drop-down menu. You can save this files anywhere, such as to a zip disk. The default setting files are located in the directory Adobe Illustrator → Presets → Save For Web Settings → Color Tables. Other files you save to this directory appear in the Color Reduction menu as well. This is a great way to keep commonly used settings at the ready.

Colors

> *What it is:* The maximum number of colors available in a color table.
> *What you should know:* Fewer colors yield a smaller file.

This setting specifies the maximum number of colors a file can contain. The highest setting is 256, but you may lower that setting to make a smaller file. A good starting point is the Auto setting, which picks a number of colors based on the contents of the image. The number of colors in a table is indicated in the lower left of the color table. Reducing the number of colors in the table can trim down file size.

The Dithering Algorithm

What it is: *The way pixels are distributed when a file is dithered.*
What you should know: *Dithering makes more colors but increases the file's size. It should be used with caution.*

Dithering distributes pixels to create the illusion of more colors. The downside is that dithering typically increases a file's size. For this reason, it's generally used only when you're using a web palette or a limited color table. Many browsers dither already, and dithering the image as well may degrade it. Before adding a dither, be sure to turn on the Browser Dither Preview and view your image at the size at which it will be displayed.

The dithering method determines how the colors are distributed throughout the image.

No Dither

With no dithering selected, Illustrator changes each image pixel to its closest equivalent in the current color table. In images with more continuous tones, like gradients, drop shadows, or meshes, no dithering usually results in harsher color transitions and visible banding. This option does produce smaller files, though.

Pattern

This method uses a predefined pattern to redistribute the colors, attempting to compensate for the lost tones. It does a poor job, and should not be used.

Diffusion

The Diffusion method randomizes the colored pixels, creating the illusion of additional colors. Most users prefer this method because it offers a slider that lets you control the amount of dithering in your image.

Noise

This method is similar to Diffusion, but it randomizes pixels more evenly throughout the image.

Dither Amount

What it is: *A setting that controls how much of the image is affected by dithering.*
What you should know: *It's only available when you're using the Diffusion dithering method.*

Available only when you set Diffusion in the Dither pop-up, this field lets you determine the degree of smoothness between color transitions. Higher values result in smoother transitions, but a larger file size; lower values result in harsher transitions, but a smaller file size.

As with the Lossy field, Dither Amount can be based on an alpha channel in Photoshop. The icon for that option appears here as well, to the right of the field, although it serves no purpose in Illustrator.

Transparency

What it is: *An option that creates transparent areas in a GIF.*
What you should know: *Partial transparency is not retained.*

The Transparency box enables you to retain a transparent area in the converted image. Pixels in a GIF are either transparent or opaque. Typically, the space between objects is transparent. You use this option to show the background color or image of a webpage behind the graphic.

If you've made objects partially opaque by using the Transparency palette, those areas will be flattened. That is, the pixels won't be transparent but will still look the same. The new color of the pixels is created by blending the transparent areas with the matte color (see the next section). This is fine and retains the flavor of the transparency, but will be incorrect if the color of the webpage background changes.

Matte

What it is: *The color of the background the objects in the file are over.*
What you should know: *The matte color should be the same as the background color in the HTML file that will house the GIF.*

You can think of the *matte color* as the background color of the art, or the color the art will be over. It is similar to the Transparency feature in two ways.

First, when the Transparency box is deselected, Illustrator paints all transparent areas with the matte color. Semitransparent areas are blended with the matte color. This produces the illusion of a transparent GIF without actually building transparency into the file.

When the Transparency box is selected, outside edges in the image are blended with the matte color in a thin, one-pixel line. This smoothes the line, creating a cleaner transition. You should matte against the background color the file will be against. If you don't, your edges will have sloppy visible fringe pixels. For information on finding this color, see Chapter 4, "Gathering the Required Information."

Click the matte color swatch to set the value numerically or choose from one of the prebuilt options in the menu at the right. The Eyedropper color option is based on the swatch color set by the Eyedropper tool. The option is not dynamic. If you change the Eyedropper swatch, you must re-select Eyedropper Color from the matte color menu.

Interlaced

What it is: An option that produces a file that loads in several passes.
What you should know: Files are larger with interlacing than without.

Select the Interlaced option to produce an interlaced GIF. These files gradually refresh on screen in multiple passes, becoming clearer with each pass. When the option is deselected, the GIF loads all at once. The result of using this option is a page that loads more quickly initially but takes longer to load overall.

PNG OPTIONS

The options for optimizing PNG-8 are the same as when you're optimizing a GIF, except that PNGs don't have the Lossy slider.

PNG-8 files can contain up to 256 separate colors. Like GIFs, they are appropriate for files with areas of solid color and sharp details, such as line art or type. A PNG-8 file uses a more advanced compression scheme than GIF, and therefore tends to be 10–30 percent smaller than a GIF of comparable dimensions.

PNG-24 files support 24-bit color. As such, they do not use a color table. PNG-24 also supports multilevel transparency, which preserves up to 256 levels of transparency to smoothly blend the edges of an image with the background color. Used with CSS layers, this makes a powerful combination. A PNG-24 file uses the same lossless compression method as PNG-8, though, and therefore tends to be larger than a JPEG of comparable dimensions.

Unfortunately, browser support for this format is still limited, particularly for PNG-24, making these options a dicey choice for everyday use.

Web Snap

> What it is: *An option that converts colors that are similar to web-safe colors to web safe.*
> What you should know: *At low values, only the colors that differ slightly from their closest equivalent are affected; at higher values, more colors are converted.*

This option enables you to pull an image into the web-safe color family incrementally. As you increase the snap value, more colors are pushed to web safe. In the dialog box's color table, any color converted to its closest browser-safe equivalent is tagged with a small white diamond. This option doesn't see a lot of use, either. If you choose to work with web-safe colors, it makes more sense to decide that up front and build your art with the web colors to begin with.

JPEG Optimization Controls

JPEG files are well suited for images with a number of continuous tones. You should think JPEG if you are using photos or images with several gradients or soft-edged effects. Figure 3.11 shows the JPEG optimization controls.

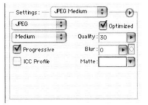

Figure 3.11

The JPEG section of the Save For Web dialog box

Optimized

> What it is: *An option that reduces the file size slightly.*
> What you should know: *Using this option doesn't reduce the size enough to compensate for its shortcomings.*

This option produces a slightly different type of JPEG, called an Optimized or Enhanced JPG. Enabling this checkbox reduces the overall file size slightly, but it produces an image that is not understood by all browsers. For this reason, most users do not activate this option.

Quality

> What it is: *An option that trades file quality for smaller file size.*
> What you should know: *Image quality and file size are connected—higher quality means higher size.*

When you save your image as a JPEG, pixel values in the image are changed to make the file more compressible. The more you allow the colors to change, the smaller the file will become. Your goal is to make the file as small as possible with damaging the image too much. Areas of solid color are especially prone to damage in the JPEG process, resulting in ugly artifacts (see Figure 3.12).

Figure 3.12

Artifacting caused by the JPEG compression

This slider allows you to set a Quality value from 0 (lowest quality, smallest size) to 100 (highest quality, largest size). Many users decide on one preferred value for all of their images—a value of 40 or 50 avoids most of the visible artifacting while producing a satisfactory file size.

The items in the pop-up menu to the left enter preset values in the Quality field. Low is 10, and Maximum is 80. These choices do not override the slider, which you can still adjust.

Progressive

What it is: *An option whose effect is similar to interlacing in GIFs.*
What you should know: *Some viewers find it irritating.*

Progressive images appear in a series of passes, giving the viewer a rough-and-ready idea of how a graphic appears before it's fully refreshed. When this box is deselected, the image is saved as a baseline JPEG, which appears in your browser one line at a time, from top to bottom.

Blur

What it is: *An option that reduces artifacting by blurring the image slightly.*
What you should know: *At low-quality settings, a small blur can improve image quality.*

The idea behind the Blur option is counterintuitive: you improve image quality by blurring it. The problem it's designed to solve is that low-quality JPEGs often produce ugly artifacts. By blurring the image slightly, you can mitigate the damage and still keep your file size low. You should take advantage of this technique only when you are seeing artifacts in your image.

ICC Profile

What it is: *An option that embeds the image's color profile into the JPEG.*
What you should know: *Most browsers can't read ICC profiles.*

When you select the ICC Profile checkbox, Illustrator embeds in the file additional details about the way the image should be displayed. The details take the form of a color profile. A group called the International Color Consortium (ICC) devised methods of describing color without using constants that may change with each device. That is, the red in your monitor may not look the same as the red in mine. This "true" version of the color takes the form of a profile. Ideally, software would adjust the values displayed to compensate for the difference between my red and yours.

This option is intended to improve the color rendering of color-critical images such as catalog items. However, the average browser cannot recognize embedded profiles. Further, doing this adds 3–4KB to the file size.

Matte

What it is: *The background color applied to your images.*
What you should know: *Transparent areas in the file are blended with the matte color.*

The matte color fills in the space between objects and blends with partially transparent objects to produce flat pixel values. If you don't set a color, the art is matted against white.

SWF Optimization Controls

There are two methods for producing SWF files. You can choose File → Save For Web or File → Export. Of the two, exporting offers more options. In general, you make SWFs with the Save For Web command if you want to integrate the Flash file with other graphics to make a complete webpage. This technique is often used with logos and text that needs to remain vectors. You typically turn to exporting when you plan to continue a SWF elsewhere and place it on a page manually.

Figure 3.13
The SWF options of the Save For Web dialog box

The additional options for exporting are listed at the end of this section. Refer to Figure 3.13 for reference with the following sections.

Type Of Export

What it is: *A pop-up menu that lets you control the conversion of Illustrator's layers to SWF.*
What you should know: *Usually you'll use the file-to-file option.*

This menu offers two options: AI File To SWF File and AI Layers To SWF Frames. Most of the time, you'll be using the former, especially in sliced files. That option generates a single, static SWF file.

The AI Layers To SWF Frames option converts the contents of the layers into frames in an animation. The effect is like a flipbook: the layers are written to frames from bottom to top, with the lowest layer being the first frame. The only timing controls available are the frame rate and looping, which makes it difficult to slow down or speed up animation. With sliced graphics, only the portion of each layer that is in the slice is included in the animation. Make sure the slice completely contains all the sections you need before saving. For more information about animation, see Chapter 9.

Read Only

What it is: *An option that protects your file from being imported into another application.*
What you should know: *Choose this option only if you're certain you won't be editing the SWF in Flash or LiveMotion.*

If you want to protect your file from being imported into another application, including Flash, select the Read Only checkbox. This prevents other people from picking up your work and reusing it.

Curve Quality

What it is: An option that reduces curve integrity and file size.
What you should know: The value 7 is a pretty good choice for this option.

The Curve Quality option trades file quality for speed of download. Using a low setting distorts curves, creating angles and lumps. A high setting preserves the integrity of the path but results in a larger file. Many users leave this option set to the default of 7, which doesn't mess up the curves and keeps the file reasonably small.

Frame Rate

What it is: An option that sets the speed at which the frames are displayed in the SWF file.
What you should know: This option is available only when you're exporting to frames.

Use this option to set the speed at which frames are displayed in the SWF file. The default frame rate is 12 frames per second (fps), which is also the default in Flash. The rate of 12fps is enough to display smooth movement and still download quickly. It's a good choice if you intend to continue working on your image in Flash.

If you're producing animation completely in Illustrator, however, 12fps can be a little high. Remember that each layer translated to one frame. At 12fps, you need a dozen layers to make a single second. For a simple fade-in, you may be fine with as few as 4fps.

Use the Loop option to instruct the SWF to play again once it completes the sequence of frames. An example of when you'd use Loop is when you're creating animated banner ads. The animation goes on and on indefinitely. Like the Frame Rate option, the Loop option is available only when you're exporting to frames.

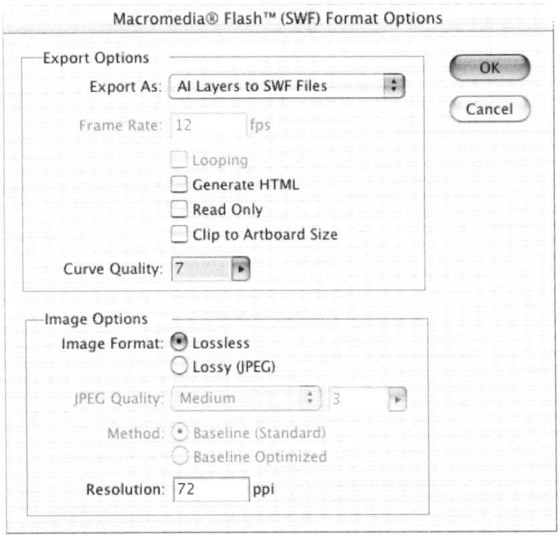

Figure 3.14
Additional options available to you when you're exporting SWFs.

File → Export → SWF Options

Additional options are available when exporting a SWF rather than using Save For Web. Figure 3.14 shows the format options for saving as SWF. We discuss the most important options in the sections that follow.

Export As: AI Layers To SWF Files

Choose AI Layers To SWF Files from the Export As menu when you want to write each layer to its own SWF file. Each new file is named sequentially for the layer from which it originated. The layer on the bottom of the stack is named `file_L1.SWF`, where `file` is the name of the original Illustrator file. Each subsequent layer is named using the same convention. If you're continuing work in Flash, this technique is redundant and usually means extra steps. If you're creating individual web graphics, though, it can be a handy way to separate elements. For example a logo and a slogan could be placed and different layers in Illustrator and then broken into separate SWF files. This enables you to use the logo with out the slogan and to adjust the two items independently on a web page.

Generate HTML

You use this option to generate an HTML document for controlling your SWF file. You don't *have* to do this; SWF files can be viewed directly in a web browser without being inside an HTML page. When viewed directly, though, SWF files resize themselves to fit the browser window and are viewed using browser default parameters. An HTML file instructs the browser to display the art at the size it was created and sets parameters for its viewing.

Image Format

Use the Image Format options to control the resolution and compression of pixels in the SWF. Pixels are passed to the SWF from raster art in the document but are also created when the objects in the Illustrator file can't be understood in Flash. This usually applies to such elements as a gradient mesh or a soft drop shadow. For a list of objects that become pixels, see Chapter 9.

Set this to Lossless or Lossy (JPEG) to compress the data. Your choice depends on the kind of pixel data you are exporting. Photographs and images with a lot of gradients are better served with JPEG compression. The Lossy option uses the JPEG format.

Resolution

Use this option to set the resolution of the pixel objects you create. The resolution affects the print quality of the objects but (unlike standard web graphics) is not related to their display size. If the SWF is intended only for online viewing, a 72ppi (pixels per inch) resolution is appropriate. If you intend to print the SWF as well, a print-ready resolution (such as 300ppi) should be considered. Increased resolution also increases file size and transfer time.

Save For Web SVG Optimization Controls

As with SWF, there are two ways to create SVG files. You can choose File → Save For Web or File → Save. Typically, you'll choose the Save For Web option when you're integrating an SVG file into a complete layout. Saving to SVG offers a more robust set of options. Details on those choices follow this section.

Figure 3.15 shows the format options for saving as SVG. We focus on the most important options in the sections that follow.

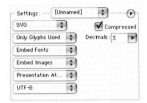

Figure 3.15

The SVG options of the Save For Web dialog box

Font Subsetting

What it is: *An option that determines which set of characters are linked to or embedded in the SVG file.*

What you should know: *Unless the text is to be dynamic, Only Glyphs Used is the best option.*

Font subsetting reduces the file size by including only some of the font information. It's worth taking a second here and noting what that implies. SVG graphics can include actual font information, not just the outlines of fonts, as SWF files do. You can select, copy, and paste text from an SVG file.

The glyph is the shape of the character. It describes the physical appearance of the letterform. In SVG files it describes both the vector shape of the letter and the on-screen appearance of the letter. Text also has a component that describes the contents of each letter, that is, whether it's an A or B. By connecting different glyphs to the same contents, you create different appearances of the same text, such as bold and italic versions of words. The more glyphs in a file, the larger it will be.

You can discard the glyphs completely; in that case, the fonts on a user's system are substituted. This results in a file that looks slightly different everywhere it goes. The Only Glyphs Used option embeds just the actual characters that appear in the document. The remaining options are typically used when text must be dynamic, such as type a user would enter, or type that comes from a server.

Font Location

What it is: *An option that embeds or links font data.*

What you should know: *Embedding is the more sensible strategy in most cases.*

Font information can be contained inside the SVF file (*embedded*) or called from an external file (*linked*). Embedding increases file size, but the characters are always available for the file to use. Linking reduces the file size of the document by storing font data in a Compact Embedded Font (CEF) file. You can't link if you're using the Only Glyphs Used option in subsetting (see the previous section). This is because the act of limiting to used characters breaks the text's connection to the font. Illustrator creates the CEF file automatically when you save. The idea is that multiple files can be linked to the same CEF, reducing file size overall.

Image Location

> What it is: *An option that embeds or links raster art.*
> What you should know: *Embedding makes a more portable but larger file.*

Use this option to link or embed raster images into the SVG. As with type, embedding raster art increases file size but ensures the art will be available as needed. Generally, art is linked when it is used by multiple documents in the same site.

You can either link or embed art in Illustrator. When you choose File → Place, you'll see a Link checkbox in the resulting dialog box. If you link rather than embed art, the link is passed directly to the SVG file. This is simple and easy to manage. Because SVG is text, you can find the link in it by looking at the source code. In this example, you can see both the object's ID and the external filename:

```
<image width="153" height="200" id="name_in_layers_palette_1_"
xlink:href="file.gif"/>
```

In cases where art is embedded, Illustrator generates a new file for the graphic. The graphic will be either JPEG or PNG, depending on its need for transparency. If the file originally placed isn't around or if the art was generated directly in Illustrator, the file will have an "ugly" name such as `FDE4198.png`. This can't be helped and there appears there is no logic to the naming, but you can rename the file and change the references in the SVG if it really upsets you. It's easiest, though, if you reserve linking for when multiple files will share the same graphic.

CSS Properties

> What it is: *Settings that determine how style attributes are recorded in the saved file.*
> What you should know: *Most users stick with Presentation Attributes.*

SVG files can contain Cascading Style Sheets (CSS) styles. CSS is a tool designed for specifying, among other things, the appearance of objects. The advantage is that you can define something once and then use it over and over again. Further, you can change the

CSS to alter the objects in the document. So if you decide that you want all of the text in a document to be blue, you can change it in the style and it will affect all the objects. This isn't a trivial task, but if you learn a little XML you can do it.

The settings in this list describe the manner in which the CSS is written. The structure of the code is important for managing the files. You may also be using the same style sheets to affect both HTML and SVG files, so you'll need to know where to find them. As with most things web, there will be a tradeoff between flexibility and speed.

The default option is Presentation Attributes, which saves the attributes in a manner that gives you the most flexibility for certain edits and transformations. You'll see the styles right at the top in the code. The Style Attributes option trades larger file size for the highest degree of flexibility in transformations. The Style Attributes (Entity References) setting gives quick delivery times and smaller file size. An *entity* is like a shortcut; you set it up once and then refer back to it, enabling you to reduce lengthy repeated code passages. Style Elements trades slower rendering speed for the ability to move style elements to HTML files.

Encoding

What it is: *Options that determine how data is written into the file.*
What you should know: *Most users stick with UTF-8.*

This option sets how the data in the SVG is written down by Illustrator. ISO 8859-1 is the common ASCII character set, used for European languages. HTML documents commonly use this code. Web pages announce to browsers that they are text documents using the ISO character set as a meta tag in their head section. As in: `<META HTTP-EQUIV="Content-Type" CONTENT="text/html; charset=iso-8859-1">`UTF 8, the default, is understood by all XML processors. The 8 stands for 8-bit, and with 256 characters available, it's suitable for a larger range of languages. Only UTF-8 enables you to include metadata, such as author information. When saving (File→ Save), you can include this data by checking the File Info option, available in the Advanced section of the SVG Options dialog but not in the Save For Web dialog box.

Compressed

What it is: *An option that switches the file from SVG to SVGZ, the compressed version.*
What you should know: *Compressed files are much smaller but you can't edit them in word processors.*

The SVGZ format is the compressed version of SVG. Illustrator can also save directly to this format and let you edit these files. The compressed versions are much smaller, making them well suited for graphics files.

The downside is that they can't be opened and edited in a word processor, like BBEdit or Microsoft Word. Since SVG is text, the files can be opened and edited like HTML. This isn't the case with SVGZ. You'll still be able to open the files in Illustrator, but not in Word.

Decimal Places (1–7)

What it is: *An option that specifies how accurate, and thus large, the file should be.*
What you should know: *Most users stick with the default setting (3), but smaller numbers may be easier to handle if you are manually editing the SVG*

This option is similar to flatness, only numerically reversed. It affects the position and sizes of points within the code. Values range from 1 (not so accurate) to 7 (too large to matter). For example, a straight line may be defined within the SVG as:

```
x1="2.222" y1="8.648" x2="45.926" y2="36.056"
```

Here, the code uses three decimal points to describe the X and Y positions of each end of the line. If you reduced the setting to 1, the numbers would round to `x1="2.2" y1="8.6"`.

For most files and users, 3 is just fine. If you are manually editing SVG, you might find it more convenient to reduce the number to 1. This makes it a lot easier to do math needed to size, animate and position objects.

Additional SVG Options via Save

What they are: *Additional choices you see when you issue the Save command rather than Save For Web.*
What you should know: *Unless you're taking the SVG to a developer, most of these options do not apply.*

Five additional options become available when you save an SVG file. Four are in the Advanced set and one in the initial Save dialog box. When you save an SVG or SVGZ file, your options are Font, Image Location, Font Subsetting, and an additional option called Preserve Illustrator Editing Capabilities.

When you save an SVG from the Save For Web dialog box, Illustrator strips the file down to its simplest, smallest size. It throws away all of the brushes, swatches, styles, and unused symbols. It also expands live objects, like blends and brushes, and converts meshes to raster art. None of this happens if you select Preserve Illustrator Editing Capabilities when you save. The file size is much larger with all of these features intact. In fact, the file is typically too large for web work. You should leave this setting enabled as you test and work through your art and then turn it off when you are ready to post.

The additional options (see Figure 3.16) become available when you click the Advanced button. Optimize For Adobe SVG Viewer is a good solid choice. The Adobe SVG Viewer is the most popular viewer out there. It is included with Acrobat and other Adobe applications, increasing its market penetration dramatically. The Optimize For Adobe SVG Viewer option speeds up the rendering time, especially when you're using SVG filters.

The remaining three options are more useful if you are working with a developer. Include Extended Syntax For Variable Data adds code that preserves any variables you built into the file. Scripts could be written by a developer to use that data, making text changes and such. Include Slicing Data adds the areas you've sliced into the SVG. You could use this option to go into the code and change how specific areas are optimized. Include File Info tucks in data you can use to track the file, such as the date it was created and modified. You can use that option only with UTF-8 encoding.

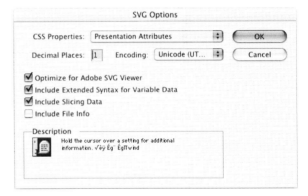

Figure 3.16

The Advanced tab of the SVG Options dialog box

So this means if you're making SVG art that isn't going to be adjusted later or massaged by a developer or IT pro, you can exclude the variable, slicing, and file information data.

Color Table Controls

What they are: *Options for files that use an 8-bit color model in the Save for Web dialog box.*

What you should know: *You'll use these tools mostly for GIFs. You will have exact control over the specific colors used in the file.*

Use the Color table to control the specific pixel colors used in a file. Only GIF and PNG images contain a Color table.

To edit a color in the table, double-click on it to open the Color Picker. The transparency color swatch (indicated by a checkerboard) cannot be edited, but it can be deleted, so be careful. You select colors by clicking on them. Shift-click to select a sequence of contiguous colors in the table; ⌘/Control+click to select noncontiguous swatches. Colors become highlighted when you click pixels of that color with the Eyedropper.

Figure 3.17 shows the Color table controls. Here's a description of each control:

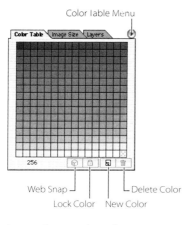

Figure 3.17
The Color table

Web Snap Shifts selected swatches to the nearest equivalent Web-safe colors. Web-safe colors are indicated in the table with a white diamond.

Lock Color Prevents colors from being snapped to web safe or from being omitted if the color number is reduced. Click again to unlock colors. Locked colors are indicated with a square tab in the lower right.

New Color Click to add the Eyedropper color to the Color table as a locked swatch.

Delete Color Click to delete selected swatches from the Color table. When a color is deleted, pixels in the image that use the color are reassigned to a nearby value—which often results in dithering. You should be careful about wiping out important colors because this dialog box offers no undo command. The easiest way to reset deleted colors is to cancel the entire dialog box and start over with the Save For Web command.

Color Table Menu The commands in the Color table's submenu enable you to sort, select, and otherwise interact with the different values.

Image Size Controls

What it is: Options in the Save for Web dialog that control the output size of web graphics.

What you should know: In addition to sizing controls, this section contains the important Clip to Artboard section.

Use the options on the Image Size tab to set the size of the pixel image produced. This doesn't affect the size of the vector graphics at all. The original size is listed for reference (see Figure 3.18). As you make changes here, you'll need to click the Apply button to preview them.

Set the width and height of the output using the pixel dimensions or the Percent field. Enabling the Constrain Proportions checkbox locks the width and height together so that they scale proportionally. As a general rule, make sure this checkbox is selected.

Figure 3.18
The Image Size controls in the Save For Web dialog box.

Likewise, you should make sure the Anti-Alias option is selected so you produce pixels with smoother edges. You can smooth hard pixel edges by changing the colors of edge pixels slightly.

The Clip To Artboard option is the best way to set web graphics to an exact size. Select this option to set the dimensions of the artwork to the Artboard size rather than to the bounding areas of the objects. Objects outside the Artboard will be cropped.

Exporting to CSS Layers

> What you're doing: *Converting Illustrator layers into CSS layers.*
> Why you're doing it: *It's easier to adjust layered items after creating HTML. This flexibility opens the door for basic motion animation, show and hide effects, and complex design possibilities.*

HTML 4 has layers similar to the layers in Illustrator. There are two ways to write layers in HTML, but the preferred method is to use the DIV tag, which is What Illustrator does. (See the section "HTML Options" for an explanation of this tag.) You can convert Illustrator layers to DIV layers in HTML by selecting the Export As CSS Layers option on the Layers tab (Figure 3.19). The contents of each layer become a separate graphic, which is then gathered in containers in the HTML. Layers are a dynamic HTML (DHTML) feature that is understood by 4.0 or higher level browsers. The contents of each Illustrator layer are written into an HTML layer, so you'd need to build layers in Illustrator appropriately before saving. Sublayers are not considered independently and become part of their parent layer.

Layers are often used in interactive pages. You see them used to create drop-down menus and disjointed rollovers. You accomplish this by showing and hiding the layers. Each layer in the Illustrator file is listed in the Layer drop-down menu. Select the layer you want to control from the list and choose from Visible, Hidden, or Do Not Export. Hidden layers are included in the file but are not displayed by default. You can use a script or link to show the layer when something happens—for example, the page loads or the user clicks a button.

When saving CSS layers, you can still use slices. Slices can generate tables or CSS layers as well. In theory, if you set both slices and layers to make layers, the slice layers will be nested inside CSS layers from Illustrator's layers. This doesn't always happen, though. The easiest approach is to decide whether to make layers and tables and then use either slices or layers to make them, but not both. The most common CSS model is to arrange your document in layers and then ignore the slice tools.

Figure 3.19
The Layers tab

CHAPTER 4

Gathering the Required Information

The more you know about how a graphic you create in Adobe Illustrator will be used on its website, the easier you'll find it to set the graphic up right the first time and make the proper choices as you go. At the very least, you should determine the area the graphic will occupy in the final webpage as well as the background color of the page it will appear on. If you know these two things, you can prepare a file that fits both its space and its background. The sooner in the creation process you know this, the less rework you'll be faced with later. This chapter explains where to find these two pieces of information in existing HTML, in GoLive, and in Dreamweaver. This chapter covers the following topics:

Dimensions of commonly used graphic elements

Creating a frame to determine pixel size in Adobe Illustrator

Determining the space a graphic should occupy in GoLive and Dreamweaver

Determining background colors in HTML

Learning page and table colors in GoLive and Dreamweaver

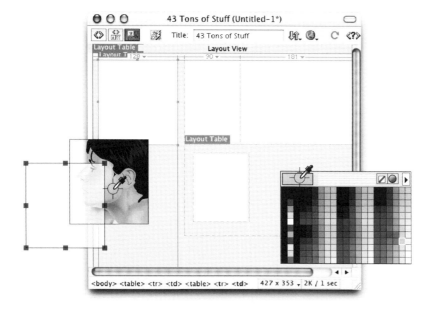

Figuring Pixel Dimensions

> What you're doing: *Determining how much space is available to your graphic.*
> Why you're doing it: *Web graphics should be used at 100 percent size. It's easier if you make them the size you'll use them. The pixel area is part of what determines your file size in bytes.*

One of the first things you should do when setting out to create web graphics is to figure out the area your art will occupy. The size is important because web graphics should be prepared at the size they will be used. If you are presenting a 100-pixel-long ad, you should create a 100-pixel-long image.

Print professionals may balk at this idea. Illustrator graphics are famous for their scalability; a single file may be used at many different sizes and still print without image degradation. Unfortunately, standard web graphics are not vector-based, and therefore they don't have this ability. The Illustrator graphic you create may be scalable, but the optimized web graphic created from it is not. So while it's possible to create an Illustrator graphic at any size and then resize as you optimize, most designers prefer to create graphics at the size they will be used.

The advantages of this approach are:

- You don't have to resize later and calculate conversion sizes.
- You get an accurate preview of how the art will appear when optimized.
- It gives you a feel for the elements in context, making it easier to set stroke weights and related settings without guessing how things will look when they're scaled.
- It enables you to see the art at the proper size without guessing about view depth.
- It provides the most accurate information about file size when you're optimizing.

If you are going to prepare SWF or SVG graphics, which are scalable, these advantages still apply. Further, the default size of those graphics in a web page will be the size at which they were created. Building them right the first time makes it easier all the way around.

Pixel and File Sizes of Common Elements

> What you're doing: *Noting the sizes of the graphics other people make.*
> Why you're doing it: *Knowing basic parameters makes it easier to decide how to build your own art; some websites standardize sizes.*

To help you get a sense of how pixel areas translate to file sizes, Table 4.1 lists typical sizes of graphic elements commonly used on websites. We present it as a guide only. Although some companies have standard sizes that they use to create graphics, there is no set rule about graphic sizing for your art, and you should feel free to add or subtract from these sizes to suit the needs of your art. Remember that larger graphics take longer to download.

ITEM	PIXEL SIZE	FILE SIZE
Buttons (navigation bar)	65 x 20	300 bytes
Button (large round)	65 x 65	2 KB
Logo (main usage)	175 x 150	7 KB
Logo (secondary usage)	40 x 35	1.5 KB
Bullet	10 x 10	100 bytes
Icon (navigation)	35 x 35	1.75 KB
Icon (e-commerce)	25 x 25	1.5 KB
Ad (banner)	275 x 50	6 KB
Ad (smaller banner)	175 x 50	3 KB
Ad (square)	100 x 100	5 KB
Illustration (large)	185 x 200	15 KB
Illustration (medium)	150 x 150	10 KB
Illustration (small)	100 x 100	6 KB

Table 4.1

Common Graphic Items and Their Sizes

Learning the Pixel Area in Illustrator

What you're doing: *Creating a box to frame the size of the graphic you'll create.*
Why you're doing it: *Creating a box helps you decide what size your graphic should be. Later, you'll use the dimensions to set up your document.*

Unless you have been given a set space to fill, deciding how large to make a graphic can be difficult. It's hard to anticipate the size an object will be until you actually see it. Once you know the size, you will be able to plan for the space in your HTML document and set the Artboard to size. This is important because when you eventually save the web version of the graphic, you will use the Artboard to crop out unneeded parts of your art. Otherwise, you'd have to take extraordinary steps to solve even everyday problems (for more information, see Chapter 5, "Preparing the Work Environment"). After a while, you'll become familiar with relative pixel dimensions and will be able to size the Artboard without first making a visual reference.

Determining the Size of a New Graphic

To visually determine the size a new graphic will occupy in Illustrator, follow these steps:

1. Choose File → New to create a new document. In the New Document dialog box, choose 640 × 480px from the Size menu and select the RGB Color Mode radio button. (This

last step isn't strictly necessary but will make it easier for you to continue working with the art later.)

2. Choose Edit → Preferences In the resulting dialog, select Units & Display Performance. From the General menu, choose Pixels. Alternately, display the rulers (View → Show Rulers) and Ctl+right-click directly on them. Then, select Pixels from the context menu. For more information about preferences, see Chapter 5.

3. Set the View Depth to 100%. The fastest way to do this is to double-click directly on the Zoom tool in the Tools palette.

4. Select the Rectangle tool and draw an area that you want the graphic to occupy. Picture the rectangle as the bounding area that the graphic must fall within. Make sure your art can completely fit in that space.

5. You may find it easy to visualize if you set the fill and stroke of the rectangle to white and black. Do this quickly by pressing D with the rectangle selected.

6. With the rectangle still selected, open the Transform palette. The values in the W and H fields represent the bounding areas a graphic could occupy. Reset the fields to test new sizes for the art.

Determining the Size of an Existing Graphic

To learn the size of an existing graphic that you intend to replace, follow these steps:

1. Choose File → Place and in the resulting dialog box navigate to the document you want to replace.

2. Unless you intend to trace from the document, don't select the Template option in the Place dialog box. There is no great reason to enable the Link option either in this case. Both of these options are intended for different techniques.

3. The graphic will appear in your document already selected. Resist the temptation to deselect it. Check the Transform palette to view the size of the graphic.

Determining the Size of a Graphic on a Website

Existing webpages may provide a good reference for art sizes. To determine the size of a graphic on the Internet, use this approach:

1. Open the webpage that contains the graphic in which you are interested.

2. Control+right-click on the image and choose Copy Image. You won't be able to copy SWF files.

3. In an open Illustrator document, choose Edit → Paste.

4. Leave the graphic selected and check the Transform palette to view the size of the graphic (Figure 4.1).
5. Delete the graphic to make sure you don't use someone else's work as your own.

Figure 4.1
Determine the size of an existing graphic with the Transform palette.

Learning Pixel Dimensions in GoLive

> What you're doing: *Getting the dimensions for a graphic from GoLive.*
> Why you're doing it: *You want to know how big to make a graphic to correctly fill the space in a webpage.*

If you are using a visual editor to generate webpages, you'll be able to see the size of the graphic you're about to create before you begin building it. This feature is very handy, especially in cases where you're building graphics for an existing page and want to set the size of your art in context.

Most professional web designers control graphic space in a webpage by using tables (layers may also be used, but they are not as common). GoLive enables you to create tables manually as well as by using the grid object. The grid is actually a table that GoLive writes in the background to aid the user. The experience is similar to designing in a page layout application; you can move objects around freely without having to adjust the table. With both the grid and a standard table, in this section we'll use image objects to figure out how large to make the graphics. Later, after creating the graphics, we'll load up the image objects with the files we've built.

PASTING AND MASKING

If you copy and paste art from webpages into Illustrator, a mask is created automatically. This doesn't happen when you open or place a file that is saved on your hard drive. The mask is a vector shape grouped to the raster art that marks the boundaries of the image. It doesn't serve an essential purpose by itself, but it can be helpful when you want to convert the image area into guides or create a vector shape that fills the exact space of the image.

To convert the clipping mask to a usable vector shape, locate the group that includes the image in the Layers palette. Twirl down the group and locate the Clipping Path object. Click-drag the clipping path straight up and out of the group in the Layers palette. The path is released from its duties in the group and becomes an ordinary path with a Fill & Stroke of None. Restyle it as you see fit or convert it to guides (View → Guides → Make Guides).

If you are working from scratch and don't yet have a webpage to put the graphic into, you'll find it easier to work with a grid. It doesn't resize itself by default (as tables do); graphic objects are easier to resize on a grid; and it enables you to place things exactly where you want.

Determining the Space for a Graphic in a GoLive Grid

To determine the space a graphic should occupy in a GoLive grid, follow these steps:

1. Open an existing GoLive page that contains a grid. If you are creating a page from scratch, start by placing a Layout Grid onto the page. The Layout Grid is the first object on the Basic tab of the Objects palette. Size the grid to fill your window by dragging the corner handle in the lower right of the grid (see Figure 4.2).

Figure 4.2

Place a grid object in the document to begin the process (top). Next, add an image object and adjust its size until you are satisfied. The dimensions of the object will be the size of your art (bottom).

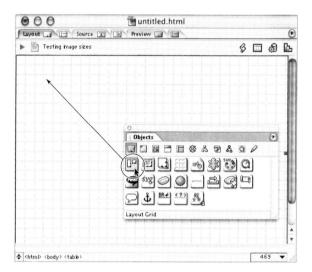

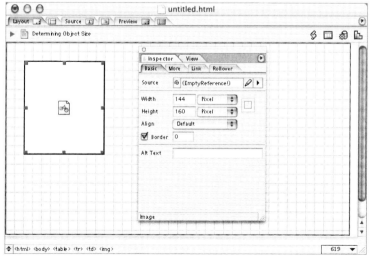

2. Drag an image object onto the layout grid from the Objects palette. The image object is fifth from the left on the Basic tab of the Objects palette. The image object serves as a placeholder for a graphic. You'll use it here to figure out how large to make your graphic. Later you'll put the graphic you built into this space and it will fit perfectly.

3. By default, a new image object is 32 pixels square. Resize it visually by click-dragging any of the corner points of the object. The Basic tab of the Inspector palette shows the pixel dimensions of the object. You can use the Width and Height fields to size the image object as well. The object will resize from the upper-left corner. That is, increased size will expand the object to the right and down. Objects around the graphic object will be repositioned to accommodate the new size, so if you don't want to mess up an existing layout, be sure you have enough room on the grid to resize the object.

Determining the Size of a Graphic in a GoLive Table

To figure the space an existing graphic occupies in a GoLive table, follow these steps:

1. Open a document that contains a table.
2. Click directly on the object. On the Basic tab of the Inspector palette (Figure 4.3), note the Width and Height of the graphic element.

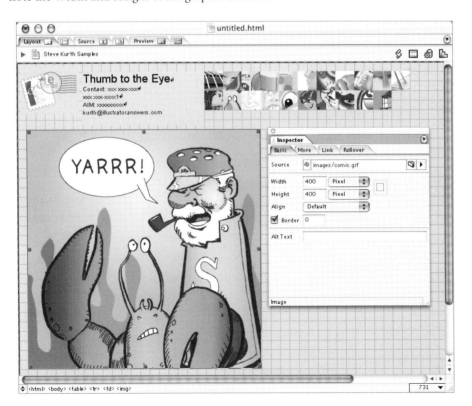

Figure 4.3

The dimensions of a selected graphic are visible in the Inspector palette.

3. If a graphic does not yet exist, drag an image object from the Objects palette into a table cell.

4. Size the graphic object by dragging one of its three corner points or using the Width and Height fields of the Basic tab of the Inspector palette. If you drag the handles, you'll notice that the graphic sizes itself about its center. The side handles set one dimension at a time (vertical or horizontal) while the corner handle sets both.

Establishing File Dimensions in Dreamweaver

> What you're doing: *Getting the dimensions for a graphic from Dreamweaver.*
> Why you're doing it: *You need to know how big to make a graphic to correctly fill the space in a webpage.*

Dreamweaver, like GoLive, has a tool for creating table cells visually. In Dreamweaver, this tool is called Layout View. Users like it because it accords them some freedom when designing a page and takes care of some of the drudgery of table creation. If you're starting a page from scratch, it makes sense to use Layout View to frame out space and establish the size of the required graphics.

Determining the Space for a Graphic in Layout View

To determine the space a graphic should occupy in Layout View, follow these steps:

1. In the Layout section of the Objects palette, click the Layout View button. The Draw Layout Cell and Draw Layout Table buttons become activated, and the Table and Layer buttons become dimmed.

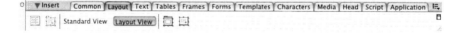

2. Click the Draw Layout Cell button and click-drag directly on the page. A rectangle follows the cursor, indicating where the cell will be created when you release the mouse. Illustrator creates a table automatically.

3. When you release the mouse, an insertion point will be blinking inside the cell. Position your cursor instead on the edge of the cell boundaries. The cell will highlight when you are over it. Click to select it.

4. When the cell is selected, boxes appear on its corners and sides. These are handles that enable you to resize the cell. Reposition the cell by dragging from its edge rather than using the handles.

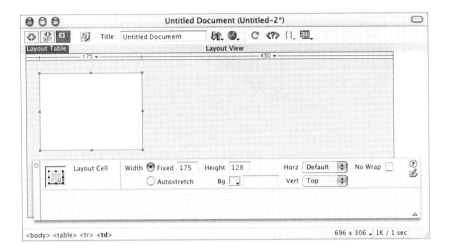

Figure 4.4

After switching to Layout View, drag out a Layout Cell to easily determine the dimensions a graphic should occupy.

5. Once the cell is the size you want it to be, note the Width and Height values in the Properties palette (Figure 4.4). Width will be set by default to Fixed (rather than Autostretch), which is what you want. These values represent the size of the graphic you need to make in Illustrator.

When Dreamweaver creates tables, it doesn't insert Width and Height properties for every cell. Usually, it inserts the width of each cell but only the height of the first cell. This makes the table efficient and flexible. However, it makes it a little harder for you to figure the dimensions of an existing cell that doesn't already contain a graphic. You could nose around in the code and figure it out, but the task is easier in Layout View.

Learning the Size of an Existing Table Cell

To determine the dimensions of an existing (non-graphic) cell in Dreamweaver, follow this approach:

1. Switch to Layout View by clicking the Layout View button at the bottom of the Objects palette.
2. Click directly on the edge of the cell. The cell becomes highlighted when your cursor is over it. The highlight color changes and handles appear when the cell is selected.
3. In the Properties palette, note the values in the Width and Height fields. These are the dimensions the Illustrator graphic should occupy.

> If the cell contains nothing at all, it will not be available in Layout View. Remedy this by typing a character into the cell in Standard View before switching modes.

To determine the space an existing graphic occupies in a Dreamweaver table:

1. Click directly on the graphic you wish to replace. Illustrator will highlight the graphic and display handles in the right and bottom sides and the lower-right corner.
2. Note the values in the W and H fields in the Properties palette. This is the size of the graphic you should create to replace the existing one.

For more information about Dreamweaver, see *Dreamweaver MX / Fireworks MX Savvy*, by Christian Crumlish (Sybex, 2002).

Understanding HTML Background Colors

What you're doing: Determining the background color of the page where you'll place your graphic.

Why you're doing it: You can use the background color of the page to create smoother outside edges in the graphics you build.

It's good to know the context art will be used in. In the case of Illustrator web graphics, knowing the background color of the page where you'll place the graphic goes beyond artistic concerns. You'll use the page's color to create the appearance of non-square graphics and to smooth the edges in graphics with transparency.

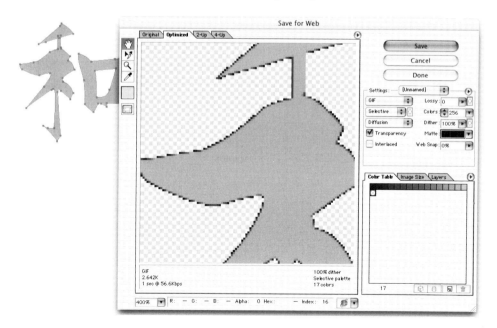

Figure 4.5

Matted edges blown up show the transitional pixels used to smooth color.

When Illustrator art is converted to a standard web graphic (that is, from a vector image to a bitmap), the edges, like the rest of the art, are translated into pixels—which are square. Where the edges of objects intersect each other, Illustrator mixes the pixel values to create a smoother transition. You can see this in the blown-up view in Figure 4.5. In Figure 4.6, you can see that without matting, the edges are noticeably jaggy. The eye doesn't notice the square pixels as easily, creating a more pleasing graphic. Where objects abut the sides of the graphic, or in the spaces between graphics, you'll see the background color of the page. Without information about this color, Illustrator can't smooth the edges. This is why you should know the color the graphic will be placed against before you finish building the art. The mixing process is called *matting*, and Illustrator does it automatically as you create the web graphic.

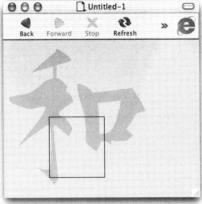

Figure 4.6

Without matting, the edge of the art looks jaggy.

The background color of a webpage can come from a number of places. In a basic workflow, the information is coded directly into the body section of the HTML. In other instances, the color can come from a CSS document to which the page is linked or from style sheets embedded in the document. Further, the color against which the graphic is placed could be the background color of a table or layer. In the next section, we'll describe where the information could live in HTML. The section that follows discusses where to find the data within an object. After that, we'll show how to find the information using GoLive and Dreamweaver.

Learning Page Background Color in HTML

What you're doing: *Determining the background color of the page from the HTML.*
Why you're doing it: *You can use the background color of the page to create smoother outside edges in your graphics.*

For print designers who are new to the Web, the structure of an HTML document may be unfamiliar, so I'll start with the basics. An HTML document has two sections: a header and a body. The *header* section stores data about what the page is and how it should be handled. It contains the document's title, as well as keywords and other metatags used by search engines. The *body* section contains the information that you see on the page. Depending on the techniques used, you can define the background color in either section of the document.

In a basic workflow, the background color is an attribute of the `<body>` tag. In HTML, items are differentiated by pairs of tags (enclosed by angle brackets) that instruct browsers how to handle information. Tags typically have an opening and a closing tag. The opening tag is the code in brackets, and the closing tag is the same but with a / before the code. For example, for bold `<b>` is the opening tag and `</b>` is the closing tag. Anything in between the tags is treated as the opening tag instructs. For example, a tag could say "here comes some text. Make the text red". Until the closing tag, all the text would be red.

Attributes (which have *values*) are additional descriptors within the opening tag that instruct browsers how to handle the data. In the previous example, the text color is the attribute and red is the value. Values appear in quotes and are separated from attributes by the equal sign, so the structure is

```
<tag attribute="value">
```

The attribute for the background color is `bgcolor`. Color values are defined in one of two ways: either by hexadecimal code or by name. Hexadecimal code is preceded by a pound sign; named text is simply named. Only 16 colors are usable directly by name: aqua, black, blue, fuchsia, gray, green, lime, maroon, navy, olive, purple, red, silver, teal, white, and yellow. Hexadecimal code is a method for writing RGB color values that uses fewer characters and thus creates a smaller HTML file. Hex code uses base 16 rather than base 10 for numbers. The numbers are alphanumeric and run 0 to F, with A being equal to 10, B equal to 11, and so on up to 16. Hex describes RGB colors with six digits, two for each color component. The first two numbers are the red component, the next two are green, and the last two are blue. Values are a measure of the degree of lightness. The numbers range from 00 (no light) to FF (pure light). So the color FF0000 would be pure red light (the first two digits) with no green or blue light (the following four digits). For more information, see Chapter 1, "Core Terms and Concepts."

In a basic HTML workflow, the background color of the page is an attribute of the `<body>` tag. The opening `<body>` tag follows the closing `</head>` tag and sets up the appearance of the page. Typically, the color of the page and the default color for text are defined as attributes of the `<body>` tag. So, the opening `<body>` tag might look like this:

```
<body bgcolor="#ffffff" text="black">
```

Here the attribute `bgcolor` is given the hexadecimal value `#ffffff`, or white, while the attribute text is given the named color `black`.

Determining the Background Color of an Existing HTML File

To learn the background color of an existing HTML file, follow these steps:

1. Open the HTML file that you want to inspect, using an application such as BBEdit, SimpleText, Word, or even your favorite web browser. If you are opening the file in a browser, you'll need to check the source code so that you can see the HTML. In

Internet Explorer, choose View → Source; in Netscape Navigator, choose View → Page Source.

2. Locate the opening `<body>` tag of the document. It should be near the beginning, just after the closing `</head>` tag.

3. See if the attribute `bgcolor` is used. If it is, select the hexadecimal number in quotes after the # sign. Copy the value (Edit → Copy) or write it down on a handy piece of paper. Later you'll paste this value into Illustrator.

4. If the body text does not use the `bgcolor` attribute or the actual color of the page doesn't seem to match the value given, that means the background color comes from someplace else and you'll have to investigate further. See the next section.

Verifying Color Values in a Page That Uses Cascading Style Sheets (CSS)

Many current web pages use Cascading Style Sheets (CSS) for the formatting of text and pages. Style sheets are a way of defining the appearance of pages that offers you greater control over items than straight HTML does. If you want to use style sheets, your web browser must be version 4 or above. It's beyond the scope of this book to describe style sheets completely, but you should be aware of what they are and how to use them effectively. For more information on style sheets, see Chapter 1.

You can either embed a style sheet in your document or link to it. An embedded style sheet is completely contained in an HTML document, whereas a linked one is merely referenced by the file. When you modify a linked style sheet, the page that uses it updates automatically. For this reason, most times you'll choose to link because you can connect more than one document to a style sheet—which means you can modify an entire site using one file. In either case, the information will appear in the head section of the document.

If a style sheet is linked to an HTML document, it will appear as follows:

```
<head>
<link href="name.css" rel="stylesheet" media="screen">
</head>
```

Here the the tag `<link>` has the attribute `href`, whose value is the reference to the style sheet file. In the example, the style sheet document lives in the same directory as the HTML file and is named `name.css`. This information doesn't tell us the actual color of the background, though. To find that out, you'd need to open the style sheet file itself. As with HTML, you can open a CSS document in a word processing application. Commonly, the code for the background color in a CSS document is an attribute of the CSS-defined `<body>` tag:

```
body   { background-color: #090cff }
```

Here the body's background color is given the value `090cff`. This is the code you would want to copy and paste for later use in Illustrator.

In some pages, the CSS lives directly in the HTML document rather than being linked externally. You'll be able to tell the difference because there is no "link" tag. In those cases, you would find the background color by looking in the head section. The `<style>` tag starts the CSS, and you should be able to identify the body:

```
<head>
    <style type="text/css" media="screen">
<!--
body {  background-color: #999900}
-->
</style>
</head>
```

The HTML that defines the background color of the webpage assigns the `<body>` tag a value of 999900, which is a dark olive green. For later use, you'd copy and paste this number. In instances where both a `<style>` and a standard `<body>` tag are used to define background color, the `<style>` tag takes precedence. You should look for the presence of both tags when you're examining files or you may miss the tag that is actually styling your page.

To download samples of style sheets and background colors, point your browser to www.sybex.com, navigate to the *Hidden Power of Illustrator* page, and click the Downloads link.

Understanding Table Background Color in HTML

What you're doing: *Determining the background color of a table by looking at the HTML.*

Why you're doing it: *An Illustrator graphic placed in a table with a background color can be matted against the color to create smoother edges.*

Tables and table elements can be given background colors, enabling you to use them as graphic elements. In cases where you intend to place a graphic into a table, you'll want to know what that color is. If you're creating the table, or Illustrator is making the table for you, it's easy to determine what the color should be. If you want to place a graphic into an existing table, you can read the HTML to determine the colors yourself.

Tables can have colors, and so can the individual rows and cells within a table. Fortunately, the attribute that determines color is the same for all three: bgcolor. This is logical, because it's the same code that's used with the `<body>` tag. The tag for a table is `<table>`, the tag for a cell is `<td>`, and the tag for a row is `<tr>`. All three require closing tags, and the cell and row tags must be placed between the opening and closing tags of a table.

For example, this table:

would be described by the following HTML:

```
<table bgcolor="#993300">
  <tr bgcolor="#990066">
    <td>row 1 column 1</td>
    <td>row 1 column 2</td>
  </tr>
  <tr>
    <td>row 2 column 1</td>
    <td bgcolor="#0099FF">row 2 column 2</td>
  </tr>
</table>
```

This code arranges the table into four cells, two by two. The table itself has a background color value of 993300, and the first row has a background color value of 990066. The final cell has its own color value as well: 0099FF. If you place a graphic in a cell instead of the text that appears here, you need to take the background color from the correct

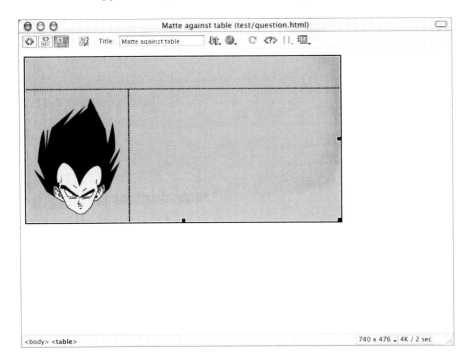

Figure 4.7
A table with four different color values

place. If the graphic appears in either of the cells in the first row, it will be the row's color, 990066. If it appears in the third cell, it will be the table's color, 993300. The last cell has its own color, 0099FF.

You can see that it's important to investigate the places color information can reside. When examining HTML that someone else has created, like the page shown in Figure 4.7, start from the graphic and work your way out. Ask yourself, is the graphic in a cell that contains color? If not, then move out to the row tag; does that contain a `bgcolor` attribute? If not, then check the table itself. Keep in mind that tables can be nested within each other.

To find where the value from each cell originates, first locate the graphic by name in the HTML. Next, move back (to the left) through the code and look for a `bgcolor` attribute. Listing 4.1 shows the HTML for this particular layout. Note the location of the `bgcolor` attributes. As you can see, the table background color in this example is specified in the row containing the graphic named *image.gif*.

Listing 4.1

The HTML for the Matte against Table Page

```
<table width="500" border="0" cellpadding="0" cellspacing="0"
bgcolor="#99CC66">
  <tr>
    <td height="75" colspan="2" valign="top"> </td>
  </tr>
  <tr bgcolor="#CC9933">
    <td width="229" height="210" align="center" valign="middle">
<img src="image.gif" width="350" height="131"></td>
    <td width="269" valign="top"> </td>
  </tr>
</table>
```

You can view this table on your browser by downloading `[table].htm` from the *Hidden Power of Illustrator CS* page on www.sybex.com.

Learning Layer Background Color in HTML

What you're doing: *Determining the background color of a layer by looking at the HTML.*

Why you're doing it: *An Illustrator graphic placed in a layer with a background color can be matted against the color to create smoother edges.*

Compared to creating tables, using layers is a slightly more advanced HTML technique that enables you to place elements in a specific position on a page. Layers offer other advantages as well, such as the ability to show or hide items, to overlap each other, and to be animated. A common example of layers is found in most drop-down menus in web pages.

Layers are actually part of a style sheet workflow and can be found in the head section of an HTML document. The code will look like this:

```
<style type="text/css" media="screen"><!--
#layer1 { background-color: #699002; position: absolute;
top: 132px; left: 228px; width: 100px; height: 100px;
visibility: visible; display: block }
--></style>
```

Here the style sheet specifies the position, size, and visibility of a layer named `layer1`. Note the familiar `background-color` attribute that follows the braces. The hex value listed here is the one you would use in Illustrator to matte your graphic against.

Determining Page and Table Colors in GoLive

What you're doing: Identifying the colors used in tables and as a background using Adobe GoLive

Why you're doing it: An Illustrator graphic placed in a table with a background color can be matted against the color to create smoother edges.

Visual editors like GoLive and Dreamweaver make it easy to identify and apply colors to objects. Let's discuss where you can find those controls so that you can spot values that have already been applied to pages and modify them as required. Remember, the goal here is to set the colors in Illustrator to match the colors over which you'll place your graphic.

As you'll see in the following steps, you set the background color of a page by using the Show Page Properties button. Clicking this button activates the Page options in the Inspector palette. To set the background color for a page in GoLive:

1. Make sure the Inspector and Color palettes are visible, as in Figure 4.8. Both are available under the Window menu.
2. If it's not already displayed, click the Layout Editor tab in an open HTML document. This view exposes the Show Page Properties button (A) in the upper left of the document window.
3. Click the Show Page Properties button. The Inspector switches to reveal the Page, HTML, and ColorSync tabs.
4. The Color checkbox in the Background section of the Page tab should be checked by default. Next to it is a color swatch (B). Click the swatch to highlight it. A black box will surround the swatch when you've selected it.

5. In the Color palette, click the Web Color List or the Web Name List button (they are the second and third from the right at the top of the palette). The hexadecimal code for the background color of the page will be indicated in the Value field (C). Highlight the value and copy it or write it down.

6. If you prefer, you can change the background color of the page. With the background color swatch highlighted in the Inspector, click on any tab in the Color palette. To bypass the Inspector palette completely, first click the color you want to apply to the page. Next, drag the large swatch from the left of the Color palette directly onto the Show Page Properties button in the upper left of the Layout Editor.

GoLive Grids

GoLive can set and identify the colors used in tables, rows, and cells. Remember that GoLive can create tables as traditional table objects but also as a grid. Reading the HTML from the Source Editor in both cases will be the same. Grids have several additional lines in the code, but uses the same `<table>` tag with the `bgcolor` attribute. The opening tag for a grid might look like this:

```
<table width="200" border="0" cellspacing="0"
cellpadding="0" bgcolor="#ff9966" cool gridx="16"
gridy="16" height="200" showgridx showgridy usegridx
usegridy>
```

Figure 4.8

To set background color in GoLive, click the Page Properties button (A) and then highlight the background color swatch in the Inspector (B) to see its value in the Color palette (C).

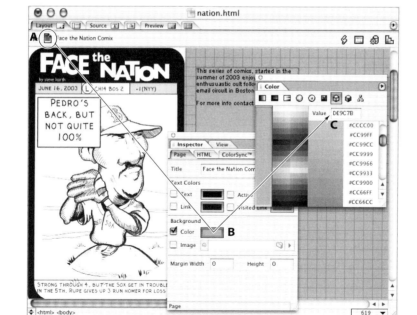

You can see that the structure here is a table with the added `cool grid` attributes. Cool grid is the proprietary code that enables GoLive to display tables as grids, enabling you to layout pages more freely. The code is typically stripped out when the file is uploaded. The key thing to note is the `bgcolor` attribute and its value.

It's easier to spot and set background colors with the Layout Editor. To use it, first make sure the Layout Editor tab is displayed. Then, select the item you want to check and highlight the color swatch in the Inspector. The Color palette shows you the color value connected to the item.

To set or check color on a grid:

1. In the Layout Editor shown in Figure 4.9, select the grid by clicking directly on it (A).
2. Click the color swatch in the Inspector palette next to the Background Color checkbox (B). To see the color value used, Control+right-click on the swatch itself. A pop-up menu appears showing the web-safe colors and the hex value of the current color.
3. The color value for the grid will appear in the Color palette in the Value field (C). To be sure you see it, set the Color palette to Web Color List or Web Name List. Click a new swatch in the Color palette to reset the grid's color if desired.

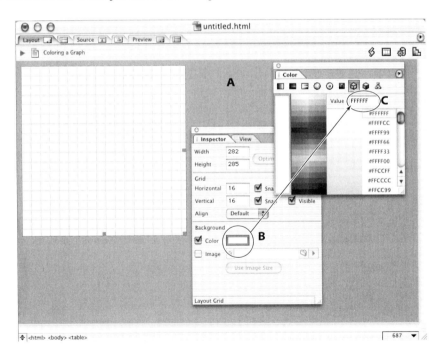

Figure 4.9

To find the background color of a grid (A), click the color swatch in the inspector (B) and then check the Color palette (C).

Traditional Tables in GoLive

The hardest part about checking tables is selecting them correctly. It's easy to miss selecting the entire table and select only a single cell or an insertion point. If this happens, you can select the cell, row, or table by clicking on the <td>, <tr>, or <table> tag respectively at the bottom of the Layout Editor (Figure 4.10). Tags are nested from left to right, so be sure to click the corresponding tag farthest to the right.

To set or check color on a table:

1. Select the item you wish to check. Either click the edge of the table to select it or click its tag as described earlier (Figure 4.10, step A).

2. The background colors of cells, rows, and tables are located in the respective tabs of the Inspector palette. Click the tab for the item you want to investigate and then look for the Color checkbox and swatch (B). Click the swatch to highlight it. A black box outlines the item to indicate it is selected. To see the color value used, Control+right-click on the swatch itself; a pop-up menu appears showing the web-safe colors and the hex value of the current color.

3. The color value for the item will be displayed in the Color palette in the Value field (C). To be sure you see it, set the Color palette to Web Color List or Web Name List. To reset the color, click a new swatch in the Color palette.

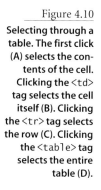

Figure 4.10

Selecting through a table. The first click (A) selects the contents of the cell. Clicking the <td> tag selects the cell itself (B). Clicking the <tr> tag selects the row (C). Clicking the <table> tag selects the entire table (D).

Layers in GoLive

GoLive calls layers "floating boxes." Identifying and setting their colors is essentially the same process as it is with tables. One difference is that they can be selected quickly in the Floating Box palette. It's the same process as before; check the swatch in the Inspector, and you can see the value in the Color palette.

To set or check the color of a floating box:

1. Open the Floating Box palette (Window → Floating Box) and click on the name of the layer you want to inspect.

2. In the Inspector palette, click the color swatch to highlight it. To see the color value used, Control+right-click on the swatch itself. A pop-up menu appears showing the web-safe colors and the hex value of the color used if it's web-safe.

3. The color value for the item appears in the Color palette in the Value field. To be sure you see it, set the Color palette to Web Color List or Web Name List. To reset the color, click a new swatch in the Color palette.

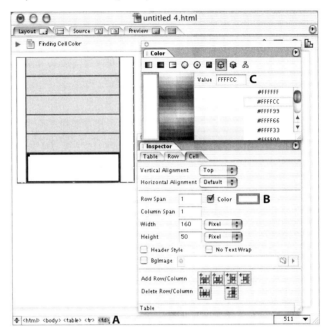

Figure 4.11

Here, a cell will contain a graphic. To find the color to matte the graphic against, select the cell's tag (A) and highlight the color swatch in the Inspector (B). The color value appears in the Color Palette (C).

Determining Page and Table Colors in Dreamweaver

What you're doing: *Determining the background color of items in Dreamweaver.*
Why you're doing it: *An Illustrator graphic placed in an item with a background color can be matted against the color to create smoother edges.*

To determine the background color of a page in Dreamweaver:

1. Open the page and choose Modify → Page Properties. You'll see the dialog box shown in Figure 4.12.

2. In the Background field, note the color value used. To modify the value, enter a new hex number in the field or click on the color swatch to access the color drop-down menu.

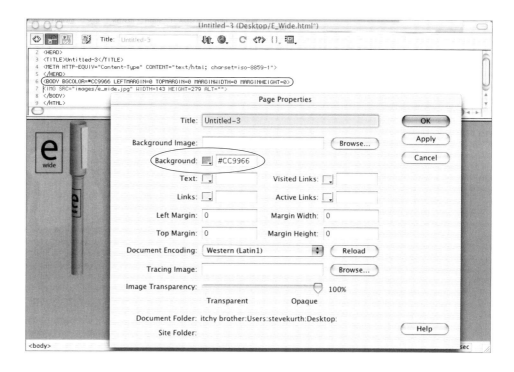

Figure 4.12

Open the Page Properties dialog box in Dreamweaver to find the value of the background color.

Cascading Style Sheets in Dreamweaver

If the color given doesn't match what you see on screen, or no color is given but the page has a background color, look for the presence of Cascading Style Sheets. As you'll recall, a style sheet overrides the attributes of the <body> tag.

1. In the CSS Styles palette (Window → CSS Styles), click the Edit Style Sheet button. Do this even if you don't see any styles listed in the palette. Linked styles and redefined HTML tags are not displayed here.

2. In the Edit Style Sheets dialog box, check for a <body> tag or a linked style that contains a <body> tag. Linked style documents appear in the main pane with (linked) next to their name. Click on one to see a list of the specific styles it contains, and then double-click the linked style to open it. In the dialog box that opens, you will be able to edit the styles in the linked document.

3. Double-click the <body> tag to edit it. In the Category pane to the left, click Background. The right side of the dialog box displays options for the page.

4. Note the value in the Background field. This is the color you should matte your Illustrator graphic against.

Dreamweaver's Design View

In Design View, Dreamweaver's Properties palette reveals any background colors that are applied to tables, rows, and cells. The trick is selecting the correct item and then looking for the Bg or Bg Color field in the Properties palette.

1. To select a table, position your cursor directly on one of its edges and click. The entire table should become selected. If you miss and select a cell instead, look to the tags listed in the lower left of the window. Click the `<table>` tag farthest to the right to select the table.

2. To select a row, position your cursor to the left of the table on the edge of the row you want to select. Your cursor will switch to a left arrow. Click to select the row.

3. To select an individual cell, ⌘/Alt click inside the cell. Alternately, click in the cell and then click the first `<td>` tag in the lower left of the window.

4. Check the value in the appropriate field (see Figure 4.13) to determine the current color of the item.

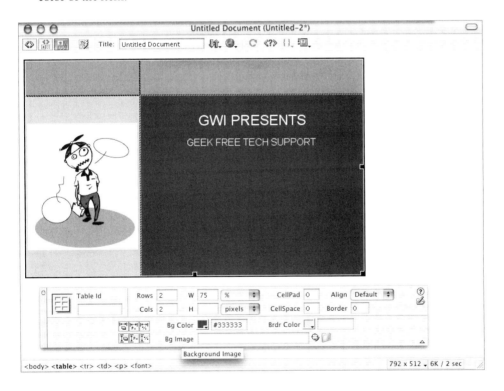

Figure 4.13

The Properties palette indicates the background color of selected items: (top) a table, (middle) a row, (bottom) a cell.

Figure 4.13
continued

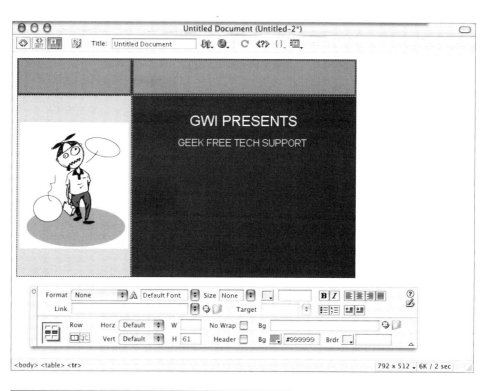

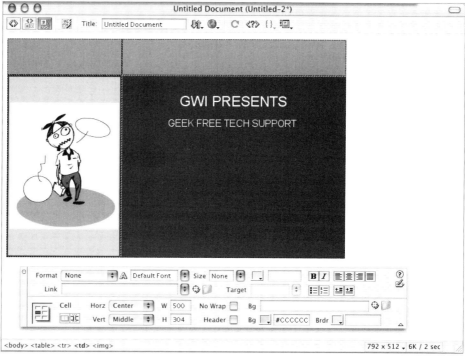

Layers in Dreamweaver

Dreamweaver's layers are managed from the Layers palette (Window → Layers). To find the colors in a layer, select the layer and then check the Bg Color field in the Properties palette (Figure 4.14).

To set or read the colors in a layer:

1. Open the Layers palette (Window → Layers). Click on the name of the layer you want to inspect. The layer will become selected.

2. Check the value in the Bg Color field in the Properties palette. This is the color you would matte your Illustrator graphic against.

Pasting Hex Color Numbers into Illustrator

Once you've copied hex code from another application, you'll need to paste it into Illustrator. The Color palette doesn't have an immediate way to do this. Instead, you'll need to paste it into the Color Picker. First make sure that you're in an RGB document. Then, double-click on the fill or stroke swatch in the Color palette or in the Tool palette. When the Color Picker opens, highlight the # field and paste in your color value.

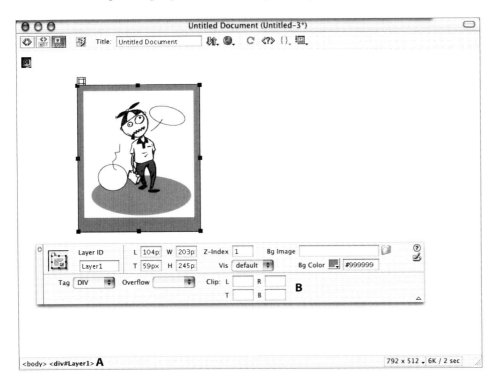

Figure 4.14

After selecting a layer (A), check the background color in the Properties palette (B).

CHAPTER 5

Preparing the Work Environment

In this chapter, we'll look at preparing documents and Illustrator itself for web work. These techniques are designed to help you with particular tasks, but they aren't necessarily required to accomplish those tasks. They will, however, save you time or streamline your work. For example, you could create web graphics without ever sizing the Artboard, but sooner or later, you'll run into complications if you don't. After setting up the document in this chapter, you'll produce the graphics (Chapter 6, "Creating Single Graphics") and optimize them for the Web (Chapter 7, "Optimizing Spot Illustrations").

This chapter covers the following topics:

Choosing typical web preferences

Creating a new document

Setting preview models

Saving and editing views

Preparing reusable color palettes

Adjusting Illustrator's defaults

Customizing shortcuts

Creating browser templates

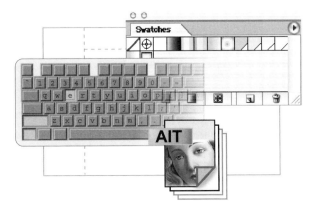

Choosing Typical Web Preferences

What you're doing: Setting up preferences and color settings for work on the Web. *Why you're doing it:* You can set common choices once rather than catch-as-catch-can as you're working.

In this section, we'll fine-tune our work environment for web work by setting basic color settings and default preferences. Preferences specify the basic behavior of your work environment and tools; color settings determine the set of colors each color mode represents and control how color conversion takes place. These settings are retained in each working session until you change them again.

PREFERENCES FOR WEB WORK

General Preferences:

- Keyboard Increment: 1 px
- Anti-Aliased Artwork: On

Units & Undo:

- Units: General: Pixels
- Units: Stroke: Pixels (or Points)
- Units: Type: Pixels (or Points)

Smart Guides & Slices:

- Slices (On, Light Red)

Color Settings for Web Work:

- Web Graphics Default

Working Spaces:

- RGB: sRGB IE-1966-2.1
- CMYK: US Web Coated. (Note that "web" refers to a web printing press. Illustrator requires you to specify a CMYK color space even if you don't intend to print.)

Color Management Policies:

- RGB: Off
- CMYK: Off
- Profile Mismatch: Ask When Opening

Set your preferences by choosing Edit → Preferences. In the Macintosh X operating system (OSX), preferences are located on the Illustrator menu. Preferences are broken into nine groups on the Preference submenu. Once inside the Preferences dialog box, you can cycle to the next or previous group of options. Many users take advantage of this by using the keyboard shortcut for General Preferences ⌘+K (on a Mac) and Ctrl+K (on a PC) and then clicking the Next button to move to the preference they need.

Set your color options by choosing Edit → Color Settings. Unlike with preferences, a single dialog box gets the job done here.

In the remainder of this section, we offer detailed descriptions and recommendations for the preferences and color settings that are involved with web work. For quick reference, the "Preferences for Web Work" sidebar summarizes the most important recommended settings.

Preference and Web Color Reference and Recommendations

This section is a quick reference for Illustrator's preferences. We list recommended settings in parentheses after each setting. (If you don't see a parenthetical recommendation, that means the setting depends on what you're doing.) Not every figure shows the recommended preference. To continue with the process of building web graphics, skip ahead to "Creating a New Document."

General Preferences

When you use the ⌘/Ctrl+K keyboard shortcut to access the Preferences dialog box, you'll start with the General tab, shown in Figure 5.1.

KEYBOARD INCREMENT (1 PX)

This setting controls how far items move when you press the arrow keys on the keyboard. At a distance of 1 pixel, it's easy to nudge items into place and align them. For finer work, you could also use a half pixel (.5 px). Keep in mind that pixels describe the distance a single pixel occupies when the document is at 100 percent view depth. The distance is not relative as you zoom in and out of the document.

If you don't want to set the preference for pixels for some reason, you may type **px** after any value in a field in Illustrator (such as the fields in the Transform palette) to express a measurement in pixels. The amount keyed in will automatically translate into the default units. Using the default preference (points), one pixel would translate into one point.

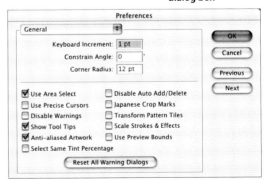

Figure 5.1
The General tab of the Preferences dialog box

CONSTRAIN ANGLE (0°)

Use this preference to set the angle of objects created with the Type, Rectangle, and Rounded Rectangle tools and to set the angle other tools will snap to when you hold down the Shift key. By default, this preference is set to 0°, which means rectangle tops will be flat and the other tools will snap to 45°, 90°, 135°, and 180°. There is nothing particularly "web" about this preference, and it should be set to 0° unless a particular job requires a different setting. It's worth noting that if you change the preference, degrees are still calculated in 45° increments. That is, if you are working on an isometric drawing and set the preference to 30°, Shift-rotating would turn objects to 75°, 120°, 165°, and 210° rather than 60°, 90°, 120°, and 150°.

CORNER RADIUS

This setting determines the size of the curve created by default when you use the Rounded Rectangle tool. You would rarely use this dialog box to set this preference. Every time you use the Rounded Rectangle tool, this preference is updated. It's easy to set the value in the document by clicking with the Rounded Rectangle tool or by using keyboard shortcuts. For information on using the Rounded Rectangle tool and making buttons, see Chapter 6.

OBJECT SELECTION BY PATH ONLY (OFF)

This preference forces you to select filled items by clicking on their paths only. Disabling this option is absolutely essential if you want to use the Magic Wand tool, and also makes it easy to select entire paths using the Selection and Direct Selection tools. When Object Selection by Path Only is deactivated, you can click the interior of a path that contains a painted fill (any Fill setting other than None) to select it in Preview mode. Without this preference, you have to click on the edge of a path to select it. This approach reduces the effectiveness of the Direct Selection tool and renders the Magic Wand useless.

When this preference is active, selecting line segments with the Direct Selection tool can sometimes be easier; an imprecise click could select the entire path instead. Some users prefer to turn on the preference, allowing them to quickly drag-select line segments. On the whole, though, Object Selection by Path Only is a better left inactive.

USE PRECISE CURSORS (ON)

This preference changes the default set of cursors from Standard to Precise. Illustrator has two sets of tool cursors: a set that looks like the tool (the Standard set) and a set that look like crosshairs (the Precise set). Many tools use crosshairs in both sets. Only a dozen or so tools (the Paintbrush, the Pencil suite, the Pen suite, the Eyedropper, the Paintbucket tools, the Symbol tools, the Magic Wand, and the Lasso selection tools) are affected by this preference. No matter which you pick as a default, pressing the Caps Lock key switches the sets.

DISABLE WARNINGS (ON)

This preference instructs Illustrator to play an "alert" sound instead of displaying a warning in the event that you attempt to use a tool in a way that produces no results. Commonly, these errors are caused by imprecise cursor placement or objects that do not support the feature you are trying to use. A typical example is clicking with the Convert Anchor Point tool anywhere except directly on an anchor point or trying to join anchor points (using the command Object: Path: Join tool) in different groups.

In practice, you should leave the warnings on until you are quite comfortable with the tools, after which you will find there is a productivity benefit to turning them off.

SHOW TOOL TIPS (ON)

This option displays the name and keyboard shortcut for a tool or palette item when the cursor is over the item. This includes named items, such as styles and brushes and custom shortcuts you create using Edit → Keyboard Shortcuts. Show Tool Tips is a great option that even highly experienced users benefit from enabling.

ANTI-ALIASED ARTWORK (ON)

This option adjusts the onscreen display of objects to make curves appear smooth. If you want to use the Pixel Preview option, you must enable this option, and you should turn it on for web work as well. For more information, see "Setting Preview Models" later in this chapter.

SELECT SAME TINT PERCENTAGE

This option affects how the commands under the Select menu behave. By default, Select → Same Fill/Stroke selects all objects with the same color definition. Sometimes this is a problem with spot colors. In a document in which all the objects are different tints of the same spot color, the Select → Same commands select everything. When this preference is activated, the Select → Same → Fill/Stroke commands select only objects with the exact same tint percentage rather than simply the same color. Tints are available only to objects styled using global swatches, such as spot colors.

Enabling this option is sometimes useful in global color workflows, usually ones based on templates. You can see examples of using global colors in Chapter 6.

DISABLE AUTO ADD/DELETE (OFF)

This option disables the ability of the Pen tool to temporarily switch to the Add A Point and Subtract A Point tools. By default, the Pen tool switches to the Add Anchor Point tool when you place it over a selected line segment, and it changes to the Delete Anchor Point tool when you place it over a selected anchor point. This behavior makes it easier for you to edit paths without switching tools. This option disables that default behavior. If you are using the Pen tool to draw a series of shapes that have common anchor points, disabling Auto Add would be useful; otherwise, leave it alone.

TRANSFORM PATTERN TILES

This option determines whether transformation tools and commands will affect patterns by default. Enabling this option sets the default behavior to include patterns in the transformation. We won't offer a recommendation for this preference because it can also be set in any transformation dialog box and in the Transform palette menu by checking the Pattern option. If you change the option in a dialog box, it changes the preference overall.

SCALE STROKES & EFFECTS

This option determines whether scaling tools and commands will affect strokes and effects as well as objects. You can also set this preference in the Scale dialog box and in the Transform palette menu. Either method is acceptable, depending on your needs. If you do start scaling stroke weight, though, make sure you get a good look at your art at 100 percent so you'll know how your art will look online.

USE PREVIEW BOUNDS (ON)

Set to On, Use Preview Bounds instructs the Info and Transform palettes to include strokes and effects when measuring an object. Because strokes extend outside the vector shape, the actual area a stroked object occupies is larger than the vector shape that defines it. Use this option to measure and transform the actual size. This preference has no effect on commands that create shapes.

Use Preview Bounds helps you learn the size of items using the Info palette, but the Transform palette has a tendency to not give you what you ask for when this preference is active. For example, if you set an object's width to 100 pixels, the palette may make the width 100.02. The difference between what you get and what you asked for is never gigantic, but it can be maddening. Nonetheless, most users activate this option for its use with the Info palette.

RESET ALL WARNING DIALOGS

When enabled, this preference clears the Don't Show Again option that may be attached to some warning dialog boxes. When you click the Don't Show Again button, all applicable warning dialog boxes will be displayed. This preference does not override the Disable Warnings preference.

Type & Auto Tracing Preferences

Use the Type & Auto Tracing tab of the Preferences dialog box (Figure 5.2) to set preferences related to typography.

SIZE/LEADING (1 PX)

You can use keyboard shortcuts to increase and decrease the size and leading (the line height of type) of selected text. This option specifies by how much the text will change each time you use the shortcuts.

A setting of 1 pixel here usually works well. Type in web graphics is often small, so a smaller preference setting works well., "Essential Illustrator Tools and Techniques."

TRACKING (20)

This option sets the increments attached to keyboard shortcuts for tracking (the space between characters and words) and kerning (the space between two characters).

BASELINE SHIFT (1 PX)

This option sets the increments attached to keyboard shortcuts for baseline shift (the distance up or down a character sits from its default position). A single pixel is a nice increment for nudging text up and down.

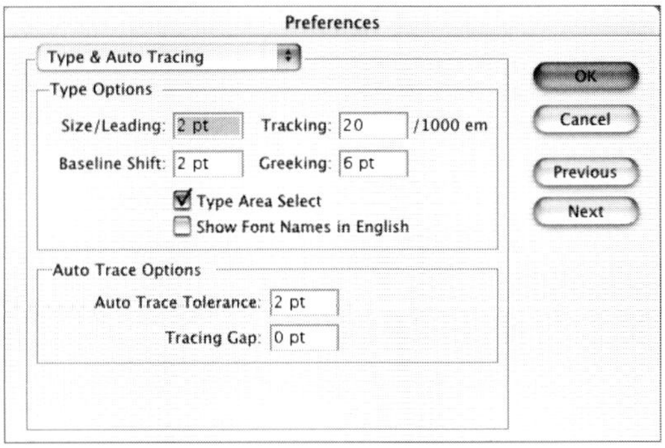

Figure 5.2
The Type & Auto Tracing tab of the Preferences dialog box

GREEKING (5 PX)

This option determines the type size at or below which Adobe uses *greeking*, the onscreen substitution of gray bars for illegibly small type. Greeking does not affect the way a file is converted to a web graphic. This measure is relative and is based on a 100 percent view depth. Using a 6-pixel greeking limit, 6-pixel type would appear to be greeked when viewed at 100 percent but not at 101 percent (it would appear larger than 6 pixels). Likewise, 12-pixel type viewed at 50 percent would appear to be 6 pixels and greeked.

A setting of 6 pixels is about as small as type can be and still be read. Set to a 5-pixel limit, type will appear greeked when it is below the legible limit. This will let you know when type is becoming too small to read. You should use your judgment, of course. The actual size of letters varies from font to font. Inspect your graphic at 100 percent view depth. If you can't read your text, it's too small. Greeking should be used as a red flag as you scale and transform your text.

TYPE AREA SELECT (ON)

This option increases the clickable area needed for selecting a type object from only its baseline to the entire space the type sweeps out. Unlike the Area Select option, Type Area Select works in outline mode and regardless of whether the type is painted. Enabling Type Area Select makes selecting type easy but can make working with complex documents cumbersome. Frequently you may find yourself selecting inadvertently instead of nearby objects. Try using it and disable it if you find that it interferes with your graphics creation.

SHOW FONT NAMES IN ENGLISH (ON)

This preference comes into play only if you are working with foreign languages, such as Japanese, Chinese, or Korean typefaces. The option displays the names of non-English language fonts in English in the type and font menus. This is important since the names of double-bit fonts don't translate correctly into Roman characters and are indecipherable.

AUTO TRACE TOLERANCE (2 PT)

This option determines the accuracy of paths created by using the Auto Trace tool. The number represents the distance from the raster edge, in pixels, that the created path may be. You can set values from 1 to 10 in 1/100th increments. The lower the setting, the more closely the created paths will follow the edge of the shape being traced. Lower settings result in paths that are closer matches but have more anchor points. Higher settings use fewer points but may be less accurate.

This is another preference that won't affect your work much. The Auto Trace tool produces acceptable results only in rare circumstances. If you need to redraw raster art, you should ideally learn to do it manually. If time doesn't permit that or you have a lot of tracing to do, consider purchasing Adobe Streamline. Streamline is a dedicated raster-to-vector translation utility that usually does a fine job of converting art.

TRACING GAP (0 PT)

This option specifies the amount of space the Auto Trace tool may omit when calculating where an edge ends. The setting allows the Auto Trace tool to skip naturally occurring gaps and divots in a scan and stick to a truer edge. The value is measured in pixels and may range from 0 to 2 in 1/100th increments. A setting of 0 turns off this function. A setting of 2 instructs the Auto Trace tool to disregard gaps of up to 2 pixels when creating an edge.

Units & Undo Preferences

Illustrator supports seven units of measure; points, picas, inches, millimeters, centimeters, pixels, and Q. Points and picas are traditional typographers units. Twelve points is equal to 1 pica, and an inch consists of 6 picas. Q is a unit of type equal to about a quarter centimeter. It is available only as a type unit. Most of the time, you'll be measuring everything in pixels. On systems with monitor resolution set to 72 pixels per inch, points and pixels are the same size. On other systems, including many PCs, they aren't the same. As such, it makes more sense to measure in pixels.

Pixel measure can take a little getting used to. In the meantime, you can use other measures in dialog boxes. You type an abbreviation (see Table 5.1) for the measuring unit into a field after the required unit, and Illustrator converts the measure to the default. For example, if you type **2** in into a dialog box, the result is 144 pixels.

Figure 5.3 shows the Units & Undo tab of the Preferences dialog box.

Table 5.1 Abbreviations for Units of Measure

UNIT	ABBREVIATION
Points	pt
Pica	p
Millimeter	mm
Centimeter	cm
Pixel	px
Inch	in or "
Q	q

UNITS: GENERAL (PIXELS)
This option sets the measuring units used for filters, effects, rulers, objects, and transformations—in fact, for any effect or tool where measuring is required, with one exception.

The ruler units of a document may be set independently of the Units: General preference. Ctrl+click/right-click directly on the rulers and choose the desired measure from the context menu. Changing ruler units in this way does not affect the preference setting.

UNITS: STROKE (PIXELS OR POINTS)
This option sets the default measuring units used for strokes. Normally, it's best to work in pixels for web work. Setting the preference to Pixels doesn't alter the Size drop-down menu in the Strokes palette, though. So if you want to leave this one set to Points, it's okay.

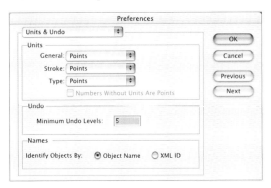

Figure 5.3
The Units & Undo tab of the Preferences dialog box

UNITS: TYPE (PIXELS OR POINTS)
This option sets the default measuring units used for type. The default unit for type is Points. Setting the preference to Pixels doesn't alter the Size drop-down menu in the Character palette, though. Many users leave this set to Points because of their familiarity with print design.

NUMBERS WITHOUT UNITS ARE POINTS
This option is used when the General units are set to Picas. When you enable this option, units typed in a dialog box without adding a "P" to specify picas are considered to be points and not picas. This makes it easier to key in sizes. For example, without this option enabled if you want to specify 8 points, you'd have to key in **0p8** instead of just **8**. This shouldn't affect your web work because you'll be working in pixels, not picas.

UNDO: MINIMUM UNDO LEVELS (5)
This option establishes the minimum number of undo steps that will be available per document. To reverse commands, Illustrator reserves an amount of random access memory (RAM) to keep track of the progress of a document. Illustrator will usually be able to undo more steps than the specified amount, but its ability to do so is based on the complexity of the documents, the number of documents open, and the tasks that must be undone. In practice, most users leave this preference set to the default value (5) because they never run into a problem undoing things.

NAMES

This option determines whether objects are identified by the object's name or the Extensible Markup Language (XML) ID in your processes, a topic that is outside the scope of this book. For a brief description of XML, see chapter 10.

Guides & Grid Preferences

These options, shown in Figure 5.4, control the appearance of guides and the document grid (displayed by choosing View → Guides → Show Guides and View → Grid).

GUIDES (OTHER, DOTS)

Establish the color of guides by selecting a color from the pop-up list or clicking on the swatch to use the Color Picker. By default, guides are the same blue color as in Photoshop. You can choose whether guides will be solid or dotted lines in the Style menu. Many users prefer to set guides to dots. This clearly identifies them as guides and not as printable lines or slices (Figure 5.5).

GRID

You can establish the color of the grid by selecting a color from the pop-up list or clicking on the swatch to use the Color Picker. Gridlines are thicker than the lines that separate them. You specify the frequency of gridlines and divisions in the Grid fields. The default settings divide the document into inches (72 pixels) and eighths of inches. The grid may appear behind or in front of objects.

In some instances, the grid is customized to match a layout; for example, you could break a graphic into quarters. This makes the grid essentially serve as prebuilt guides. For instance, when working on a 400 × 100-pixel graphic, you could set the preference to a gridline every 100 pixels with 1 subdivision. If you do this, be advised that the grid squares itself to the zero point of the rulers. By default, the rulers zero in the lower-left corner of the document, as shown at the top of Figure 5.6. Most users prefer to line up the grid from the upper-left corner of the document, as shown at the bottom. Drag from where the rulers meet to the upper-left corner of your document to reset the grid.

Figure 5.4

The Guides & Grid tab of the Preferences dialog box

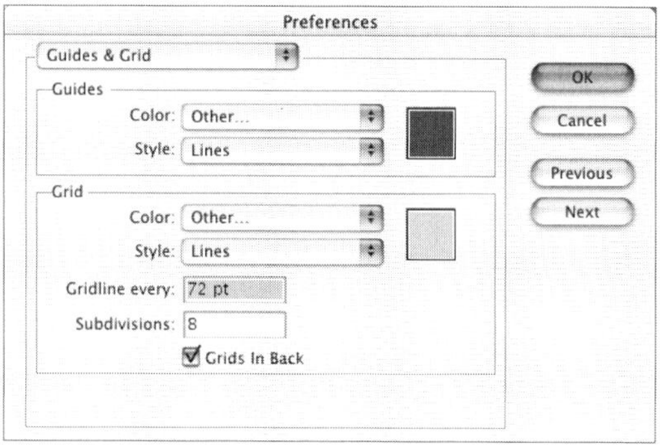

CHOOSING TYPICAL WEB PREFERENCES 139

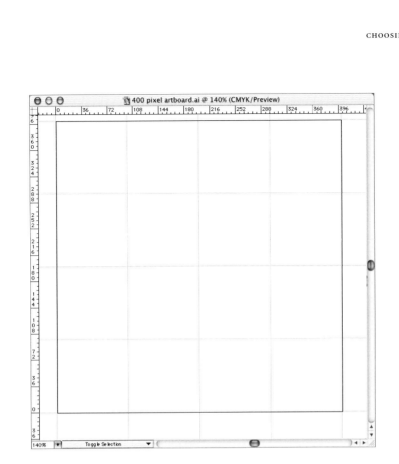

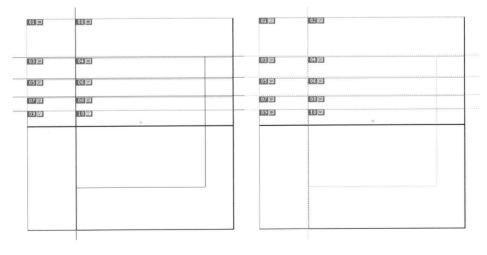

Figure 5.5
Guides set as lines may be confused with slices and paths (top), but are easily identified when viewed as dots.

Smart Guides & Slices Preferences

These options (shown in Figure 5.7) determine what is displayed when you use the Smart Guides feature (View → Smart Guides) and the display of slices (View → Slices). Most users consider Smart Guides distracting and don't activate them. You will likely be using slices, though, if you intend to produce entire HTML pages in Illustrator. See the section "Slicing" in Chapter 8 ("Creating Complete Pages") to learn more about this technique.

SLICES (ON, LIGHT RED)

This preference sets the display of slices. The Show Slice Numbers option displays the number and style of slice in the upper-left corner of the slice. It is essential that you leave this option on. If you deselect it, slices are nearly impossible to distinguish from other objects. The color setting is less important, but you should avoid changing it often—once you're accustomed to looking at slices, it can be distracting to change their color.

Hyphenation Preferences

Use the options shown in Figure 5.8 to determine which default language Illustrator uses to hyphenate and which words Illustrator will not hyphenate at all. If you don't want Illustrator

Figure 5.6

Two views of a 400-pixel Artboard with a grid division every 100 pixels. Left, note that the grid aligns with the lower-left corner of the Artboard. Right, dragging from the zero reset point into the document resets the rulers and the grid. Here, the zero point is dragged to the upper-left corner.

to break a word—a proper noun, for example—add it to the Exceptions list by typing the word in the New Entry text box and clicking Add. These exceptions are not related to the Learned Words list. This preference set isn't specifically related to web work but can come in handy. Hyphenation is especially important in web graphics. Web graphics invariably contain a limited amount of words. Consequently, bad hyphenation is glaringly obvious.

DEFAULT LANGUAGE (U.S. ENGLISH)

Use this menu to select the default dictionary used for hyphenation. Unless you're working in a foreign language, you'll want to use U.S. English.

Plug-ins & Scratch Disks Preferences

The preferences shown in Figure 5.9 control from where Illustrator loads its plug-ins and which drives are used for temporary memory.

PLUG-INS FOLDER

The plug-ins folder contains the startup documents Illustrator uses to set the default swatches, symbols, brushes, and styles in a new document. To indicate the location of the plug-ins folder Illustrator should read at startup, click the Choose button and navigate to the folder you want in the resulting dialog. In most workflows, this preference remains set at the default (the plug-ins folder located inside the Illustrator folder). In some environments, you may want to establish multiple plug-ins folders to switch among. That way, you can isolate tools you use or set up a number of startup documents with different default brushes, swatches, styles, and symbols.

For more information, see "Adjusting Illustrator's Defaults" later in this chapter.

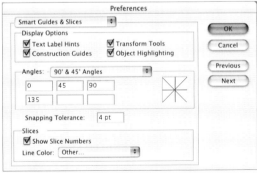

Figure 5.7

The Smart Guides & Slices tab of the Preferences dialog box

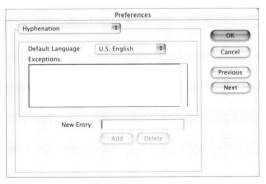

Figure 5.8

The Hyphenation tab of the Preferences dialog box

SCRATCH DISKS

Use these settings to determine the volumes Illustrator will use as scratch disks. When Illustrator runs low on RAM, it temporarily uses available disk storage space as RAM. The volume it uses is called a *scratch disk*. This process is less efficient than real RAM and will run more slowly. Some users partition disk space or purchase additional drives strictly for this purpose. If you have more than one drive attached to your system, you could set a primary and secondary scratch disk.

Files & Clipboard Preferences

The preferences shown in Figure 5.10 handle data in and out of Illustrator. The Clipboard is used to store data temporarily that you have copied or cut. It is a principle model of shuttling small amounts of data between applications.

APPEND EXTENSION (ALWAYS)

Use this option to determine how Illustrator handles the file extension when saving files. If you choose Ask When Saving, you'll see a checkbox in the Save dialog box for adding the file format extension. The Always setting adds the extension by default, and None does nothing at all.

This preference does not affect the Save For Web dialog box, which always adds extensions.

UPDATE LINKS (ASK WHEN MODIFIED)

Use this option to determine how linked external files should be treated in the event that they are edited in another application. The Manually setting takes no action; users must update links themselves. Automatic refreshes the link without telling you about it, and Ask When Modified displays a prompt. Most users stick with Ask When Modified. It enables you to stop and inspect the effect of the changes.

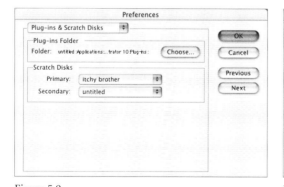

Figure 5.9

The Plug-ins & Scratch Disks tab of the Preferences dialog box

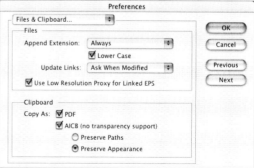

Figure 5.10

The Files & Clipboard tab of the Preferences dialog box

USE LOW RESOLUTION PROXY FOR LINKED EPS (ON)

Use this option to display the embedded preview of a linked EPS file. This choice increases redraw time and improves productivity at the cost of poorer quality onscreen display.

CLIPBOARD (PDF, AICB)

This option specifies the format copied data is recorded in. The PDF format supports transparency, whereas the AICB (Adobe Illustrator Clip Board) format must either render transparency as pixels (Preserve Appearance) or discard transparent effects (Preserve Paths). The format you choose may affect the results when you're pasting into other applications. Some applications can support PDF pasting; some cannot. Further, some support PDF pasting but do not accept the transparency. For example, Photoshop 6 does not recognize compound shapes when they are pasted from a PDF Clipboard. It correctly sees vector shapes, but it does not recognize the compound shape and fails to give you the option to create a Shape layer. To gain the most options when pasting, enable both formats.

Color Settings

It may seem redundant to establish a color space for a color mode. For the Web, you'll be working in RGB documents. RGB is the color mode; it specifies the way color is described—in this case, by setting numerical levels for red, green, and blue color components. *Color space* defines the specific set of colors used. The intention of establishing a color space is to improve the ability to forecast color on the monitor and to establish a profile for color management. Typically, you won't be using color management online. Although it's technically possible, the implementation of it is spotty and problematic.

The color space most users choose for web work is the sRGB space. This color set describes the colors most typical PC monitors use. By working with this limited set of colors, you'll reduce the risk of color shifting online. As you work in Illustrator, you'll be able to forecast the effects of displaying your work on different monitors. For more information, see "Setting Preview Models" later in this chapter.

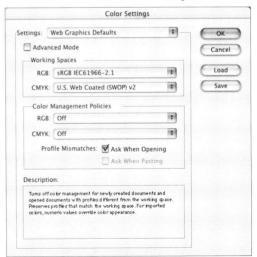

Figure 5.11

The Color Settings dialog box

Color Settings Options

When setting out to work in Illustrator, it's a good idea to take a moment and establish your color settings. These options determine, among other things, how Illustrator handles color conversion from mode to mode. Since many users convert existing CMYK print graphics to RGB web graphics, these options are especially important. To establish them, choose Edit: Color Settings (Figure 5.11).

SETTINGS (WEB GRAPHICS DEFAULTS)

When you first choose the Color Settings command, this pop-up menu offers a list of factory-installed setups. Choosing one resets the values as necessary throughout the dialog box. Most users will be well served to select the Web Graphics Defaults option.

There are several areas where you might want to change the default settings. If you do this, it would be handy to save your new settings as a separate file. Do this by clicking the Save button after choosing the setup you want. Illustrator automatically places the file in the `Application Support\Adobe\Color\Settings` folder on your system. The name of the file you save subsequently appears in the Settings pop-up menu.

ADVANCED MODE (OFF)

Check this box when you need to enable the Conversion Options settings or to expand the profile options in the menus. None of these options applies directly to web work and can be ignored.

WORKING SPACES: RGB (SRGB)

Use this command to establish the working RGB space. The RGB pop-up menu lists the following items when you deselect the Advanced box:

Monitor RGB With this option enabled, Illustrator uses the current color space of the monitor. If desired, profile your monitor using the Adobe Gamma utility to modify the display. The problem with this approach is that as a graphics professional, you might have a better monitor than the general public. As such, your monitor working space is bigger than the space that your audience can see.

Adobe RGB (1998) The recommended choice for print work, this option displays a much wider color range than sRGB, Apple RGB, or ColorMatch RGB. Adobe intends this color space to be a viable option for prepress professionals who require the largest gamut possible. If you think your audience is principally high-end users, or you are working in a controlled environment (such as intranet delivery), this might be a good choice.

Apple RGB Based on the range of an Apple 13-inch Trinitron monitor, this option is the color space used by many other design applications.

ColorMatch RGB This option represents the range of a Radius PressView monitor.

sRGB Short for standard RGB, this option represents the color space of HDTV, and is promoted primarily by Hewlett-Packard and Microsoft. Many users use this space for web graphics, because it displays the same characteristics as most PC monitors. As such, it is the smallest of the RGB spaces. By using a small space, you work with the same colors that most of your audience can see. This is especially important if you intend to use non-web-safe colors.

WORKING SPACES: CMYK (US WEB COATED)

Use this setting to establish the working CMYK space. Although it might seem that a CMYK space is of little use to web professionals, you should remember that the space is used as a reference when converting colors. That is, when you choose File → Document Color Mode, Illustrator has to do some math to convert one set of colors to another. Telling it what the CMYK colors look like helps ensure accurate color. Converting color modes is reasonably common as you prepare existing print graphics for the Web. Therefore, we have recommended a commonly used set of CMYK colors. We've recommended US Web Coated since it is commonly used for print graphics.

PROFILE MISMATCHES (ASK WHEN OPENING)

These options determine how Illustrator responds when you open an image that conflicts with the established working space.

Ask When Opening When this option is selected, Illustrator displays a Profile Mismatch dialog box, which enables you to accept, change, or refuse the current color-management policy. When the option is deselected, the current policy is automatically followed. If you use the settings we recommend, you will see a dialog box whenever you open a document that contains a profile other than sRGB. The default choice in the dialog box is to discard the embedded profile because the color-management policy is to discard it (the Off setting).

Ask When Pasting This option is important if you routinely copy information from one image and paste it into another. When you select Ask When Pasting, Illustrator displays a Profile Mismatch dialog box, which lets you accept, change, or refuse the current color-management policy. When the option is deselected, the current policy is automatically followed. This option isn't available when Color Management Policy is set to Off.

Creating a New Document

> What you're doing: *Creating and setting up a new document to begin working on graphics.*
> Why you're doing it: *You want to establish the correct environment for single web graphics.*

Chapter 4, "Gathering the Required Information," showed you how to determine how much space will be available for your Illustrator graphic in various kinds of web documents. Here, we'll use the information we gathered about the document's size to help us appropriately size the optimized graphic. In the following sections, we'll also set some basic options to facilitate production.

The process of creating a new document is straightforward: Choose New from the File menu or press ⌘/Ctrl+N. In the resulting dialog box (Figure 5.12), you'll set two options. You can do this quickly, and you can adjust the options later as needed.

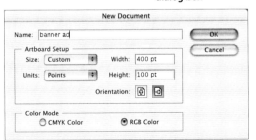

Figure 5.12

The New Document dialog box

Setting the Artboard

The most important part of creating a new document is setting the Artboard. You should set the Artboard to the same size that the final art will be. For example, if you're building a 400-pixel × 50-pixel banner ad, you should set your Artboard to 400 px × 50 px.

There are several reasons why you should do this, but the best one relates to the Clip To Artboard option in the Save For Web dialog box. To understand this, let's explore the concept of the bounding box.

The *bounding box* is a rectangular area that is just large enough to cover all of the items selected. This includes parts of items that are invisible, such as items that are masked or the baseline for path type, but not items that are hidden. When you're optimizing web graphics, Illustrator uses the bounding box of all the visible objects to determine the size of the graphics. This behavior creates a problem if you are using features that create bounding boxes that are larger than the visible area of your work. For example, Figure 5.13 (left) shows a banner ad with type on a path. In the Save For Web dialog box on the right, you can see that the path has created a bounding box that will leave space around the image. Figure 5.14 illustrates a solution: build the graphic on a correctly sized Artboard so that it can be clipped to fit the available space. When saving, the Clip To Artboard option removes the excess area around the graphic.

Figure 5.13

The bounding box of a banner ad with path type (shown here) is wrong when saving for the Web (next page). The result is a graphic that would need to be cropped to avoid white space.

CREATING A NEW DOCUMENT   **147**

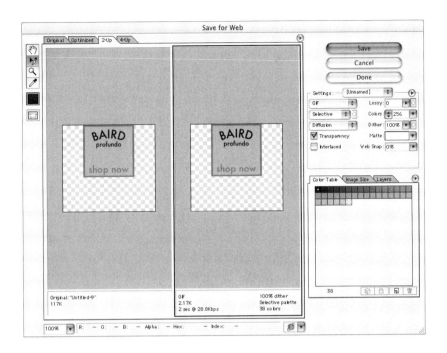

Figure 5.13
(continued)

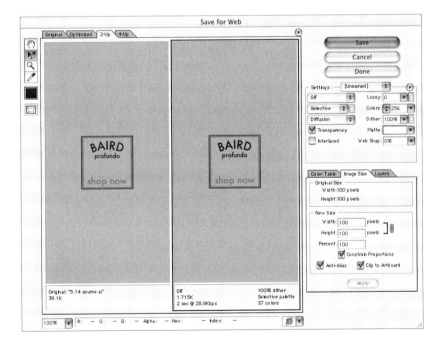

Figure 5.14
The same graphic built on a correctly sized Artboard can be clipped to fit upon optimizing.

It's possible to simplify the art that is causing the bounding box error by turning type to outlines (by choosing Type: Create Outlines) or expanding masks, but this can get complicated and limits your options for changing the art later. The best bet is to build the Artboard to the size you want the graphic, use whatever features you want, and then clip to the Artboard when you save for the Web. That's what we've done in Figure 5.15. This is why we went to such trouble in Chapter 4 to find what the size the final graphic would be.

Figure 5.15

Here, care was taken to size the Artboard correctly. Now the artist needn't worry about the bounding box of objects (top). Art can be anywhere in the document but is neatly cropped out in the Save For Web process (bottom).

Once you determine the size you'll use, set the width and height in the Artboard section to the same value.

The basic process for changing the size of the Artboard isn't difficult. You can't control the location that the Artboard space is added or subtracted from, though, so it's best to set the size as early in the process as possible. When the Artboard size is adjusted, space is added or subtracted evenly on all sides from the center.

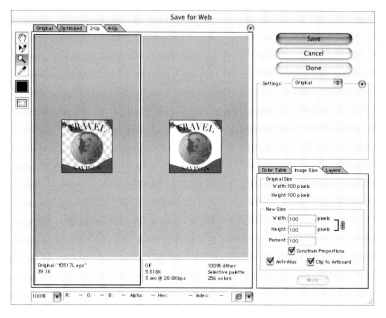

To change the size of the Artboard:

1. Choose File → Document Setup ⌘+Option+P/Ctrl+Alt+ P. In the Document Setup dialog box, choose the Artboard setting.
2. Set the size of the Artboard by entering values in the Width and Height fields, or choose one of the prebuilt options from the Size menu. Once you click OK, Illustrator resizes the Artboard from the center.

Common Setup Options

After creating a new document, you typically open palettes and set the options you need for doing your work. These settings can be incorporated as part of a template or default settings. For information, see the section "Preparing Reusable Color Palettes" later in this chapter.

The first option to turn off is the page tiling. Page tiling is the dotted rectangle on the Artboard that indicates the area the currently selected printer can print in (the imageable area). In small documents, the page tiling Artboard is positioned in the lower left of the imageable area. This often means that the tiling takes up a large percentage of the Artboard, which makes it quite distracting. This art is not destined for printing, so you can disable page tiling by choosing View → Hide Page Tiling.

Next, you'll want to turn on your rulers (View → Show Rulers) and choose the palettes you'll need for working. Rulers are useful for checking the positioning of items as well as for creating guides. You may notice that rulers intrude into the document space and could cover up some of the Artboard. If this happens, choose View → Fit In Window to reveal the entire document.

Finally, open the palettes you need. Most designers prefer to limit the number of palettes open to only those they intend to use. For web work, this often includes the web-safe Color palette. To open that palette, choose Window → Swatch Libraries → Web. Some users also prefer to set the Color palette to the web-safe set. To do this, choose Web Safe RGB from the Color palette menu. Keep in mind that it is possible to create non-web-safe colors with the Color palette, even when set to web-safe option. This usually happens when converting existing colors. Remember, just because a color is defined in hexadecimal notation does not mean it is web safe.

Setting Preview Models

What you're doing: *Changing the onscreen display of a file.*
Why you're doing it: *You want to predict what your image will look like as a web graphic or in different color models.*

There are two reasons you'd want to change the onscreen display of your art:

- You'll be posting a different kind of file online.
- The file will be viewed on different kinds of computers.

Both of these factors affect how that art will appear.

Illustrator art is not often used online in the format you are creating it. Unless you are making a file that will be saved as a Shock Wave Flash (SWF) or Scalable Vector Graphic (SVG) file (see Chapter 10, "Creating Scalable Vector Graphics (SVG)"), the art will be converted to pixels for online viewing. This is a fundamental change in the way the file digitally represents the image; therefore, it can cause some shifting of appearance. Typically, edges are not as crisp, and small type becomes less legible. You can anticipate this potential trouble area by using the Pixel Preview command.

Choose View → Pixel Preview to display a file onscreen as it would appear if it were transferred to pixels. The underlying vector shapes are not changed (as they are with the Object → Rasterize command) in the process. Figure 5.16 illustrates the difference in the display. You can see that the previewed version on the right has noticeably jagged edges compared to the original on the left. In almost every case, the difference will be visible only if you are zoomed in on the graphic greater than 100 percent. At the size it will be used online (100 percent), the art should preview crisply. The principal use for this command is to inspect the effect rasterization will have on edges. In some cases, you use it to determine whether objects are positioned correctly.

> When Pixel Preview is active, Illustrator displays the text "Pixel Preview" next to the color mode in the title bar of the document.

Although Pixel Preview is a good option for forecasting the final appearance of your art, it can be distracting to leave on during everyday use. As you zoom in, the pixel edges appear blurrier. That is correct but useless information for a web workflow: your art will be viewed at 100 percent size in the web browser all the time.

Consider this strategy. Choose Window → New Window to create a separate window for your document. Each window the file has can be set with different viewing options, but any changes you make to the actual art is reflected in all of the windows. Set this new window to 100% view depth and Pixel Preview. Illustrator will display your art as it will appear online. Go back to the original window for the document and proceed to work without the special view option.

In that same, second window, you may also want to turn on the Proof Colors option. Proof Colors changes the onscreen appearance of art based on a predefined color profile. To use this option, first set the color space you want to emulate and then enable the Proof Colors

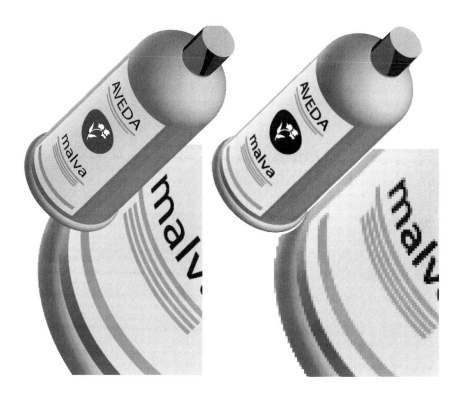

Figure 5.16
A file as it normally appears (left) and with Pixel Preview turned on (right). Note the change in the appearance of the edges.

option. Typically, you set Proof Colors to Windows RGB (choose View → Proof Setup → Windows RGB). This sets the document to display in the color space most of your audience will be using. After choosing the Proof Setup, select View → Proof Colors. Generally, the result is that the image darkens overall. As with Pixel Preview, when this option is active Illustrator displays the color profile used next to the color mode in the title bar of the document.

Saving and Editing Views

What you're doing: Saving view options to be recalled later.
Why you're doing it: You want to speed up selecting commonly used view settings.

The View → New View command enables you to save the current view settings of a document. You can then recall those options later. This trick saves you time zooming in and out and changing back and forth between view options. You can save multiple views in the same document, making it easy to switch back and forth between various groups of settings.

When you choose View → New View, you'll be prompted to name the current view. After you do, the saved view appears in the View menu, as shown in Figure 5.17. Select the saved view to return to the view options that were in effect when you created the view. To delete or rename views, choose View → Edit Views.

Figure 5.17
Here we've saved a new view and named it Proof Colors.

The following view options are included in each saved view:

- The view depth percentage
- The part of the document displayed
- The visibility and preview mode of each layer
- Any special view options, such as Pixel Preview or Proof Colors

The visibility of individual objects is not recorded.

So, a common use for a new view is to set a view that previews the file as it will appear online. To do this, set the view depth to 100% (View → Actual Size) and then choose View → Pixel Preview and View → Proof Colors. Then, choose View → New View. In the resulting dialog, give the view a name, such as "online preview." Other common views, shown in Figure 5.18, are close-up versions of key areas in outline mode and full views with specific layers turned on and off.

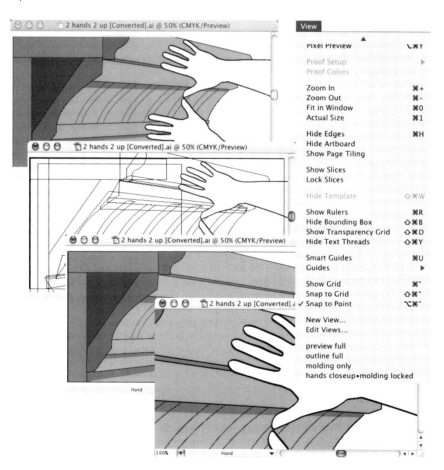

Figure 5.18
A document (left) and common saved views

Preparing Reusable Color Palettes

What you're doing: Creating color resources for use later
Why you're doing it: You want to save rework time later and manage important resources, such as color swatches.

Sets of colors tend to fall into three categories: the colors you need every day, the colors you need every time you do work on the same project or for the same client, and colors that you will need only once. In this section, we'll create color sets and then store them to match each of these needs. We'll also cover monochrome strategies and techniques that make it easier to capture color families.

Colors in Illustrator are saved as swatches and live in the Swatches palette. Gradients and patterns are saved there as well, and they are perfectly applicable to this discussion. Each document has its own Swatches palette and thus its own set of colors, gradients, and patterns. This means that the swatches you save today will not automatically be available in the document you create tomorrow. If the colors you're saving are ones that you'll use regularly, you'll want to be able to get at them easily. First, we'll go over swatch types and creating them; next, we'll discuss how to manage them.

There are several ways to create a color swatch. All of them work with the Swatches palette (Window → Swatches), and some also use the Color palette (Window → Colors).

Saving a Color as a Swatch

To save the active fill or stroke color as a swatch, click the New Swatch button at the bottom of the palette. The active fill or stroke is the one that is forward in the tool and Color palette. If the active attribute is already a swatch, this button duplicates it. You take this route when you already know what the current item is and want to save it quickly. An important issue to consider is that the swatch is given a default name, such as "New Color Swatch 1," which is not descriptive. You can rename the swatch by double-clicking on it and typing a new name, or you can avoid the issue altogether by holding down the Option[Alt] key when clicking the New Swatch button or choosing New Swatch from the Swatch palette menu. This opens the Swatch Options dialog box as the swatch is created.

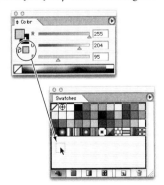

Figure 5.19
Creating new swatches by dragging directly into the palette

There may be times when you need to make swatches out of attributes that are not active (forward in the palette). To save either the current fill or the stroke as a swatch, drag it directly from the Color, Gradient, or Tool palette into the Swatches palette, as shown in Figure 5.19. Note that you shouldn't drag the *object* into the Swatches palette—just the icon for the attribute.

So, a common technique for saving an existing color as a swatch is to first select an object that contains the color you want to save. This sets the current fill and stroke to those of the object. Confirm that the color selected is the one you want to save by checking its values in the Color palette. From there, drag the item you want to save directly into the Swatches palette. This technique works for files with path objects and simple fills. In some files created by high-end users, however, the color swatch created may not match the visual appearance of the item. This may be the case if you have used some styles as well. To pick up color values from raster art, see "Creating a Color Swatch from Imported Art" later in this chapter.

Creating a Color Swatch without Selecting

Selecting an object each time you want to create a swatch can be cumbersome. You may accidentally move the object or apply a new swatch to it in the course of repeated selecting. To avoid this, use the Eyedropper tool instead (Figure 5.20). With nothing selected, and the attribute (fill or stroke) you want to sample forward in the Tool and Color palettes, click with the Eyedropper on an object. The item's fill and stroke are sampled without the object being selected. Click the New Swatch button in the Swatches palette to save the color as a swatch.

Creating a Color Swatch from Imported Art

Raster (pixel) art and images that have been placed are handled differently by the Eyedropper tool. When you click with the Eyedropper on these files, it registers a fill and stroke of None. Shift+click with the Eyedropper to sample color values from these images.

A common example occurs when you're re-creating existing web graphics. Web graphics are often copied and pasted into Illustrator to be redrawn and modified. To take color values from these images, Shift+click with the Eyedropper tool on the color you want to sample. Then, create a new swatch from the color.

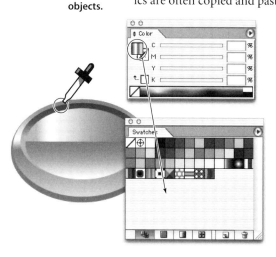

Figure 5.20

Use the Eyedropper to sample colors and create swatches without selecting objects.

When you're choosing sample colors from imported photographs, it's easy to get sidetracked by sampling over and over again in an effort to find the "true" color of an image. This is often a fruitless venture. The flavor of a color is often a combination of the surrounding colors and the overall impression of the image, rather than the specific RGB numbers. When trying to pick representative values, sample from middle-to-quarter tones. Don't click in the highest highlights or the deepest shadows. And if the color seems wrong, try again—you may have found a misrepresentative pixel. Once you've made a few good swatches, consider using the color family technique (see the section "Creating a Family of Colors" later in this chapter) to make up the remaining values. See color insert.

Creating a Global Swatch

When you save a color, you can choose to create a *global* swatch. A global swatch is different from other swatches in two ways. First, it is connected to the objects that use it. When the color definition for the swatch changes, so do the objects that use the swatch color. If you apply a global swatch to an object and then later adjust the color mix of the swatch, the object is updated automatically, as illustrated in Figure 5.21. This does not happen with regular (non-global) swatches.. Global swatches are used a lot in templates for this reason.

The second way global swatches differ is that they can be applied as tints of themselves. In fact, they show up as a single tint slider in the Color palette rather than color components. In Figure 5.22, you can see how important this is to consider as you define colors you expect to save as global swatches. You can only make them lighter; you cannot make them darker without adjusting the basic color definition. The fact that you can only lighten the color comes up if you are going to create lighting effects, such as a beveled button. Global colors at 100% tint should be the dark version of your color, not the middle value.

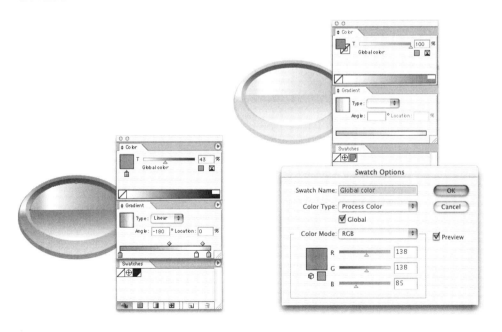

Figure 5.21

On the left, the object and its gradient have been styled with a global swatch. As the design changes, the swatch mix is adjusted and the change is automatically applied to all of the objects and gradients (right).

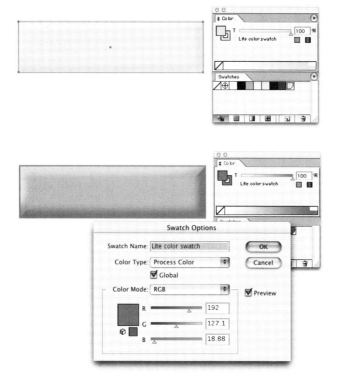

Figure 5.22

The image at the top uses a series of global color tints, but the basic definition is too light. There is nowhere to go but down, creating too light an effect. At the bottom, the core swatch is darkened and the image falls into place.

Creating a Family of Colors

Color families are a series of colors related in some way. They can be tints of the same colors, or a mix of two prominent colors in the design. You'd want to look at color families when auditioning colors for a design or building color resources for a site. To quickly set up a series of swatches:

1. In the Swatches palette menu, make sure the color swatches are showing and choose Select All Unused. From the same menu, choose Delete Swatches. This clears the palette of unneeded items.

2. Create a square in the document with the Rectangle tool. Give the square a stroke of None and a fill of a key color in your design. This color may be one you've sampled from an imported image.

3. Select the square and drag it horizontally to the other side of the document. Add the Option/Alt key as you drag to create a copy.

4. Using the Color palette, adjust the color in the duplicate square. For example, you could add black ink to the color or switch to HSB and reduce the saturation of the

color, as in Figure 5.23. To create a series of colors blending to gray and then to the color's opposite, choose Complement from the Color palette menu.

5. Set the Blend Options (Object → Blend → Blend Options) to Specified Steps. Specify a value based on the number of swatches you wish to create of each color variation. For example, you may want to see four sequentially desaturated versions of the color. Select both squares and choose Object → Blend → Make.

6. Select the Eyedropper and click on an intermediate square. Click the New Swatch button in the Swatches palette to create a new color swatch from the color.

7. Repeat the process to generate all the swatches for the variation (Figure 5.24). Next, adjust the color in either square and repeat.

Converting a Color Table to Swatches

When you convert an image into a GIF, each pixel has to be one of up to 256 specific colors. The set of colors you can choose from may be created from the image itself or loaded from an external file. This file is called a color lookup table (CLUT). Photoshop uses these tables as well, and many users want to convert the CLUT into swatches. And with good reason—a lookup table often contains a neat summarization of the colors in an image.

Figure 5.23

Here, two rectangles are created from the first. The second is the same color as the first except with a nearly 0% Saturation value. The third is the Complement of the first. (See also color insert.)

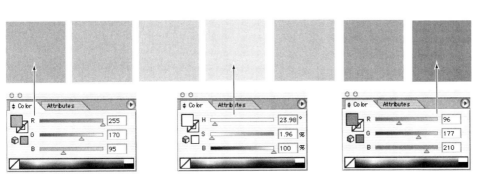

Figure 5.24

A series of swatches created from the intermediate objects. After making the swatches, you can go back and adjust the colors in blend objects to create a new sequence of colors. (See also color insert.)

Unfortunately, there is no way to handle the conversion directly. You cannot load a CLUT as a swatch library or open the file in Illustrator. Two techniques enable you to convert this information to Illustrator swatches, but neither is automatic. The second option, which creates the swatches for you, also requires Adobe Streamline. First, here's the Illustrator-only procedure:

1. Create a new document in Illustrator.
2. Choose File → Save For Web. In the Settings section, choose the GIF format (technically, you could also choose PNG-8). This enables the Color Table section of the palette. Make sure the Transparency option is deselected, or Illustrator may not load the complete table.
3. From the Color Table section menu, choose Load Color Table and navigate to the CLUT that you want to convert. The Color Table should fill with the swatches. Figure 5.25 illustrates the process so far.
4. Take a screen capture of the swatches. On the Mac, press ⌘+Shift+4 and draw a rectangle around the Color Table section of the palette.

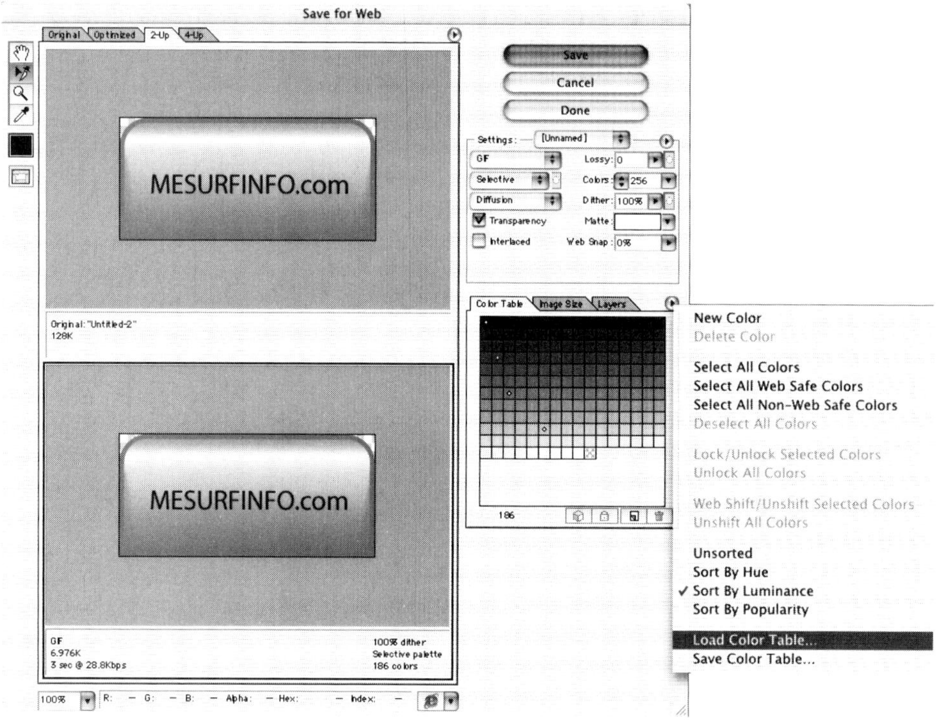

Figure 5.25
Load the CLUT you want to convert to swatches.

5. Place the screen capture file into Illustrator (File → Place). From here, you'll need to Shift+click with the Eyedropper tool on the image to sample the RGB color values of each square. Save each sample as a swatch (Figure 5.26).

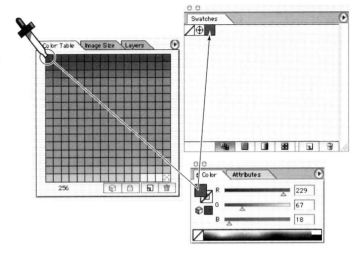

Figure 5.26
Convert the screen capture into swatches.

If Adobe Streamline is part of your toolkit, you can save yourself some Shift-clicking. To do this, follow steps 1–3 from the previous list to create a screen capture of the Color Table. Then:

1. Open the screen capture of the Color Table in Streamline. Streamline supports the popular TIF and PICT formats.

2. Choose Options → Color/B&W Setup. In the resulting dialog box, choose Limited Colors from the Posterization drop-down list; enter **255** in the Maximum # Of Colors text box; and select the Add New Colors To Custom List option, as shown in Figure 5.27.

3. Choose File → Convert. It doesn't matter how accurate a job Streamline does of tracing the image, as long as it adds the correct colors to the Custom Color list. Check this by choosing Options → Custom Color to see the color values of swatches added. You may also want to consider renaming the colors at this point. By default, each will be named Auto Color and numbered sequentially.

Figure 5.27
Use these options in the Color/B&W Setup dialog box in Streamline.

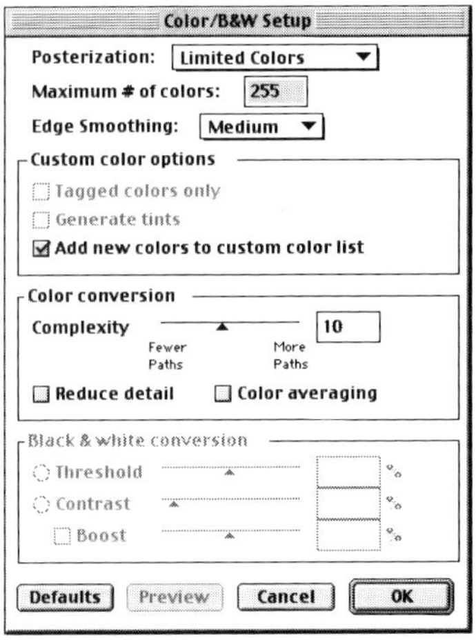

4. Save the file by choosing File → Save Art. Choose either the EPS or AI format and open the converted file in Illustrator. You can delete all the art on the page, since you are concerned only about the swatches. The newly created swatches will be saved as spot colors with CMYK definitions. This is fine, but if you prefer you can convert them collectively to RGB. To do so, first select them all by clicking the first swatch (not including the None or Registration swatch) and then Shift+clicking the last swatch. Double-click on an any swatch to open the Swatch Options dialog box and set the Color Mode to RGB.

Saving and Loading Swatches

Because swatches are saved with each document, the next document you create will not have the custom swatches you've created automatically. You'll need to load them as a library each time you want to use them. To do this, first save the document in a place where you can find it easily. Save it in either the

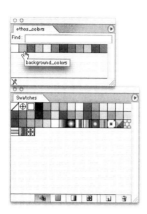

Figure 5.28

Saved swatches open as a library; add them to the current document's swatches by clicking on them.

EPS or AI file format. The entire contents of the Swatches palette will be loaded, so you may want to delete unused items from the palette.

To load the swatches for use in a new document, first make sure it is saved and then choose Window → Swatch Libraries → Other Library. Navigate to the document that contains the swatches you want. As we mentioned earlier, the entire contents of the Swatches palette are loaded as a library. Add each library item to the document's Swatches palette by clicking on them or dragging them into the palette. Figure 5.28 illustrates the process.

Saving Swatches for Semi-Regular Use

If you work on the same jobs regularly, you may want to save client swatches in a place that makes them easy for you to access. After you've prepared a document with the swatches, save them in your `Adobe Illustrator\Presets\Swatches` folder. Next, quit and relaunch Illustrator. The document will be available for you to open as a library by choosing Window → Swatch Libraries and selecting your document. If you want the library open every time you launch Illustrator, choose Persistent from its menu (Figure 5.29). Only files loaded from the preset folder in this way may be set as persistent libraries.

Although it's not strictly necessary, you may want to pay some extra attention to your persistent libraries. A little organization will make it easier if you need to go back and edit the contents of the library later. A common setup is to delete all of the elements on the page except for representative squares for each color. Deleting all of the default swatches

Figure 5.29

After saving a file in the `Swatches` folder (left), you can designate it as persistent (right) so that it will open along with Illustrator by default.

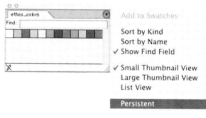

makes sense, as does taking the time to name the swatches used. Many users opt for the numeric color-naming convention, choosing to call a swatch by its RGB components. For example, a swatch might be named *R:FF B:99 G:0* (or in Windows, RFFB99G0) instead of *orange*. This way, you will know the components of a color from the name and tool tip pop-up and will be able to use it in HTML editors as well.

Saving Swatches for Everyday Use

Some colors are so important that you may want access to them in every session. Although you can't automatically change the contents of the Swatches palette of documents you've already created, you *can* change the contents of the next document you create.

To do this, you'll need to edit the Startup document. Illustrator copies the swatches from a reference document it uses into each new file you create. So, if you change the contents of this reference file, you change what goes into the next document you create.

Illustrator has two reference documents: one for RGB files and the other for CMYK files. For web graphics, you'll want the RGB version. Start by opening the document (`Adobe Illustrator\Plug-ins\Adobe Illustrator Startup_RGB`). Then, add swatches as you see fit to the Swatches palette. You could open and use libraries to move existing swatches as well.

Many users also delete swatches and resources that they don't use. Don't worry about removing defaults; all of the default swatches (and brushes, styles, and symbols) are available as libraries from the `Preset` folder. This means you can at any point choose Window → Swatch Libraries → Default_RGB to recall the old choices. If you are completely snarled, you can even duplicate a preset file, rename it `Adobe Illustrator Startup_RGB`, and put it in the `Plug-ins` folder. This resets the factory default options.

Swatches are set when the document is created. This means that if you change the color mode of a document (by choosing File → Document Color Mode), you are changing the color mode of the existing swatches only and not loading the set.

Adjusting Illustrator's Defaults

What you're doing: *Changing the default swatches, resources, and settings of new documents.*
Why you're doing it: *Your goal is to save time setting common options and importing resources.*

The more you work in Illustrator, the more you will want to customize the basic settings it uses. You can adjust the default preferences and preview settings as well as the document resources. Document resources are the brushes, styles, swatches, and symbols in a file. You can permanently change the resources used in new documents or change the list of library files at the bottom of the Window menu. You typically change the preset libraries when you want a set of resources on hand but don't need it to be part of every document you open. For example, the swatches for a regular client might be saved as a library. This gives you ready access to the client's colors but doesn't affect every new file you make. For information on this process, see the section "Saving Swatches for Semi-Regular Use" earlier.

When you create a new document, Illustrator takes the default resources and view settings from a file named either `Adobe Illustrator Startup_RGB` or `Adobe Illustrator Startup_CMYK`, depending on the color mode of the file you create. These files live in the `Plug-ins` folder inside the Illustrator `application` folder. By changing the contents of these startup files, you change the default settings used for new documents going forward.

To set the defaults for web work, start by opening the `Startup_RGB` document. Enable the view options you like to use. For example, many users activate the rulers (View → Show Rulers) and the grid (View → Show Grid) and hide the page tiling (View → Hide Page Tiling). Next, add or subtract items from the Swatches, Symbols, Brushes, and Styles palettes as you see fit. Many users remove the default symbols and styles completely. You can recall the default options if you need by choosing the default libraries (Window → Style Libraries and Window → Symbol Libraries).

Keep in mind that the default fill and stroke on the toolbar is connected to the default style in the Styles palette. By default, it's a white fill and a one-point black stroke. The keyboard shortcut is D. If you want, you can reset the default style. Suppose you prefer a thicker stroke or a fill of None by default. Specifying these preferences in the startup document resets the default for all new documents of that color mode. To do this:

Figure 5.30

Option/Alt+dragging a new style onto the default style resets the default.

1. With the `Startup_RGB` document open and active, set the fill and stroke options as you would like them to be for the new default.

2. Choose New Style from the Styles palette menu.

3. Hold down the Option/Alt key and drag the new style on top of the default style, as shown in Figure 5.30. The icon for the style remains the default black-and-white icon, but the settings are combined with the new style settings.

4. Save the file.

The next RGB document you create will have the new, custom default settings. To activate them, click the default attribute icon in the toolbar or press D on the keyboard.

Customizing Shortcuts

What you're doing: *Creating shortcuts for commonly used commands.*
Why you're doing it: *You want to expedite selecting often-used commands and options. Many of the web-oriented commands do not have keyboard shortcuts out of the box.*

Many of Illustrator's commands can be run either from a menu command or a keyboard shortcut. Users typically consider keyboard commands easier and faster. If you don't like the shortcuts as they are out of the box, you can edit them. Knowing how to customize shortcuts is particularly useful for web work where many common commands do not have shortcuts by default. For example, no shortcuts exist for any of the commands in the Slice submenu.

> You can find a downloadable keyboard shortcut set (.kys file) at:
> `http://www.illustratoranswers.com/downloads.`

There are two ways to create shortcuts: you can edit the existing shortcut set, or you can create an action and assign it a keyboard shortcut. *Actions* are often used to automate a sequence of commands. Unfortunately, many of the sequences used in a web workflow, such as setting default text in a no-image slice, are not recordable in this way.

To edit the default shortcuts for single commands, choose Edit → Keyboard Shortcuts or press ⌘+Option+Shift+K on the Mac or Ctrl+Alt+Shift+K on a PC. The Keyboard Shortcuts dialog box opens. Shortcuts are grouped together in sets that can be saved as files, which enables you to load and unload them and to share them with co-workers. If you begin with the default set, it will automatically create a new custom set. In this example, we'll add a keyboard shortcut for the Object → Slice → Make command.

1. Choose Edit → Keyboard Shortcuts (Figure 5.31, top).
2. Locate the menu that says Tools by default and toggle it to Menu Commands. The large pane in the center will switch to show nested menu commands instead of tool icons.
3. Choose the Slice submenu from the Objects menu.
4. On the Slice submenu, click to the immediate left of the Make command, in the Shortcut column (Figure 5.31, center). A field appears, enabling you to set a new shortcut. Key in a new shortcut (Figure 5.31, bottom).

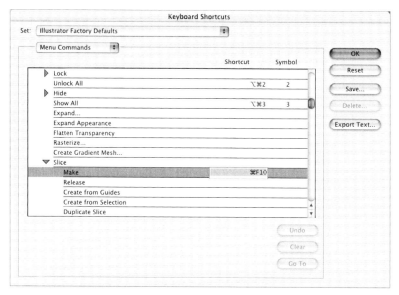

Figure 5.31
To reset a keyboard shortcut, choose File → Edit → Keyboard Shortcuts, then locate the command you want to change and enter a new keystroke combination

5. If you choose an "illegal" shortcut (one that is in use by the system) or one that is already in use in Illustrator, an alert will appear in the bottom of the dialog box. If you choose an illegal one, try again. In the event that you have chosen a shortcut that is in use and you want to keep the custom one, click the Go To button at the bottom of the dialog box to jump to the "usurped" command. From there, you can reassign a shortcut to that command.

6. Click the Save button to save the new set. If you don't do this, the set will still work, but it will be called Custom, making it harder to manage and share.

Creating Browser Templates

What you're doing: *Setting up reusable documents to facilitate designing complete web pages.*
Why you're doing it: *It's easier to build pages with some references in place.*

When you're setting out to build a complete web page (rather than a single graphic) in Illustrator, you have several issues to consider. First, you must take into account the size of your Artboard. You use the Artboard to size your art when saving for the Web, but how big should you make it? If you make it too large, viewers with laptops may miss some of your material. Additionally, you may prefer to design the page in the context that it will be used in—inside a web browser.

You can find browser templates at http://www.illustratoranswers.com/downloads.

In this section, we'll construct a template you can use when making full pages. We'll set up the Artboard to accommodate users with typical monitors but drop guides to anticipate the views of smaller ones. Additionally, we'll set up a browser interface to help users view the document in context.

The first factor to consider is size. It's important to know not the size of the monitors themselves, but rather the resolution they are set to display. For example, a PowerBook may have a 14-inch display surface but could be set to a 640 × 480, 800 × 600, or 1024 × 768 resolution. The first number here is the width; the second is the height. The "resolution" in this case refers to the total pixels on the monitor, not the relative number in an inch, as it does in other areas. The monitor size stays the same, but at different resolutions, or display settings, the visible area is different (Figure 5.32). Some systems are able to go bigger and make more choices available, whereas others can display only at a fixed size. Consequently, the amount of a document that users can see without scrolling will vary depending on the kind of monitor they have, the settings it is capable of displaying, and the user's preferences. It also means that you should concern yourself with total pixels and not pixels per inch.

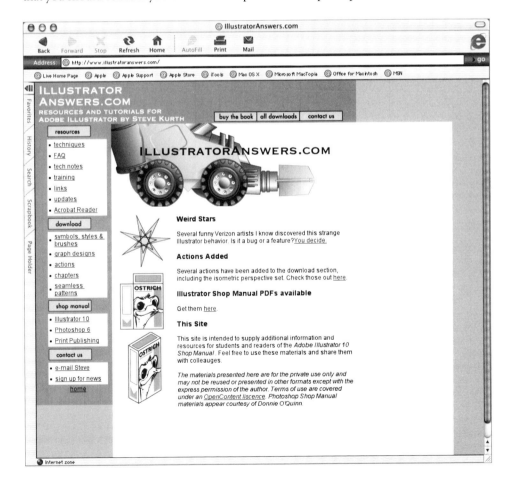

Figure 5.32

The same web page viewed on an 800 × 600 monitor display (show here) and on a 1024 × 768 monitor (next page).

Figure 5.32
(continued)

The total viewable area of a web page is reduced by the browser's interface. We'll set up an Artboard to accommodate the largest browser and then create guides to display smaller imageable areas. The total usable areas of common resolutions, after subtracting the space taken up by browser interface, are listed in Table 5.2. Remember that to see this area, a user will need to maximize the window, not always a common occurrence on Macs. Also keep in mind that these numbers are rounded for simplicity.

To create a browser template:

1. Choose File → New. In the New Document dialog box, specify **955** for the Width and **600** for the Height setting. Set the color mode to RGB. These options set up a document with an Artboard of the largest size you will likely use. You may also choose one of the smaller sizes from Table 5.2. Remember, we'll use the Artboard to set the size of our table when outputting HTML, so choose a size that you are comfortable with.

2. Choose View → Hide Page Tiling. Doing so gets the dotted lines out of your way so that you can see the page without the (unnecessary) printing boundaries.

Table 5.2

The Usable Areas of Common Monitor Resolutions

MONITOR RESOLUTION	MAXIMUM USABLE AREA
640 × 480	600 width, 300 height
800 × 600	760 width, 420 height
832 × 624	795 width, 470 height
1024 × 768	955 width, 600 height
Web TV	544 width, 378 height

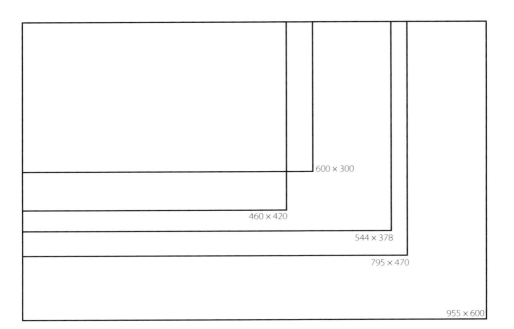

Figure 5.33

The Artboard describes the largest maximized viewing area; each rectangle bounds one of the other common maximum sizes.

3. Rather than dragging guides out of the rulers to show the various image areas, we'll convert rectangles to guides. This approach will make the guides less obtrusive. To do this, select the Rectangle tool and click in the upper-left corner of your document. In the resulting dialog box, specify a Width setting of **795** and a Height of **470**. Repeat this process for the other sizes in Table 5.2. Figure 5.33 shows the relative sizes.

4. To remove the distracting center points of the rectangles (which are retained when they are converted to guides), first select all the rectangles you've created. Then, choose Window → Attributes, and click the Don't Show Center button, as shown here:

5. With the rectangles still selected, choose View → Guides → Make Guides or press ⌘/Ctrl+5.

6. This step is optional; it isolates the guides on their own layer so that they can be shown and hidden quickly. Open the Layers palette and double-click on Layer 1. Rename it `Guides` and select the Lock box. This prevents you from putting art on the Guides layer later on.

7. To add a browser image or two, first create a screen capture of the browser. Open Internet Explorer and maximize your window. It will be easier if you open a blank page. The Mac has a built-in screen capture utility; press ⌘+Shift+3 to capture the whole screen. Create a new layer and drag it below the Guides layer. This is an important step; you'll want it on its own layer to facilitate hiding it later on. You may want

to name the layer for easy identification as well. Choose File → Place to import the screen capture. Don't bother linking the art, because you won't save any file size and doing so will only create complications.

8. Position the screen capture so that the inside upper-left corner is in the upper-left corner of the Artboard. Lock the layer to prevent you from accidentally removing or adding art to the layer. Repeat for other browser interfaces as needed (Figure 5.34).

9. Create a final layer at the top of the stack to begin your actual art. When you choose Save For Web, be sure to hide the browser windows so that they won't be included, or select the Crop To Artboard option.

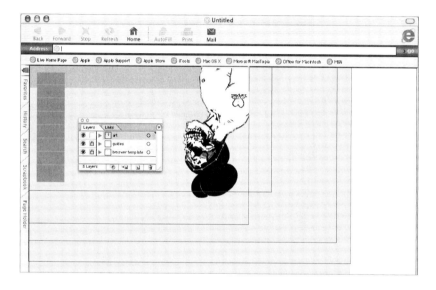

Figure 5.34

A screen shot of a browser window. The art is placed on its own layer below the guides. Turn the layer on and off to preview your page in context.

CHAPTER 6

Creating Single Graphics

This chapter explores the process of creating spot illustrations for use online. We examine the often-misunderstood Appearance and Styles palettes and their role in standardizing graphics. We also discuss setting up typical art and optimizing it for the Web. For more information on that topic, see Chapter 7, "Optimizing Spot Illustrations."

This chapter covers the following topics:

Streamlining your work with the Styles and Appearance palettes

Developing styles

Building common buttons

Creating common symbols and icons

Producing background images

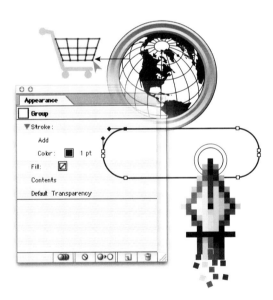

Streamlining Your Work with the Graphic Styles and Appearance Palettes

What you're doing: Setting up complex art motifs and storing them as reusable items. *Why you're doing it:* You can speed up and standardize the art creation process and take advantage of hierarchical styling.

Most designers are comfortable with the basic process of applying fills and strokes to objects, and this chapter assumes you already know how to do that. In this section, we explain how to apply effects using the Graphic Styles and Appearance palettes. We show you how to expedite repetitive tasks and delve into some advanced styling techniques. Many designers do not understand how to use these palettes effectively, so we devote some attention to the mechanics of these tools. We also present practical examples that illustrate how to create common web graphics.

Objects, Layers, Groups, and Appearance

Before we begin, let's discuss *object styling hierarchy*, which involves two important concepts. First, objects can have multiple fills and strokes. Second, the way objects appear can be controlled by the attributes of the item (such as effects applied to a fill alone), the object itself, the group that contains the object, or the layer or sublayer on which the object is positioned. As illustrated in Figure 6.1, if an object leaves a group or layer that supplies its appearance, the art changes.

Figure 6.1
This art has a drop shadow because it's on a layer with a drop shadow (left). When the art is moved off the layer (right), the shadow is updated.

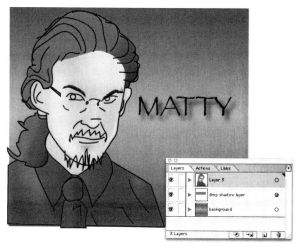

Given this, you've probably grasped that groups and layers can have attributes as well. This includes the fills and strokes that you can add to your object in addition to the object's own attributes. Objects, groups, and layers can have a paint style (which consists of fills and strokes), transparency, and effects. The fills and strokes themselves may also have transparency and effects. This is what we mean by the styling hierarchy.

An object may appear transparent, for example, as a result of any of these conditions (or even a combination of them):

- The object has a transparent fill.
- The entire object is transparent.
- The object is on a transparent layer or group.

To organize the appearance of your objects, you use the aptly named Appearance palette (Figure 6.2), which lets you define and organize motifs. You then use the Graphic Styles palette to save and manage those patterns. The Layers palette allows you to target items to receive the motifs, and you can use the Effects menu to modify your objects.

The Appearance Palette

The current selection appears in bold in the top section of the Appearance palette, listed by object type, such as *path* or *compound path*. If no object is selected, the palette will display *no selection*. The name of the style connected to the object, if any, will appear after the object's name, and you'll see a thumbnail of the object next to it.

The options that affect your selection are listed from the top down in the Appearance palette. Layers and groups that affect the object are listed first, and then the object itself. A horizontal line then separates the object from its attributes.

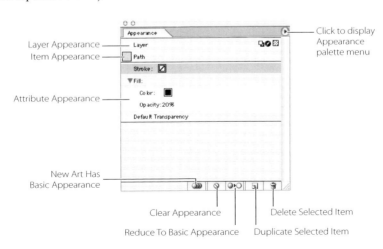

Figure 6.2

The Appearance palette

THE LAYER APPEARANCE

Anything listed above the current selection in the palette indicates that layers or groups affect your object's appearance. An icon specifies how your object is affected; for instance, a checkerboard indicates transparency; an *f* in a circle represents an effect. The default fill and stroke icon indicates that a fill or stroke attribute is applied to your object. You can click on a layer or group name in the Appearance palette to target that item. All the objects governed by that layer or group are selected, and the Appearance palette switches to show that item's attributes.

THE ITEM APPEARANCE

As we mentioned earlier, the current selection is indicated in bold with a thumbnail next to it. The selection is often an object, but it could also be a layer or group. If objects of various kinds are selected, the field will read *Mixed Objects*. If you've selected multiple objects of the same type, the palette displays the type. In the event that all the selected objects have the same appearance attributes, those attributes will be listed as well.

You can apply the current contents of the Appearance palette to unselected objects by simply dragging and dropping the thumbnail onto objects in your document.

THE ATTRIBUTE APPEARANCE

The attributes of your selection are listed in this section of the palette. If the object is a layer or a group, any effects or transparency applied to the layer or group will be listed here. You'll also see the word *Contents*, which describes the items in the layer or group. You can double-click effects anywhere in this palette in order to edit them.

If your selection is an object, fills, strokes, effects, and transparency will be listed here. If you've applied a style to your object, this section also displays the name of that style. A swatch indicates the color of each fill and stroke. You'll see the brush stroke, stroke weight, and dashed status here as well. You can reposition items by dragging them up and down in the palette. A guide shows you where the item will reside when you release the mouse. If you've applied more than one fill or stroke to your object, the palette indicates the last item you selected by placing a small box around the item's swatch. This is referred to as the *cardinal*, or focal fill or stroke. Illustrator uses this attribute when considering the object for commands that require a single attribute, such as Select → Same → Fill. This is also the attribute that Illustrator retains if you later simplify the appearance.

An upside-down triangle indicates that you've assigned effects or a transparency attribute to a fill or stroke. You can move effects from fills to strokes by dragging. As you drag, double triangles highlight the attribute on which the item is to be dropped. If you drop the effect "loose" in the Attribute section, Illustrator applies it to the entire object. If you want to duplicate an effect, simply Option/Alt+drag.

NEW ART HAS BASIC APPEARANCE

Use the New Art Has Basic Appearance button to specify how the next object you create will be treated. New Art Has Basic Appearance discards all effects, including those attached to attributes. Additional fills and strokes are also removed, and the object's opacity is set to 100%. This is the "basic appearance": an appearance with only one fill or stroke, and no effects or transparency. To retain the exact settings currently in the Appearance palette, click the button again to toggle to New Art Maintains Appearance.

CLEAR APPEARANCE

Click the Clear Appearance button to remove all attributes from your selection. The object is left with a single fill and stroke, both set to None.

REDUCE TO BASIC APPEARANCE

Click the Reduce To Basic Appearance button to discard all effects, including those attached to attributes. Additional fills and strokes are also removed. The object's opacity is set to 100% and its blend mode to Normal. However, opacity masks are not released. Objects whose transparency is controlled by an opacity mask are not affected when you click this button.

Reducing a group to the basic appearance removes group attributes only, which means the members of the group are not affected. Any effects that are attached to the objects will remain.

DUPLICATE SELECTED ITEM

The Duplicate Selected Item button duplicates the currently selected fill, stroke, or effect. Any effect or transparency attached to the item is duplicated as well. Illustrator places the duplicated item over the original item in the Appearance palette. This technique is often used to create multiple fills and strokes for objects. To add fills or strokes to layers and groups, choose Add New Fill or Add New Stroke from the Appearance palette menu.

DELETE SELECTED ITEM

The Delete Selected Item button clears the current fill, stroke, effect, or transparency setting. Objects must have at least one fill and stroke. If you delete the last fill or stroke, it isn't removed, but its value is set to None. Likewise, deleting the object's transparency setting sets it to the default transparency. You may also drag items directly onto this button to delete them.

THE APPEARANCE PALETTE MENU

The Appearance palette menu lets you modify the appearance of your objects and edit styles. You can access the menu by clicking on the black triangle in the upper right of the palette. Let's look at the commands you'll find on this menu.

Add New Fill Use this command when you want to create a new basic fill. The fill will be the same color as the cardinal fill, but it won't have any custom effects or transparency settings. The position of the new fill depends on what you've selected in the Appearance palette. If an attribute is selected, the new item will be over it. If nothing is selected, the new item will be added over the highest fill. If the name of the object is selected, the fill will appear at the top of the Appearance palette.

Add New Stroke Use this command when you want to create a new basic stroke. The stroke will be the same color as the cardinal stroke, but it won't have any custom effects or transparency settings. Illustrator determines the position of the new stroke in the same way it does a new fill.

Redefine Style In cases where the current appearance started as a style but has since been modified, the Redefine Style command saves the changes to the original style. For example, you may start with the default Blue Goo style and decide to change the drop shadow settings. Before you begin editing, the style's name appears at the top of the Appearance palette. Once you edit the effect, Illustrator removes the style's name from the palette. Click this button to rewrite the Blue Goo definition to match the current settings in the palette.

When you redefine a style, objects that use the style are updated automatically. This includes symbols and envelopes that contain styled objects. Symbol sets and instances that you styled using the Style Stainer tool are not updated automatically. To update them, you would have to remove the style and then reapply the new one.

Appearance, Stacking Order, and the Bounding Box

Fills, strokes, and effects applied to layers and groups may be in front of or behind the contents of the layer or group. The "stacking order" doesn't matter for some effects, but it can play a large role in some cases and certainly affects paint styles. In Figure 6.3, we've added a stroke to the layer on which our art is positioned. On the left, the stroke is behind the contents of the layer, creating an outline. On the right, the stroke is in front of the contents, overlapping each object.

Figure 6.3

Adding a stroke behind (left) and in front of (right) the layer contents

 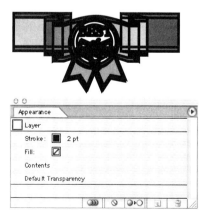

By default, transform effects are applied after a group's or layer's contents. When you move a transform effect above the contents of a layer or group in the Appearance palette, you affect *each* item based on its bounding box. When you apply the effect below the contents, the bounding box of *all* the items controls the effect. It is as though the contents of the layer are flattened into a single shape and that new shape is then transformed. In Figure 6.4, on the left we've applied a twist effect above the contents of a group. Each member of the group is twisted by the specified amount. On the right, we've applied the twist below the contents in the Appearance palette. The effect is stronger because it takes into account the bounding area of the entire group rather than of each member.

Typically, fills and strokes are placed behind the contents of the layer or group. Designers take this approach when they want to create a motif or provide an attribute to which they can apply an effect. Let's look at some examples in the next section

Applying Appearance and Effects

To apply multiple fills or effects to an item, first determine which item should receive your attention. As Figure 6.5 shows, there is a big difference between styling an attribute, an object, a group, or a layer. Judging how to apply the appearance and effects takes experience. Keep in mind that when you apply an effect to a group or layer, all the items within the group or layer will be affected as a unit.

Once you've determined where the appearance should reside:

1. Target the item to which you want to apply the effect. If this item is a layer or group, click in the target circle in the Layers palette. If the target item is an object, select it. If it is a single attribute, such as a fill or stroke, select the item that contains the attribute and then click on the attribute in the Appearance palette.

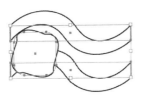
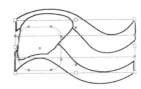
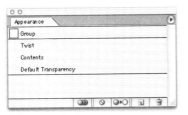
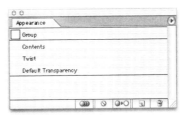

Figure 6.4

Placing a twist effect above (left) and below (right) the contents layer

Figure 6.5

The same drop shadow effect applied to objects (left), a complete group (center), and a single attribute, here the stroke (right).

2. Set the appearance as desired. To create additional fills or strokes, choose Add New Fill Or Stroke from the Appearance palette menu. Then, style the fills and strokes as you normally would, using the Color, Swatches, or Brushes palette. To apply an effect, choose it from the Effects menu. To apply transparency, set an opacity value in the Transparency palette.

3. Examine the results and adjust accordingly. Double-click on effects in the Appearance palette if you want to edit them.

Saving Appearances as Graphic Styles

Graphic styles capture the contents of the Appearance palette for later use. You can record all of the fills, strokes, transparency, and effects that populate the palette so you can apply them to other objects. Further, objects that use the graphic styles are connected—if a style definition changes, Illustrator updates the objects automatically. Graphic styles, even basic ones, are handy for quick, consistent styling of objects throughout a website or document. Figure 6.6 shows the Graphic Styles palette.

Graphic Styles

This section of the palette displays the Graphic Styles available within your document. You can click on an icon to apply that style to the object(s) you have selected. Graphic Styles are listed by name (in list view) or as thumbnails (as shown in Figure 6.6), which is the default view. When you're in list view, smaller thumbnails also appear next to the style name.

Figure 6.6

The Graphic Styles palette

You can also select a style in the palette and edit, duplicate, or delete it. To select more than one style at a time, use Shift+click for contiguous graphic styles and ⌘/Ctrl+click for noncontiguous Graphic Styles. Alternatively, highlight the palette by holding down Option+⌘/Alt+Ctrl and clicking on it; once the palette is highlighted, you can select a graphic style by typing its name.

To reorder the graphic styles in the palette, simply click on a style and drag it into a new position. As you drag, a black bar indicates where the style will appear when you release the mouse. If you want to replace a style, Option/Alt+drag a style on top of the one you want to replace. This technique is handy when you want to replace the default style.

If you want to change a style's name, first double-click on the style. When the Style Options dialog box opens, type your new name and click OK. Style names appear when the palette is in list view or as tool tips when in thumbnail view.

Break Link To Style

Click the Break Link To Style button to sever the connection between an object and a style. The object retains its appearance but is not updated when you redefine the style.

Any time you alter the attributes of an object that uses a style, the link to the style is broken automatically.

New Graphic Style

Use the New Style button to create new graphic styles and to duplicate existing styles. For example, click this button to record the appearance of a selected object as a style. When you do, Illustrator creates a new style with a default name. The current contents of the Appearance palette define the style. If you want to name a style as you create it, hold down Option/Alt) as you click the button and then type the new name in the resulting Graphic Style Options dialog box. You can drag selected styles onto this button to duplicate them.

Delete Graphic Style

After finishing work on a file, many designers delete unused graphic styles to reduce file size and avoid confusion. Use the Delete Style button when you want to delete styles. Deleting a style does not change the appearance of objects that use that style.

First select a style in the palette and then click the button to delete it, or you can drag selected graphic styles onto the button. Once you click the Delete Graphic Style button, Illustrator displays an alert dialog box. To bypass the warning, Option/Alt+click the button instead.

The Graphic Styles Palette Menu

Open the Graphic Styles palette menu by clicking on the black triangle in the upper-right corner of the palette. The commands in the Styles palette menu let you change the appearance of the Graphic Styles palette and edit styles. Many of the commands have the same functions as palette buttons. Let's look at the ones unique to the menu:

Merge Graphic Styles Use this command to create a new style that contains the appearance settings of at least two existing graphic styles. Generally you use this command to create style variations. Your new style will contain all the attributes of the graphic styles you used to generate it. This typically results in a style with multiple fills and strokes. The items are added from top to bottom in the order in which the original graphic styles appeared in the palette.

To merge graphic styles, select them in the palette and then choose the command. A dialog box prompts you to name your new style.

Select All Unused Use this command to select all of the graphic styles in the palette that have not been applied to objects. Typically you do this so you can delete all the unnecessary styles at once.

Sort By Name Use this command to place the graphic styles in the palette in alphabetical order. This command works whether the palette is in thumbnail or list view.

Thumbnail View Use this command to display graphic styles as square swatches. This is the default view, and it takes up the least amount of monitor space. The swatches show an approximation of what the style looks like when applied to a square. Hold your cursor over a style to see its name as a pop-up tool tip. Graphic styles fill the palette from left to right and top to bottom in this view.

Small List View Use this command to display graphic styles as small square swatches with the names next to them. The small swatches show an approximation of what the style looks like when applied to a square. Graphic styles fill the palette from top to bottom in this view.

Large List View This command displays graphic styles using larger swatches—the same size as those used in thumbnail view. This view takes up a lot of monitor space but provides a complete view of the thumbnail and the style name.

Override Character Color Use this option to set the fill and stroke attributes of characters to None when you're applying a style to text. Activating this option makes the style appear the same when applied to type as it does when applied to other objects. When you deselect the option, the attributes of the type are retained.

This option affects colors applied to characters but not to text objects. You must select a character with one of the Type tools in order to edit its attributes.

Style Options Use this command to open the Style Options dialog box. Graphic styles have only one attribute: their name. So, to change the name of a style, you can use this dialog box. You can also access this dialog box by double-clicking on the style. Keep in mind that you cannot rename the Default style.

Creating Typical Appearances

What you're doing: Setting up appearance and graphic styles for objects and groups.
Why you're doing it: You want to create effects that you can reapply to other objects.

In this section, we describe a series of typical motifs that you can create using the Appearance palette. Although they may not be applicable to every webpage, these examples illustrate the use of appearances. You can modify these techniques to suit the art you're creating. For more information on optimizing graphics for web deployment, see Chapter 7.

Group Outlines

In a group outline, you can apply a stroke effect around a group of objects, as shown in Figure 6.7. The individual objects' strokes are retained. As you reposition or add objects to the group, the appearance updates automatically.

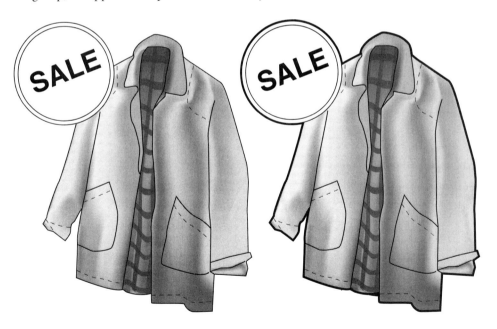

Figure 6.7

The basic objects (left) and with a group outline applied (right)

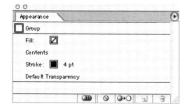

Figure 6.8

The Appearance palette for a group outline has the group's stroke behind the contents of the group.

To use the group outline feature, follow these steps:

1. Group the desired objects (Object → Group). Leave the group selected.
2. From the Appearance palette menu, choose Add New Stroke.
3. The Appearance palette displays a new fill and stroke for the group. The stroke should be highlighted at the top of the list. Set the width and color of the stroke now.
4. Drag the new stroke below the contents in the Appearance palette, as shown in Figure 6.8. The strokes of the items in the group are in front of the group's stroke, making them visible. Use the Direct Selection tool to select group members and adjust as you see fit. Select the whole group to adjust the group stroke.
5. Click the New Style button in the Graphic Styles palette to save the appearance.

The Group Perspective Drop Shadow

In this section, we show you how to use a group fill to apply the distortion effect needed to create a perspective drop shadow, as shown in Figure 6.9. By adding a fill to the group, you protect the objects in the group from the impact of the distortion.

To create a group perspective drop shadow, follow these steps:

1. Group the desired items (Object → Group). Leave the group selected.
2. From the Appearance palette menu, choose Add New Fill.
3. The Appearance palette displays a new fill and stroke for the group. The fill should be highlighted. Using the Swatches or Color palette, set the color of the fill. You may want to apply transparency or a blend mode as well. In Figure 6.9, we applied the Multiply blend mode.
4. Choose Effects → Distort & Transform → Free Distort.
5. In the Free Distort dialog box, drag the top two anchor points to create the shadow shape, as shown in Figure 6.10.

Figure 6.9

The basic objects (left) and with a group perspective shadow applied (right)

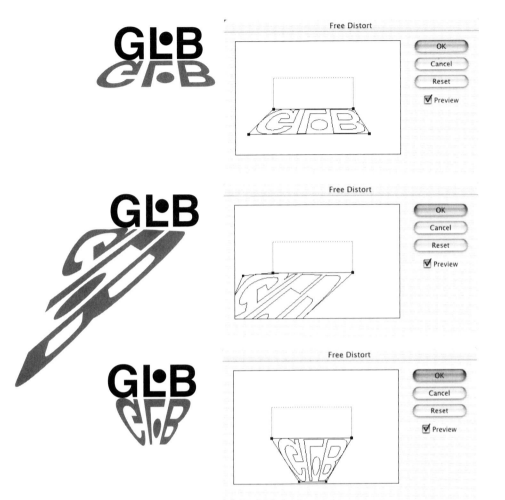

Figure 6.10

Various free transform effects

6. Drag the fill below the contents in the Appearance palette, as shown in Figure 6.11, so that the original group items are visible. Save the appearance as a style if you want and use the Direct Selection tool to adjust group members as needed.

Figure 6.11

The Appearance palette for a perspective shadow

Setting Strokes Behind Type

Strokes on small type can obscure the fills and make your text difficult to read. Consider a block of type as a group whose members are the individual characters. Just as groups can have attributes different from those of their members, type blocks can have fills and strokes different from those of their characters, as shown in Figure 6.12.

Figure 6.12

Default type (left) and with strokes behind fills (right)

To set strokes behind your type:

1. Select the type rather than the characters by using a Selection tool and not a Type tool. The Appearance palette will display *type* rather than *character*.
2. Choose Add New Fill from the Appearance palette menu.

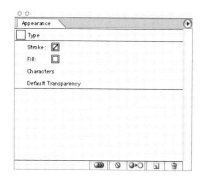

Figure 6.13

The Appearance palette for strokes on the outside only

3. The new fill appears over the characters in the Appearance palette, as shown in Figure 6.13. Set the fill to the color of the characters. The fill of the type will obscure the inside of the character's stroke.
4. Remember that only half of the stroke on the characters will be visible. If you want a stroke of a specific size on the outside of the letters, set the character's stroke to twice that value.

Applying a Stroke to a Gradient Mesh

A gradient mesh can't accept a stroke. This is true even if you add another stroke to it in the Appearance palette. You can sneak around this by grouping the mesh to itself (choose the mesh and choose Object: Group) and applying a stroke to the group. Figure 6.14 shows the result.

To apply a stroke to a gradient mesh:

1. Select a gradient mesh and choose Object → Group.
2. Choose Add New Stroke from the Appearance palette menu. Set the stroke color and width as needed.
3. Although the new stroke is above the group's contents, it doesn't automatically appear in this case. To trick the stroke forward, choose Effect → Path → Offset Path. In the resulting dialog box, set the Offset distance to 0.

Figure 6.14

A gradient mesh (left) and with a stroke applied (right)

In some circumstances, you may be grouping more than one mesh to create a three-dimensional object. In that case, you'll want to move the group's stroke behind the contents of the layer and double its width. This keeps the stroke from crossing the meshes and leaves the width the same.

The Outline Live Type Effect

The technique we'll describe in this section creates the outline effect shown in Figure 6.16, which is similar to ones created with compound shapes. The key difference is that as an appearance, this result can be saved as a style and applied to other objects with a single click.

Figure 6.15

The Appearance palette settings for creating a stroke on a gradient mesh

Figure 6.16

The original text (left) and with the outline effect applied (right)

1. Set the type you want to combine and track it tightly so that the individual characters overlap. (Tracking is located in the Character palette. It's the field with the shaded A V icon.)Figure 6.17 shows the settings you want. Usually a tracking setting of –100 is plenty. You must give the text a stroke to make the effect work. In Figure 6.17, we used a white fill and a black stroke.

2. Choose Effect → Pathfinder→ Add. The overlapping sections of the characters will be combined to make a single shape.

3. Choose Add New Fill from the Appearance palette menu. Color the new fill and drag it below the characters in the Appearance palette (Figure 6.18).

4. Select the new fill in the Appearance palette and choose Effects → Path → Offset Path. Set a distance to push the fill away from the text, creating the appearance of a fat stroke.

5. There are two ways to create a stroke around the offset fill. One is to offset the stroke the same amount and use the command Pathfinder → Add Effect to add an effect to the stroke as well. Your other option is to duplicate the offset fill and reduce the offset amount by the desired thickness.

Figure 6.17

The tracking section of the Character palette

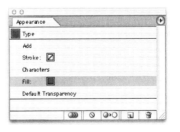

Figure 6.18

A new fill behind the characters

You'll need to recolor the second fill as well, as shown in Figure 6.19. This second approach is slightly less complex than the first.

6. When saving the appearance as a style, be sure that Override Character Color is not selected in the Graphic Styles palette menu. This preserves the core character attributes that are at the heart of this technique.

Auto-Expanding Buttons

In this section, we explain how to add a series of automatically expanding rectangles or ellipses around an object. As Figure 6.20 illustrates, this approach simplifies the process of creating buttons because the shapes are automatically centered and updated as the core text is modified. You do this by creating a separate fill for the object or group and using the Convert To Shape effect.

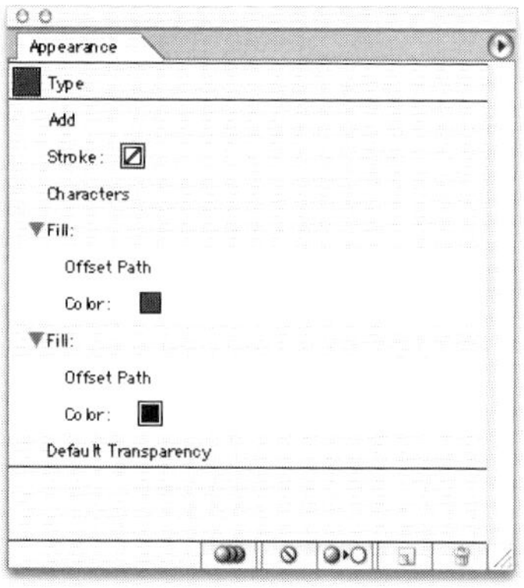

Figure 6.19
A second offset fill with a different distance and color acts as a stroke.

To use this technique:

1. Select the item you want to receive the effect.

2. Choose Add New Fill from the Appearance palette menu.

3. Drag the new fill below the characters (for text objects) or contents (for a group or layer).

4. With the new fill selected in the Appearance palette (Figure 6.21), choose Effect → Convert To Shape → Rounded Rectangle. This command converts the underlying fill into a rectangle, leaving the text unchanged. Decide the button shape you want to use. For our example, choose a rounded rectangle with a 5-point relative extra width and height.

5. To create a stroke around the rounded rectangle, color the original fill black. Then, duplicate the fill that you converted to a rectangle. Do this by clicking the word *Fill* in the Appearance palette and clicking the Duplicate Selected Item button at the bottom of the palette (Figure 6.22).

Figure 6.20
Text by itself (left), with the appearance applied (center) and after editing the text (right)

Figure 6.21
Add a second fill below the contents to accept the Convert To Shape effect.

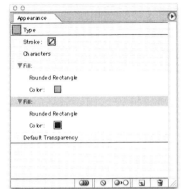

Figure 6.22
A second fill added with a smaller offset (the values used are not displayed in the Appearance palette). This reveals the previous fill, making it appear to be a stroke.

6. The new fill will be in front of the previous one. Double-click the rectangle effect to modify the size. Set it to a smaller size than the previous one and change the color.

7. Add additional fills and strokes or apply effects to the existing ones as you see fit. Save the appearance as a style. If you're going to apply the style to text, make sure that Override Character Color is not selected in the Graphic Styles palette menu.

Building Common Buttons

What you're doing: *Building art that will be used as buttons in your webpages.*
Why you're doing it: *Users love buttons.*

This section discusses the art of building buttons in Illustrator. We're limiting the topic to creating the actual button shapes. You'll find details on adding links to the buttons in Chapter 8, "Creating Complete Pages."

BUT SHOULD YOU?

You can create a lot of special effects with Illustrator. Shiny buttons, drop shadows, and glowing edges are easy enough. However, just because you *can* produce these effects, that doesn't mean it's a good idea in every case. Let your good design sense guide you to use Illustrator's tools to create the impression you want, rather than the tools guiding your design sense.

Anticipating Save For Web Issues

Pixel file formats are all based on rectangular spaces. This doesn't mean you need to create rectangular designs; it only means that the final file will be a rectangle. When you optimize, Illustrator creates a rectangle that is just exactly large enough to cover all of your art and uses it as the boundaries of the file.

This behavior creates a small problem. Curved edges in raster art are smoothed by a process called *anti-aliasing*. Anti-aliasing adds a thin strip of transitionally colored pixels that blend one part of an image into another. Without this process, edges look jagged and hard.

In Chapter 5, "Preparing the Work Environment," we described how to work around this problem by creating an Artboard and making it the size you want your art to be or using crop marks to frame your art. This approach makes the most sense. But if you don't know how big you want your art to be until after you create it, you may need to work around the curved-edge issue. Be aware that this technique will not work when you have masks and hidden art. In those cases, it is better to clip to the Artboard. In simpler files, you can do this using a layer style:

1. Make sure your art is set up the way you want it. Target the layer that contains the art by clicking on the target circle in the Layers palette. If the document contains more than one layer, you may want to consider creating a new layer and then dragging all the other layers into it, as shown in Figure 6.23. In this way, you retain the layer structure and you can perform this technique without flattening the file. Later, you can drag the layers out to return the document to its original state.

2. In the Appearance palette menu, choose Add New Fill. Drag the new fill below the contents of the layer in the Appearance palette. If you intend to matte your art against a specific color, apply that color to the fill now.

3. Leave the fill highlighted in the Appearance palette and choose Effects → Convert To Shape → Rectangle. In the Shape dialog box (Figure 6.24), click the Relative radio button and enter **1 px** in the Extra Width and Extra Height text boxes.

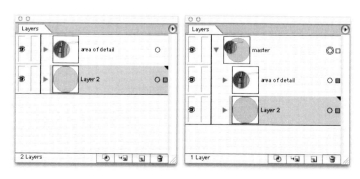

Figure 6.23

The original Layers palette (left) and after creating a new layer and dragging the other layers in (right). Note the target circle on the master layer is highlighted.

4. Save the appearance as a style in case you need it again later. Illustrator doesn't do a very good job of noticing the added size of the rectangle effect when it is applied to a layer. To fix this, make sure the layer is still targeted and choose Object → Expand Appearance. Illustrator creates a new rectangle from the effect.

5. Choose File → Save For Web and optimize your graphic as you see fit. To return your file to the way it was before, choose Edit → Undo repeatedly until you are back to where you were. Undoing does not remove the file you created when you chose Save For Web.

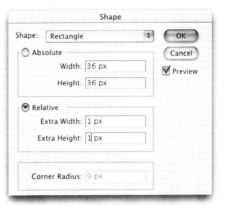

Figure 6.24
The Shape dialog box with an extra pixel added all the way around. This will provide space for the anti-aliasing.

Preparing Typical Buttons

In this section, we examine techniques for creating commonly used button graphic styles, including beveled edges, glows, and drop shadows.

The Basic Bevel

You can use Illustrator's 3D effect to create bevels, like the ones in Figure 6.25, or you can create them manually. Building them by hand is more time consuming, but it gives you more control in the process.

When using the 3D effect, keep in mind that the Surface controls will likely change the color of your original object. You're trading flexibility and ease of use for exact control. Also remember that you can expand the appearance of the button afterward to create standard paths.

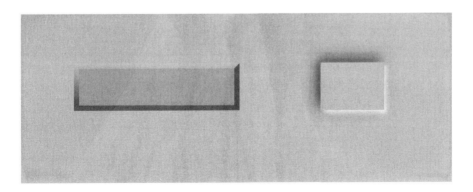

Figure 6.25
Basic bevels

To create a basic bevel:

1. Create a rectangle the size of the button you want. In our example, we want the button to have a black outline around it, so we'll apply a black stroke as well as a fill. This is an important consideration. If your object has a stroke, you'll need to bevel the fill only. Otherwise, the art will look awkward.

2. If your art has a stroke, click the fill attribute in the Appearance palette. This will apply the bevel to the inside of the rectangle only.

3. Choose Effect → 3D → Extrude And Bevel. In the 3D Options dialog box, first set the Rotate option to Front. This sets the X, Y, and Z fields to 0, leaving the rectangle straight up. Next, choose a bevel style and height. For our example, select a Classic Narrow bevel with a height of 30 pixels.

4. Set the Surface and Lighting controls to color the button. For our example, select Diffused Shading with the default options. Also, position a white light in the upper left, as shown in Figure 6.26.

Figure 6.26

3D Options and the resulting bevel

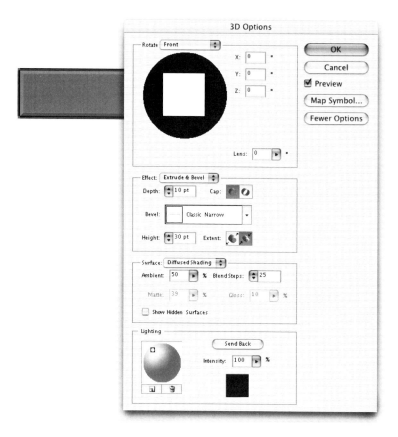

Creating bevels by hand means doing a little "path surgery." There are several variations on the theme described here, but these will get you started:

1. Use the Rectangle tool to drag out a button the size you want. It will need to be large enough to encompass the text for the button face. For our example, we want a button 100 pixels long by 25 tall, so click once with the Rectangle tool in the document and dial in exactly that.

2. Leave the rectangle selected and choose Edit → Copy. This shape will end up being the highlighted side of the bevel, so style it with the fill you want for the highlight after copying it but don't give it a stroke. Many users apply a linear gradient, running from a light version of the color to the shadow color. In this example, the gradient runs from 10% gray to 75% and has an angle of −90°.

3. To create the inside face of the button, choose Object → Path → Offset Path. In the Offset Path dialog box, select a negative offset value. You can leave the other options at their defaults. For our example, choose −5 pixels. This creates a new rectangle in front of the original one. Set the fill of this object to the color you want for the face of your button.

4. Make sure that View → Snap To Point is active. Position the Direct Selection tool over the lower-right anchor point in the outer rectangle. A white box appears when your cursor is in the correct position. Click-drag the anchor point directly onto the upper-right anchor point of the inner rectangle. The cursor display changes to indicate when you are exactly on the anchor point.

5. Leave the shape selected but switch to your Pen tool. Unless you have activated the Disable Auto Add/Delete option (Edit → Preferences → General), the Pen tool should display a plus sign when positioned over the selected path. Click anywhere on the long lower diagonal of the path. Then switch back to the Direct Selection tool and drag the new anchor point directly onto the lower-left corner of the inner rectangle.

Figure 6.27

The stroke on the shadow with the default settings looks awkward when it crosses from behind the highlight side (left). After we position it behind the fill in the Appearance palette, it looks better (right).

6. Back in Step 2, you copied the unaltered rectangle. At this point, choose Edit → Paste In Back to create the shadow side of the bevel. Style this with a darker version of your color scheme. For our example, use a 75% black. To create a stroke around the entire shape, apply the stroke to the shadow at twice the width you want it to be, and then drag the stroke attribute below the fill in the Appearance palette. This solves the stacking order issue of the stroke with the highlight side. In Figure 6.27, we've set the stroke to 100% black to make it contrast with the shadow.

Figure 6.28
Soft outer bevels

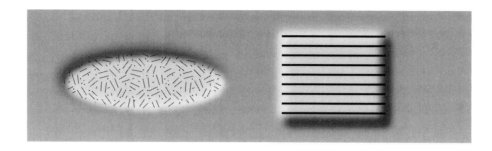

In this next variation on the bevel, you'll create an outer bevel. As shown in Figure 6.28, an outer bevel is basically two drop shadows of different colors set at opposite angles from each other.

1. Create the shape that will be the face of the button. In this example, we've selected an oval with a pattern fill.

2. Leave the object selected. Choose Effect → Stylize → Drop Shadow. In this example, we produced the shadow side first. Leave the Mode and Opacity settings at their defaults (Multiply and 75%) and select the Color option. Click the swatch and dial in black as the value. Set the remaining values to position the shadow where you want it. For this example, use 3 and 3 to make it appear as though light is coming across the object from the upper left.

Figure 6.29
After reversing the direction of the "shadow" effect, the highlight side of the bevel falls into place. This appearance is a good candidate to be saved as a style.

3. After dismissing the dialog box, immediately choose the Drop Shadow command again. This time, set Color to white, Mode to Normal, and Opacity to 75%. Reverse the positives and negatives in the offset fields to set the highlight opposite the shadow. For our example, use –3 and –3. Figure 6.29 shows the Appearance palette.

The Pill

There are many variations on Illustrator's pill-shaped button. The pill shape is basically just a rounded rectangle. From there, your artistic sensibilities and tastes determine how it looks. Figure 6.30 shows three variations.

To set up the pill shape, using the Rounded Rectangle tool begin to click-drag a path. Don't release the mouse immediately, though. When you reach the length of button you want, press the right-arrow key on the keyboard. This will round the height sides of the shape, creating the basic pill (Figure 6.31).

Figure 6.30

Three typical pill-style buttons

LIGHTING PILL-SHAPED BUTTONS

When creating lighting effects, consider the effect light has on rounded objects. For each color there will be a middle value, a highlight, and a shadow version of the color. You can create these different colors each time, but if you intend to make single-color buttons and you plan to change or reuse them later, you should consider a global color or symbol workflow. In this example, we'll use a global color. This technique enables you to work in tints of a color that can be swapped out later on.

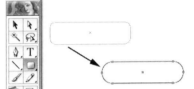

Figure 6.31

Begin dragging with the Rounded Rectangle tool (left). When the rectangle is at the correct length, press the right-arrow key to round the sides.

To create a three-dimensional pill that you can recolor later:

1. Create the basic pill shape as shown in the previous example. Be sure to use the size you want and take care to consider Artboard sizing issues. While you can change the size of the button later, it will be easier if you set it up right from the beginning.

2. Choose a color for the button. You can do this by auditioning combinations in the Color palette or picking from one of the existing swatches. For this example, select R: 255, G: 177, and B: 102. All other colors in the body of the button will be lighter shades of this one, so don't start too light.

3. Save the color as a swatch. Do this by Option+clicking (on a Mac) or Alt-clicking (on a PC) the New Swatch button at the base of the Swatches palette. Using Option or Alt opens the New Swatch dialog box (Figure 6.32) automatically as you create the swatch. This is important because you want to select the Global option in this dialog

box. This option creates a connection between the swatch and any objects that use it, enabling you to swap out color values later.

4. Close the New Swatch dialog box. If you haven't already, apply the swatch color to the fill of the button. Now select the Mesh tool. Click once on the inside of the button shape in the upper left (Figure 6.33) to create two intersecting mesh lines. Resist the urge to recolor the anchor point now.

5. Position the Mesh tool so that it is directly over the vertical mesh line in the middle of the button. A plus icon will appear next to the tool, indicating that you can click to add mesh points. Be sure to click directly on the mesh line rather than in the fill area so that you don't create unneeded points. Repeat this twice more along the vertical mesh line to divide the button into quarters, and once more over a horizontal mesh line to produce the mesh shown in Figure 6.34.

6. Using the Direct Selection tool, select the two inside mesh points on the top horizontal mesh line. You can do this easily in outline mode (View → Outline) by carefully dragging a marquee around only those two points. In the Color palette (Figure 6.35), set them to a 40% tint of your global swatch color.

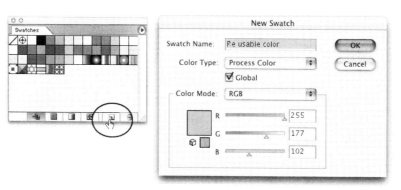

Figure 6.32
To begin setting up a button color you can swap later, Option+click (or Alt+click) the New Swatch button (left) and select the Global option in the resulting dialog box (left).

Figure 6.33
Click once in the position indicated to convert the path to a mesh. Exactness isn't important, but this point will become the highlight location for the button, so use some care.

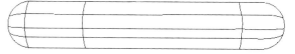

Figure 6.34
The button divided by four mesh lines horizontally. Now you're ready to color the points.

7. Some light will reflect onto the bottom side of the pill as well, so select the bottom two mesh points in the same manner and set those to an 80% tint of the color.
8. To let a little light creep in, select the left interior mesh point on the next-to-the-lowest horizontal line and color it a 75% tint of the swatch. Experiment with other tints and mesh points as you see fit.
9. If you need to change the base color of the button, double-click on the swatch to reset its color definition (Figure 6.36 here and Figure C.xx in the color section). Illustrator updates the button automatically.

Figure 6.35

The top two mesh points are set to 40% tints of the color and the bottom two to 80% tints. Your mileage may vary depending on the amount of light you want and the color you choose, so use your judgment about the percentages.

You can also achieve a simple lighting effect by using a basic gradient. Again, for flexibility in monochrome designs and to repurpose the art elsewhere, we'll use global colors.

1. Create the basic pill shape as described in the previous technique. Leave it selected.
2. As in the previous example, the colors will all be tints of a global swatch. Once you've defined the swatch that will be the base color for the button (see the previous example), you can create the gradients. Begin by clicking on the thumbnail of the current gradient in the Gradient palette to activate the palette. Set the angle of the gradient to –90°.
3. Click on a gradient slider to select it and then Option+ click (on a Mac) or Alt+click (on a PC) on the global swatch to color the slider with the gradient (Figure 6.37). You'll repeat this several times, each time adjusting the position and tint of the slider. Consider the following settings:

Location	Tint%
0	15%
25	25%
60	0%
61	70%
100	30%

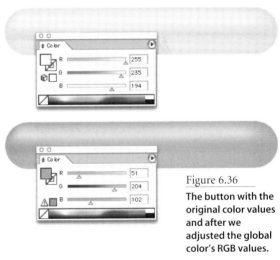

Figure 6.36

The button with the original color values and after we adjusted the global color's RGB values.

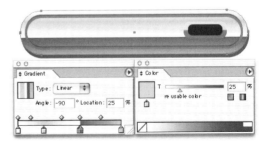

Figure 6.37

Our gradient settings create a sharp color transition in the button.

4. The button should have the gradient applied to its fill. If it doesn't, do so now. To create the inset stripe for the button, leave it selected and open the Appearance palette (View → Appearance). Set the stroke to a suitable width in the Stroke palette (1 pixel for this example) and the Color palette (a 100% tint of the global color for this example).

5. With the object still selected, click the stroke in the Appearance palette. Choose Effect → Path → Offset Path. Set it to a negative amount using a miter join. The miter join won't affect this technique but may come in handy if you save the appearance as a style and apply it to other objects later. The offset distance you choose will vary depending on the size of the button you're making. For this example, use a −5 pixel distance. Save the appearance (Figure 6.38) as a style to reuse later or if you want to recolor the global swatch to adjust the color theme.

Figure 6.38
The completed button and corresponding Appearance palette

The Tab

Tabs are rounded rectangles with flat bottoms. They look like the tabbed separators used in notebooks and are common devices in navigation interfaces, such as the ones illustrated in Figure 6.39.

Setting up the basic tab structure is straightforward. As with other buttons, you can include more complex effects if you desire.

1. Decide how large you want to make the tabs. In this example, the tab is 60 pixels long and 25 pixels high. If your rulers aren't showing, turn them on by choosing View → Show

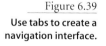

Figure 6.39
Use tabs to create a navigation interface.

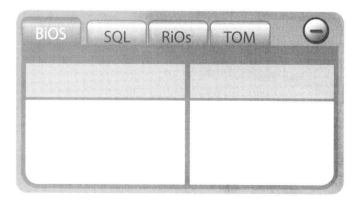

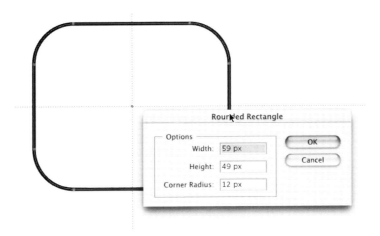

Figure 6.40

Half of a stroke's weight is on either side of the path. Subtracting the weight from the size object you want gives you the size path you ought to make.

Rulers. Drag a guide from the vertical ruler into the document and then an intersecting one from the horizontal ruler. This step isn't strictly necessary, but it will make aligning things easier later on.

2. Position the Rounded Rectangle tool directly on the spot where the guides meet and Option+click (on a Mac) or Alt+click (on a PC). In the resulting dialog box, set the width to the size you've chosen, but make the height twice the size you need. Set the corner radius as you see fit. If you intend to use a stroke, don't forget to account for its weight. Do this by subtracting the stroke weight from the value you want and enter that number here. The resulting path's total area will be the size you need. For our example, enter a width of 59 and a height of 49 (Figure 6.40).

3. Now you'll cut the path in half to create the tab shape. Select the Scissors tool and position the cursor on either side of the path where it intersects the horizontal guide (Figure 6.41). Click with the tool to cut the path at that point and repeat the process on the other side. Select and delete the lower half of the shape.

4. Click on the vertical guide with the Text tool to begin entering text for the face of the tab. Press ⌘+Shift+C (on a Mac) or Ctrl+Shift+C (on a PC) to center the type about the guide.

5. You can color the tab to suit your website. For our example, use a 5-pixel stroke

Figure 6.41

Cut the path with the scissors on the points indicated (left) and delete the bottom half to create the tab (right).

(R: 140, G: 140, B: 140) and a gradient fill. The gradient is linear, −90°, and has the following gradient sliders:

Location	R G B
0%	180 180 180
13%	255 255 255
26%	220 220 220
100%	140 140 140

6. To further give the impression that the tab is rounded, use the Pen tool to draw the curved shape shown over the left side of the tab. Give the path a fill of R: 140, G: 140, B: 140 and set to 30% opacity in the Transparency palette (Figure 6.42).

Figure 6.42
A curved, partially opaque path is used to create a lighting effect.

7. To create the mirror image on the other side of the tab, select the Reflect tool and position it directly above the vertical guide. Option/Alt+click on the guide. In the Reflect dialog box, select the Vertical Axis radio button and click the Copy button (not the OK button).

The Interface Buttons

Objects that emulate the ones used in browsers and computer operating systems, like the Close button in Figure 6.43, are often created as part of an interface design. At first blush, they seem simple enough, but correct alignment of the individual elements can take some doing. In this example, we'll use the Object → Path command to solve these problems.

To create an interface button:

1. Click in the document with the Rectangle tool. In the resulting dialog box, dial in a 14-pixel width and height. Give the square a 1-pixel stroke and a fill of None. Make the stroke medium dark gray (R: 166, G: 166, B: 166) but not black.

2. Choose Object → Path→ Outline Stroke. This turns the stroke into a filled shape, resulting in a compound path. If you had given the original path a fill, it would have been retained as its own object—just one more element to stumble over.

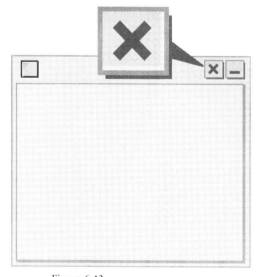

Figure 6.43
Examples of interface buttons

3. Choose Object → Compound Path → Release (or press ⌘+Option+8 on a Mac or Ctrl+Alt+8 on a PC). This allows you to use the inside of the stroke as its own object and give it a separate fill. The whole reason for working in this way is to be able to use the anchor points in the inside square for alignment. Select the inside square and give it a fill. Use the color R: 230, G: 230, B: 230. This will be in the interior highlight, so don't be too concerned that it is too light.

4. Leave the inner square selected and click the upper-left reference point in the Transform palette. The width and height of this item should be 13 pixels each. Enter **12** in either of the two fields and press ⌘+Option (on a Mac) or Ctrl+Alt (on a PC) and then press Return (or Enter). Illustrator creates a new square in the upper-left corner perfectly aligned with the inner square (Figure 6.44). Give it a darker fill—say R: 200, G: 200, B: 200. This is why we outlined the stroke in the first place—there isn't an easy way to align an item with the stroke edge.

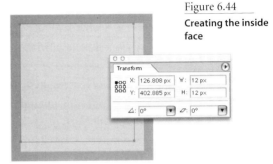

Figure 6.44

Creating the inside face

5. To create the drop shadow on the right side, first select the outer rectangle. Choose Edit → Copy And Edit → Paste In Back (or press ⌘+F on a Mac or Ctrl+F on a PC).

6. Offset the newly pasted item by pressing the right-arrow and then the down-arrow key on your keyboard. Make the shadow a darker color. Our example uses R: 117, G: 117, B: 117.

7. Finish it off by adding a rectangle for the "minus" sign. To create the closing "x", you could rotate a rectangle 45°, and then copy-rotate it 90°.

The Dome

The dome is a basic rounded button (Figure 6.45). It consists of two inset circles with similar color themes and a blur to help the transition. In this section, we examine some common gradient-creation techniques.

You'll set up your dome as follows:

1. Click with the Ellipse tool in the document to create the outside circle. In our example, the circle is 60 pixels wide and tall.

2. Give the circle a fill and no stroke. The fill you use should not have a tone that's too light or too dark. You're going to create highlight and shadow versions of the color. Starting with very light or dark colors will make it harder to create distinction. For our example, use R: 218, G: 125, B: 55.

Figure 6.45

Examples of dome-style buttons

3. Leave the circle selected and Option+click (on a Mac) or Alt+click (on a PC) with the Ellipse tool on the center point of the existing circle. Use the resulting dialog box to create a 50-pixel perfect circle. You should have two concentric circles with the same fill.

4. Next, you'll create a gradient based on the fill color you've just built. Begin by selecting the outer circle. Drag the fill swatch from the Color palette into the gradient bar on the far left. A diamond will appear to indicate that you are about to set the color of the gradient slider (Figure 6.46). Repeat this for the 100% position gradient slider.

5. The 100% slider should be active in the Gradient palette. You need to darken it. One way to do this is to switch the color palette to an HSB display. With this done, drag the B slider to the left. For our example, set the B slider to 20%. This is not a very scientific method for setting colors, so be sure that you've inspected your results by choosing View → Proof Setup → Windows RGB Active.

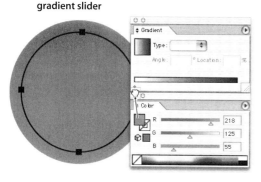

Figure 6.46

Dragging the color swatch onto the gradient slider

6. Click on the 0% slider in the Gradient palette. You'll lighten this one, so leave the Color palette in HSB and drag the B slider to the right.

7. Select the interior circle and choose Effect → Blur → Gaussian Blur. Our example uses a 5-pixel Gaussian Blur. This smoothes the color transition and creates a rounded bevel effect.

The Inside Shadow

You can create the internal shadow illustrated in Figure 6.47 by knocking the character or icon out of the button's surface to reveal a colored object below. Apply a drop shadow to create the internal shadow. Then, hide the parts of the shadow that fall outside the button area by using a clipping mask.

To create an internal shadow:

1. Create the shape for the face of your button. You'll use this shape again and again, so be sure it's what you want. For our example, the button is a relatively simple 60-pixel perfect circle.

2. Set the fill to the color you want the positive area of the button to be. That is, if you want a red triangle on the face of the button, set this circle's fill to the color red. For this example, use R: FF, G: 33, B: 33.

3. Choose Edit → Copy. To simplify the process for later use, also choose Object → Lock → Selection.

Figure 6.47

An example of a button with an internal shadow

Figure 6.48

Reset the gradient at the left by clicking and dragging from A to B to produce the effect at the right.

4. Choose Edit → Paste In Front. Reset this circle's fill to the color you want for the face of the button. For this example, choose the prebuilt swatch Black, White Radial. Use the Gradient tool to reset the positions of the gradient, as shown in Figure 6.48. This makes the lighting effect match the drop shadow you'll build.

5. Next, you'll create the art for the face of the button. In this example, we used the @ symbol to make an e-mail button, but it could just as easily be a triangle, arrow, or text snippet. It's not necessary to turn type into outlines for this technique, so resist the urge. The color of the art you create for the face of the button doesn't matter, but it should be atop the previously created shape.

6. Select both the button face art and the circle and then open the Pathfinder palette (Window → Pathfinder). Click the Subtract From Shape Area button, as shown in Figure 6.49. The underlying color should take the place of the button face art. The top object is now negative space, revealing the items below it. This is vital for the inner drop shadow.

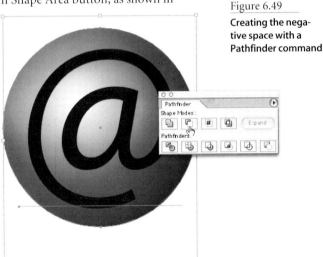

Figure 6.49

Creating the negative space with a Pathfinder command

7. Leave the compound path selected and choose Effect → Stylize → Drop Shadow. Set it as you choose. Try not to use a shadow that is too diffuse or large. The effect will not be clear. In this example (Figure 6.50), you'll want a small offset and blur amount. We choose 1 pixel for X, Y, and blur and the default values for the other shadow options.

8. To trim the shadow from the outside of the button, you'll make a clipping group. First, choose Edit → Paste In Front to put another copy of the first circle at the top of the stack. Next, choose Object → Unlock All to make the original circle available.

9. Select all the objects and choose Object → Clipping Mask → Make. As shown in Figure 6.51, this crops the areas of the selection outside the topmost circle—in this case, the drop shadow areas outside the button. In the Layers palette, the mask will be named Clipping Path.

A key component of this technique is the compound shape created by the Pathfinder palette. Compound shapes don't expand type, which means you can reset or resize as you see fit. Be aware that if you want to choose a different font, as shown in Figure 6.52, you'll need to select the characters. That is, you'll need to use the Type tool rather than the Selection tool.

Figure 6.50
The drop shadow applied to the compound path

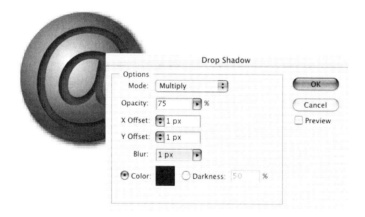

Figure 6.51
The clipping group

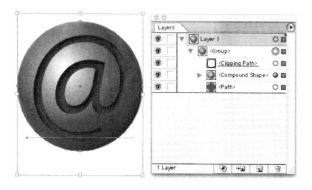

Buttons and Symbol Workflow

In many cases, you'll want to use buttons over again but in a slightly modified state. Perhaps a new job has come up that could use a button similar to one you already have, except you need the button to look greener. Or you want to quickly reverse the colors in a button to make a rollover. Using Illustrator's highly misunderstood Symbol technology, you can make these changes in a hurry without altering your original art.

Figure 6.52

Resetting the text in the compound shape

The plan is to create the art you want to adjust or recolor and then convert the art to a symbol. Once the art is converted, you'll place instances of the symbol on your page (Figure 6.53). You'll do this because symbols can be recolored using the Symbol Stainer and Symbol Styler tools. This is easier than rebuilding gradients based on new colors. Further, once the coloring is completed, you'll be able to convert the instances back into regular objects to continue editing them.

Of course, in a web workflow you can use symbols for more than just recoloring objects. For more on symbols, see Chapter 9, "Creating Animations," and Chapter 10, "Creating Scalable Vector Graphics (SVG)." For now, though, consider using symbols to recolor items as follows:

1. Create the objects that you want to recolor. For this example, we'll use objects from a button face.
2. Select the objects and click on the New Symbol button at the base of the Symbol palette. You could also drag the objects directly into the Symbols palette (Figure 6.54) or choose New Symbol from the Symbols palette menu.

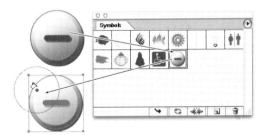

Figure 6.53

Convert your button to a symbol and then place it on the page as an instance. This enables you to swap colors quickly.

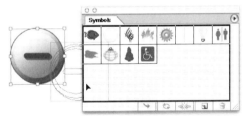

Figure 6.54

Creating a new symbol

3. You no longer need the original items that created the symbol, so you can delete them. Click the Place Symbol Instance button at the base of the Symbols palette to add an instance of the symbol to the document. Leave this selected.

4. Select a solid color fill in the Color palette or from an existing swatch and choose the Symbol Stainer tool from the Tool palette.

5. Click directly on the instance with the Symbol Stainer. The tool partially recolors the instance with the fill color, creating a monotone appearance. Click and hold down longer to increase the effect. Option/Alt+click to reduce the effect, returning the art to its original state (see Figure 6.55, also Figure C.xx in the color section).

Preparing Rollover Buttons

Most readers are familiar with the concept of a *rollover*. Art that changes its appearance in reaction to mouse behaviors is called a rollover. A popular example is the rollover button, a graphic that changes as the cursor crosses over it, alerting users that they can click in that location.

Typically, you create rollovers from multiple graphics using JavaScript. The code in the webpage substitutes one graphic for another when the mouse does a specific thing, such as entering an area. You can also create rollovers inside Flash (for more information, see Chapter 9). Illustrator does not have the ability to generate this JavaScript itself, but Dreamweaver, GoLive, and ImageReady all do. If you're going to incorporate the rollover into a page that you are already working on in a visual editor such as Dreamweaver or GoLive, you should build the rollovers there. You'll find that approach easier than trying to incorporate the HTML that ImageReady creates.

You can set up the different states of a rollover in Illustrator and then finish your work in one of the other applications. In this section, we describe how to set up common rollover versions of buttons.

Figure 6.55

From left to right, the original art, after we clicked with the Symbol Stainer twice, and after we Option-clicked

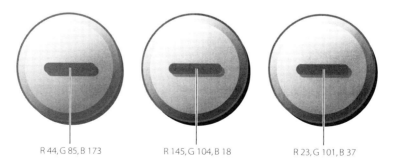

Sizing

As with other web graphics, you'll need to be acutely aware of the size of the graphics you're creating. This is especially important for rollovers, because each version of the graphic must occupy the same space when placed on the page. That means if you size one version of the graphic differently, it will appear distorted. As you can see in Figures 6.56 and 6.57, this can be distracting, even if users can detect only a slight difference.

If you intend to use graphics of different sizes as rollovers, there are two quick ways of working around the sizing issue in Illustrator. The simpler option is to set the Artboard to the size of the largest graphic and then use the Clip To Artboard option when saving. Some artists find it inhibiting to use the Artboard and prefer instead to create a bounding box manually. To do this, create a rectangle with a fill and stroke of None in the document that completely surrounds the art. If you're saving different layers as different files, be sure the invisible box is duplicated into the same position on all the layers.

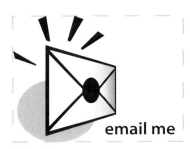

Figure 6.56

Rollover size differences. The rollover version doesn't have the same bounding area but appears the same size.

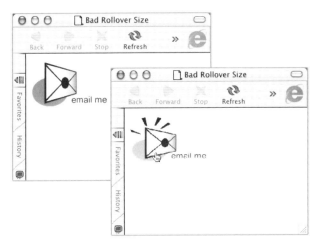

Figure 6.57

The result on mouseover. The rollover version is distorted to fit the space the original occupied.

Setting Up Rollover Versions of Buttons

The easiest way to set up alternate versions of art for rollovers in Illustrator is to use layers. This makes it easy to isolate the different versions, which speeds up saving and previewing files. If you intend to complete the rollovers in ImageReady, it makes your work much easier.

To set up a rollover version of the art:

1. Create the art you want to use as the "up," or default, state of the button.

2. Open the Layers palette and choose Duplicate Layer from the Layers palette menu. Alternatively, you could drag the current layer onto the Create New Layer button at the bottom of the palette (Figure 6.58). Double-click on the new layer to set its options. Rename the layer `over_state` so that you won't confuse your versions.

3. Hide the bottom layer by clicking on the eye icon next to it in the Layers palette. This gets the art out of your way for the time being. Later, you'll turn the visibility back on as you save the art.

4. Alter the art in the over state to create the rollover. This step could involve using different colors for the text and background, adding elements, or recoloring the art. This is a prime example of how you can use symbol staining, as described in the previous section. Be careful of using techniques that create larger bounding boxes, though, such as masks and path type.

5. Decide where you are going to finish the rollovers: in ImageReady, or in Dreamweaver, or GoLive.

   If you are going to finish the rollover in ImageReady, first export to a Photoshop native file. Otherwise, you'll create two graphics from the Save For Web dialog box here in Illustrator. In either case, the first step is to turn on the visibility of the original layer.

6. To export to Photoshop: choose File → Export. In the Export dialog box (Figure 6.59), give the file a name and place to live and choose Photoshop (PSD) in the Format field. After you click Export, you'll see the Photoshop Options dialog box. Enable the options RGB, Screen (72 ppi), Anti-alias, and Write Layers.

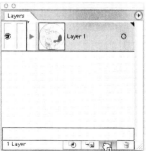

Figure 6.58
Duplicating the current layer

7. If you're going to finish the rollover elsewhere, you need to trick the Save For Web dialog box into creating a separate file from each layer. Choose File → Save For Web. Set the formatting options as you see fit (for more information, see Chapter 3). In the Layer tab of the dialog box, activate the Export As CSS Layers option. Then click Save.

8. In the Save Optimized As dialog box, set the Format option to Images Only. Click the Output Settings button and then choose the HTML options. In that section, select Generate CSS in the Slice Output section, and then click OK. Illustrator generates a separate file for each layer, naming it sequentially. The lowest layer—in this example the up state of the button—will have the default name and higher layers will be given the number extensions. That is, if your file was named button and you saved it as a GIF, the up state file would be named normal.gif and the over state would be named normal-01.gif.

You now have either a Photoshop native file or a series of web graphics for use in a visual HTML editor such as GoLive or Dreamweaver. The following techniques outline the basic procedures for creating rollovers in these applications.

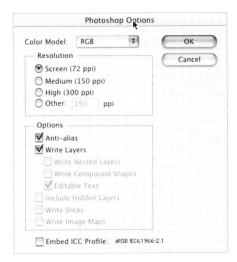

Figure 6.59

The correct settings in the Photoshop Options dialog box

Completing the Rollover in GoLive

GoLive 6 is well suited for creating rollovers and enables you to create one from any standard web graphic:

1. Drag an image object from the Objects palette onto the page in GoLive (Figure 6.60).

2. In the Inspector, click the Rollover tab and click the Browse button to the right of the Normal field. Navigate to the file you want to use as the up state version (Figure 6.61).

3. Activate the Over option and then the Preload option (Figure 6.62). As before, use the Browse button to navigate to the second graphic. Optionally, add a message to appear in the lower left of the browser when the user mouses over the graphic. This technique is often used to tell users where the link will take them.

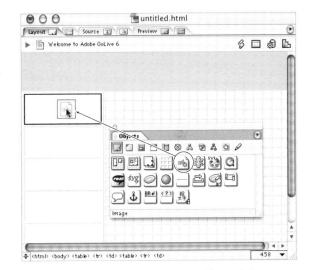

Figure 6.60

Dragging an image object onto a page. Here, we're placing it in a table cell

Figure 6.61
Adding the default state of the rollover

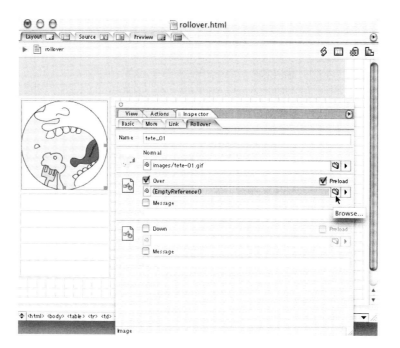

Figure 6.62
Adding the Over option

Completing the Rollover in Dreamweaver

Dreamweaver utilizes a special object for rollovers. In fact, there are two: the Rollover Image object and the Navigation Bar object. If you intend to place a series of horizontal or vertical rollovers, a navigation bar is an excellent choice. However, there can be only one on a page. For rollovers that won't be next to each other, you'll want the Rollover image object.

1. Click where you want to place the rollover and then click the Rollover Image button in the Common tab of the Insert palette.

2. In the Insert Rollover Image dialog box that appears (Figure 6.63), use the Browse buttons to populate the Original Image and Rollover Image fields. Make sure the Preload option is activated. Finish it off by adding the link location in the When Clicked, Go To URL field.

Completing the Rollover in ImageReady

After exporting a PSD file from Illustrator, you can complete the rollover effect in ImageReady. Open the exported PSD in ImageReady and follow these steps.

1. Hide the top layer by clicking on the Visibility icon in the Layers palette (Figure 6.64).
2. Choose Window → Rollovers. From the Rollovers palette menu, choose New Rollover State.

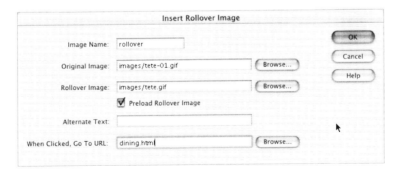

Figure 6.63
Filling in the rollover options

3. In the Layers palette, hide the bottom layer and show the top one (Figure 6.65). This sets the appearance for the over state.

4. Set the options you want in the Optimize palette and then choose File → Save Optimized. From the Format drop-down list, select HTML And Images.

GoLive users may also consider using the Photoshop document as described here in ImageReady as a *smart object*. The rollovers we built here will carry over to be generated automatically in GoLive.

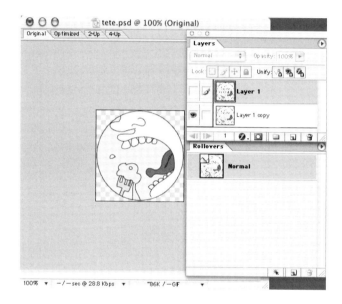

Figure 6.64
Create the appearance of the up state by hiding the top layer

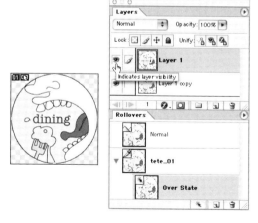

Figure 6.65
Adjusting the appearance of layers in the rollover state

Symbols and Icons

What you're doing: *Creating symbols and icons for web pages.*
Why you're doing it: *Many web pages use graphic elements in their interfaces.*

The faces of buttons and graphics often contain icons to help users identify their purpose. While some objects seem straightforward to create, such as triangles for forward and backward navigation, others take a little bit more work. In this section, we'll create art that might occupy the face of typical buttons.

It should be mentioned here that icons for buttons make good candidates for converting to symbols, especially in cases where you may be designing multiple interfaces from the same basic template. For information, see Chapter 8, "Creating Complete Pages."

The first question is whether or not to build these icons from scratch. A fair amount of clip art is available that you can modify so that it doesn't look so canned. Another good source is fonts. Two popular choices, Zapf Dingbats and Webdings, both provide reasonable fodder for web button art. For example, the) and + characters in the Zapf Dingbats typeface look like this:

If you're going to use fonts to create button art, you should be aware that text has negative space. That is, areas that aren't part of the fill color are transparent. In our previous example, the inside of the envelope is see-through. If you want to color that part, you'll need to convert the font to vector shapes.

You can do this by first selecting the text with a Selection tool (not a Text tool) and choosing Type → Create Outlines or Object → Expand. When type is converted in this way, each character becomes a compound path that is grouped to all the other characters that you expanded. You may want to ungroup them if you intend to treat each character differently (Object → Ungroup). To address the internal shapes, select the expanded type and choose Object → Compound Path → Release. However, this may cause confusion, since all of the internal shapes will be the same color as the external shape. The objects will also be grouped to each other by default. Use the Direct Selection tool to select and recolor each internal object. Be aware that some shapes may be behind others. Here is the text after converting to outlines (left), releasing the compound path (center) and then recoloring.

Home

The Home button indicates that a single click sends the user back to the default page of the website. To build it, you'll use basic objects combined as a compound shape.

To build an icon for your Home button:

1. Define the space the art will occupy. If you're going to add the art to an existing button, consider opening the file and isolating the button to a new locked layer. For our example, you'll use a 30-pixel round button, so set the Artboard to 30 pixels square (Choose File → Document Setup to change the Artboard size as described in Chapter 5).

2. To create the house image for the Home button, begin by using the Rectangle tool to create a 12-pixel square. This will be the main part of the house.

3. Next, make a 4 × 6-pixel rectangle and position it for the door. A second 3 × 5-pixel rectangle will serve as the chimney. Both rectangles should overlap the house slightly.

4. To create the roof, you have a number of choices. A straightforward approach is to click in the document with the Polygon tool and enter a radius of 12 and 3 sides. The radius here is the distance from the center to the anchor points; the actual size of the polygon will be much larger. Once you've created the triangle, lower the pitch of the roof by selecting the top anchor point with the Direct Selection tool and pressing the down-arrow key on the keyboard a few times (Figure 6.66).

5. Select all of the items and choose Add To Shape Area in the Pathfinder palette. Illustrator combines the shapes to create the outline of the house. To "knock out" the door, select that rectangle with the Direct Selection tool and click the Subtract From Shape Area button in the Pathfinder palette (Figure 6.67). As a compound shape, the house has a single fill and stroke for all of the paths that comprise it. However, the paths are independent and you may adjust and modify them for size and position until you are satisfied with the house.

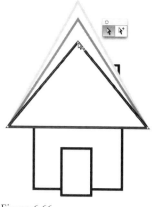

Figure 6.66
Select the top anchor point (left) and lower it with the down-arrow key (right).

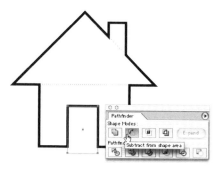

Figure 6.67
With the objects combined as a compound shape, you can adjust the individual elements to fine-tune the icon.

Forward/Back

Forward and Back buttons are often used in conjunction with slide shows and sequential pages. The Forward button also sees use as a "go" button in forms and navigation menus.

There are a number of ways to create these buttons. First, typefaces provide a series of canned arrows. You can locate and insert these characters using the command Type → Alternate Glyphs. To do this, first click in the document with the Type tool. Next, choose a likely font from the base of the Glyphs palette. The glyphs in Figure 6.68 are from ITC Zapf Dingbats. Scroll through the choices until you locate the button you want. Double-click the button to insert it into the page or to replace highlighted text. Figure 6.68 shows the results.

A second option for creating navigation buttons quickly is available through the shapes built into the Add Arrowheads effect and filter. The choices available in filters and effects are the same. Using the filter is slightly quicker, but less flexible. To create shapes from the filter:

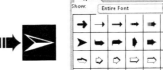

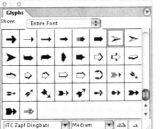

Figure 6.68
Inserting glyphs that will be converted to buttons

1. Select the Line tool and click in the document to create a straight line. In the dialog box, set the length of the line to 10 pixels and a 0° angle.

2. Choose Filter → Stylize → Add Arrowheads. Use the forward and back arrows to navigate to the arrowhead design you are interested in. Don't worry about the Scale percentage; you'll be able to adjust the art later. The example shown in Figure 6.69 is item 2 of 27.

3. The arrowhead objects are added to the line as members of a group. Since you don't want the line shape, use the Direct Selection tool to select the line segment. Delete it to leave only the arrowhead design.

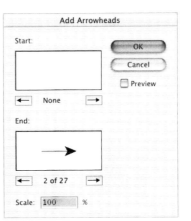

Figure 6.69
The Add Arrowheads dialog box

E-mail Me

E-mail button art often tends to be @ symbols or to follow a postal theme. Postmarks, envelopes, and stamps are common.

You learned in earlier sections how to use symbol fonts to create button art. This is possible here. In Zapf Dingbats the) character yields the envelope symbol. The Wingdings typeface has postal icons as well. Note the glyphs shown in Figure 6.70.

Creating an Envelope Object

Create the envelope shape from scratch as follows:

Figure 6.71
Scaling the bottom two anchor points to create the top flap

1. Using the Rectangle tool, create the basic outside shape of the rectangle. In this example, the rectangle is 35 pixels × 25 pixels. Set it to the default fill and stroke (by pressing D on the keyboard).

2. Copy the rectangle and choose Edit → Paste In Front.

3. Using the Direct Selection tool, Shift+click on the top two anchor points to deselect them. Switch to the Scale tool and scale the points toward the center as shown to create the top envelope flap (Figure 6.71).

4. The top two corners of the stroke may stick out beyond the rectangle shape. Remedy this by reducing the Miter limit in the Stroke palette until the corners bevel.

Figure 6.70
Postal icons available in the Wingdings typeface

5. Select the rear rectangle and repeat the process of copying and pasting in front. This time, Shift-click with the Direct Selection tool on the bottom two anchor points to deselect them. Again, scale toward the center to create the bottom flap.

6. Finish up as you see fit. In the example shown, we rotated the letter 20° (double-click the Rotate tool and enter **20°**) and gave the rear rectangle a drop shadow (Effect → Stylize → Drop Shadow).

Creating a Postmark Button

In this example, inspired by the logo for the Mac OS X Mail application, the postmark is over a stamp.

This art has two separate challenges: clipping the curved lines in the postmark directly at the outer circle and creating the looping border for the stamp. The postmark problem would be easier if the outer circle had an opaque fill.

To create the postmark:

1. Use the Pen tool to draw one of the curved lines on the right side of the postmark. If you have a hard time using the Pen tool, use the Line tool to create a 40-pixel-long straight line. Leave it selected and choose Filter → Distort → Twist. In the resulting dialog box, choose –30°. Give the line a stroke and make it the color you want (here we used R:163, G: 163, B: 163) and a fill of None.

2. Using the Selection tool, drag the twisted line straight down a few pixels. As you drag, press Option/Alt+Shift. This will produce a copy offset from the original (Figure 6.72).

3. Choose Object → Transform → Transform Again to create additional copies of the line.

4. Click in the document with the Ellipse tool to create the outer circle in the postmark. For our example, make the circle 35 pixels wide and tall. Position it so that it overlaps the curved lines as shown here. Choose Edit → Copy.

5. Select the curved lines and choose Object → Path→ Outline Stroke to convert the strokes to fills. You're doing this so that you can chop them by the circle.

6. Select the circle and choose Object → Path → Divide Objects Below. The wave shapes are broken in two along the line of the circle. Select the objects on the left half with the Selection tool (Figure 6.73) and delete them.

7. Choose Edit → Paste In Front to return the circle to its original position. Polish it off by creating additional concentric circles of reducing stroke weight. For our example, create circles that are 31 and 23 pixels across.

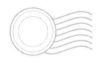

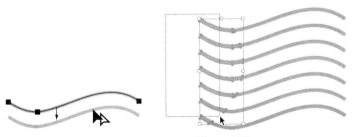

Figure 6.72
Creating duplicate lines

Figure 6.73
Selecting the objects on the left half

Creating the Stamp Button

You can create a Stamp button by combining rectangles and rounded rectangles. The trick will be to evenly space the rounded rectangles to create the effect. You have a couple of ways to do this. You could use the Align palette to distribute the objects within a set space. You could also create an object blend between two identical rounded rectangles. This approach has the advantage of enabling you to change the number of rectangles on a side at any time without having to distribute them a second time. Follow these steps:

1. Click in the document with the Rectangle tool to create a rectangle 25 pixels wide and 35 tall. This will be the basic shape of the stamp. Give it a white fill and a dark gray 0.5 pixel stroke.

2. Create a second rectangle 20 pixels wide by 30 pixels tall. This will be the inside section of the stamp. Align it with the center of the previous rectangle.

3. To create the rounded sides of the stamp, you'll make a series of object blends and combine them to the original circle. Click in the document with the Rounded Rectangle tool. In the resulting dialog box, set the width to 5 pixels and the height to 2.5 pixels. Set the corner radius to any value 2 pixels or higher.

4. Using the Direct Selection tool, drag from the upper-left anchor point in the rounded rectangle to the upper-left corner of the large rectangle (Figure 6.74).

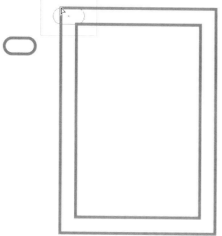

Figure 6.74
Dragging from one anchor point to another makes it easy to align objects

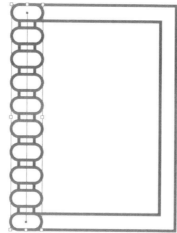

Figure 6.75
After creating a second rectangle, blend the two to create the rest in the series automatically

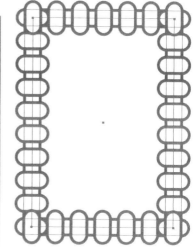

Figure 6.76
Four object blends used to create the sides of the stamp

5. Again, using the Direct Selection tool, drag from the lower-left anchor point of the rounded rectangle to the lower-left corner of the large rectangle. As you drag, hold down Option/Alt to create a duplicate (Figure 6.75). Shift+click on the first smaller rectangle to add it to the selection and choose Object → Blend → Make.

6. Set the number of intermediate objects in the blend by choosing Object → Blend → Blend Options and setting the Spacing option to Specified Steps. For this example, use eight objects. You can also get the options for a selected blend by double-clicking on the Blend tool.

7. Leave the blend selected. Using the Direct Selection tool, drag from the upper-right anchor point of one of the top rounded rectangles to the upper-right corner of the large rectangle. Press the Option/Alt key as you drag to create a duplicate.

8. Repeat the process you used to create the vertical sides to create the top and bottom sides (Figure 6.76). You may find it easiest to copy and paste one of the existing blends, rotate it 90°, and reposition the rounded rectangles as shown.

9. Select the blends and the large rectangle and click the Add To Shape Area button in the Pathfinder palette. The shapes all unite, creating the stamp shape. Combine the stamp with the postmark from the previous example to get a result like this:

Creating a Shopping Cart Icon

The Shopping Cart icon isn't particularly difficult to construct, and it illustrates a useful technique.

To create a Shopping Cart icon for your button:

1. Start by creating the shape for the thick left side and base. One way to do this is to start with a rounded rectangle. The one in our example is 30 × 22 pixels with a 3-pixel corner radius. Give the object a fill of None and a 2-point stroke with rounded caps.

2. Leave the rounded rectangle selected and switch to the Free Transform tool. Click and drag from the lower-right corner to the left. After you start to drag, press ⌘+Option+Shift/Ctrl+Alt+Shift. This creates a perspective effect.

3. Use the Direct Selection tool to select and delete the four upper-right anchor points.

4. Select the Pen tool and position it over the upper-left anchor point. A forward slash icon (/) will appear to indicate that you are about to continue the path. Click, reposition the mouse to the left, and click again to create the handle of the cart.

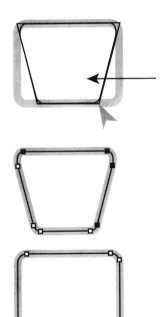

5. Switch to the Rectangular Grid tool and click about three quarters of the way up the bar side of the cart. In the resulting dialog box, choose the options shown in Figure 6.77.

Figure 6.77

The Rectangular Grid Tool Options dialog box

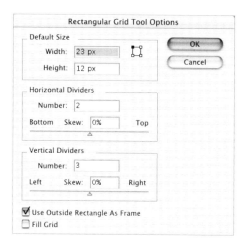

6. Set the stroke weight of the grid items to 1 point. Switch to the Free Transform tool. Click and drag from the lower-right corner to the left. After you start to drag, press ⌘+Option+Shift/Ctrl+Alt+Shift. This creates a perspective effect.

7. Finish the cart by creating 4-pixel perfect circles with the Ellipse tool to represent the wheels and handle.

Producing Background Images

What you're doing: *Creating images that you will use as backgrounds for webpages.*
Why you're doing it: *Background images are a common feature of many pages.*

HTML has a provision for including background images. These kinds of graphics appear behind pages, tables, layers, and even text. By default, background images tile, as shown in Figure 6.78. This means the image repeats next to itself to fill the entire page area.

You can control how images tile by using Cascading Style Sheets, but this feature behaves differently in different browsers. In the interests of compatibility, we'll work around tiling. This is usually done by creating an image that tiles seamlessly to create a wallpaper effect or that is so long no one notices the tiling because it extends beyond the page.

Figure 6.78

An image (left) and how it appears when used as a background image (right)

Left-Side Art

Long background images have art on the left side. They don't need to be very tall to work correctly (minimum 1 pixel), but should be quite long (at least 1200 pixels or more). That way, you don't see them tiling on the right. These images are typically GIFs, which enables you to have low file sizes even for large images.

When you build these types of images, try to keep the height of the graphic as thin as possible. Backgrounds that are simple color shifts, such as a gradient, can be as thin as a single pixel. Other patterns, such as stripes or wave forms, should be taller. In this section, we provide some basic examples.

The Gradient Fade Effect

Figure 6.79 shows the gradient fade background image we'll create.

To create the gradient fade:

1. Make a new RGB document to start your work. Click once in the image with the Rectangle tool. Set the size of the rectangle to 1200 pixels width and 1 pixel high.

2. Apply the gradient you want for the background to the rectangle. Be sure to set the color you want in the right at the 0% position in your gradient. The 100% color in the gradient will be the background of most of the webpage.

3. Click-drag with the Gradient tool from the left side of the rectangle to where you want the gradient to stop.

4. Choose Save For Web to preview the fade.

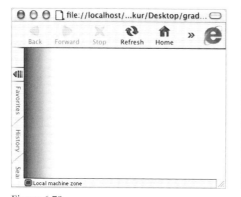

Figure 6.79
A gradient used as a background image

Figure 6.80
A webpage with a short stripe background image

Short Stripes

Figure 6.80 shows a pattern of stripes used as a background image.

1. Make a new RGB document to start your work. Click once in the image with the Rectangle tool. Set the size of the rectangle to 1200 pixels width and 4 pixels high.

2. Zoom in on the rectangle so that you can see it clearly. Using the Direct Selection tool, position your cursor over the upper-left anchor point. Click-drag from the anchor point to the lower-left anchor point. Hold down the Option/Alt key as you drag to duplicate the rectangle as you drag it.

3. Click off the rectangle to deselect all of the objects. Set the view depth to 100% so that you can gauge distances correctly. Select the Knife tool and position the cursor over the area where you'd like the stripes to stop. Hold down Option/Alt+Shift and click-drag completely across both rectangles.

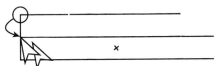

4. The two rectangles are chopped into four. Switch to the Selection tool and drag out a marquee to select the two long right-side rectangles. Give them a fill; keep in mind that the color you choose will be the principle background color of the page.

5. Select the top-left rectangle and give it a fill color that's different from the long two on the right. You'll do the same with the lower-left rectangle to create the repeating stripe patterns.

Use the Save For Web command to preview the image as a background.

The Wave Pattern

Figure 6.81 shows a wave pattern you can use as a background image. To create this pattern:

1. Create a new RGB color mode document to start your work. Click once in the image with the Rectangle tool. Set the size of the rectangle to 1200 pixels width and 40 pixels high. The height here may take some trial and error. The height is going to be the frequency of the waves. Our example is based on a 40-pixel height.

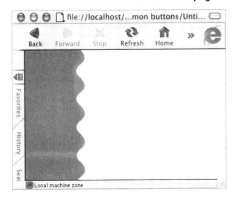

Figure 6.81
A wave pattern background image used in a webpage

2. Choose View → Actual Size (or press ⌘/Ctrl+1) so that you can judge distances accurately. Make sure your rulers are visible (View → Show Rulers) and drag a vertical guide into the document where you want the wave to fall in the image.

3. Pan in on the area where the guide fell. If you're comfortable with the Pen tool, use it to create the curve you see in the image that follows. Make sure that the end anchor points both fall on the guide. If you aren't comfortable using the Pen tool, select the Line tool instead. Position your cursor on the top of the rectangle and click. In the resulting dialog box, set the length to 40 pixels and the angle to –270°. Choose Filter → Distort → Twist. In the Twist dialog box, set the angle to –60°.

4. Position the Pen tool at one ending anchor point on the path and click. Shift+click on the far-left corner of the large rectangle and continue Shift+clicking around until you close up the wave shape. Fill the wave form with color.

5. Choose Save For Web to preview the pattern.

Seamless Patterns

Seamless patterns attempt to disguise the tiling to make it less visually jarring (Figure 6.82). You accomplish this by repeating elements that cross the Artboard in exactly the same position on the other side of the Artboard. When saving for the Web, you'll clip the graphic to the Artboard, removing the parts that drape outside. When the image tiles, the corresponding parts match up, creating the seamless pattern (Figure 6.83).

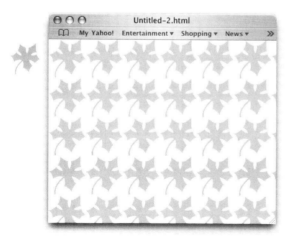

Figure 6.82
A design and how it appears in a webpage

Figure 6.83
The same design converted to a seamless pattern and used in a webpage

To set up a seamless pattern:

1. Create a new RGB document. Set the Artboard size to the size of the image you wish to use as a pattern. For our example, the Artboard is 100 pixels square.
2. Click in the upper-left corner of the Artboard with the Rectangle tool and create a rectangle that's the same size as your Artboard. You'll use this rectangle to help you position objects later.
3. Create the elements you want to use in your pattern. As you do, try to avoid having a single object cross two sides of the square. Also, try to keep objects from crossing the square entirely and from crossing directly across from each other.
4. Select all of the objects, including the square. Using the Direct Selection tool, position your cursor on one of the anchor points of the square and drag to another anchor point on the square. Press Option (or Alt) as you drag. This makes a duplicate of the square and the pattern tiles (Figure 6.84). You need to do this only for the sides of the square where an object crosses the Artboard, but you could easily repeat this process for all four sides of the rectangle.
5. Check for objects that cross each other on the sides of the center square. Reposition them as needed.
6. At this point, you could use the Save For Web command and be done. It is good trade craft, though, to delete any objects that are not needed. Delete all the squares except the first one and any objects that do not cross the first square.
7. Choose File → Save For Web. In the Image Size tab, select the Clip To Artboard option. Continue the Save For Web process as outlined in Chapter 3.

Figure 6.84

Duplicating the elements that cross the Artboard. Note that the rectangle enables you to do this exactly.

Previewing HTML Results

When creating background images, you may want to check your work without actually exporting files. Overwriting files as you check and recheck art can be tedious. Use this technique to inspect how your art will look used as a background image:

1. Prepare the art you want to use as a background image.
2. Choose File → Save For Web. For information on this dialog box, see Chapter 3. Choose Save.
3. In the Save Optimized As dialog box (Figure 6.85), choose HTML And Images from the Format drop-down list and then click the Output Settings button.

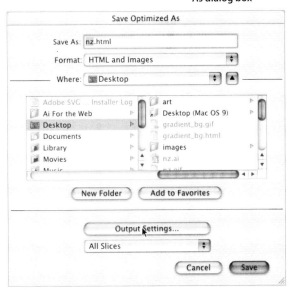

Figure 6.85

The Save Optimized As dialog box

4. In the Output Settings dialog box, select the Background option and choose View As → Background.
5. Click OK to dismiss the Output Settings dialog box and then close the Save Optimized As dialog box by clicking Save.
6. Back in the Save For Web dialog box, click the Preview In button to check the results of your file as a background image in the browser of your choice.

The image appears as a background image in a temporary webpage. The dimensions, settings, and file size, along with the HTML used, are displayed in a copy block as well (Figure 6.86).

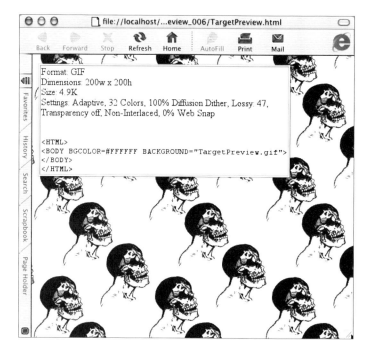

Figure 6.86

A preview of a web graphic as HTML

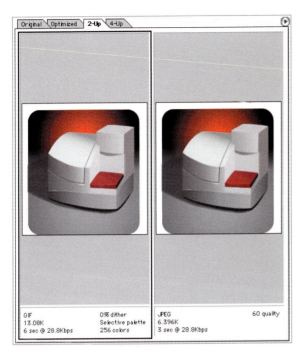

◄**Figure C1** With a limited number of colors available, GIFs are best suited for graphics that have large areas of flat color rather than ones with a lot of color changes. An image with gradients, gradient meshes, feathers, drop shadows, or raster art may be better served as a JPEG file. Although this image has areas of solid color, it is too large when optimized as a GIF (left) because of the gradients. Optimizing it as a JPEG (right) reduces the file size.

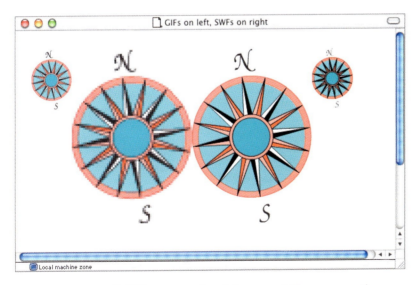

▲**Figure C2** Because SWF files are vector based, they are scalable; you can use the same file at different sizes on the same webpage without the edges becoming fuzzy. Here, the SWF logo at different sizes on the right shows none of the degradation its pixel-based GIF counterparts on the left do. [Chapter 1]

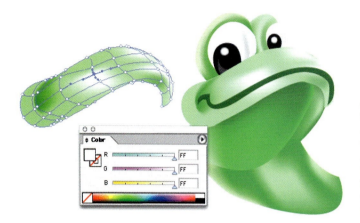

◀**Figure C3** *Meshes* break an object's fill up into a chicken-wire array of points. The segments between the points are controlled by direction points, with up to four on each anchor. Each point can also support its own color. Values are blended between anchor points in all directions, based on the curve of the segments. As you reposition the points and segments, the colors are updated to match.

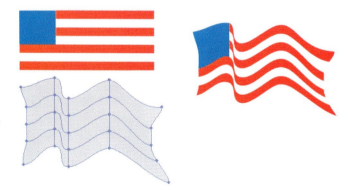

▶**Figure C4** *Envelopes* use the same interface and tools that meshes do, but the curves used describe the way the object is reshaped rather than the way color is blended. Here you see the original object, the envelope form, and the resulting object. [Chapter 2]

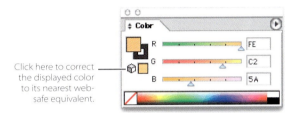

Click here to correct the displayed color to its nearest web-safe equivalent.

◀**Figure C5** In the Web Safe RGB color model, each color component slider in the Color palette is bracketed with six stops, representing the web-safe combinations. When your cursor is snapped onto one of those combinations for all three color sliders, the color is web safe. If a color isn't web safe (which is most of the time), Illustrator displays the In Web Color button. Click it to correct a color.

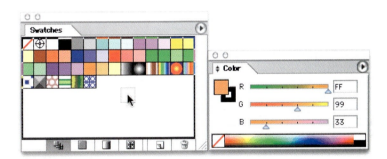

▲**Figure C6** Use the Swatches palette to store the colors you use in a document. To save a color as a swatch, drag a color swatch from the Tool or Color palette directly onto the Swatches palette. [Chapter 2]

▲**Figure C7** Blend modes are based on complex math that often makes them seem obscure and difficult to anticipate. While many users report a hit-or-miss strategy of trying different modes until they find an effect that pleases them, it is important to remember that each mode was created as a production aid. When used correctly, blend modes are often part of a more focused technique. Here you see the effects of the Normal, Overlay, and Color Burn modes applied to the text. [Chapter 2, Chapter 6]

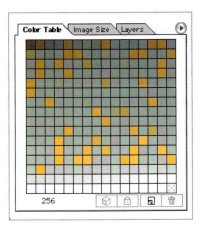

◀**Figure C8** Working with the Color table. Web Snap shifts selected swatches to the nearest equivalent web-safe colors. Web-safe colors are indicated in the table with a white diamond. Lock Color prevents colors from being snapped to web safe or from being omitted if the color number is reduced. Click New Color to add the Eyedropper color to the Color table as a locked swatch, or click Delete Color to delete selected swatches from the Color table. The commands in the Color table's sub-menu enable you to sort, select, and otherwise interact with the different values.

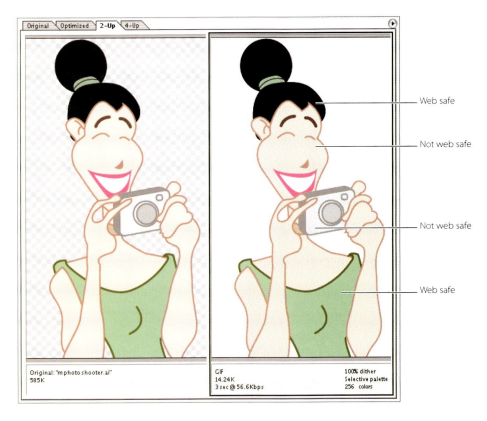

▲**Figure C9** Illustrator offers preview tools so you can see how an image will look in a site visitor's browser as you are optimizing it. Here, the Browser Dither option is used on the right to show which colors in the original image on the left are web safe and which are not. [Chapter 3]

▶**Figure C10** An important part of optimizing an Illustrator graphic for the web is knowing how much space is available for it in the page design. The software you use to generate the page can provide this information. Adobe GoLive, for example, offers an Inspector palette that displays the dimensions of a selected graphic.

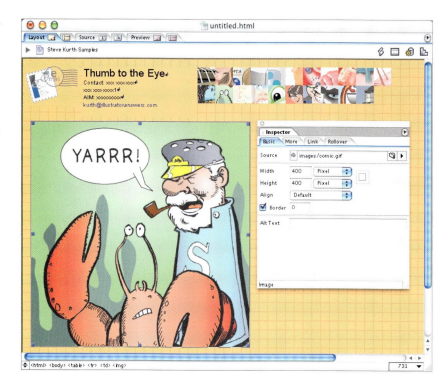

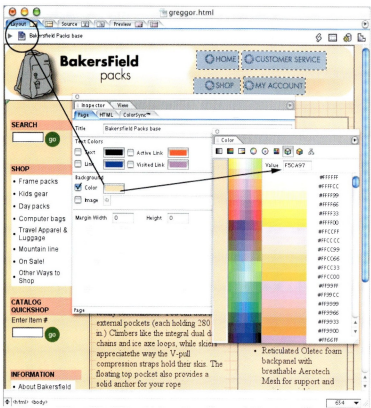

◀**Figure C11** Knowing the exact background color used in a web design allows you to match that color in your Illustrator graphic. GoLive also has a Page Properties display that lets you click a Background color swatch to see its hexadecimal value. Write this value down to use in Illustrator. [Chapter 4]

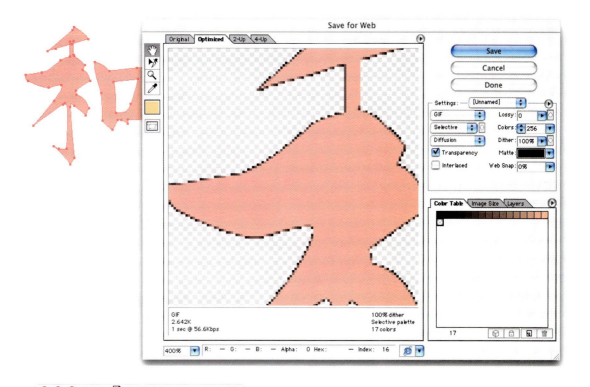
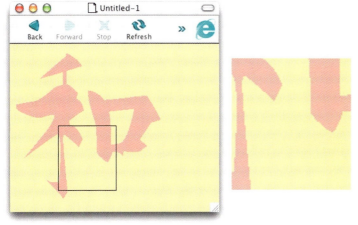

◄▲**Figure C12** When Illustrator art is converted from a vector image to a bitmap for use as a web graphic, the edges, like the rest of the art, are translated into pixels—which are square. Where the edges of objects intersect each other, Illustrator mixes the pixel values to create a smoother transition. You can see this in the blown-up view on the left. On the right, you can see that without matting, the edges are noticeably jaggy.

▲**Figure C13** When you're choosing sample colors from imported photographs, it's easy to get sidetracked by sampling over and over again in an effort to find the "true" color of an image. This is often a fruitless venture. The flavor of a color is often a combination of the surrounding colors and the overall impression of the image, rather than the specific RGB numbers. When trying to pick representative values, sample from middle-to-quarter tones, as we've done here. Don't click in the highest highlights or the deepest shadows. And if the color seems wrong, try again—you may have found a misrepresentative pixel. Once you've made a few good swatches, consider using the color family technique (illustrated next) to make up the remaining values. [Chapter 5]

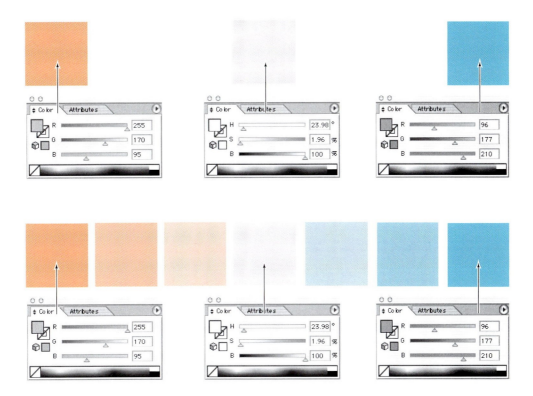

▲**Figure C14** A *color family* is a series of colors related in some way. They can be tints of the same colors, or a mix of two prominent colors in the design. You create a color family as a series of swatches. Top: Two rectangles are created from the first. The second is the same color as the first except with a nearly 0% Saturation value. The third is the complement of the first. Bottom: More swatches are created from the intermediate objects. After making the swatches, you can go back and adjust the colors in blend objects to create a new sequence of colors. [Chapter 5]

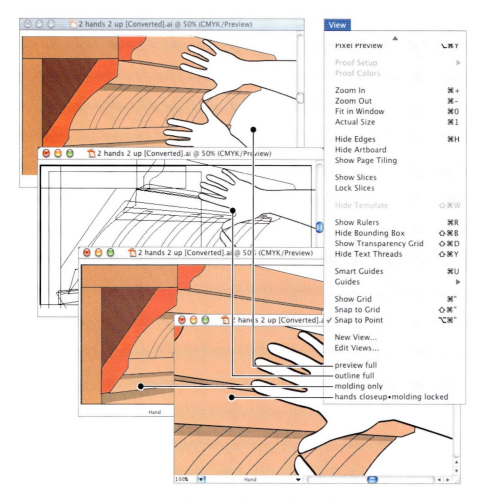

▲**Figure C15** Illustrator's features for tailoring the workspace to your needs are just as important for web productivity as the tools for creating and optimizing graphics. By creating named views of a drawing, you can quickly switch between different aspects of it to work on. [Chapter 5]

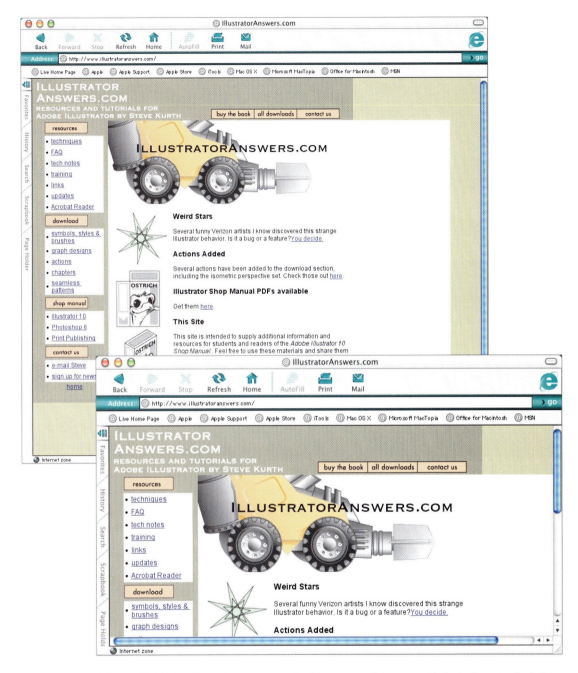

▲**Figure C16** Using Illustrator, you can create a browser template to reuse the basic elements of a design and see it in the context of a browser. The first thing to consider in designing such a template is the resolution setting you expect your site visitors to use. Here is the same webpage viewed on an 800 × 600 monitor display (top) and on a 1024 × 768 monitor (bottom). [Chapter 5]

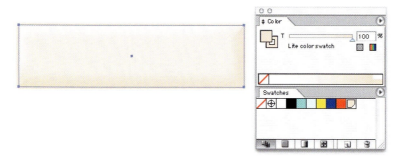

▲▶**Figure C17** Saving a color as a global swatch. Because the swatch definition is attached to any file that contains the color, modifying the swatch changes every image that uses the color. 1024 × 768 monitor (bottom). [Chapter 5]

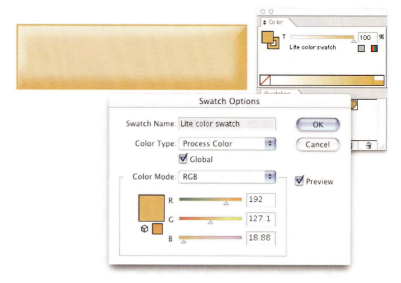

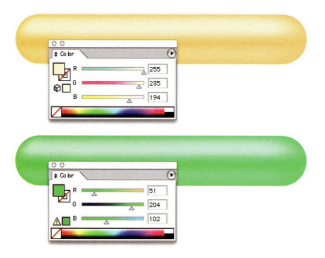

◀**Figure C18** This button will be used many places on a site. Redefine the global color swatch used to fill it, and all the instances of the button will update immediately. [Chapter 5, Chapter 6]

▲**Figure C19** Illustrator's Symbols technology allows you to make quick modifications to instances of a symbol (like these buttons) without altering your original art. Here you see the effect of the Symbol Stainer: (left) the original art, (center) after we clicked with the Symbol Stainer twice, and (right) after we Option-clicked to reduce the effect. [Chapter 6]

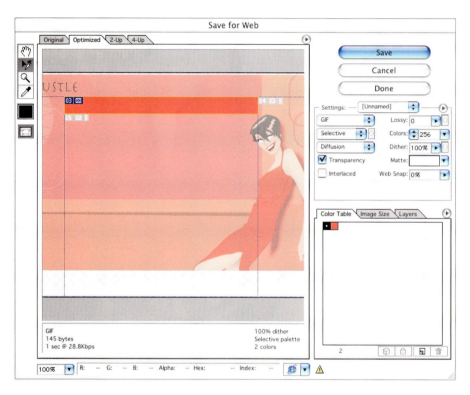

▲**Figure C20** You can use Illustrator to create complete webpage designs, typically as templates for a site layout. Slices you create in Illustrator can be used as either CSS layers or HTML tables. Illustrator numbers your slices from left to right and top to bottom. Here we are previewing a slice in the Save For Web dialog box. [Chapter 8]

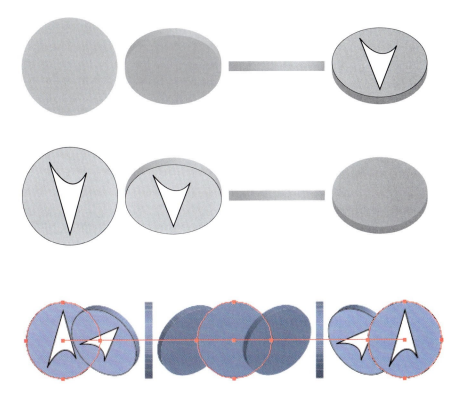

▲**Figure C21** Illustrator's tools can help you add animation to your site, too. For example, to make a button spin, you can draw the basic images (top) and then use Blend (bottom) to create an animated loop.

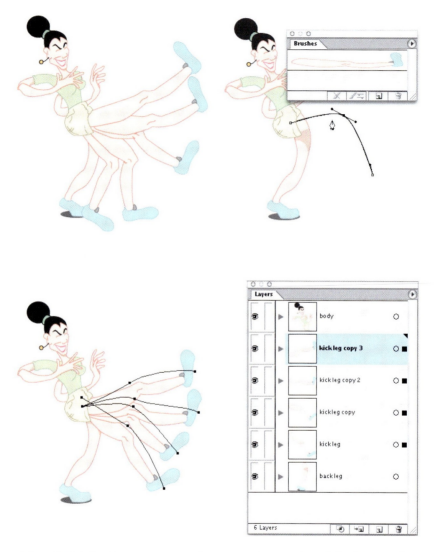

▲**Figure C22** Animating even a cartoon character can be a complex task, but Illustrator's tools help simplify the process. Instead of drawing each position of the kicking leg separately, you can draw it once and convert it to a brush. Then apply the brush to paths you define for the various positions, saving each one as a separate layer.

CHAPTER 7

Optimizing Spot Illustrations

In this chapter, we'll walk through the process of optimizing individual graphics for use in a webpage. We cover the sequence of steps to be taken, the choices involved, and how to assess each decision. For a reference guide to all the Save For Web options, see Chapter 3, "Save For Web Reference."

This chapter covers the following topics:

Optimizing sections of a file

Following the basic optimization steps

Automating your optimization process

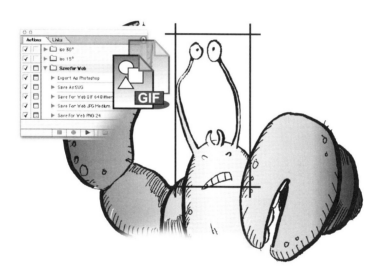

Optimizing Sections of a File

In some cases, you may want to optimize a specific part of a file. Perhaps you're interested in only a particular section of the image, or Illustrator is including too much white space around your art. There are several ways to "crop" an optimized image. In previous chapters, we advised you to set your document's Artboard to the size of the graphic you want to make. This is good advice, but it's not always practical for existing documents. In this section, we discuss several other options that will enable you to alter the part of your image that will become a web graphic. You'll want to use these techniques prior to saving for the Web.

Cropping to a Defined Area

> *What you're doing:* Choosing which section of a file will be exported when you run the Save For Web command.
>
> *Why you're doing it:* The goal is to create a single, cropped web graphic without slicing the document. This technique is handy when you're interested in only one area of your document or when you want to set the final graphic to a specific size.

The Crop Area option enables you to set the area that you see in the Save For Web dialog box quickly and reversibly. A single file is generated based on the area that you specify. Later, if you change your mind, you can reset or discard the crop area and create additional graphics without ruining the art in Illustrator.

First, draw a rectangle around the area that you want to use as the cropped image. If you are building web graphics to a specific size, click in the document with the Rectangle tool to enter the exact size. The rectangle can be anywhere in the stacking order, and it can have any fill and stroke attributes. For convenience, you should create a new rectangle rather than using an existing one and give it a black stroke and no fill. Position the rectangle over the part of the document you want to use and choose Object → Crop Area → Make. Illustrator converts the rectangle so that you see just the crop marks at its corners. When you choose the Save For Web command, you should see only the area inside the rectangle, as shown in Figure 7.1.

> **OTHER USES FOR CROP MARKS**
>
> Crop marks affect the output of other file formats as well. Most formats that you export to (using File → Export) will crop the art upon export based on crop marks. Saving to Scalable Vector Graphics (SVG) has the same results. Saving to Encapsulated PostScript (EPS) with crop marks doesn't affect the results when you're working in Quark, but it does influence Photoshop's rasterizing of the file. PDF files always crop to the Artboard size.

 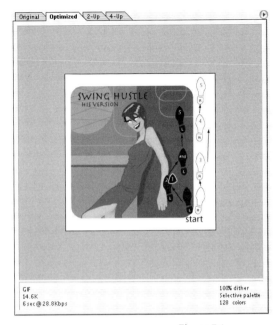

Figure 7.1
Crop marks in a document and the resulting Save For Web dialog box

Crop marks are not like trim marks (Filter → Create → Trim Marks). You cannot select, modify, or hide them. If you want to move the crops, you'll need to release them (Object → Crop Area → Release) and then re-create them. This process is a little cumbersome, so be sure to position the rectangle carefully before converting it.

Once you've finished saving or exporting, you can release the crop marks if you find them distracting. Or you may consider putting the rectangle on its own, hidden layer, and you can recall it later if you need to optimize the file again.

Slices

What you're doing: *Slicing the document into parts and then outputting only the one you want.*
Why you're doing it: *The goal is to isolate parts of a document in a flexible format.*

Slices break a document into rectangles that are assembled in a table in an HTML document. Even if you aren't interested in producing a complete page, you can use the technology to output a specific part of a document. The upside of this technique is that it's easier to modify slices than crop marks or layers. To begin, create a slice, select it in the Save For Web dialog box, and then choose Selected Slices in the Save Optimized As dialog box. You can create a slice for this purpose in one of two ways: by using the Slice tool or by creating an object slice.

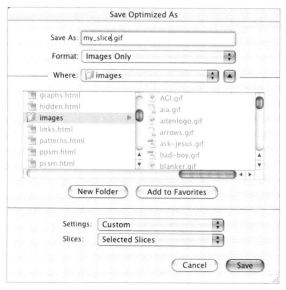

Figure 7.2

Enable the Selected Slices option in the Save Optimized As dialog box.

Once you specify the size and location, use the Slice tool to create a static slice. Click and drag with the tool to establish the desired area. The modifier keys for the Slice tool are the same as for the Rectangle tool. Hold down the Shift key as you drag to create a perfectly square slice; hold down Option/Alt to drag from the center instead of a corner. You can reposition the slice as you create it by holding down the spacebar. For more information on using the Slice tool, see Chapter 8, "Creating Complete Pages."

Object slices are based on the bounding area of an object. As you edit the object, Illustrator updates the slice automatically. For example, you can base a slice on a group and the slice will expand as items are added to the group. Create an object slice by selecting an item (or in the case of layers, by targeting it in the Layers palette) and choosing Object → Slice → Make.

You can see that each option has a specific purpose. If you want to use a specific section or parts of objects as the graphic, use the Slice tool. If you want to show a set of objects you've connected in a layer or group, you'll find object slices useful. However, be aware that object slices sometimes shave the edges of curved selections slightly.

Once you've generated your slice, choose File → Save For Web. Use the Slice Select tool to highlight the single slice that you want to save. Then, set the optimize settings and click Save. In the resulting Save Optimized As dialog box, choose the Selected Slices and Images Only options (see Figure 7.2). Then, click the Output Settings button. In the Saving Files section of the resulting dialog box, deselect the Put Images In Folder option. That way, you avoid confusion by writing the file directly into the directory you name rather than creating a new one.

Although slices can be visually distracting, try to resist the temptation to delete them when you're done. Instead, choose View → Hide Slices to get them out of your way. Because it's not uncommon to have to re-create web graphics, getting the positioning correct the first time is important. Having the slices hidden saves you from attempting to rebuild them.

Layers

What you're doing: *Creating separate web graphics from each layer.*

Why you're doing it: *You can capitalize on your existing document structure rather than creating new graphics. This is a good technique to use when you're preparing rollover button states, animation, or interface graphics.*

There are two common reasons for exporting Cascading Stylesheets (CSS) layers. Either you intend to create a complete web page and want to manipulate objects separately, or you want to separate a single file into multiple graphics by content. For example, you may be a given a file containing several company logos on a single sheet. Instead of copying and pasting the art into multiple files for saving, you can position the art on separate layers within the same file and choose Save For Web only once. This makes the Illustrator file easier to handle as well.

When you choose the Export As CSS Layers option in the Save For Web dialog box, Illustrator creates a separate graphic for each layer. The bounding area of each layer is used for the graphics, rather than the bounding area of the entire document or the edges of slices. This makes for easier manipulation later in an HTML editor. For example, a navigation bar placed over a background graphic can be repositioned in Dreamweaver because the background object would be complete rather than segmented.

If a file doesn't already contain layers (and many Illustrator users do not use them extensively), you will need to create them. To do this:

1. Decide the content that should be connected. That is, figure out which things should be on the same layer. Generally, you want every complete set of items to be together on a layer. This will vary from file to file, but should be suggested by the contents of the art. For example, all the objects that combine to create buttons may be grouped as separate layers and all of the objects that define the rest of a navigation bar as another.

2. In the Layers palette, click the New Layer button to generate a layer. Select the items to be moved to the layer and drag the selection icon in the Layers palette from the current layer to the new layer you've created for the art. If more than one item is selected, be sure to drag the selection icon next to the layer name rather than the item name. Dragging item selection icons moves only a single item, forcing you to reselect.

3. Note that the Save For Web command considers nested layers to be part of their parent layer and does not give you the opportunity to make them into unique graphics. To promote a sublayer, locate it in the Layers palette and drag it up above the name of the layer it is currently in. A black bar will appear above the old layer to indicate the new position the layer will have in the stacking order. If you've applied styles to layers, you'll need to reapply them to the new layers to retain the art's appearance.

4. Once you're ready, choose File → Save For Web and enable the Export As CSS Layers option (see Figure 7.3). By default, Illustrator will create a graphic for every layer. If you don't need a specific graphic, select it from the Layer menu and choose the Do Not Export option. Choose Save and then click the Output Settings button. In the Saving Files section, deselect the Put Images In Folder option.

Figure 7.3

Click here to generate a new file from each layer in your document.

Troubleshooting with Slices and Layers

What you're doing: Using the previous techniques to fix the two most common problems with Save For Web.

Why you're doing it: There is no way to fix your problem other than manually.

The biggest problem with the Save For Web command is how Illustrator defines bounding areas. Often the area is either too small or too big. Slices offer a workaround when the bounding box is too small, and layers can help when it is too large.

Web Graphic Too Small

Typically, there are two instances when a web graphic will be considered too small. The more common case is when Illustrator does not include the outermost anti-aliased pixels in the web graphic. This causes a slightly hard edge on the farthest sections of graphics (see Figure 7.4).

The other instance in which Illustrator builds the bounding area incorrectly is when effects are applied to layers and groups. Illustrator looks at the bounding area of the paths and not the total area described. The result is that the bottoms of drop shadows are cropped and similar problems.

If you can't clip to the Artboard, you can use slices to solve this problem:

1. Make sure nothing is locked and choose Select → All.
2. Choose Object → Slice → Create From Selection. Leave the newly created slice selected.
3. In the Transform palette, set the reference point to the middle. Next, add a pixel to both the width and height of the slice. This will leave a half pixel on either side of the object, which is usually enough to smooth out the edges. Or you could add a full pixel on either side by increasing the width and height by 2.

If your image is sliced already, you'll need to adjust the size of the outer slices individually.

Web Graphic Too Big

When you use some effects on objects, Illustrator attaches a too-large bounding area around the image. A drop shadow is a good example. Figure 7.5 shows the bounding area of a web graphic created by a drop shadow on the object. Path type and masked areas are other reasons for a too-large graphic. Both include areas that are defined but invisible. Illustrator counts the invisible areas as part of the file, even though they can't be seen.

Once again, working on a correctly sized Artboard is the best solution. Slices are a possible workaround here, but because Illustrator sticks with the overall shape used, you will end up with multiple slices. The easiest solution is to add crop marks on a new layer:

1. Pan in on the area of the graphic you are concerned about. This will enable you to be more precise.
2. Create a new layer and name it `crop marks`. On that layer, draw a rectangle with a black stroke and a fill of None over the area you want to keep.
3. Adjust the rectangle as you see fit and choose Object → Crop Marks → Make.
4. Save the graphic as you would normally. Later you can choose Object → Crop Marks → Release to return the path to a rectangle.

Figure 7.4

The outer edges of this saved-for-web graphic have been cut off, leaving a hard edge, because of the incorrectly clipped edge pixels.

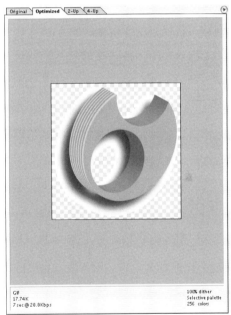

Figure 7.5

The bounding area for the graphic includes too much white space beyond the shadow.

Basic Optimization Steps

In this section, we'll examine the process of optimizing spot web graphics. We'll help you make sense of the sprawling options available to you for creating graphics. First, let's look at options for creating the graphics themselves; then, we'll propose a step-by-step model for optimizing.

Output Options

> What you're doing: *Choosing a command for creating web graphics.*
> Why you're doing it: *There are several cases in which using Save For Web is less useful than other options.*

Illustrator offers three ways to create a web graphic. You can use the Save For Web command, you can save or export to a specific web format, or you can save or export to a non-web format and optimize in another application. You'll most often use the Save For Web command, but there are circumstances in which the other two models make sense.

Saving to a Web Format

Saving or exporting (File → Save And File → Export) to a web format is typically only done in a couple of specific cases. You can export to JPEG and SWF, and you can save to SVG and SVGZ. If you've chosen to use SVG, saving is fine. Usually people save to SVG as they test files and then save to compressed SVGZ when they have finished. Saving to SVG has more options than Save For Web, and the lack of preview is less debilitating there.

Exporting is less common for creating web JPEGs. In fact, there is no good reason to do it. The export option for JPEG is intended for high-resolution graphics. Export is used for SWFs, though, particularly those that you intend to continue working with in Flash or LiveMotion. Exporting gives you a larger set of options and enables you to control what happens to raster art.

Optimizing in Another Application

Creating non-web graphics for optimization in another application usually means one of two things: you intend to work with the file in Photoshop or ImageReady, or you want to create a SmartObject in Adobe GoLive. SmartObjects in GoLive are graphics that use the `livesrc` attribute. GoLive uses this attribute to create a connection between the high-resolution version of the art and the web version, enabling you to re-optimize at any time and to automatically update the web version as the high-res graphic changes. This approach facilitates graphic management and enables some additional GoLive features, such as variables. The `livesrc` attributes can be stripped out automatically upon upload.

When you place an Illustrator native or EPS file into a GoLive document, you will be given the option to create a new SWF, SVG, or bitmapped file from the art. All of the save and export settings that you would have in Illustrator are replicated in GoLive. A key difference is that there is no Clip To Artboard option. If you are going to use this technique and you are concerned about the bounding area of your graphic, you may want to consider the Crop Area trick from the section "Troubleshooting with Slices and Layers."

Another option is to export to the Photoshop native format. Do this when you want to convert layers into frames in an animated GIF or states in a rollover button. Some users also export to Photoshop because they want to use tools there that aren't available in Illustrator. It's possible to open or place Illustrator art within Photoshop as well. This process doesn't retain layers, though, and is usually a better option only when you're compositing Illustrator art with Photoshop work.

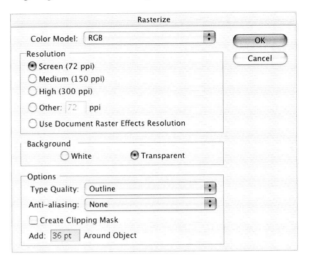

Figure 7.6

The Rasterize Effect settings for small type

Pre-rasterizing art

What you're doing: *Applying the rasterize effect to (small text) objects before choosing Save For Web.*

Why you're doing it: *You can control how the art is anti-aliased and create crisper edges for some objects.*

Making small text look crisp on screen can be a challenge. The anti-aliasing that is so important for most objects actually works against small type. The added pixels make the thin lines blurry, resulting in type that looks soft. Illustrator does not have controls that enable you to control the anti-aliasing of objects when you save for the Web, but it does have these controls when you're rasterizing objects in the document.

Instead of converting the objects to pixels, which would ruin the text for further copy changes, you should apply rasterization as an effect (Effect → Rasterize). This leaves the text intact but adds instructions about how the text should be converted to pixels. Objects with this effect will preview and print as rasters, so be careful to remove this effect if you intend to use the art for print as well.

To add the rasterization, choose Effect → Rasterize. Enables the options shown in Figure 7.6 for best results with small text. Figure 7.7 shows examples of alternate settings.

Figure 7.7

Six-, 8-, and 10-point type rasterized with the different settings

Optimizing GIFs

What you're doing: *Attempting to create a GIF file that is both small enough for efficient web transfer and of sufficient high quality to convey its message effectively.*
Why you're doing it: *Even small changes can affect the overall appearance and load time of your graphics.*

Optimizing web graphics requires judgment calls. While you can set up basic options to speed up the process, you will still need to assess each image quickly to ensure quick and clean output. When creating a GIF, follow these general steps:

1. Confirm that your image is correct.
2. Choose File → Save For Web.
3. Compare file formats.
4. Adjust GIF options.
5. Reduce and adjust colors.
6. Save your settings.

Confirm That Your Image Is Correct

The first step is to check your image quickly to make sure that it contains nothing that you didn't intend to include. Look at it at a setting of 100% View Depth. Some users also turn on View → Pixel Preview to get a look at the art as rasters. Check for spelling errors (Type → Check Spelling) and missing or hidden objects. If your art features masks, type paths, or invisible objects, you may have to worry about the bounding area. Check it quickly by making sure that nothing is locked, clicking the Select tool, and choosing Select → All. The bounding box will cover the area the web graphic will occupy. If it's bigger than you expected, consider the options listed for restricting the area or using the Artboard clipping technique. Many artists like to run the Cleanup command (Object → Path → Cleanup) to remove unneeded elements from their art as well. This command automatically selects and deletes stray points, as well as other elements that you may stumble over.

Choose Save For Web

Once you are satisfied with the image, choose File → Save For Web to begin optimizing your image. In the Save For Web dialog box, click the 2-Up tab. This will give you a side-by-side comparison of your original art and the optimized version. Your goal is to make the two look as similar as possible while making the optimized file's size as small as possible. In the Preview menu, choose 56K. Transfer time isn't as important as file size, but this will provide some perspective. Also, deselect the option Browser Dither. You'll use it later, but it can be too distracting initially.

Compare Formats

If you've used raster art, gradients, meshes, or soft-edge effects, your file may be better served as a JPEG. Quickly check by choosing JPEG Medium from the Settings menu and note the file size at the bottom of the Optimized pane. If you see a significant difference in file size, you should consider switching formats. Also check the basic visual differences between the files. Color may shift slightly in the different iterations, especially in the areas of solid color. When two colors next to each other both shift, the difference becomes very noticeable. Keep an eye on gradients to see how much they band. Also watch the solid areas and edges for ugly artifacting (odd smudges created by compression) and dithering. All of these defects can be mitigated, but you're trying to get a sense of the visual and file size differences between the two formats. Don't simply assume that all of your art should be GIFs.

Depending on the nature of your image and your level of comfort with HTML, you may also consider going back and slicing the image. If you use this approach, you can choose to optimize part of the image as a JPEG and the rest as a GIF. You'd typically use this solution when mixing photographs with vector art or when combining meshes and gradients with flat areas.

Adjust GIF Options

Chapter 3 (the section titled "GIF Optimization Controls") outlined the GIF settings in the Save For Web dialog box. When you choose the GIF settings for an image you're optimizing, you must first pick a color-reduction algorithm. The menu you'll use isn't labeled; you can find it directly below the File Format menu. Most users prefer either Selective or Adaptive. (For details about the differences, see Chapter 3.) You can audition the two models quickly, but it's unlikely that your eye will see a large difference, especially in files that have limited amounts of color. You can also choose from previously saved custom color tables or knock the image down to grayscale.

Next, decide whether you want to include transparency. Transparency is indicated in the Preview pane by a gray-and-white checkerboard. Areas between objects are transparent by default. If you are going to use transparency, you should matte the art against the background color that the art will be placed against. (We discussed finding a background color value in an HTML file in Chapter 4, "Gathering the Required Information.") To set a specific color, click the Matte swatch to open the Color Picker and enter the color's hex number in the # field.

Your next step is to decide whether you want to use interlacing. Some users activate this option, but most do not, preferring the smaller file size instead.

Turn dithering off for the time being. You may add it later to help smooth color transitions (see the next section).

Reduce and Adjust Colors

Your goal is to reduce the number of colors in the image (and thus its file size) while maintaining the appearance of your image. Essentially, you're carving away the fat in the file until only the data required to describe the art is left.

Using the Color field, reduce the number of colors in the image incrementally until you see a noticeable change in the preview version of the image. The change will take the form of image banding. Color transitions will clump up and become noticeable. You will see this especially in gradients. For example, in Figure 7.8 banding becomes noticeable with fewer than 64 colors, and there is much less difference in file size and download time between 64 and 32 colors than between the original and 64 colors. So with this image, 64 colors seems to be our point of diminishing returns.

Before increasing the number of colors, try to reduce the banding by turning on dithering. Most users choose the Diffusion option, because it enables you to set the amount of dithering with a slider. If dithering isn't enough, then increase the number of colors in the table. Be aware that you can enter your own values into the field as well as choose the preset values. As you add and reduce colors in the file, keep checking the file size at the base of the Preview pane so that you can evaluate the file savings versus quality lost.

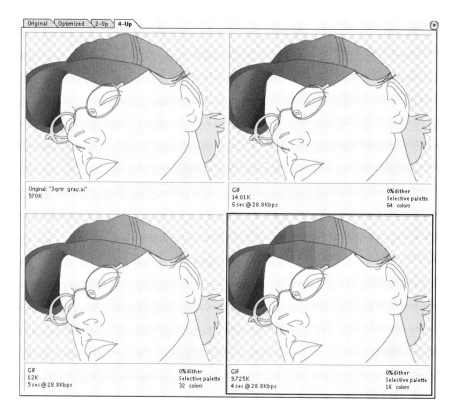

Figure 7.8
With fewer colors in the table, gradients start to band.

As you work down the file size, you may lose colors that are important to you. To prevent this from happening, first click on the colors in the Preview pane with the Eyedropper. Then, find the highlighted color in the Color table (which corresponds to the color you clicked on). Click the Lock icon at the base of the Color table to protect the color from being deleted as you reduce the colors in the image.

You can try to squeeze a little more size out of the file by increasing the Lossy field setting slightly. This setting will damage your image at larger values, so be cautious. The damage will take the form of ugly patterning or dots in the image. At the first sign of this, decrease the value until you don't see that effect anymore. You should be able to shave a few kilobytes off your file size using this technique.

WEB-SAFE COLORS

Chapter 1, "Core Terms and Concepts," introduced the controversial concept of a "web-safe" Color palette. As we explained, the idea is that in order to ensure that all visitors see exactly the colors you intend, your site should use only a set of 216 colors common to Macintosh and Windows systems at their 8-bit settings. Critics argue that very few monitors capable of only 256 colors are sold these days, and that no colors are absolutely "safe"; there are always small variations between monitors.

If you decide to stick with the web-safe palette for an image you're optimizing, turn on the Browser Dither option in the Preview menu. All the non-web-safe colors should appear flecked and spotty. The only way to fix this is to use web-safe colors. You can do that while in the Save For Web dialog box or back in Illustrator in the page itself. The fastest way to do this is to increase the Web Snap value in the Save For Web dialog box. Colors that are close to web safe will be pushed into that set. To set a specific color in the image to web safe, click on it with the Eyedropper tool. Next, locate the color swatch in the table and click the Snap To Web Safe button at the base of the palette. As you increase the number of web-safe colors, browser dithering should be less noticeable. This technique will alter the colors in the image, though, so use it with caution.

Save Your Settings

Once you've established a group of options that work well for the kinds of images you're producing, save the collection as a set. You can do this temporarily by holding down the Option/Alt key and choosing Remember. The Remember command saves the current set temporarily. Once you capture a set of options this way, you can audition additional settings and then recall the earlier ones by holding down Option/Alt again and choosing Reset. This is useful because there is no Undo in this dialog box. That is, you can't pick a setting and then reverse it. You have to reset it manually or with this function.

For a more permanent solution, choose Save Settings from the Optimize menu. This command defaults to saving a file into the directory Illustrator\Presets →Save For Web Settings →Optimize. You should name the file something that will make sense to you a year from now. A good practice is to name it based on the settings, such as "GIF 256 matted." Once you save the file, you can recall those settings the next time you need to optimize a similar image.

Optimizing JPEGs

> What you're doing: *Trying to make a JPEG that loads quickly and efficiently in a browser yet retains its original high-quality appearance.*
>
> Why you're doing it: *Even small changes can affect the overall appearance and load time of your graphics.*

Optimizing web graphics requires judgment calls. Fortunately (or not), you have fewer choices to make when creating JPEGs. This fact makes the save process simpler, but you will still need to assess each image to ensure quick and clean output. When creating a JPEG, follow these general steps:

1. Confirm that your image is correct.
2. Choose File → Save For Web.
3. Compare file formats.
4. Adjust JPEG options.
5. Reduce and adjust quality.
6. Save your settings.

Confirm That Your Image Is Correct

Follow the same general steps as listed for GIF images to be sure your image is ready for posting.

Choose Save For Web

Once you are satisfied with the image, choose File → Save For Web to begin optimizing. In the Save For Web dialog box, click the 2-Up tab. This will give you a side-by-side comparison of your original art and the optimized version. Your goal is to make the two look as similar as possible while making the optimized file's size as small as possible. In the Preview menu, choose 56K. Transfer time isn't as important as file size, but this will provide some perspective. Also, disable Browser Dither.

Compare Formats

JPEG is a good choice for images with a lot of continuous-tone data. Images with large areas of flat color, though, tend to reproduce poorly. To be certain JPEG is the right choice, switch to GIF and compare the file size and content of the image. If the image seems worse, switch back to JPEG.

Adjust JPEG Options

We outlined the basic JPEG options in Chapter 3. Most web developers turn off ICC Profile, a high-end tool intended to ensure color accuracy by embedding data about the color. Most browsers can't read this profile. The Progressive option, in which images upon loading appear in progressively sharper focus, is also little used. You might enable this option if you have very large images. The Optimize option is controversial. Older browsers do not understand files that use this option, and it doesn't reduce the file size greatly. For these reasons, many users prefer not to enable it. If you've made the choice to use CSS or other dynamic HTML (DHTML) structures in your website, though, you might as well turn it on.

Set the matte color as needed. This will be the color against which all the transparent areas in the file are blended. You typically use the same setting as the background color the art will be placed over. (For details on finding that color, see Chapter 4.) Click the color swatch next to the Matte field to enter a custom color in the Color Picker.

Reduce and Adjust Quality

Set the Compression Quality option at Medium to begin your adjustments. Compare the optimized version with the original. If the two look the same, reduce the quality slider until the image begins to show degradation. This will take the form of blotchy sections of color in the solid areas. If you're close to your file size goal and want to keep the current quality setting, consider raising the Blur value slightly. Doing so can mitigate the damage caused by compression and keep your size down.

Blur may not work, though; in that case, you'll need to increase the Quality setting of the image. Use the Quality slider to do this rather than the preset stops. This will enable you to more precisely balance size and quality.

Save Your Settings

As with a GIF, you can Option/Alt+click the Done button to save the current set of options temporarily or save the options permanently as a set.

Automation

If you find yourself optimizing images the same way over and over again, you might consider putting some automation in place. There are two approaches: You can write a script or you can prepare an action. Scripting provides a greater level of control over the process, but you need to be able to write scripts, and that is well beyond the scope of this book. For more information, see the sidebar "Illustrator Scripting Resources." On the other hand, anyone can set up an action and run it in Batch mode to process a whole folder full of files. Once created, actions are available to all documents.

Actions are best suited for simple, repetitive operations that don't involve if/then decision making. For optimizing web graphics, this means that actions will work best with batches of images where the input is all principally the same. If you are optimizing files that vary substantively from one another, you should consider taking part in the process yourself. For example, actions can record the scaling applied to a web graphic but not its final size. If you're creating a web gallery and all your art starts at the same size, an action would work. If they're not, and you want them to be, you'll need to weigh in on the matter yourself. Often, breaking a procedure into several smaller actions solves the problem most simply.

Output settings are not recorded in actions. They are a preference and are retained until you reset them. Before running an action, verify your output settings.

ILLUSTRATOR SCRIPTING RESOURCES

Scripting is a great way to empower your work. Illustrator supports both AppleScript and Visual Basic. Scripts run faster than actions and support logic functions, making them more flexible as tools. Their creation requires specialized skills, and not every user may want to invest the time involved in mastering those skills. Often, it makes sense to farm out creating your highly specific scripts to professionals.

To get started on scripting, check out Adobe's scripting guide for Illustrator:

www.adobe.com/products/illustrator/pdfs/illustrator_scripting_guide.pdf

Additional information can be found at the user forums at

www.adobeforums.com

but the forums tend not to be very active. Users may also consult *Adobe Illustrator Scripting with Visual Basic and AppleScript*, by Ethan Wilde (Adobe Press). The book is fine, but some of the examples aren't particularly realistic and only one deals specifically with web issues.

Illustrator ships with four pre-made web optimization actions. You can use these or create your own, based on your specific optimization preferences. Find actions in the Actions palette (Window → Actions). Actions are grouped into sets, which appear as folders in the palette. You can save and load sets as independent files. You'll find this approach useful for managing actions and sharing them with colleagues. The commands for loading and saving actions are located in the Actions palette menu:

You can download a web-optimization and file-management action set at www.sybex.com.

Building an Action

> What you're doing: *Setting up a series of steps that Illustrator will repeat when instructed.*
> Why you're doing it: *The goal is to simplify the process of optimization and prevent errors.*

In addition to the optimization you want to automate, actions that involve saving or exporting require you to name a destination for the files that are produced. You can move the files later or manually override the locations, but you will need to set a destination up front. In the steps that follow, you'll set up a destination folder and an action that writes the web files it optimizes into that folder automatically. The optimization choices you make in your own actions may differ from this example, but the overall procedure is the same.

1. Create a new folder or directory for the web files. If you are working on only a single web site, you can omit this step and write the web graphics directly into the site folder with your action.

2. If you don't have a file open, create a new one. Open the Actions palette and click the Create New Set button at the base of the palette. In the resulting dialog box, name the set `Web Optimize`.

3. Click the Create New Action button at the base of the palette. In the resulting dialog box, make sure that the action is being saved in the Web Optimized set and assign the action a descriptive name. In this example, we'll create an action that makes a 128-color GIF without transparency, so we'll name the file `GIF128_no_60%`. The 60% refers to the amount of dither we'll apply. You can add function keys and colors later as needed. The Begin Recording circle at the bottom of the palette should switch from black to red, indicating that Illustrator is following your every move.

4. Choose File → Save For Web. In the Save For Web dialog box, set the options you want to associate with the action. Remember, the things that you set here will be repeated by the action. This includes matte color, so make careful choices.

5. Click Save and navigate to the directory you created in step 1. If you're producing only one web site, write the file into the appropriate location in the website folder

(often the Images folder). Remember that output settings are not scripted into the action. You can set them here and make them the default options, but if they are changed before the action is executed, the new defaults will be used.

6. Dismiss the dialog box by clicking OK and click the Stop Playing/Recording button at the base of the palette.

Repeat these steps to create additional actions for different web settings. To run the action, select it in the palette and click the Play Current Selection button at the base of the palette. Note that by default the Toggle Dialog button to the left of the action's name is activated. If you leave the button activated, Illustrator opens the Save For Web dialog box as the action is run, which enables you to adjust the options as you go. To execute the action without displaying the dialog box, click the Toggle Dialog button. Doing so is especially important if you are batching a large series of files.

Batch Actions

What you're doing: *Running an action on an entire directory of files.*
Why you're doing it: *You want to optimize several files automatically while you do something else.*

The Batch command executes an existing action on a series of files. The command works best when the input files are mostly the same or when you want to make the same set of changes to a large number of files. For example, suppose you need to web-optimize a folder full of client logos. After having created an action that represents the way you'd like to convert the files, follow these steps:

1. Select the action you want to run in the Actions palette. This step isn't strictly necessary—you can choose the action later—but most users find it helps to ensure that you're running the correct action.

2. Choose Batch from the Actions palette menu. The set and action that you chose in step 1 should be selected in the dialog box that opens.

3. In the Source field, choose Folder. This tells Illustrator that you want it to open files to use in the action. Click the Choose button and navigate to the folder that contains the files you want to optimize. Select the Include All Subdirectories option if you want the action to run on folders inside the one you chose as well.

4. In the Destination section, select the option Save And Close. That way, Illustrator will open the files, optimize them based on the action's settings, and then close them afterward. The directory for saving the web graphics is built into the action, so you don't need to do anything else.

5. Click OK. The action executes and optimizes all the files in the folder you specified.

CHAPTER 8

Creating Complete Pages

In this chapter, we show you how to generate HTML pages and graphics directly from Illustrator. Typically, you'll do this to create a template or basic design idea for a website. After creating an initial design in Illustrator, you may adjust the page code from Illustrator by hand or in a visual HTML editor like Dreamweaver or GoLive. It's rare to generate all the pages and interactivity for a site in Illustrator because Illustrator lacks a robust set of HTML creation tools. Nonetheless, Illustrator's graphic tools make it a solid and flexible choice for laying out a basic page or page elements quickly.

This chapter covers the following topics:

Creating HTML pages

Creating slices

Managing slices

Setting slice options

Using CSS layers

Building links

Creating a complete layout

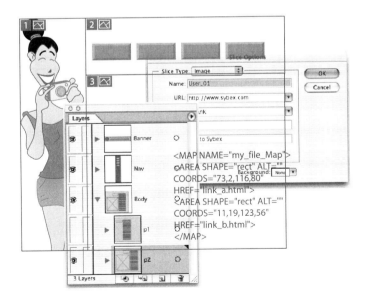

HTML Page Layout in Illustrator

The Save For Web dialog box, covered in Chapter 3, "Save For Web Reference," is Adobe Illustrator's primary tool for creating complete HTML pages, just as it is for optimizing graphics. Like the dedicated web authoring tools noted in the chapter introduction, Save For Web generates HTML based on the options you choose in its various windows. In previous chapters, we assumed that the page itself would be created in other software and that graphics would be created and optimized in Illustrator for the purpose of incorporating them into those external pages. Our primary concern was finding for each graphic an optimal balance between image quality and downloading efficiency. Optimization is still important when you're creating whole page designs in Illustrator, but now you also need to address the overall layout of the page and its completeness—does it have all the basic elements?

As we discussed in Chapter 1, HTML can describe space using tables, layers, or both. This section examines both, although we have a clear preference for layers because of the flexibility they provide. In either case, the use of Illustrator layers to organize a file is vital, and opens up avenues for generating multiple pages from the same document.

HTML pages typically contain at least three major sections: a banner, navigation elements, and a body. The *banner* identifies the site and contains the logo. It's typically at the top of a page. The location of the *navigation elements* varies by layout, but the elements are usually grouped together. The *body* section holds the content of the page. In this instance, the term is not connected to the <body> tag. All of the visual content in an Illustrator document appears in the <body> of the HTML.

Figure 8.1
The sections of a typical webpage

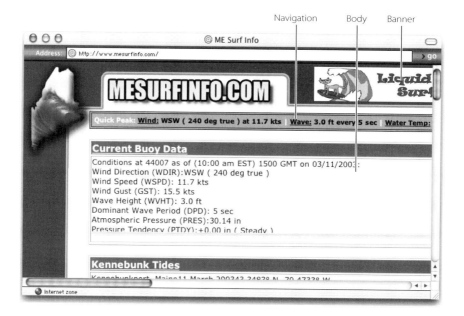

The sections are shown in Figure 8.1. In many sites, the banner section remains relatively constant, while the body section changes with each page. The banner and navigation elements may also change to indicate the current section of the website.

In Illustrator, we'll separate these three sections into layers. This approach helps organize the document and sets up Cascading Style Sheets (CSS) output. The file can still be sliced, and the slices can produce tables or nested CSS layers. By adding alternate versions of the core layers, you can generate additional pages or create alternate designs for the same content. Figure 8.2 shows the Layers palette for a webpage design. Note the hidden layers. For more information on CSS, see the section titled "CSS Layers" later in this chapter.

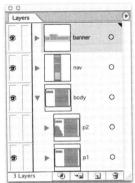

Figure 8.2

The Layers palette for a webpage. Sublayers are used to switch content in the body section.

Slicing

Back in Chapter 1 we discussed the problem of graphic space in HTML. We said that basic HTML requires that a complete page be in the form of a rectangular design. To position graphics in specific locations, you must divide the large rectangle into a series of smaller ones. The effect is similar to a jigsaw puzzle made up entirely of rectangular pieces of varying sizes. In this metaphor, slices become the pieces to the puzzle. As you create slices, Illustrator adds its own automatically to complete the larger puzzle.

We also noted in Chapter 1 that the two basic techniques for positioning elements precisely on a page involved using tables or CSS layers. Slices can be used to generate CSS layers, but they are more commonly associated with tables. In either case, it's important to divide the space somehow when creating complete pages. By segmenting the art, you'll get the chance to adjust segments of the page differently. For example, it's common to create a single slice for the body content section of a page and then add HTML text to it in Dreamweaver or GoLive.

Slices divide the entire document into a grid or rectangles. They appear in the document as highlighted rectangles, each with a small icon in its upper-left corner. The icons show the slice number, which is generated automatically; the type of slice; and its link status (see Figure 8.3). As you learned in Chapter 3, slices can be designated in Illustrator as *image* (which all slices are by default) or *no-image*. No-image slices represent areas in the HTML file that are not filled with a graphic. Illustrator has a special kind of no-image slice, known as HTML text. These slices convert Illustrator text objects to basic HTML text, recording the basic size and color of the text. As the text changes on the page, the slice resizes itself and the HTML in the slice is automatically updated. The number assigned to each slice corresponds to its position in the document. The upper-left slice is number 1. The numbers proceed in rows left to

Figure 8.3

Image, no-image, and linked slices

right and top to bottom. As slices are added and modified, the numbers may change. By default, the slice numbers are included in the filenames of the files they produce. For example a GIF from slice 2 in the file banner.ai will be named banner_02.gif.

All of the slices in a document need to combine to create a rectangle. This is a function of the way HTML works. Standard HTML supports only rectangular, non-overlapping graphics. As you create slices on the page, Illustrator adds its own slices to complete the rectangle. These slices are called *auto slices*. You can't change the options of auto slices; they are all image slices. Illustrator also generates a transparent spacer graphic for empty areas in the table. Auto slices are also linked, meaning that they are all optimized the same way when you save for the Web. You will have an opportunity to unlink individual slices when you save, but not before. If you need to work with a specific area, it's best to create it as a slice.

The alignment of slices affects the efficiency of a table. The more slices in your table, the more complicated the table will be and the slower the file will download. Look at Figure 8.4. Because page elements aren't cleanly aligned, extra slices are required, which makes the table more complex. If it doesn't disrupt your design, you should try to align slices to produce a more efficient file.

Figure 8.4
Unaligned items result in additional slices. The same layout adjusted slightly is a faster download.

Standard and Object Slices

What you're doing: *Generating slice areas in a document.*
Why you're doing it: *You want to set boundaries for cells in tables or locations for CSS layers. Through these devices, you can position objects where you want them in a webpage.*

Illustrator slices are based on the bounding area of objects. You can generate slices from objects, groups, or layers that already exist in your document, or you can create them from scratch.

To convert an existing item to a slice, select it and choose Object → Slice → Make. An object created in this way is known as an *object slice*. The object itself defines the slice boundaries. As you move or edit the item, Illustrator automatically updates the slice to match. Object slices are typically used when site developers aren't locked into a specific layout. For example, buttons in a navigation bar might be converted to slices. As you size and adjust the position of the buttons to try out new designs, the slices update on the fly.

When you create a slice from scratch using the Slice tool or any of the Object → Slice → Create commands, you create a rectangle with a fill and stroke of None that is automatically set to an object slice. It will be named <slice> in the Layers palette. In this respect, the slice is not connected to any preexisting content on the page. This command is commonly used to create slices of a specific size or in an exact location. By generating them as separate objects, you can adjust and position your art without affecting the slices. Because these slices are handled differently, we'll call them *standard* slices.

You work with the Slice tool in the same way you do the Rectangle tool; Option/Alt+drag with the Slice tool to create a slice from the center; Shift+drag to create a perfectly square slice; spacebar+drag to reposition the slice while in the process of drawing it.

The slice-rectangle is still an editable path. You can select it, transform it, rotate it (as shown in Figure 8.5), and give it printing attributes. The option for editing slices is useful but can lead to unexpected results if you are not familiar with it. Later in the chapter, you'll learn about options for protecting slices from accidental change. When you want to activate a slice to change its options or divide it, click the slice's number with the Slice Select tool . You can also activate the slice by clicking directly on the slice rectangle, but this is sometimes harder to do, since the presence of other slices may create a disparity between the slice-rectangle and the slice area.

The tools you use with object slices are not the same ones you use with standard slices. Object slices can't be combined or divided using the commands in the Slice submenu, and they aren't affected by the View → Lock Slices command. In general, you should use object slices to define elements in a layout that are flexible or singular. For example, you might use the Slice tool to break apart the background of a page and then make object slices from the button objects. Standard slices may also be required when the bounding area of an object doesn't correspond to its appearance. For example, a clipping mask group may produce a slice much larger than you need. Work around this by manually creating a standard slice or positioning other slices over the clipping group to crop it.

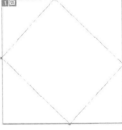

Figure 8.5

A slice created with the Slice tool and then after we adjusted it. Note that the slice path becomes visible and the bounding area is used for the slice.

Stacking Order and Slices

What it is: *The way overlapping area in slices affect one another and the final output.*
What you should know: *The slice on top subtracts from the slice areas of the objects underneath.*

Stacking order matters to slices. The highest slice in the stacking order is used to determine where to divide the graphic. Slices underneath are re-formed to accommodate the space. So, if you resize a slice that is under another one in the stacking order, it won't have any effect on the slices above it. Likewise, if you position or create a slice over an existing one, it will subtract from the slice area of the underlying ones and may force them to divide. This behavior can be confusing, because the bottom slice object doesn't change but its area does, and everything is renumbered. In fact, putting a slice over another may force the lower one to produce more than one slice area. As you move slice objects forward and backward (Object → Arrange), Illustrator redraws the slice areas, as shown in Figure 8.6. After creating the first slice (top), we place a second slice over it. The new, top slice becomes slice 1 and the original slice becomes slices 3 and 5. Illustrator generates slices 2 and 4 automatically to complete the rectangle. Bringing the first slice to the front unites it and forces slice 1 to split. Although the slice areas are split, the slice objects remain whole and editable.

When a slice splits because of overlapping objects, the resulting slices are linked and share the same options. For example, if you attach a URL to a slice that is forced to output as two separate graphics, both graphics will serve as a link in the final HTML.

To keep the slice objects clear in your mind, refer to the Layers palette frequently. Slices are clearly listed there, making it easy to keep straight the objects that are dividing the document. Keep in mind that one slice object may produce multiple slices on the page.

Creating Slices from Guides and Selections

What you're doing: *Generating standard slices from guide areas or selections.*
Why you're doing it: *The goal is to create slices without using the sometimes-clumsy Slice tool.*

Slices can also be generated from existing items without becoming object slices in two ways: they can be created from the location of guides and from the bounding area of a selection.

Choose Object → Slice → Create From Selection to create a slice based on the bounding box of the currently selected objects. If more than one object is selected, the overall bounding area is used and not the areas of each object in the selection. The resulting slice is not updated as the objects it was based on are edited. This command isn't frequently employed. Most often, it's used to generate a slice from a series of ungrouped objects, such as a button and a related graphic. Additionally, it can be used to create multiple slices based on the size of an existing object. For example, to set up a series of evenly sized slices based on the size of an existing button, you could create a slice from the selection and then Option/Alt+drag the slice with the Selection tool to create duplicates of it. This approach can be a quick way to generate uniform slices to a specific size.

Figure 8.6
Overlapping slices cause underlying ones to split. As the stack is reordered, the split slice is united.

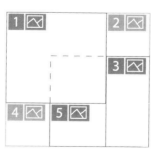
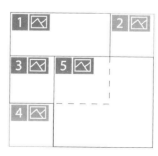

Take care not to inadvertently select unlocked guides when using this command. The result will be gigantic, thin slices that will overload the Save For Web command.

Guides can be used to create usable slices, though. The command Object → Slice → Create From Guides creates standard slices in a document where the guides intersect. The command isn't available when a selection is active.

Create From Guides is commonly used in conjunction with Object → Slice → Clip To Artboard. By default, Create From Guides adds slices to the document to fill the collective bounding area of all the objects in the document. Clip To Artboard sets the boundaries to the edge of the Artboard, regardless of the presence of objects. This fixes the geography of the table or layer produced to the size of the Artboard, rather than the area of the objects in the document. If you don't use the Clip To Artboard option, Create From Guides adds slices based on the location of guides and the objects in the document, as shown in Figure 8.7. With Clip To Artboard active, if there are no objects in the document, Create From Guides makes slices to fill the Artboard.

Create From Guides is especially valuable if you use guides to compose a document. Many users position guides in a document and then align objects to them.

Figure 8.7

Slices created from guides clip to the bounding areas of the objects by default. When Clip To Artboard is activated, slices fill up the document.

Dividing and Combining Slices

What you're doing: *Splitting and joining standard slice cells.*
Why you're doing it: *The goal is to create perfectly aligned cells in an area or to reduce the presence of unneeded cells.*

It's often hard to create perfectly aligned slices with the Slice tool. You may miss slightly when dragging, creating overlaps and unwanted auto slices. Instead, use the command Object → Slice → Divide Slices to break a large slice into smaller slices. The resulting slices will be uniformly sized and perfectly aligned. Any excess slices created in the process can be combined to simplify the document. For example, you can create a slice around a complete navigation bar and then divide it to create slices for the buttons, as shown in Figure 8.8. From there, the slice heights may be adjusted to center the slice content, if desired.

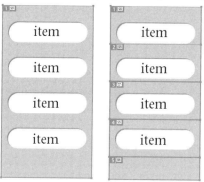

Figure 8.8
A slice is drawn around a navigation bar and then divided.

Slices can be divided horizontally, vertically, or both. To divide a slice:

1. Select it by clicking on its icon with the Slice Select tool. You can also select the slice object with any of the other selection tools, but the Slice Selection tool is usually easiest. Shift+select additional slices you wish to divide at the same time.

2. Choose Object → Slice → Divide Slices. In the resulting dialog box, choose to divide the slice horizontally, vertically, or both, as shown in Figure 8.9. This is usually easier if you turn on the Preview option. For each direction chosen, you can divide the slice up evenly or into slices of a set size. If you choose a specific size that isn't evenly divisible, the right- and bottommost slice will be sized with the remainder.

3. When you divide, slices descend in the stacking order left to right and top to bottom from the upper left. The top-left slice is above all the others, with the slice to its right just below it. As you adjust the size of the slices, don't forget that the area of slices in the front take precedence over those behind, as shown in Figure 8.10.

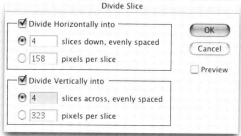

Figure 8.9
The Divide Slice dialog box

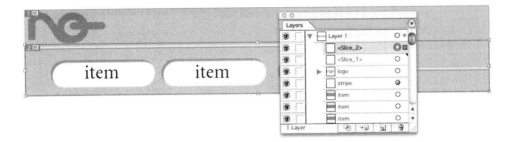

Figure 8.10
After dividing this page's header slice in half (top), we want to increase the bottom slice's height. If you make the top slice smaller, you'll create an auto slice between them. Instead, bring slice 2 forward before adjusting (bottom).

Locking and Hiding Slices

What you're doing: *Setting the visibility and editability of slices.*
Why you're doing it: *You can prevent unwanted changes in a slice grid or get the distracting elements out of your way.*

Slices have two special commands that help you manage them. View → Hide Slices turns off the display of all slice boundaries. The slice objects themselves remain editable, but the distracting slice display is hidden. When slices are shown again, any changes made to the slice objects are updated.

View → Lock Slices prevents you from changing any standard slices. The slice display remains visible, but the slice objects themselves are all locked and dimmed in the Layers palette. Unlocking them individually in the Layers palette will have no effect. You must select the command a second time to make the slices available for editing. Be aware that object slices are not affected by this command. This exception is somewhat illogical, since editing the position of an object slice will most likely affect the locked slices.

Setting Slice Options

What you're doing: Creating no-image slices and adding attributes to slices.
Why you're doing it: You want to make links and leave space for HTML code (sometimes straight text but more commonly HTML tables with text and graphics) to be added later.

Slice options set the basic behavior of slices and add functionality to them. You'll use the Slice Options dialog box principally to create no-image sections and to add links to slices. After selecting a slice, use the command Object → Slice → Slice Options to open the dialog box shown in Figure 8.11.

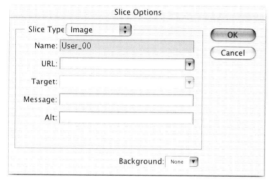

Figure 8.11
The Slice Options dialog box

Recall that there are three types of slices: image, no-image, and HTML text. Image slices produce graphics when you use the command File → Save For Web. This is the default setting for all slices. No-image slices contain text. Commonly, this text is HTML. Graphic information in the slice is not exported when you save for the Web. Frequently, you'll use no-image slices to leave space in the body of an HTML page for content that will be inserted later.

HTML text slices write styled HTML into a cell based on the text in an object slice. This option is available only to type objects that have been made into object slices. This includes area type, which means you can convert a complete column of text. HTML text records the size, color, and styling (such as bold or italic) of the text in the slice, even if the text is styled differently from word to word. As the text in the slices changes, the HTML text is updated to match. This option yeilds somewhat sketchy results, though, and requires special attention. It's not commonly used.

Use the Background option to set the background color of the slice. This step adds a `bgcolor` attribute to the cell or layer code in the HTML. You can specify one of the colors on the list or select a custom color from the Color Picker by choosing Other. The Eyedropper color is the last color picked in the Save For Web dialog box. This option is available for all slice types.

Image Slice Controls

For an image slice, the Slice Options dialog box offers the following controls, illustrated in Figure 8.11.

Name Use this to option to name the graphic that the image slice will generate. When you're saving slices as CSS layers, names are also attached to layers in the code. By default, names are sequential numbers. Many users prefer to add descriptive names to facilitate code revision and file reuse. Slice names do not appear on the page in Illustrator. Non-web-safe characters (letters not supported by all servers) in the name are converted upon export. For example, spaces become dashes.

URL Enter a web address in this field to generate a link to another webpage. The link will be written into the HTML generated when you execute the Save For Web command. The cell will act as a button, linking viewers to the address entered in this field. The entry may be an absolute or relative URL. Unlike image map links, this field supports JavaScript snippets. For example, enter `javascript:window.close()` in the field to create a link that closes the current window.

Target The Target option is used in conjunction with the URL option to specify where a link opens. This option is commonly used in a frame document or to spawn new windows. Frames have names in HTML documents. Enter the name of a specific frame in the Target field or use one of the defaults listed: _blank creates a new webpage for the link, leaving the current page open; _self replaces the page with the referenced page in the same frame (this is the default action in most browsers); _parent loads the link into the frame that encases the current frame; and _top replaces the entire frameset with the link.

Message Text entered in the Message field appears in the browser status bar. This option is commonly used to provide details about the link, particularly when the URL itself is not descriptive. When you use this feature without using the URL option, a null (#) link is generated in the HTML so that the message can be displayed.

Alt The `Alt` tag supplies alternate text to the browsers. The text is displayed while images are loading and on browsers that are set to not display images. `Alt` tags are required in some environments in order to comply with the Americans with Disabilities Act (see the sidebar). The visually impaired use software that reads the contents of webpages to them. When the reader software encounters a graphic, it reads the `Alt` tag.

THE AMERICANS WITH DISABILITIES ACT

The Americans with Disabilities Act (ADA) has a number of far-reaching effects on web designers and developers. Many universities have also extended the provisions made there to include access for financially disadvantaged web users. Check with your web administrator to learn the requirements in your environment. To find out more about the ADA, consult the website `www.ada.gov/websites2.htm` For a guide to webpage building within these requirements, see `www.access-board.gov/sec508/guide/1194.22.htm`.

No-Image Slice Controls

For a no-image slice, you have the following options, shown in Figure 8.12.

Text Displayed In Cell Use this field to enter text that appears in the cell. Typically, you'd enter HTML in the cell. Non-HTML text that you enter will still appear in the cell in the webpage, but it won't be styled. Text object slices will populate the cell with HTML that describes the size, color, and style of the text. This result is similar to the HTML text slice option (described next) except that it is not dynamic and will not update as text changes. However, unlike HTML text, the text in this field is editable and can be manually adjusted as needed.

Text Is HTML When this option is deactivated, text displayed in the field is displayed exactly as typed. HTML characters such as < and > appear as typed rather than being understood as code.

Cell Alignment Use the Cell Alignment pop-up menus to set the horizontal and vertical alignment of the text within the cell.

HTML Text Slice Controls

For an HTML text slice, you have the options shown in Figure 8.13.

Text Displayed In Cell You cannot modify the information in this field. To change the HTML text, edit the text in the object slice directly on the page. As you change the content, size, and color of the text on the page, the HTML is rewritten. This command does not generate CSSs or record font information. It will not preserve the exact look and feel of the text.

Cell Alignment Use the Cell Alignment pop-up menus to set the horizontal and vertical alignment of the text within the cell.

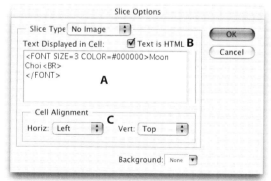

Figure 8.12
No-image slice options

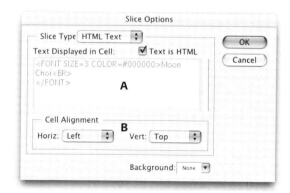

Figure 8.13
HTML text slice options

CSS Layers

Illustrator can generate CSS layers from slices and from Illustrator layers. When you use both options together, the layers from the slices are nested inside the CSS layer generated from the Illustrator layer the slices were on. Nested Illustrator layers are not exported as nested CSS layers. Sublayers are treated as though the parent layer were flattened.

You can convert Illustrator layers to CSS layers by activating the Export As CSS Layers option in the Save For Web dialog box. You convert slices to layers by choosing Generate CSS in the Slices section of the Output Options dialog box. For information on these options, see Chapter 3.

Exporting as CSS lets you use complex techniques and retains the organizational structure of documents. Commonly, each section of a document is organized on its own layer. Additional elements, such as drop-down menus and floating content, are created as layers. After export, JavaScript is added to activate the showing and hiding of specific layers.

Unfortunately, Adobe GoLive 6 does a poor job of opening HTML files from Illustrator that contain CSS layers. Layers often appear out of position and incorrectly stacked. Typically, this results in layers stacked vertically in the document, and you must reposition them and convert them to floating boxes if desired. The only circumstance in which GoLive 6 routinely interprets CSS from Illustrator correctly is when you're converting slices to CSS with references by ID (see Chapter 3) and the Export As CSS Layers option deactivated. Dreamweaver interprets the files without a problem. This failing is a GoLive problem; the code Illustrator produces displays correctly in the browser.

Building Links

Illustrator enables you to define objects as buttons that you can click to go to another webpage. It calls these areas *image maps*. In HTML, an image map defines clickable areas and the links associated with them by using a coordinate system. The map then becomes an attribute of the graphics that use it. The <map> tag looks like this:

```
<MAP NAME="my_file_Map">
<AREA SHAPE="rect" ALT="" COORDS="73,2,116,80" HREF="link_a.html">
<AREA SHAPE="rect" ALT="" COORDS="11,19,123,56" HREF="link_b.html">
</MAP>
```

> **MORE ON CASCADING STYLE SHEETS**
>
> For a detailed reference on CSS layers themselves, consult *Cascading Style Sheets: The Designer's Edge*, by Molly E. Holzschlag (Sybex, 2003).

Here, two rectangle areas (`rect`) are defined by coordinates and given an `HREF` link destination. Objects use the map by referencing it by name. The reference is an attribute of the `<img>` tag. In this way, a single image can link to more than one location:

```
<IMG SRC="button.gif" WIDTH=100 HEIGHT=75 BORDER=0
ALT="click me" USEMAP="#my_file_Map">
```

Image maps can be combined with slice links. That is, art that has a URL attached to it may be contained within a slice that also has a link. When this happens, Illustrator integrates the slice link into the image map, thus enabling all of the links you generate to work correctly. The code looks like this:

```
<A HREF="http://www.sybex.com">
<IMG SRC="graphic.gif" WIDTH=136 HEIGHT=164 BORDER=0 ALT=""
USEMAP="#Untitled_1_Map"></A>
<MAP NAME="Untitled_1_Map">
<AREA SHAPE="rect" ALT="" COORDS="14,30,120,130" HREF="secondlink.html">
<AREA SHAPE="rect" ALT="" COORDS="0,0,136,164" HREF="http://www.sybex.com">
</MAP>
```

Here, the link to www.sybex.com takes up the entire area of the graphic. The graphic is 136 × 164 pixels and the map coordinates are 0,0 (the upper left) and 136,164 (lower right), which means the entire area is covered. The result is one link in the center to one location, and links everywhere else to a second location.

SWF and SVG files use different linking models. In these files, the links exist inside the graphics themselves, rather than in the HTML that wraps them. SVG files use the `xlink` code connected to the familiar `<a>` (anchor) tag. Here's an example:

```
<a xlink:href="myfile.html">
```

The important thing to remember is that in standard GIFs and JPEGs, the links will exist only in the HTML. You cannot place the graphic into different pages and expect the link to work there. In SWF and SVG files, the links reside in the graphics, making them more portable to other files.

Creating Basic Links

What you're doing: *Adding links to objects that will be coded into the optimized files.*
Why you're doing it: *Your goal is to build working pages and add links to SWF and SVG files built completely in Illustrator.*

As we mentioned earlier, links are slightly different in the various kinds of web-optimized files. Fortunately, links are all created using the same process. To create them, follow these steps:

1. Choose View → Attributes to open the Attributes palette. If the palette doesn't display the Image Map section, choose Show All from the Attributes palette menu.

2. Select the object that will serve as the link. You can use any single path, but not groups and layers. You're creating an area that users will be able to click to go to a new page. Set the Image Map field to either Rectangle or Polygon. Rectangular maps set the bounding box of an object as the clickable area. Rectangles require only four coordinates. Polygons create a more accurate clickable area by using more points (see Figure 8.14). The result is also a larger file. Keep in mind that image map areas can overlap one another. Areas in front take precedence over areas in back. It's in such cases that you'd want a more accurate image map. Some users also prefer to use polygonal maps for any object other than a rectangle because of the way Internet Explorer (IE) displays links; IE places glowing edges around link areas. The result looks slightly odd when a circular hotspot is surrounded by a square.

3. In the URL field, type in the link location. Illustrator accepts both relative and absolute addressing in this field. You can also enter null links that you can replace later. If you're entering absolute addresses and you're connected to the Internet, you can check the URL you entered by clicking the Browse button. Clicking that button opens the system's default browser to the location specified. This technique doesn't work for local addressing, even if you've saved the document to a specific directory already.

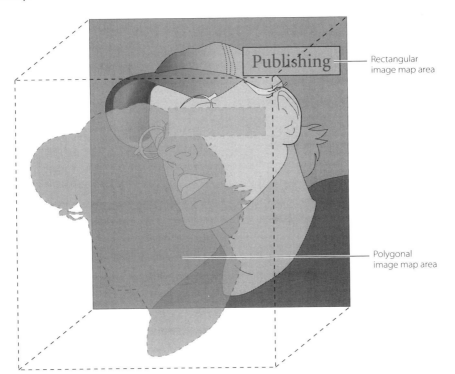

Figure 8.14

Rectangular and polygonal image maps

4. As you type in links, Illustrator records them for later use. By default, it records the last 30 entries, which is the maximum it can store. These URL addresses are available for all open documents. Choose a saved address from the pop-up menu at the right side of the URL field. There is no way to modify the entries listed there; you can't lock, edit, or delete them. If you find the list growing out of control and want to start over, choose Palette Options from the Attributes palette menu. Reduce the number in the Number Of URL Entries field to 1. After closing the dialog box, open it again and return the value to 30.

Invisible Links

What you're doing: Creating invisible hotspots for links.
Why you're doing it: You want to create a link that covers part of or more than one item, or you want to solve slicing problems.

In some cases, you'll want to create invisible objects for image maps. In some cases, an image doesn't lend itself easily to mapping specific shapes to links. For example, in Figure 8.15, we'd like a link to cover all of the objects on the right—that is, all of the dance steps. You cannot attach an image map to a group or a layer, so an additional object is needed.

The process for creating an invisible link is the same as for creating a visible one, with one key exception. Image maps for standard HTML output graphics can be created using an object with a fill and stroke of None. Link objects for SWF and SVG files must have fills. To make them invisible, set their opacity to 0%. So, in a standard web output, you'd create a rectangle with a fill and stroke of None over the areas you want to link, and then add the link in the Attributes palette.

Figure 8.15
On the left, no obvious object is available to attach the link to, so on the right, we create a new, invisible one.

For SWF and SVG files, most users set up an invisible symbol to create links. This is a common technique in Flash, but it works for SVG and standard web output as well:

1. Create a rectangle of the approximate size you want to use for the hotspots. The exact size isn't important, but it will save you time later if things don't have to be scaled too dramatically. Ideally, the rectangle should have a solid color fill and no strokes or effects. Some users color them a light cyan, since that color is used for invisible items in Flash.

2. With the rectangle selected, click the New Symbol button at the base of the Symbol palette. Delete the rectangle from the page and drag the new symbol out of the palette onto the page. Resize it as needed and position it over the link area.

3. Use the Attributes palette to attach links as described in "Creating Basic Links." In the Transparency palette, set the opacity of the symbol to 0%. Repeat as needed to complete the linking in the document.

SWF Links and Rollovers

What you're doing: *Setting transparency rollover effects in SWF files.*
Why you're doing it: *You want to either create or prevent a default rollover behavior for SWF links.*

Adding links to SWFs in Illustrator is not always a bug-free process. The process for attaching links is the same as it is for making image maps. You add links in the Attributes palette. In some cases, though, they refuse to "take," forcing you to remove objects and try again. Also, the interface enables you to apply image maps to groups, even though they don't work upon export. This often leads to confusion when you're attempting to create links to the groups created automatically when some objects are expanded. Remember to create links from basic shapes.

Another hit-or-miss feature is transparency rollovers. You can't create complex show-hide rollovers in Illustrator, but you can generate transparency effect rollovers. When you add image maps to partially transparent objects, the opacity of the object changes slightly when users mouse over them in the exported SWF. The result is a rollover effect, which happens by default—but not all the time. Further, you can't control the amount the opacity changes, nor can you create any other type of rollover directly in Illustrator. To set up a transparency rollover:

1. Create the object that you want to use as a button. For best results, make the object a basic path, rather than a group, text, or a symbol instance.

2. In the Transparency palette, set the opacity of the object to less than 100%. The opacity must be set for the entire object, rather than a specific fill or stroke.

3. In the Attributes palette, select a rectangular image map and enter a URL. The address may be relative or absolute.

4. Use the Save For Web command to create a SWF. The generated SWF will have a transparency rollover built into the button.

When adding links to SWFs, your best bet is to anticipate this behavior and either accept it or work around it. If you don't want this rollover effect, create an invisible button as we described earlier to hold your image maps. Completely transparent objects don't create rollovers—only partially transparent ones.

Slice Links

What you're doing: *Adding links to image slices.*
Why you're doing it: *You want to build working pages with links based on slice areas.*

Another way to create basic links is to build them into the slices. This approach sidesteps the limitation of not being able to image-map groups. You can create a slice from a group and then add the link to that. As the group changes, the slice is updated to match. Most people use slice linking except when they want a single file to link to more than one location.

Slice links are written into the HTML as an <a> tag pair nested inside the <td> tag set created by the slice. That way, everything in the cell acts as a button. Here's an example:

```
<TABLE> <TR> <TD>
    <A HREF="location.html">
        <IMG SRC="images/link.gif"></A></TD></TABLE>
```

An exception occurs when an object with an image map is completely contained within a slice. In that case, Illustrator may write the slice link's code as a portion of the image map. This irregularity can be hard to anticipate, so be careful when using the two technologies together.

Also, if an object contains an image map and you slice it into more than one piece, Illustrator creates multiple image maps to support each new graphic created by the slice. This behavior can also lead to frustration in the editing process. In such cases, look for the simplest area that describes your hotspot. In many instances, as with navigation bars, this will be the slice area. If that's not the case and you need to move things around, consider creating invisible buttons. This solution will give you the most flexibility.

To add a link to an image slice:

1. Choose Object → Slice → Slice Options.

2. In the URL field, enter the address of the link. You can use relative or absolute addressing here.

3. If desired, add a target as well. A common use for the Target field is to create a link that opens in a new browser window. That way, your page stays open when linking to another site. You can do this by entering the text **_blank** into the Target field.

Text Links

What you're doing: *Creating links on type from scratch, or from point or area text within Illustrator.*
Why you're doing it: *The goal is to build working pages with links based on slice areas.*

Using slices, you can also create *text links*. A text link is a hyperlink attached to type instead of a graphic. These links are not commonly used in Illustrator because the process of creating them is somewhat awkward. The technique is best suited to single-word links, such as text buttons. The problem is that you have to enter the links as HTML in the Slice Options dialog box for a no-image slice. If you have anything more than a word or two, it's easier to edit the HTML outside of Illustrator.

In most cases, text links in Illustrator are meant to be placeholders. For example, in the design phase of a website creation, you may fill a section of a table with a simple link to a more complete version of a page component. You can accomplish this using a no-image slice. You can also base a no-image slice on actual text. Illustrator can pick up basic size and color attributes of text-based slices and convert them to HTML—which makes it a little easier for you to anticipate the final appearance of your webpage.

To create placeholder links:

1. Create the slice that represents the link area. (In Figure 8.16, a slice is a placeholder for a complicated navigation bar that is being created by a colleague writing HTML code directly. This slice will link to that page during the initial design phase and then later be connected to a replacement graphic or replaced completely.

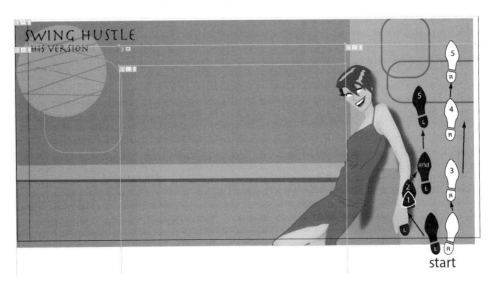

Figure 8.16
A slice holds the place of a navigation bar that will be added later.

2. Choose Object → Slice → Slice Options. In the Slice Type menu, select No Image. Set the Cell Alignment options to position the text within the cell. In the example shown, we chose Center and Middle to set the text in the horizontal and vertical center of the cell.

3. Make sure that the Text Is HTML option is activated and enter the link in the Text Displayed In Cell field. To create a link, at minimum use the code <a href="link_name.html"> *text you want in cell* </a>. If you want to save the file in a directory other than the one that contains the link, be sure to include the correct relative addressing.

4. The text you enter in the Text field will not appear on the page in Illustrator. You will see it only in the HTML generated by a Save For Web command. The Save For Web dialog box displays an alert icon to help remind you of this (see Figure 8.17). When you see that icon, consider previewing the page in the browser before you save it.

5. Keep in mind that you can paste large chunks of HTML into the Text field. Sometimes users paste columns of text containing links. You won't be able to preview the HTML until you see it in a browser, but you can do this in a pinch.

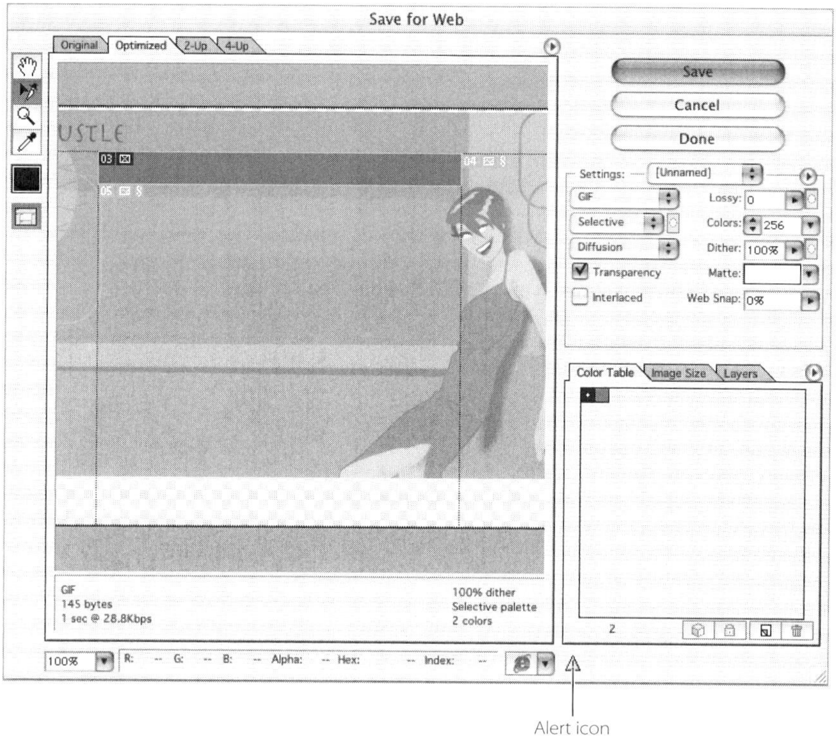

Figure 8.17
The alert icon indicates that the optimized preview is not what you'll see in the final output, in this case because of text in the no-image slices.

Alert icon

To create text-based links on the page:

1. Enter the text you're going to make into a link. To better anticipate the actual webpage, use a typeface and size congruent with basic HTML. By default, Illustrator uses the `<FONT>` tag (which is deprecated in HTML 4, meaning that its use is discouraged and that it won't be supported in future versions) when it converts type. It doesn't add the `FACE` attribute, but it does use `SIZE` and `COLOR`. Since style sheets aren't created automatically, you'll have to guess at sizing type. Consult the following chart for a starting point:

HTML Character Size	Point Size in Internet Explorer 5	Point Size in Netscape 4.7
7	48 pt	36 pt
6	32	24
5	24	18
4	18	15
3	16	13
2	13	10
1	10	10 tracking -75

Of the two models, Illustrator follows the Netscape version more closely. That is, 18-point type becomes size 5 characters and not size 4.

2. Select the text on the page and choose Object → Slice → Make. This command creates a dynamic slice from the text, updating it as the text is changed.

3. Choose Object → Slice → Slice Options. In the Slice Options dialog box, choose No Image. The HTML for the text will populate the Text field. The Text Is HTML option should be activated by default; do not deactivate it. After the first `<FONT>` tag, insert `<a href="link_name.html">`. Then after the text in the cell and before the closing `<FONT>` tag, add the `</a>` tag.

4. Choose File → Save For Web. Set the optimization options as you would normally. Be sure to choose Save HTML And Images in the Save Optimized As dialog box. Next, check the HTML produced closely in as many platform/browser combinations as you can. Remember that you are looking for type reflow. Text may be resized, but the slice size remains static.

Building a Common Layout

In this section, we'll use the templates created in Chapter 5, "Preparing the Work Environment," to a build basic page design. The directions in this section are intended to show a common model for using the tools; you should adjust the instructions for your own needs and environments. Follow along with these examples by downloading the template files from www.sybex.com. On the Sybex site, navigate to the page for this book and click the Download link.

Building L Pattern Pages

What you're doing: Creating a webpage design with a banner across the top and a navigation bar on the left side.

Why you're doing it: Because of flexible window sizes, the top and left sides of the page are typical places for important page elements.

In this section, you'll set up a basic webpage: a banner across the top and navigation along the left side. You'll also set up a body area and build a background image to account for longer pages. The end result will look like Figure 8.18.

The plan here is to set up a template page in Illustrator and then add the contents of the body section later. To do this, you'll need to account for the fact that the body section may be different sizes with different content. As discussed in Chapter 1, table cells expand to fit their content. You'll use this basic design for several pages in the site. If a page has too much data for the body section, it may pull apart the page, resulting in a mess.

The easiest way to address this design completely within Illustrator is to use CSS layers. You'll isolate the banner and navigation bar sections on one layer and the body section on another:

1. Start by creating a new document in the RGB color mode, 760 × 420 pixels. This is the usable area of an 800 × 600 display. Later, you'll create a second document to produce the background graphic.

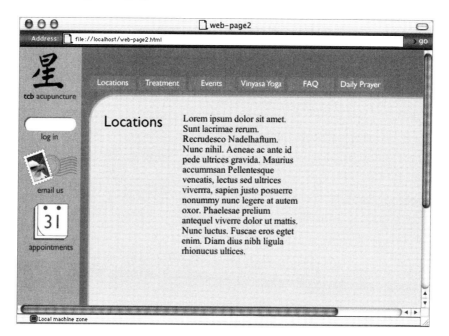

Figure 8.18
A basic L pattern webpage

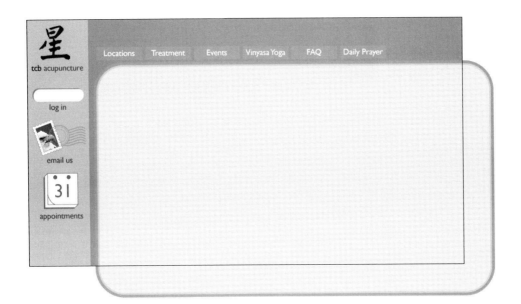

Figure 8.19
Adding the basic page elements

2. Position the company logo in the upper-left corner and add the rounded rectangles, buttons, and icons, as shown in Figure 8.19. Note that shapes drape over the edge of the Artboard. This is fine because you will clip to the Artboard on output. Make sure the elements are located where you want them.

3. Add a layer for the body section. For this example, add a simple text headline for the page content. To keep things straight, name the layer **Body**.

4. You're ready to slice the document. Because you intend to output CSS layers, you can't isolate slices on a separate layer. Each layer must contain its own slices. Start by clicking on Layer 1 to activate it. Using the Slice tool, draw a large rectangle over the left section of the page. Next, choose Object → Slice → Divide to break the slice into sections, as shown in Figure 8.20.

5. Using the Slice Select tool, select and adjust the slice positions to capture graphics completely. You're doing this so that you can add links to the objects and because you may want to use these icons in a different context later. Remember as you adjust the slice positions that the divided slices will be stacked top to bottom from left to right.

6. Set the slice options for each of the banner slices individually. You'll want to name the slices based on their contents and add links. In this example, you aren't concerned about the large hit areas the links will have. If that were a concern, you could have used image maps to limit the clickable areas.

Figure 8.20
The left section divided

7. Next, select the navigation buttons on the left. In this instance, the rectangles in the buttons and the text are all grouped together. You could have chosen to select just the outer rectangles to create a slice, but turning the group into an object slice will be useful later if you need to reuse the button set. Next, choose Object → Slice → Make. As before, you should adjust the name and link options for each slice.

8. The basic framework is set. Now highlight the body layer, and using the Slice tool, draw a rectangle over the section you want to use as the body. Select the headline text and convert it to a slice. In this example, the text is to the side and doesn't affect the previous slice. Using the Slice Select tool, highlight the first slice you created on this layer and convert it to a no-image slice. The results should look like Figure 8.21. At this point, save the document.

9. Chose File → Save For Web. In the Image Size section, select the Clip To Artboard option. In the Layers section, enable Export As CSS Layers. Leave the other options in that section at the default settings. As you optimize the various slices, you will have access to only the slices on a given layer at a time. Use the Layer menu in the Layers section of the dialog box to specify the active group. You could attach the background image at this point by opening the Output Options section and entering the name of the file you're going to create. In this case, though, you will adjust the HTML anyway, so let's add it manually in Step 11. Be sure to export both HTML and images.

Figure 8.21

Slicing the body layer. Note the no-image slice.

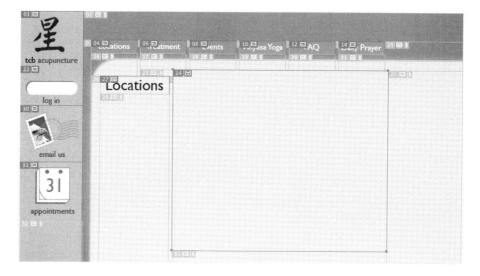

10. To create the background image for this file, create a new document. Make the file RGB, 1000 pixels long and 1 pixel tall. In the original document, select and copy the large rear rectangle and rounded rectangles on Layer 1. Return to the new background document and Choose Edit → Paste In Front. Resize the rear rectangle so that it extends the length of the Artboard. Be careful not to reposition the rounded rectangles. Choose File → Save For Web. In the Image Size section of that dialog box, select the Clip To Artboard option and save the file.

11. You must adjust the HTML file to add the background image and to set the margins for the document to 0. If you don't reset the margins, the background image may peek out at the top left of the image and create an awkward look. Making these changes in Dreamweaver or GoLive is straightforward, but if you don't have these applications, open the HTML file in a text editor and add the bolded text shown here. Note that we are also saving the background file (bg.gif) in the images folder of the directory the HTML file resides in:

```
<BODY BGCOLOR=#FFFFFF LEFTMARGIN="0" TOPMARGIN="0"
  MARGINWIDTH="0" MARGINHEIGHT="0"
  BACKGROUND="images/bg.gif">
```

CHAPTER 9

Creating Animations

Illustrator is not an animation program. It has only limited tools for creating animations and is typically not the final source of any web animation.

Animation can be in the form of Shock Wave Flash (SWF), GIF, or Scalable Vector Graphics (SVG) files. Illustrator can produce animation directly in the SWF format only. For all other kinds of animation and rollovers, Illustrator can set up the objects or rollover states, but you must complete the animation in another application.

In this chapter, we'll look at the mechanics of preparing animations and handing files off for completion elsewhere. This chapter covers the following topics:

Creating stop-frame animation

Creating fade-in animations

Creating 3D animation

Creating 360° rotation

Creating guided movement

Creating art brush animation

Converting layers to frames in ImageReady

Creating banner ad animation in ImageReady

Pasting to Flash symbols

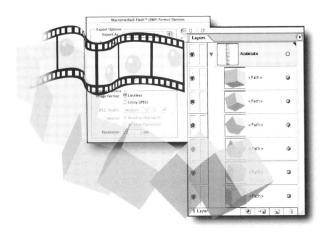

Creating Simple Animation in Illustrator

The only kind of animation that Illustrator can generate on its own is a sequential SWF. Each frame of the animation must follow the previous one in a linear fashion. There are no timing controls. You cannot define how long individual frames are displayed, and you must create each frame of the animation as a separate layer. This process lends itself to only the crudest, most straightforward animations. Examples include the basic motion and fade animations common to banner ads.

Even with these, you will quickly reach the limits of what Illustrator can do. Even basic changes typically require you to rebuild the complete animation, and establishing recurring elements can be tedious.

You must consider three things when setting out to create an SWF from Illustrator:

- The relationship of layer content to frames
- The size of the file you create
- The translation of some features to the SWF format

The basic metaphor in Illustrator for animation is that each layer, including nested layers, is a frame in a cell animation. The lowest layer in the palette is the first frame of the movie.

Frames play back at a fixed rate, which you set when you export to SWF. The default is 12 frames per second (fps). This is the default in Flash as well. It provides smooth motion but can be cumbersome in Illustrator. A two-second animation would require you to produce 24 layers. By using as few as 6 fps, you can reduce the size of your file, making it load faster, and still provide acceptable animation for banner ads.

Since the contents of each frame are determined by the contents of layers, anything that you want to appear in all the frames has to be on each layer. This means that if you want a background color besides white, you need to build a box for the background and make sure that the box is on every layer. (In Figure 9.1, we've created a background image but placed it only on layer 1, so it doesn't appear in subsequent frames.) Placing an object on each frame's layer can lead to a glut of objects, causing your file size to balloon. You can mitigate this by using symbols for recurring elements.

Figure 9.1

The contents of the Layers palette and the resulting animation frames. Because the backdrop is not repeated on every layer, it shows up only in the first frame.

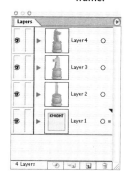

Other features are not understood and will either be discarded or converted to raster art, causing the file size to bloat. You can work around some of the limitations, but you should be aware of this as you're creating the art.

Features that do not translate include:

Blending modes SWF files can understand transparency, but not these advanced attributes. If you want to use these features, consider selecting all of the affected objects and choosing Object → Flatten Transparency before converting to a symbol. Soft-edged transparency effects, such as the blurs and feathers often used with opacity masks, result in raster art upon export.

Beveled and square caps and joins SWF recognizes only rounded caps and joins; all others are converted.

Many text features Illustrator simulates text rotation, kerning, leading, and tracking by breaking text into portions. The underline and strikethrough options are discarded outright, and glyph scaling causes type to disappear intermittently. The best option for complete text fidelity is to convert text to outlines.

Features that are rasterized include the following:

- Gradient meshes
- Gradients with more than eight gradient sliders
- Pattern fills
- Soft-edged effects, including opacity masks

Try to avoid using these features in your work if you can. It will make the process of creating SWFs simpler and more predictable. Additionally, use some care when using the Symbol Stainer and Symbol Styler tools. These tools increase the size of the SWF by creating additional symbols. Changing the opacity of a symbol instance adjusts the Alpha value of the symbol in Flash; it doesn't create additional symbols.

Creating Stop-Frame Animation

What you're doing: *Creating a basic SWF animation from Illustrator step by step, in this example a wipe reveal.*

Why you're doing it: *The goal is to create animations without using additional applications.*

One way to set up SWF animation from Illustrator is to create a model that follows traditional stop-motion techniques. In this very manual process, you'll duplicate and adjust

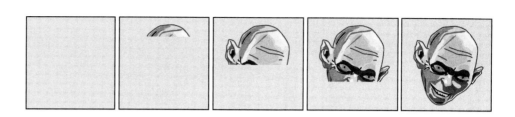

Figure 9.2
The frames in a wipe-reveal animation

the contents of a series of layers. This strategy is useful in animations that require exact attention to each frame or when automated techniques aren't possible. In the following sections, we provide details for using effects and blends to create layers automatically. First, let's walk through the steps for a wipe reveal, as shown in Figure 9.2. The contents of the banner ad will be exposed top to bottom using a basic mask technique.

1. Determine the geographic size the SWF will occupy. As with most web graphics, it's easiest to prepare the Artboard to match the size of the graphic and clip to it. Create a new RGB mode document and set the Artboard size to the size of the final animation.

2. Prepare the art that will be used in the animation. In most cases, it will be easiest to set up all the elements that will be used first and then animate them. SWF files will have a white background unless you create additional elements.

3. As you complete elements for the animation, convert them to symbols. Do this by selecting the art and clicking the New Symbol button in the Symbols palette, as shown in Figure 9.3.

4. After creating a symbol from the art, you need to replace the original items with symbol instances. In this case, the entire contents of the ad will stay in place while a clipping mask is animated to reveal the art. So after creating the symbol, delete the original image from the page. Then drag its symbol out of the Symbols palette and into position. This step may seem redundant, but it reduces file size overall.

5. Using the Rectangle tool , draw a thin rectangle over the top of the image, as shown in Figure 9.4. Select the rectangle and the symbol on the page and choose Object → Clipping Mask → Make. Use the Direct Selection tool to select the symbol instance and choose Object → Lock → Selection.

Figure 9.3
Creating a new symbol

6. Leave the clipping mask rectangle selected and choose Duplicate Layer from the Layers palette menu. This will create a second layer over the previous one with the new, duplicate clipping mask selected. Resize the mask to reveal more of the underlying symbol. Repeat this process of duplicating and adjusting the mask until the image is completely revealed. Keep in mind that each layer will be a frame and that you'll export this art at around 8 fps.

7. Choose File → Export and select the SWF format. In the SWF Options dialog box, choose the AI Layers To SWF Frames option. Set the rate to 8 fps. Don't check Looping; activate the Clip To Artboard Size option. Click OK to create a single-run SWF that reveals the contents of the ad as it loads.

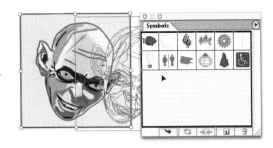

Figure 9.4

A thin rectangle is used to mask the contents of the layer.

Motion and Opacity Animation

What you're doing: Creating frames for an animation automatically, using blends. Why you're doing it: You can quickly create the in between states of objects for animation.

Illustrator's blends are often used to set up frames for sequential animations. When combined with transparency, effects, and brushes, blends can quickly generate a series of object adjustments that are difficult to achieve in other applications. Figure 9.5 shows sequential blends that are ready to be converted to animation frames.

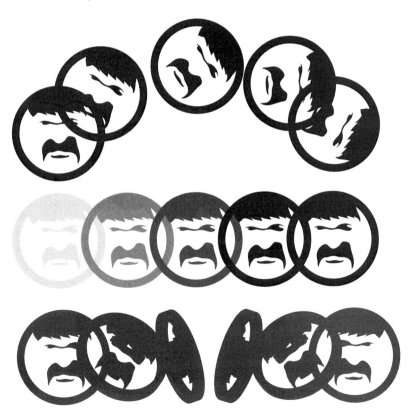

Figure 9.5

Blends used to create motion, opacity, and 3D animation

The process you'll use here will be the same whether you intend to export the file as a SWF or create an animated GIF in ImageReady. In both cases, you'll set up at least two instances of objects and create a blend between them. From there, you'll expand the blend, ungroup the results, and send each object to its own layer. This second half of the process is much less flexible than the first. If the results aren't what you wanted, it's usually easiest to undo the last four steps of the process and rebuild from the blend. Additionally, the process of sending objects to independent layers doesn't account for things like background art that isn't animated. You'll need to manually adjust the frames to add other items. Further, keep in mind that blends may not automatically give you what you want. You may have to manually go in and adjust each frame instance to create the effect you want, particularly if you have specific goals in mind.

Creating a Fade-In Animation

Fade-in animations reveal art by increasing opacity sequentially. The result is the sort of reveal that is used commonly in movies and commercials. Follow these steps:

1. Create a new RGB document. Be sure to set the Artboard to the size of the final graphic.

2. Create the art that you want to blend. If there is incidental art such as backgrounds, create that as well. In this example, we'll have a logo fade in over a custom background, as shown in Figure 9.6.

3. Select the logo and click the New Symbol button in the Symbols palette. Delete the art on the page and drag the newly created symbol back out onto the page. This step seems redundant, but it helps reduce file size in the animation. Repeat the process for the background art. Choose Object → Arrange → Send To Back to move the background art behind the logo.

4. Position the logo instance on the page where you want the animation to start. This is the position the art will begin to appear. Drag a second instance of the symbol onto the stage and position it where you want the logo to end up.

Figure 9.6

The frames of an animation for a typical fade

5. Select both instances of the symbol (but not the background) and choose Object → Blend → Make. A series of intermediate objects should appear between the two, as in Figure 9.7. Illustrator creates the number of intermediate objects by default. Later we'll choose an amount based on the timing of the animation. At this point, the starting, ending, and blend images all look the same, because we haven't adjusted the transparency yet.

6. Use the Direct Selection tool to highlight only the first instance of the symbol, the one where the blend starts. In the Transparency palette, set the Opacity to 0%. You can make additional edits as well, such as scaling the starting logo down slightly or adjusting its position.

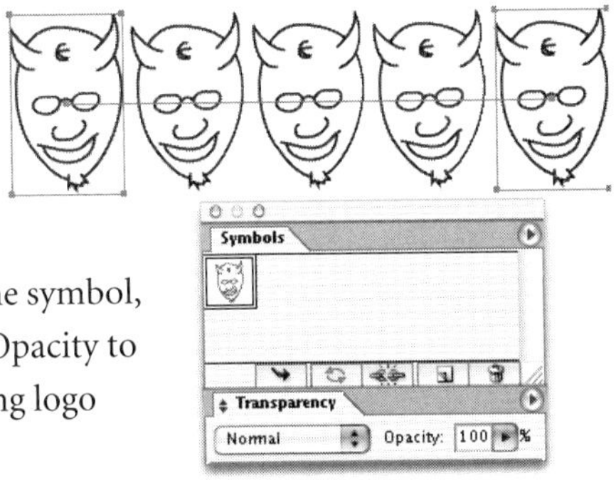

7. To set the number of intermediate objects in the blend, leave the instance selected and choose Object → Blend → Blend Options. (You can also double-click on the Blend tool to open this dialog box.) Set the blend options to Specified Steps and choose the number of frames you want to create. The steps indicate the number of objects in between the two original items, so consider those objects as you determine how many frames to create.

8. By default, the blend will take place in a straight line between the two instances. The shape of the blend is called its *spine*. The easiest way to adjust the blend direction is to replace the spine with another path. To do this, first create another path. It can be open or closed, but it's typically an open path created by the Pen tool. Be aware that intermediate objects in a blend are pushed away from direction points on a spine. If you want to create an even progression, make sure that both ends of the spine have curve handles, as shown in Figure 9.8. After creating the new path, select it and the blend (and nothing else) and choose Object → Blend → Replace Spine.

9. Be sure the blend and the intermediate objects are as you want them and save your file. The next few steps are less flexible and you may want to revert the file (File → Revert) after exporting the animation. This strategy establishes a version of the file you can fall back on if you want different iterations of the animation or you want to use the file differently later. Select the blend and choose Object → Blend → Expand. This command will create real objects out of the blend shapes and group them together.

Figure 9.7
Two versions of the logo blended. Adjusting either instance will automatically update the blend.

Figure 9.8
A custom spine for a blend. Note that the steps in the blend are affected by the position of curve handles.

10. Leave the former blend selected and choose Object → Ungroup. This command enables you to distribute the objects to different layers.

11. Next we'll distribute the items onto their own layers so that they can be exported as frames. There are two ways this can work. Illustrator can send each object on a layer to its own layer independently, or it can send objects along with all of the other objects in the layer progressively. The first model is called Release To Layers (Sequence), and the second is Release To Layers (Build). The build option is intended for cases in which you want to progressively add items to an animation, such as letters in a word. The sequence model is intended for motion animations, like our current example. Figure 9.9 illustrates the difference.

The wrinkle arises when you want additional items in the frame of a sequence animation, such as the background objects shown in Figure 9.9. When you use the sequence model, the background art becomes its own frame rather than part of each frame. The simplest thing to do is to release to layers using the build model and then delete the extra blend instances on each layer. You could avoid this step by grouping the items to the background before blending, but that approach makes it much harder to position and adjust elements in the blend.

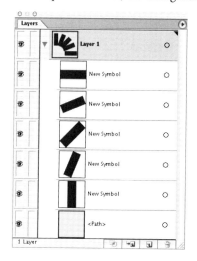

Figure 9.9

A Layers palette and the resulting frames of a sequence and build animation

12. After distributing to layers and adjusting as needed, you can export to SWF. In the SWF Options dialog box, choose the AI Layers To SWF Frames option. Set the rate to 8 fps. Typically, this kind of animation doesn't loop. Be sure to activate the Clip To Artboard Size option. Then, click OK to create a single-run SWF that resolves the logo as it loads.

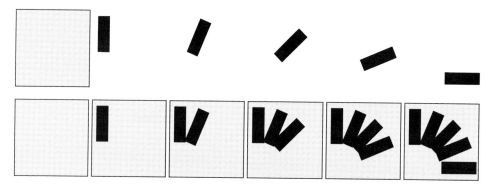

Creating 3D Animation

In this example, you'll use the three-dimensional (3D) effect and blends to create animation frames. The 3D effect is new to Illustrator CS. You use it to extrude and bevel basic objects to create the appearance of 3D art. Art isn't truly 3D, but by adjusting the settings of the effect applied to objects, you can spin and rotate an object completely, creating different views of the art. You can apply symbols to the facets of the extruded object to supply certain details, such as product information. For example, to create a 3D box, you would first extrude a basic rectangle. You save the surface details of the box as a symbol and then apply that symbol to one of the box faces. The surface details are distorted automatically to match the box. To set up 3D animation:

1. Create a new RGB document. Be sure to set the Artboard to the size of the final graphic. For this example, make it 400 × 100 pixels.

2. Create the art that you want to blend. Let's simplify this document by creating only the objects we intend to rotate. As shown in Figure 9.10, our goal is to extrude a flat logo and then flip it along the length of a banner ad.

3. If the art has negative space that you want extruded correctly, make sure that it's transparent and not white. You can check this quickly by choosing View → Show Grid. If you have white areas you want to knock out, consider using the Subtract From Shape Area command in the Pathfinder palette.

4. The 3D effect works best with simple, colored shapes. If your logo relies on strokes and gradients or has stroke design elements that are not related to its shape, first convert the logo to a symbol. Then, remove any strokes and non-shape elements from your logo. Illustrator reapplies the appearance of the logo, now saved as a symbol, to the 3D object after the basic shape is extruded. See Figure 9.11.

Figure 9.10

The frames for a 3D animation

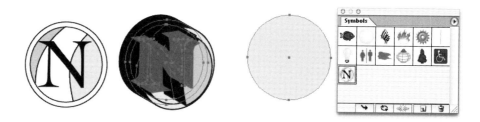

Figure 9.11

The design elements cause problems for the 3D effect. Convert the logo to a symbol, and then remove everything but the core elements from the logo.

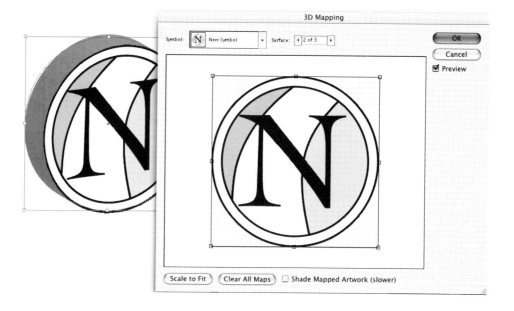

5. Select the logo and choose Effect → 3D → Extrude & Bevel. This opens the 3D Extrude & Bevel dialog box. Set the Rotate options as desired to specify the starting position of the logo. For this example, we want the logo to flip up and over, so start with x: −150°, y: 30°, z: 15°, as shown in Figure 9.12. The other options are a matter of preference. For this example, set a 10-pixel extrude depth with no bevel. Choose a diffuse shading and leave the lighting options at the default settings.

6. In the 3D Extrude & Bevel dialog box, Map Symbol. This is where you'll bring back the details in the logo face. In the 3D Mapping dialog box, cycle through the surface fields to find the front of the extruded object. The face will be highlighted in red in the document and displayed in the main panel of the dialog box (see Figure 9.13). Select the symbol you created in step 4; it should fit perfectly. Activate the Preview option to be sure that you have the correct face.

7. Accept the settings in the 3D Mapping and 3D Options dialog boxes to get back to the document. Select the extruded logo with the Selection tool and Option/Alt+drag it to the far side of the document. With the new copy still selected, open the Appearance palette. Locate the 3D Extrude and Bevel (Mapped) effect and double-click on it. This will open the Extrude & Bevel dialog box dialog box, where you can reset the view of the object. For this example, use the Off-Axis Front preset angles and leave the Effect and Surface options at the same settings.

8. Select both versions of the art and choose Object → Blend → Make. Intermediate objects should emerge between the two and appear to be twisting in space. Leave the objects selected and double-click the Blend tool to set the options for the blend. Click Specified Steps and dial in the number of additional frames you want to generate.

9. Adjust the blend by changing the position or options of the base objects. To create a curving blend, you can also replace the spine as described earlier. Once you're satisfied with the blend, save the document; you may need to revert it (File → Revert) later.

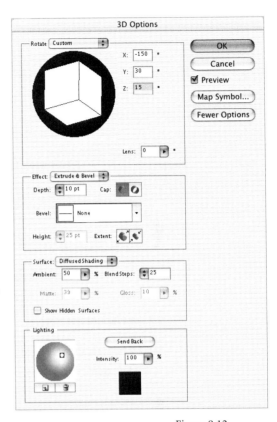

Figure 9.12

The 3D options used to create the first frame of the animation

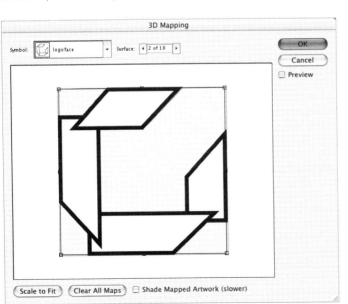

Figure 9.13

Mapping the logo back onto the surface of the extruded object

10. With the blend selected, choose Object → Blend → Expand to create paths from the intermediate objects. Choose Object → Ungroup to make the objects independent from each other.

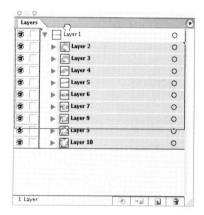

Figure 9.14
Dragging sublayers out of the current layer

11. Make sure the layer on which the objects reside is highlighted and choose Release To Layers (Sequence) from the Layers palette menu. This command creates new sublayers from each object. In some complex documents, SWF files fail to recognize sublayers. To ensure that this doesn't happen, highlight all of the sublayers in the palette and drag them out of their current layer so that they are independent layers, as seen in Figure 9.14.

12. Choose File → Export to generate a SWF from the file. Or, export as a Photoshop document to generate an animated GIF.

Creating Seamless 360° Rotation Loops

Many people use blends to create 3D loop animations in order to make a logo or button spin. One typical technique uses a loop animation as an over state for a button. The button spins in three dimensions when the user mouses over it.

You can use Illustrator to set this up, but one of the limitations of using blends is that you can't automatically specify the direction of rotation for intermediate shapes. For example, in Figure 9.15, the blend objects go from the front of the object (x: 0°, y: 0°, z: 0°) to the back (x: 0°, y: 180°, z: 0°). While the middle intermediate object is at a correct setting (x: 0°, y: 90°, z: 0°), the other blend objects are rotated in y and z as well.

Nonetheless, you can still use blends to prepare the frames and then adjust accordingly. In the example that follows, you'll blend the objects over a distance so that you can see the frames clearly and adjust their settings. Next, you'll reposition the blend items and create the animation. For this example, you'll spin a button forward 360°, as shown in Figure 9.16. Because of the complexity of the vector shapes used, this kind of file is usually smaller when optimized as an animated GIF rather than a SWF.

1. Create a new RGB document. Be sure to set the Artboard to the size of the final graphic (for this example, make it 50 × 50 pixels).

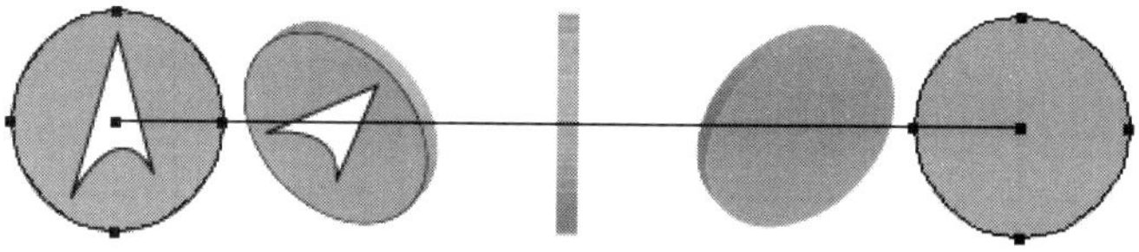

Figure 9.15
A front-to-back 3D effect blend incorrectly rotates in x and z as well as the intended y.

2. Create the art that you want to blend. Refer to the section "Creating 3D Animation" for instructions for setting up negative space, basic shapes, and symbol maps.

3. Once you have the art as you want it, drag it to the far left side of the document so that you have plenty of room to see what you're doing. Choose Effect → 3D → Extrude & Bevel. For this example, use the Front preset angles, a 10-point extrude, and diffuse lighting. The button should look like it does in its up state.

4. Option/Alt+Shift+drag a copy of the button halfway across the document. (Adding the Shift key keeps the objects aligned, making it easier to adjust them later.) Double-click the 3D effect for the copied object in the Appearance palette. Set the Rotate menu to Back.

5. Option/Alt+Shift+drag a copy of the second button the rest of the way across the document. Double-click the 3D effect for this third object in the Appearance palette and set the Rotate menu to Front.

6. Select all three versions and choose Object → Blend → Make. The document should look like Figure 9.17. Set the number of intermediate objects in the blend by choosing Object → Blend → Blend Options. Click Specified Steps and set the count to 3. This will create six total objects. When added to the three that already exist, this makes a nine-frame animation. Since the animation loops, you'll use the first frame as the last; this means you'll need to remove the last frame to end up with eight frames. If you're doing work that requires finer animation, consider adding more steps to the blend.

7. Choose Object → Blend → Expand. This command creates actual objects from the blend and enables you to adjust the incorrect angles of the intermediate objects. Choose Object → Ungroup. Do this so that later you can reposition the objects and release them to layers easily.

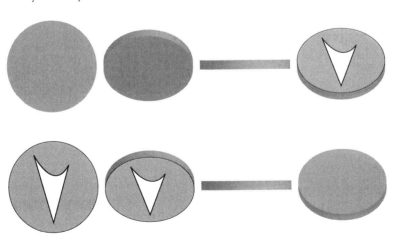

Figure 9.16

The frames for a 3D animation

8. Select the second object in the sequence and double-click the 3D effect in the Appearance palette to reset its rotation. In our example, the logo spins forward, so set the angles to x: –45°, y: 0°, z: 0°. In this example, all of the objects have y and z rotation of 0°. Select and set the remaining objects' x rotation in increments of 45°, as shown in Figure 9.18.

9. Delete the last object in the sequence so that you have eight objects. Since the animation loops, the final frame will become the first, creating a smooth transition. If you leave this object in the document, the animation will stall slightly at the first frame.

10. Select all of the objects and align them. If you used the Shift key in step 4, all you need to do is click Horizontally Align Centers in the Align palette. Position the objects in the Artboard so that they output in the correct location.

11. Choose Release To Layers (Sequence) from the Layers palette menu. Because nested layers sometimes cause problems, Shift+select all the layers and drag them out of their current layer to make them independent layers.

12. Export the file to SWF or to PSD to make it an animated GIF in ImageReady. If you choose SWF, be sure to set the AI Layers To SWF Frames options, set the rate to 8 fps, and enable the Looping option. if you choose PSD, set the color model to RGB, set the resolution to 72 ppi, and activate the Anti-Alias and Layers options.

Figure 9.17

The blend that will be used to create 3D rotation

Figure 9.18

The degrees of x rotation applied to each object in the sequence.

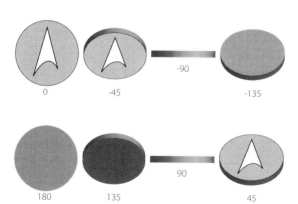

Creating 2D Rotation Animation

Frequently, animation calls for objects to spin or rotate in two dimensions. A wrinkle arises, though, when you're using blends to create intermediate frames for rotation animation. For example, suppose you want a clock hand to turn 90°. If you set up two versions of the arm and blend them, as shown in Figure 9.19, the result is a blend of shapes, not a rotation of the arm. These results can be handy for morphing one object into another, but not for the kind of sequential art we want to make.

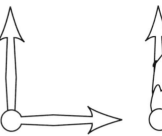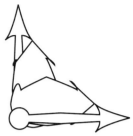

Figure 9.19

Blending two rotated versions of the art does not result in rotated intermediate objects.

The way around this is to use symbols. When you're blending between symbols, Illustrator retains the basic shape of the items and blends based on position and rotation. To blend between symbol instances:

1. Create the art that you wish to blend. In this example, use the hand of a clock.
2. With the art selected, click the New Symbol button at the base of the Symbols palette. Once you've done this, delete the art on the page.
3. Drag the symbol you've created out of the Symbols palette and onto the page. Position it where the original non-symbol version of the art was.
4. To create a rotated version of the symbol, Option/Alt+click the center of the bottom of the symbol with the Rotate tool, as shown in Figure 9.20. This sets the position of rotation about the bottom center and opens the Rotate dialog box.
5. Set the angle of rotation to –90° and click the Copy button. Illustrator creates a second symbol at the 3 o'clock position. Select both objects and choose Object → Blend → Make. Illustrator creates the blend with the object shapes intact. From here, you can expand the blend and release to layers to create animation frames.

Figure 9.20

Positioning the Rotate tool to set the point of transformation

Creating Guided Movement Animation

In stop-frame animation, you move each object manually to create an animation. In this section, you'll automatically create a series of objects using a scatter brush. This will set up a series of shapes oriented in the direction of the path. That way, you can quickly set up complex object sequences that you can then expand and release to layers. This technique works best when objects aren't moving in simple straight lines, like the cursor shown in Figure 9.21.

To create guided movement animation:

1. Create the art that will be animated. For best results, build the art the size you expect to use it in the animation and create it oriented in the direction you want it to move. For this example, choose an overhead view of a car. You want it to move left to right, so create it headed in that direction. With the art selected, click the New Brush button in the base of the Brushes palette.

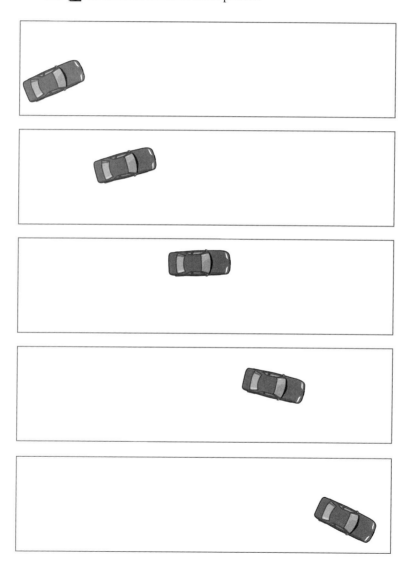

Figure 9.21

The frames for a guided movement animation

2. In the New Brush dialog box, choose Scatter Brush. For the time being, set the Rotation Relative option to Path and leave the other options at their defaults.

3. Create the path that the animation should follow. For this example, create a loose line with the Pencil tool across the length of a 400 × 100-pixel banner ad. With the path selected, click the new scatter brush you've created. The results should be similar to those shown in Figure 9.22.

4. Inspect the results of the brush on the line. To adjust the size and spacing of the objects, double-click the brush in the palette. Adjust the Size and Spacing options to create the size and number of objects in the path.

5. After adjusting the brush options, choose Object → Expand Appearance. This command creates objects that can be released to layers. Choose Object → Ungroup and then select Release To Layers (Sequence) from the Layers palette menu. The original path you applied the stroke to will be the bottom layer in the stack. Delete this layer by dragging it into the trash icon at the bottom of the Layers palette.

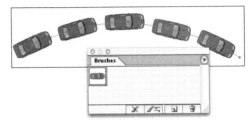

Figure 9.22

A path with a scatter brush applied to it becomes the basis for a motion animation.

6. Select all of the layers and drag them out of their current layer to make them independent layers. They will be in the reverse order for the animation, so Shift+select all of the layers and choose Reverse Order from the Layers palette menu.

7. The file should be ready to export as a SWF or a PSD to be finished in ImageReady.

Distorted Object Animation

In this example, you'll use an art brush to create iterations of an object for animation frames rather than redrawing it each time. This is useful in cases where objects are bending or twisting and you don't want to create the art from scratch each time. In the example in Figure 9.23, a leg is animated in the process of kicking. Rather than drawing each position of the leg separately, you'll convert the leg object to a brush and then duplicate and adjust it to produce each position. After the art is complete, you export the file either as a SWF or a PSD for animating in ImageReady. Keep in mind that if you intend to

Figure 9.23

The frames for a brush stroke animation. Here, the kicking leg is a series of open paths with brush strokes.

animate the art as a SWF, you'll need to include the non-animated elements (in this case the body and rear leg) in every frame.

1. Set up the art to be animated. In this example, the body of the girl is set on one layer and the back leg is on another. A third layer is sandwiched in between for the kicking leg. On this layer, create the art that you want to animate straight up and down. Try to create the art the size you intend to use it on the Web. Don't start by creating one of the action poses; it will be harder to adjust as a brush, as shown in Figure 9.24.

2. Select the art to be animated and click the New Brush button at the base of the Brushes palette. Choose New Art Brush in the New Brush dialog box. In the Art Brush Options dialog box that results, the most important setting is Stroke Direction. You want to set the arrow to follow the direction the art flows in. For our leg example, the Stroke From Top to Bottom is correct, because it approximates the direction the leg will be drawn. Keep this direction in mind as you create the strokes that will use the brushes. Start at the top of the leg and draw toward the foot.

Figure 9.24

Creating the art to be animated. Note that the art is on its own layer and not yet bent or posed.

3. Using the Pen tool , create a path that describes the shape you want to animate. In our example, the path should have three anchor points: one at each end and a knee in the middle (see Figure 9.25). For best results, make smooth points with direction handles instead of sharp corners. For this example, use the Pen tool instead of the Brush tool because you want to control the position of each anchor point. After positioning the path, leave it selected and click the new art brush you created in Step 2 to apply it to the path.

4. Duplicate the layer the kicking leg is on. Option/Alt+click the newly created layer's lock icon. This leaves only the new layer unlocked, which makes it easier to select the new frame of the animation. Using the Direct Selection tool, reposition the brushed path to create the next step in the movement. As you do, keep in mind that the position of direction points affects the shape of the brush as well. In our example, curving the lower segment slightly helps arch the toe.

Figure 9.25

The curved path has an anchor point at the knee to facilitate animating the kicking motion. This is easier to create with the Pen than the Brush.

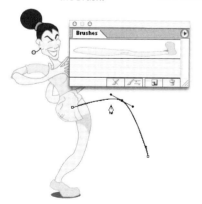

5. Repeat step 4 to create additional versions of the animated sequence, as shown in Figure 9.26. In our example, you need to adjust the thigh point as the leg is raised to create the correct appearance of motion. You could try to use a blend to create the intermediate brush shapes, but the results tend to call for so much editing that it's easier to duplicate and adjust.

6. Choose File → Export to create the animation. In this example, the presence of other objects lends itself to animating in another application, rather than directly as a SWF. The additional objects are easy to handle in Flash or ImageReady, but they are cumbersome to manipulate directly in Illustrator. Export to the Photoshop format to continue working with the art in ImageReady or to SWF to continue working in Flash. When exporting to Flash, most people use the Layers To Frames option and then pull the file apart in Flash to create the symbols they need.

Export for Animation

We've noted that Illustrator is better at producing frames for animation than generating the actual animation itself. In this section, we'll look at exporting to ImageReady and Flash and animating in ImageReady. Space prohibits a discussion of animating in Flash. For information on using Flash, check out *Flash MX Savvy*, by Ethan Watrall and Norbert Herber (Sybex, 2002). Also note that Adobe's solid LiveMotion application produces SWF files as well. Further, it can accept a native Illustrator file without enduring the export process. LiveMotion suffers from poor market share, though, making it a marginal player in the SWF creation game.

ImageReady is included free with Photoshop. Many users, however, are unaware of its existence. The application is well integrated with Photoshop, enabling you to shuttle an open image directly between the two applications and even back to Illustrator. GoLive users will also enjoy that rollovers generated in ImageReady are included when native PSD files are placed in GoLive as SmartObjects. In this next section, we'll convert an Illustrator file to animated GIF in ImageReady.

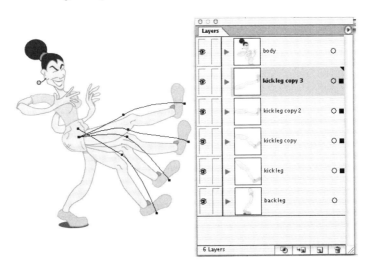

Figure 9.26

Additional layers used to develop the kicking motion

Converting Layers to Frames in ImageReady

What you're doing: Exporting to the PSD format and converting layers to animation frames in ImageReady.
Why you're doing it: Illustrator has no tools for creating animated GIFs.

In this section, we'll break out the basic process for converting Illustrator files into animated GIFs. This section assumes you've created layered Illustrator files such as those described in the previous sections. As you prepare those files, keep in mind that ImageReady can generate intermediate frames, like those produced by Illustrator blends for the position, layer effects, and the opacity of layers. This means that if all you want to do is move text from one side of the screen to another or fade it in, and you intend to finish the file in ImageReady, there's no sense in creating frames for the movement in Illustrator.

Layer effects are similar to effects in Illustrator, but they can be applied only to layers and not to individual objects. Effects that you apply to a layer in Illustrator do not translate to layer effects in ImageReady. The appearance of the objects will be unchanged, but they will not convert to editable items in ImageReady. Once again, this means that if you intend to animate effects, such as a pulsing outer glow, you may find it easier to apply the effects in ImageReady rather than creating multiple layers in Illustrator.

Transparency applied to layers is translated upon export. That is, if you target a layer and reduce its opacity or apply a blend mode, the resulting PSD will contain those settings as well, enabling you to adjust them in ImageReady. Transparency applied to objects is retained but isn't editable in the exported file. This means that if transparency is something you want to adjust (as when you're creating a fade animation), you'll want to apply it to the layer in Illustrator and not to the objects. To set the transparency of a layer, click the circle to the right of its name in the Layers palette to target the layer, and then adjust the opacity in the Transparency palette. To convert an Illustrator file to an animated GIF in ImageReady:

1. In Illustrator, confirm that the file is correct and as you want it. Make sure your layers are organized correctly. Inspect the art at 100% size. This will be the size of the web graphic you create. You cannot clip to the Artboard when exporting. The only way to alter the size of the export is to include crop marks. Do this by using the Rectangle tool to draw a box around the area you wish to export. With the rectangle selected, choose Object → Crop Marks → Make.

2. Choose File → Export. In the resulting Export dialog box, choose the Photoshop (psd) option and give the file a name and place to live. In the Photoshop Options dialog box, choose Color Model: RGB, Resolution: Screen (72 ppi). In the Options section, be sure to select the Anti-Alias and Write Layers options.

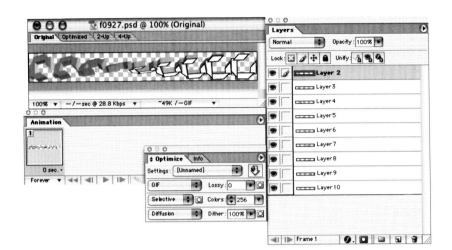

Figure 9.27
Setting up to animate a file in ImageReady

3. Launch ImageReady and open the file you created by choosing File → Open. On most systems, PSD files are associated with Photoshop, so double-clicking the file you export will likely not open it in ImageReady.

4. In ImageReady, open the Layers and Animation palettes, as shown in Figure 9.27. Both palettes are available from the Window menu.

5. Each frame in the Animation palette records the visibility options, effects, and position of layers. Each frame in the palette records these settings and the amount of time delay before the next frame is displayed. If your layers are set up correctly from Illustrator, creating the animation is a snap. Choose Make Frames From Layers from the Animation palette menu. From the bottom layer up, a frame is generated for each layer and the visibility of each layer is sequentially activated to match.

6. The first frame will be selected in the Animation palette. Shift+click the final frame to select them all. With all frames selected, click the Frame Delay Time menu to set the timing for all frames, as shown in Figure 9.28. Set to No Delay, short animations may play too quickly. The only way to really tell how long a file will load and play is to experiment with actual posted files. Animations played on a local computer often play much faster than posted versions. In many cases, a .1- or .2- second delay slows down animations enough for users to register them visually.

7. Set the Looping options as desired; typically, you'd choose either Once or Forever. The Forever option is used for looping animations, such as animated banner ads. Animations that play once are often logos and art used as eye candy when a page initially loads.

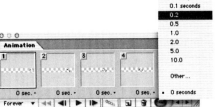

Figure 9.28
Setting the delay on a series of frames

8. In the Optimize palette, make certain the File Format option is set to GIF. Set the other options as you see fit (see Chapters 3 and 7 for details). Note that the file size at the bottom of the Optimized pane indicates the total size, including all frames of the animation. Choose File → Save Optimized to generate the animated GIF.

Creating Banner Ad Animation in ImageReady

What you're doing: *Exporting to the PSD format and manually adjusting layer visibility and timing to create banner ads.*

Why you're doing it: *Illustrator has no tools for creating animated GIFs.*

Figure 9.29

Frames in an animated banner ad

In cases where you haven't created all of the frames of an animation in Illustrator, you'll need to use ImageReady's tools to create animations. This process is common for the slide show style animation often used in text-oriented banner ads. In this section, you'll lay out the ad shown in Figure 9.29 in Illustrator and then animate the sequence in ImageReady. In the interest of completeness, we'll also show you how to use ImageReady's tweening capability. *Tweening* is the process of generating animation frames based on two existing ones. The generated frames represent a sequential blending of the frame content. Some users refer to this as "morphing." ImageReady can tween basic attributes such as layer position, opacity, and effects, but it cannot morph content, such as turning a pencil into a flower.

1. In Illustrator, confirm that the file is correct and as you want it. Typically, the rear object in the file will be a rectangle the size of the ad you're creating. For our example, you'll create a 125-pixel square ad. To be accurate, you'll create a 124-pixel square with a 1-pixel stroke. The remaining items will be separated onto individual layers, as shown in Figure 9.30.

2. Choose File → Export to create a Photoshop native file. Open the file from within ImageReady rather than by double-clicking on the newly created file.

3. Make sure that the Layers and Animation palettes are visible. If you have any plans to alter the contents of the file, now is the time to do so. It will be confusing to make changes after the file contains animation frames. These changes include applying any layer effects, or adding or repositioning layers. Click on the visibility icons of all the layers that will not be shown initially. This should create the appearance of the file as it first appears when it loads.

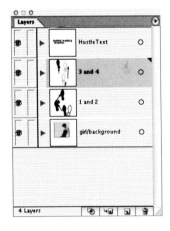

Figure 9.30

The layout of the ad in Illustrator's Layers palette. Note that text that will be shown separately is isolated onto different layers.

4. Set the frame delay to the value you'll use most in the document. You can set each frame's delay independently, but since each new frame is a duplicate of the previous one, you'll save time by setting the delay now.

5. Click the Duplicate Current Frame button at the base of the Animation palette. In the Layers palette, change the visibility of the layers to display the second message in the banner ad, as shown in Figure 9.31.

6. In this next frame, you'll use ImageReady's tween to create a fade. First, create a new frame for the animation. Next, reset the visibility of the layers to display the next message layer. Then, select Tween from the Animation palette menu. Choose Tween With: Previous Frame, set the number of frames to add (for this example, choose a

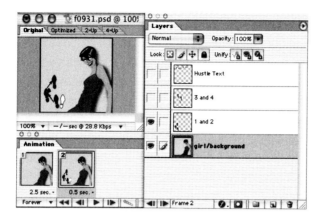

Figure 9.31
Creating the second frame in the animation. Note that the background layer stays visible.

conservative 2). Set the tween to affect All Layers and be sure to activate the Opacity option. Two new frames are generated, fading one layer out and another in. Position tweens are used much as Illustrator blends are to create the appearance of motion of a layer. Create motion tweens by actually moving the layer, not by creating multiple layers.

7. Repeat this process to complete the visibility of messages. Next, set the delays of frames to fine-tune the display of the ad. The time used will vary depending on the goals of the animation and the number of layers. Frequently, the delay on the first frame is longer than on the subsequent ones. While it is patently illegal to use others' works as your own, you can investigate frame delays on posted GIFs you admire. Do this by Control+clicking (on a Mac) or right-clicking (on a PC) on the animated GIF in a web browser and choosing the Download File To Disk option. Opening the downloaded GIF in ImageReady will display the frames and delays used in the animation.

8. Check the Optimize palette to make sure you're creating a GIF with the options you want and choose File → Save Optimized.

Pasting Illustrator Art into Flash

What you're doing: Copying and pasting art from Illustrator to Flash.
Why you're doing it: You want to avoid the logistics of converting to symbols or pulling apart imported SWF frames in Flash.

In previous sections, we discussed exporting Illustrator files to the SWF format and the features that are not directly translated. In cases where you intend to do the bulk of your animation in Flash, you may find exporting cumbersome. To be most useful, art needs to be converted to symbols either in Illustrator or Flash. This process can be a headache, especially for legacy files. In one application or the other, you'll need to tear the file apart, create symbols, and replace art on the page with them.

A second option is to copy and paste between the applications. This strategy makes sense when you're moving small amounts of data back and forth. It involves fewer steps and enables you to retain control of the process. On the downside, it's a manual process. You'll find it best to paste directly into a new symbol in Flash. Follow these steps:

1. Open the Files & Clipboard Preference dialog box. On the PC, preferences are located under the Edit menu; on the Mac, they are under the Illustrator menu. Set the Clipboard option to PDF Only.

   This Clipboard does a much better job of translating color values and pasting simpler object groups than the Adobe Illustrator Clipboard (AICB). You'll need to keep your eye on this, though. In some cases, the PDF Clipboard becomes confused by complex objects, such as expanded art brushes, and misplaces anchor points. It may also draw envelopes with coarse, inaccurate edges. If this happens, your best bet is to return to Illustrator and export a SWF. It's also possible to activate the AICB Clipboard and copy and paste again. The AICB Clipboard usually misplaces color values, though, and pastes nested groups for basic objects.

2. Inspect the art to be translated. Remove any transparency on the art, because it is more flexible to reapply it in Flash as an Alpha effect on the symbol. In most cases, effects do not need to be simplified.

3. Select the art that you want to translate. You should try to select art that is logically connected. For example, if you were animating a face, you might convert the face shape, nose, and hair to a single symbol. You would convert eyes, eyebrows, and the mouth, which would be animated separately, as separate symbols and later nest them in Flash. After you select your art, choose Edit → Copy.

4. Switch to Flash. Choose Insert → New Symbol. Give the new symbol a name and behavior. In most cases, you'll be creating Movie Clip or Graphic symbols. Click OK to enter symbol-editing mode. Choose Edit → Paste to add the art from Illustrator to the symbol.

5. In the event that you want to edit the Illustrator vectors in Flash, you will need to choose Modify → Ungroup. If you pasted using the AICB Clipboard, you may need to ungroup four or five times to get down to the actual vectors. From here, proceed as you would normally in Flash. For more information on working with Flash, see *Flash MX 2004 Savvy*, by Ethan Watrall and Norbert Herber (Sybex, 2004).

CHAPTER 10

Creating Scalable Vector Graphics (SVG)

Scalable Vector Graphics (SVG) is an open-source vector file format understood by web browsers. You can think of it as a free alternative to SWF files, since both are web vector formats. The format offers some appealing features but faces problems of browser limits and market penetration. These challenges are not insurmountable, and as newer browsers are introduced, SVG could become an important force on the Internet.

One of the drawbacks of SVG has been that it was traditionally hand-coded. Illustrator is one of the only professional-grade graphics applications that can generate SVG code. And while Illustrator CS writes better SVG than its predecessor, creating interactivity still requires you to write JavaScript. In this chapter, you'll learn to prepare static SVG graphics and to prepare some basic interactivity directly from Illustrator.

This chapter covers the following topics:

SVG features and limitations

Creating SVG files

Adding interactivity to SVG

Applying SVG filters

Customizing SVG filters

SVG Basics

The first thing you should know about SVG is that it is a text language. You can open and read these files in word processing applications. The code is English language and mostly understandable by humans. For example, a red rectangle might be coded as

```
<rect x="100" y="100" width="100" height="100"
    style="stroke: red; stroke-width:1; fill: red"/>
```

You can see the code for the x and y positions (on a coordinate grid system), size, and color attributes of the rectangle. You could write or edit this code by hand, but it's somewhat impractical to do so. Nonetheless, that is how most SVG was produced up to the release of Illustrator 9.

SVG code is based on Extensible Markup Language (XML). XML is a set of parameters that defines how computer languages for the Web should be written. The code in an SVG file may even start with an XML declaration (a sentence that says "I am an XML document"). XML may or may not become the next big thing on the Web. In 1998 the W3C, or World Wide Web Consortium (a group responsible for setting standards for the Web), established XML in an effort to simplify coding. Since then, due to the involvement of different companies with different agendas, things have gotten much more complicated. If you research the subject a bit, you're likely to find as many experts who believe XML is sublime and revolutionary as those who think it is bloated and indulgent.

XML hasn't yet replaced HTML. The popular browsers don't completely understand XML, and as a result, you need a plug-in to view SVG graphics. A number of plug-ins are available; the most popular one is Adobe's SVG Viewer. The most complete version of the viewer is the 3.0 release, which is installed with new versions of Adobe software, including Acrobat.

The SVG plug-in enjoys a good market share, but it is by no means universal. As browsers advance, the need for a plug-in may evaporate, but currently it's a serious consideration.

SVG files can be compressed. This happens when you save the file and create an SVGZ rather than SVG file. The compressed version can be up to 80 percent smaller than its counterpart, but you cannot adjust it with a text editor. Illustrator can open and edit both versions. You can find details on the saving options in Chapter 3, "Save For Web Reference."

Benefits and Drawbacks of SVG

To help you weigh the pros and cons of choosing to use SVG, let's look at both sides of the balance sheet.

SVG Benefits

There are a number of just plain good things about SVG—particularly when compared with SWF files.

SCALABLE ART

SVG art on a webpage can be scaled up or down. In addition to the flexibility this accords a designer (the same file may be used at different sizes in a layout), users can pan in or out. Control-click (Mac) or right-click (PC) on an SVG graphic on a webpage to access a context menu. Users can use the top two commands on this menu to zoom in or out, as shown in Figure 10.1.

TEXT IS TEXT

When an SVG file is saved, characters in the document can remain text—which means they can be selected, copied, and pasted as text objects. The font information that defines the appearance of the characters can also be included in the file. The result is text in the webpage that appears as you intended and that can be indexed by search engines. Compare this with SWF files, where text is converted to outlines. The text appearance is retained but not the underlying functionality of the characters. Rendering text as SWF files do prevents the text from being read by screen readers, making the file inaccessible to the visually challenged.

OPENESS, LINKING, AND INTERACTIVITY

SVG enables developers to adjust and add interactivity and animation. Most of this happens by attaching external Javascript documents to the SVG documents. From there, some commands are included in the SVG to activate the commands inside the Javascript files. This works because SVG files are "open" to linking other data in.

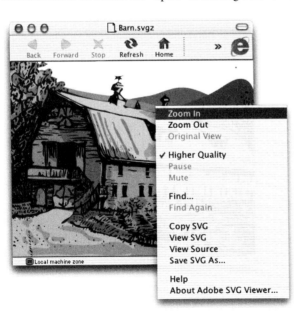

Figure 10.1

SVG files feature a context menu that users can access to zoom in on art.

This open structure enables you to link other files to an SVG document for added functionality or flexibility. For example, the same Cascading Style Sheets (CSS) used to control a webpage may be linked to define the appearance of text and objects of an SVG graphic. As the style sheets change, the SVG art is updated automatically. A common example in Illustrator is to link text or raster graphics to the SVG to reduce the load time of multiple files. JavaScript documents are also frequently linked to provide the backbone of commands for interactivity and rollover effects. Additionally, graphic content can be driven from databases. That is, the content of an image can change as data changes. This is often done by showing and hiding elements within the SVG file. For example, the available seats on an airplane can be culled from a database. As each seat is sold, the graphic representing the seat can be hidden, switched to a different graphic, or dimmed.

These features may seem esoteric to a beginning user or average designer. Consider this instead; you can open and inspect the code of an SVG file in any word processor. The nuts and bolts of the file are on display for you to adjust and edit. Likewise, other files and formats can hook into this code to expand its utility. This isn't the case with SWF files, where the code is hidden. This spirit of openness is well in keeping with the best intentions of the Web.

SVG TEXT FILTERS

Just as the fill and stroke of paths can be coded as text, common filters, such as blurs and drop shadows, can be coded as text. The result is a vector file that doesn't require large amounts of pixel information. For example, you can set a fuzzy drop shadow behind art as an SVG filter. In an SWF file the shadow would become pixel art, adding significantly to the document's file size. As an SVG text filter, the drop shadow does not add to file size. Figure 10.2 shows the difference.

SVG Pitfalls

The benefits sound pretty convincing, but when considering whether to use SVG art in a webpage, you also need to keep the following factors in mind.

REQUIRES CODE

Setting up even basic interactivity, such as a rollover, in an SVG file requires you to write some code in Illustrator. The code isn't complex, but it must be precise and there isn't an easy way to do it visually or to test the results in Illustrator. With a little practice in Flash or LiveMotion, you can set up reasonably complex animation and interactivity. There are no visual tools for interactivity in Illustrator. You will have to enter or attach some code and then test it.

As documents become structurally complex, Illustrator can also be a little quirky with its code. Things that work in one circumstance may not work in another. The best solution is to understand the SVG code so that you can tweak and repair it, or enlist the aid of a developer.

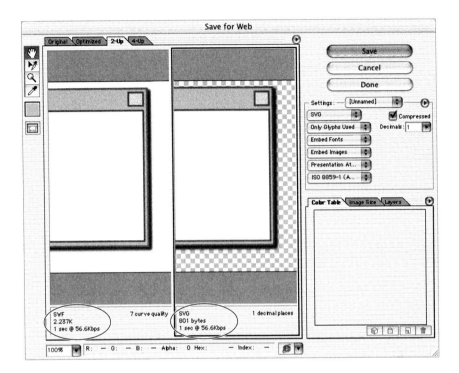

Figure 10.2
The same art saved as an SVG (.7KB) and SWF (3KB) from Illustrator. The SWF must save the shadow as raster art, accounting for the increased file size.

REQUIRES A PLUG-IN

As with SWF, SVG requires a plug-in so that current browsers can understand the files. In the future this limitation may be remedied, but it's currently an important consideration. Adobe has reported 50 million installations of the software. This amounts to about 10 percent of the online population. Compare that figure with the 90 percent penetration the SWF plug-in enjoys. It should also be noted that the SVG plug-in weighs in at about 2.3MB while the SWF plug-in is about 200Kb.

HTML uses the <EMBED> tag in the body of HTML to refer to SVG files rather than the common <IMG> tag. An attribute of this tag, Pluginspace, calls the plug-in is about 200Kb.

The values and attributes of the <EMBED> tag are naturally different than those of <IMG>, but the SRC attribute will be familiar to you if you've used HTML:

```
<EMBED NAME="file_name" SRC="file_name.svgz" WIDTH=100 HEIGHT=200 ALT=""
PLUGINSPAGE="http://www.adobe.com/svg/viewer/install/" TYPE="image/svg-xml"
WMODE="transparent">
</EMBED>
```

INCOMPLETE SUPPORT

Internet Explorer on the Mac doesn't give plug-ins access to JavaScript. This causes some interactivity to fail on the Mac side in that browser.

Creating SVG Files

In Chapter 3 you learned that to create an SVG file from an Illustrator document you simply save the document as SVG, from either the Save For Web or the Save dialog box. You'll typically use Save For Web if you are integrating an SVG file into a complete layout, and Save if you plan to hand off the file to a developer for further scripting.

This section details how to prepare and create SVG files directly from Illustrator.

SVG Attributes

What they are: *Elements within the <SVG> tag that set the size and viewable areas of the graphic.*

What you should know: *By default, the two areas are the same. You can change the values by editing the SVG file in a text editor, but most users won't need to unless art was created at the incorrect size, or you are working with a developer to create specific panning or cropping effects.*

SVG separates the total area that a graphic takes up and the viewable area it presents. To understand this, picture a clipping mask group. The bounding area of the graphic represents the overall size of the objects in the group; the clipping mask size represents the viewable area. In SVG the total area is called the *canvas* and the mask space is called the viewBox.

The canvas size is set by the width and height attributes in the <SVG> tag that Illustrator generates, and the viewBox is defined as a sequence of four numbers. The first two are the x and y coordinates of the upper-left corner of the viewBox; the second pair contains the coordinates of the lower-right corner. By default, these numbers will work out so that they perfectly display the image content.

The code looks like this:

```
<svg width="100" height="100" viewBox="0 0 100 100">
```

In this example, the canvas size is 100 pixels square. The viewable area is also 100 pixels square and completely covers the image. The viewBox coordinates are based on the upper-left corner of the original Illustrator art. It would be tempting to use the viewBox attribute as you would a clipping mask in Illustrator. This solution isn't as straightforward as it would seem. The scalable nature of vectors and the role of the width and height SVG attributes combine to make this sort of editing complicated. It makes more sense to crop in Illustrator using the Crop Marks function.

Without width and height attributes, SVG files scale uniformly to fit the current window. This is a common technique for pop-up ads. Delete the width and height attributes from within the confines of the <SVG> tag and save the file. If you want to allow the art to distort non-uniformly, you could add the code `preserveAspectRatio="none"` after the view-Box sizes within the `<SVG>` tag, but this is typically only done to retrofit existing art into a layout it wasn't designed for.

SVG Elements Tags

> What they are: *How SVG files name Illustrator objects.*
> What you should know: *Illustrator CS improved this capability to include more general objects.*

It's important to understand how the objects you create in Illustrator are rendered in SVG. Illustrator objects are converted into tags with attributes. We describe the objects and their attributes in the sections that follow. Prior to Illustrator CS, all paths were written using the `<path>` tag. This method isn't particularly flexible. Be aware that SVG code from Illustrator 9 and 10 will be harder for developers to adjust.

You can assign names to SVG objects and groups to help you identify them. Commonly, this is done for layers, but names can be attached to objects as well. By default, objects in Illustrator are named by their class. That is, each path is named `<path>`. These generic names are not translated to SVG. To rename objects, double-click them in the Layers palette and type the new name over the old one. To ensure that this custom name translates to the SVG file, choose Preferences → Units & Undo. In the Names section, make sure that Object Name is selected.

Style Attributes

In SVG, tags are painted with attributes that will be familiar to Illustrator users. Most are named the same and use similar units of measure. Style attributes can be connected to an object or a group. The code will look like this:

```
style="fill:#FFFFFF;stroke:#000000;stroke-width:2"
```

The `style` attribute will be inside an `<element>` tag. Each `style` attribute is separated from its value by a colon, and each value is separated from the next attribute by a semicolon. Fills and strokes you apply in Illustrator will be translated to this sort of code when the file is saved to SVG.

FILLS

Fill attributes can be solid colors, gradients, or patterns. Solid color fills are named with hexadecimal notation, starting with the pound sign. This will be very familiar to people with some hand-coding experience. Patterns and gradients are slightly more complicated. When you save an SVG file, patterns and fills are defined within the code first and then attached to objects; this process happens automatically. Just as in Illustrator, the pattern or gradient is assigned a name. Objects then connect the fills to the name. You should be aware of this in the event that you need to edit SVG code manually. Illustrator tends to name its gradients by the objects that use them. Here, the code for the default black and white gradient is named oaf_1_:

```
<linearGradient id="oaf_1_"
gradientUnits="userSpaceOnUse" x1="0.5" y1="25" x2="44" y2="26">
<stop  offset="0"  style="stop-color:#FFFFFF"/>
<stop  offset="1"  style="stop-color:#000000"/>
<a:midPointStop  offset="0"  style="stop-color:#FFFFFF"/>
<a:midPointStop  offset="0.5"  style="stop-color:#FFFFFF"/>
<a:midPointStop  offset="1"  style="stop-color:#000000"/>
</linearGradient>
```

Later in the code, the ellipse oaf uses the gradient by linking to it:

```
<ellipse id="oaf" style="fill:url(#oaf_1_);stroke:#000000;"
cx="22.47" cy="26.257" rx="21.97" ry="18.182"/>
```

Patterns work in the same way.

STROKES

Strokes are colored with the same structure as fills. As in Illustrator, strokes can use patterns in SVG. Additionally, strokes have other components you need to be concerned with.

The thickness of a stroke is set using the attribute stroke-width. If no value is given, it is assumed to be 1 pixel. Joins and caps are controlled with the stroke-linejoin and stroke-linecap attributes, respectively. Miter join strokes can also use the stroke-miterlimit attribute. Use stroke-dasharray to set up dashed lines. Values for these attributes are the same as they are in Illustrator. For example:

```
<rect x="1" y="1"
style="fill:#FFFFFF;stroke:#000000;
stroke-width:2;
stroke-linecap:round;
stroke-dasharray:12 5;"
width="125" height="180"/>
```

Note that this is a rectangle (rect) with a two-point dashed line. The line has 12-point rounded dashes and 5-point gaps.

TRANSPARENCY

SVG supports most of the transparency functions that Illustrator does. A minor difference is that opacity is expressed as a decimal rather than percent. So a circle with a 65 percent opacity would be expressed as 0.65. The code might look like this:

```
<circle style="opacity:0.65;
fill:#FF9900;" cx="40" cy="40" r="40"/>
```

When transparency is applied to fills and strokes rather than complete objects, Illustrator handles it by flattening the art and creating a group. See "<g>" below.

Blending modes and opacity masks in Illustrator are expressed using `adobe-blending-mode` and `Adobe_OpacityMaskFilter`, respectively. These attributes work when you're using the Adobe SVG Viewer 3. The names of blending modes in SVG are the same as they are in Illustrator (without the spaces). Should the need arise, you can change the mode by typing in a new name. For example, if you think an image looks too harsh using the Hard Light blending mode, you can open the file in a text editor and replace `hardlight` with `softlight`:

```
<ellipse style="fill:#FF9900;
adobe-blending-mode:softlight;"
cx="42" cy="43" rx="42" ry="43"/>
```

APPEARANCE

When objects have complex appearances, Illustrator renders them as multiple objects within the SVG. The objects are grouped together but are expressed as multiple items. In SVG, the tag `<g>` groups items. This applies to objects with multiple fills and strokes, but also to compound shapes, brushes, and objects with effects or transparency applied to their fills or strokes. For example, to represent an object with a solid red stroke and 50 percent opaque red fill, you'd use this code:

```
<g>
    <circle style="opacity:0.5;fill:#FF0000;" cx="74" cy="74" r="73"/>
    <circle style="fill:none;stroke:#FF0000;" cx="74" cy="74" r="73"/>
</g>
```

This is mildly awkward because SVG supports the `fill-opacity` and `stroke-opacity` attributes. The same circle can be expressed as:

```
<circle style="fill:#FF0000;stroke:#FF0000;fill-opacity:.5;"
cx="74" cy="74" r="73"/>
```

A similar thing happens with compound shapes. The rendering of the complex appearance becomes too literal. Because of this, some users prefer to expand objects before saving and apply fill and stroke opacity in the SVG code rather than in Illustrator.

<rect>

The `<rect>` tag tells Illustrator to draw a rectangle. You can include attributes describing the rectangle's size, position, and coloring as well. In Illustrator `<rect>` tags look like this:

```
<rect x="50" y="50" style="fill:#FFFFFF;stroke:#000000;stroke-width:2"
width="50" height="150"/>
```

The x and y values set the position of the upper-left corner of the object. The position 0,0 is in the upper left of the SVG file. The `style` attributes set the fill and stroke (using hexadecimal notation) to white and black. Note that the width and height of the rectangle are given here in pixels.

Rounded rectangles from Illustrator are currently drawn as `path` objects. This is unfortunate because the `<rect>` tag supports rounding using the `rx` and `ry` attributes. Either of these may be included with a positive value to round a rectangle. The code for rounding the previous rectangle's corners 10 pixels is as follows:

```
<rect x="50" y="50" style="fill:#FFFFFF;stroke:#000000;stroke-width:2"
width="50" height="150" rx="10"/>
```

<polygon> and *<polyline>*

Illustrator uses `<polygon>` to describe any closed path entirely made of straight lines. For open paths with straight lines, it uses `<polyline>`. In both cases, a series of x and y coordinate sets describes the position of anchor points in the path. The following example describes a five-pointed star:

```
<polygon style="fill:#FFFFFF;stroke:#000000;"
points="48.2,1.6 59.3,35.5 94.9,35.5 66.1,56.5 77.1,90.4
   48.2,69.5 19.4,90.4 30.4,56.5 1.5,35.5 37.2,35.5 "/>
```

<line>

The `<line>` tag describes a straight, open path. Paths made with Illustrator's Line tool become `line` elements. Lines have the same `style` attributes as other objects but only two anchor points. This code shows how you'd indicate the position of the points:

```
<line style="stroke:#FF0000;stroke-width:2;"
x1="0.7" y1="0.7" x2="195" y2="180"/>
```

<circle> and *<ellipse>*

A circle is described in SVG by the coordinate position of its center and its radius. The `cx` and `cy` attributes set the center location and the `r` attribute its radius, as in this code:

```
<circle style="fill:#FFFFFF;stroke:#000000;"
cx="44.4" cy="44.4" r="43.9"/>
```

As you know, an ellipse is a circle with different horizontal and vertical radiuses. The `rx` and `ry` attributes describe the horizontal and vertical radiuses, respectively. If they are the same, the result is a circle. This means that you can convert ellipses to circles by making the values the same, as in this code:

```
<ellipse style="fill:#FFFFFF;stroke:#000000;stroke-width:2;"
cx="44.4" cy="35.3" rx="43.9" ry="43.9"/>
```

<path>

Most custom vector shapes in Illustrator (elements other than circles, squares, basic lines, and polygons) are converted to the path element. Prior to Illustrator CS, all vector shapes became path elements. Anything you drew with the Pen or Pencil tool, or any customized shape you created, became path elements. The code for describing paths is complicated. Fortunately for you, Illustrator takes care of this task for you, eliminating the need to calculate.

Paths in SVG use the d attribute (which stands for draw), and it connects to several different actions. Further, the actions can be relative to the path or absolute. Capitalized code is absolute; lowercase is relative. The most commonly used ones in Illustrator are M for moveto (without drawing) and c for curveto, which draws a cubic Bezier curve to the point specified. Other commands you may encounter are L for lineto (draws a straight line to the point), H for horizontallineto, V for verticallineto, S for smoothcurveto, A for elliptical arc, and Z for closepath.

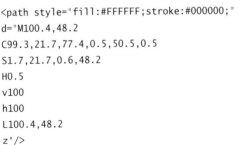

Figure 10.3

A shape with both straight and curved lines

To give you a sense of how the code works, here's the SVG for the shape in Figure 10.3. Spaces are added for clarity. The instructions start on the right shoulder of the arc, curve through several points, and then smooth (curve down) to the opposite shoulder of the arc. Next, the line adjusts itself horizontally slightly before going straight down 100 pixels, horizontally 100 pixels, and then back up to where it started. The z command closes the path.

```
<path style="fill:#FFFFFF;stroke:#000000;"
d="M100.4,48.2
C99.3,21.7,77.4,0.5,50.5,0.5
S1.7,21.7,0.6,48.2
H0.5
v100
h100
L100.4,48.2
z"/>
```

<image>

The <image> tag is used for raster art. It has attributes that define the position and size of the art. As noted in Chapter 3, raster art can be linked or embedded. In the event that it's embedded, the raw code for the file will follow the tag. Humans can't read this code. If the art is linked, the reference will be included as an xlink, as in:

```
<image width="98" height="93" id="XMLID_1_" xlink:href="756FC232.jpg" />
```

<g>

The `<g>` tag is used for groups. Illustrator groups and layers both translate to `<g>` tags when saved as SVG files. Groups can be nested, one inside another, and this is common. Groups are given names, or IDs, based on the layer name in Illustrator. Transparency and SVF filter effects applied to layers in Illustrator may be translated to `style` attributes for the layer. The SVG for a layer with 60 percent opacity would be:

```
<g id="Layer_1" style="opacity:0.6;">
```

Other effects applied to layers have a habit of descending to the objects on the layer. This preserves the appearance of the objects but creates frustratingly inflexible code. For example, if you rotate a group of rectangles 45° by applying the effect Distort & Transform, the resulting SVG looks like this:

```
<g><rect x="10" y="20" transform="matrix(0.7 -0.7 0.7 0.7 -31 43)"
style="fill:#FFFFFF;stroke:#000000;" width="56" height="78"/>
<rect x="51" y="-20.4" transform="matrix(0.7 -0.7 0.7 0.7 10 60)"
style="fill:#FFFFFF;stroke:#000000;" width="55"
 height="75"/>
</g>
```

We could have applied a transformation to the group to produce the same effect. That approach would make it easier to script interactions and animations that use the transformation effect. For most users, this won't make any difference, but you should be aware of this when developing SVG.

<symbol> and *<use>*

The `<symbol>` tag corresponds directly to an Illustrator symbol. The `<symbol>` tag defines but does not draw the items it describes; the `<use>` tag calls the defined symbol for drawing on the page. Items converted to symbols in Illustrator are grouped automatically, and this passes to the SVG. The code looks like this:

```
<symbol  id="New_Symbol_" viewBox="-24.7 -24.7 49.5 49.5">
    <g>
        <circle style="fill:#FFFFFF;stroke:#000000;" cx="0" cy="0" r="24.2"/>
    </g>
</symbol>
```

This symbol is a basic circle. The circle's position (0,0) is relative to the `viewBox` of the symbol, not the document. Instances of the symbols are coded:

```
<use xlink:href="#New_Symbol_"
width="49.5" height="49.5" x="-24.7" y="-24.7" transform="matrix(1 0 0 -1
98.8506 24.7422)"/>
```

A symbol set is coded as a group of `<use>` tags. Transparency and effects attached to instances are applied as styles to the `<use>` tag.

Code Reuse

What it is: *Using an entity and the `<defs>` tag.*
What you should know: *Illustrator uses these conventions to reduce file size. Developers should be aware of this when massaging the code Illustrator generates.*

SVG promotes the idea of recycling repeating code snippets. The idea is to define a chunk of code and then refer to it later in the code. This keeps the overall file size down and reduces the potential for errors when you're hand-coding. Although you won't edit these snippets often by hand, you should be aware that Illustrator takes advantage of its reusability features as it writes code. In some instances, it does so superfluously. There are two key instances of this: entities and the `<defs>` tag.

Entities

Entities create shortcuts. A chunk of code is first set and given a name. Later if you want to use that string of code again, you type an ampersand, the name of the entity, and a semicolon. Illustrator uses this structure to define namespaces. So, first it defines the entity:

```
<!ENTITY ns_svg "http://www.w3.org/2000/svg">
```

Here the URL describing the SVG namespace is given the shortcut `ns_svg`. Then, when it sets up the `<SVG>` tag, Illustrator connects the namespace by using the entity:

```
<svg  xmlns="&ns_svg;">
```

This may seem like a redundant structure, but the extra level of abstraction provides more utility for developers. In complicated applications, there may be additional `<SVG>` or other tags nested within the XML wrapper. For basic graphic designers, just be aware that the more options you activate in the Advanced section of the SVG Options dialog box when you save, the more entities Illustrator will write.

The *<def>* Tag

The `<defs>` tag defines elements that can be reused later. Code is wrapped within the `<defs>` and `</defs>` tags. Later, if you want to use the code again, you call the wrapped elements by name. In hand-coding, this approach is used often for setting up filters, gradients, and animation. Illustrator uses it principally for clipping paths. In the following example, a rectangle masks ellipses. First, Illustrator defines the rectangle shape and gives it a name:

```
<defs>
<rect id="XMLID_2_" y="15" width="90" height="40"/>
</defs>
```

Next, the defined rectangle (XMLID_2_) is used as a clipping path (XMLID_3_). The # sign links the defined path:

```
<clipPath id="XMLID_3_">
<use xlink:href="#XMLID_2_" />
</clipPath>
```

With the path defined, the masked objects are defined with the clip-path as an attribute:

```
<ellipse clip-path="url(#XMLID_3_)" fill="#FFFFFF"
 stroke="#000000" cx="40" cy="30" rx="35" ry="30"/>
<ellipse clip-path="url(#XMLID_3_)" fill="#FFFFFF"
 stroke="#000000" cx="76.515" cy="50" rx="30" ry="25"/>
```

Adding Interactivity to SVG Files

In this section, we'll look at scripting interactive behaviors into SVG files. Although it's possible to script SVG animation using layers as frames, you won't have much success using this technique directly in Illustrator. We'll limit our discussion to creating links and three types of rollovers.

Basic linking is not complex. The process is the same as it is for adding links to SWF files—you add an image map using the Attributes palette.

To create rollovers and other effects, though, you'll need to use the SVG Interactivity palette. The palette itself is spare. The basic process involves linking a file that contains JavaScript commands (a .js file) to the SVG document and then selecting objects that act as buttons. In the SVG Interactivity palette, you'll then script events that call the appropriate commands in the associated JavaScript file. The JavaScript file will be linked to the resulting SVG web graphic. You must write the path to it correctly, and it must be present and available to the SVG file when you post your file online.

Users who are familiar with JavaScript or who have access to developers can create custom JavaScript files. For the rest of us, Adobe installs a file named events.js with Illustrator. You'll find a copy of that file in Adobe Illustrator CS\Sample Files\Sample Art\ SVG .localized\svg. Commands in this file can be used to perform the rollovers we'll describe in the section "SVG Rollovers."

SVG Linking

What you're doing: *Attaching links to objects.*
Why you're doing it: *You want to add interactivity to SVG files.*

SVG can write links using the <a> and <xlink> tags. These are technically two different ways of linking, but they are used together. For simplicity's sake, let's focus on the familiar <a> tag portion. If you begin to edit SVG yourself, you will find that you can write links without the <a> tag, but Illustrator does so by default. To use xlink, the browser needs to be informed what kind of object the tag represents. Illustrator does this by first setting entities for the namespace URLs and then declaring them in the <SVG> tag.

Objects, groups, and layers can act as links in SVG files. Do not attach links to paths with fills and strokes of None. Although these objects are still written into the SVG, the links do not work correctly. To create invisible linking areas, use objects with fills and an opacity of 0 percent. To add a link to an SVG or SVGZ file, follow these steps:

1. Select or target the object that will serve as a button.
2. In the Attributes palette, select Rectangle from the Image Map menu. You aren't really creating an image map, but this will activate the URL field so that you can enter a URL.
3. Enter the link address in the URL field or choose a recent one from the URL pop-up menu. For e-mail links, use the code `mailto:` followed by the e-mail address.
4. Save the file as an SVG or SVGZ file.

Targets for Links

Targets instruct browsers where to open links. Commonly, they are used in frame documents or to spawn new windows for links. You can't set a target for an SVG link directly in Illustrator. To create one, you edit the SVG code in a text editor. Use these steps:

1. Create the link as you normally would in Illustrator. Note the URL you are attaching—you will need to locate it in the SVG code.
2. Save the SVG file. Don't select the SVGZ format because you would not be able to edit it.
3. Open the file in a text editor.
4. Scroll through the text until you find the URL you entered in step 1. If you have a hard time finding it, look for the <g> ID for the layer the link was on. The code will look like this:

    `<a xlink:href="your_link.htm">`

5. Within the link, add the text **target ="name"**. To open the link in a new window, use `"new"` instead of _blank:

    `<a xlink:href="your_link.htm" target ="new">`

6. Save the file.

As we mentioned earlier, the links you create using the `xlink` tag aren't exactly the same as HTML links, but they can be used to do many of the same things. For example, instead of setting a target, you can also use an `xlink:show` value. The code `xlink:show="new"` opens the link in a new window. The code `xlink:actuate` specifies when the link should be opened. Commonly, this code is used to open a link when a page opens or closes. So, to open the document `file.htm` in a new window when the document loads, you'd use this code:

```
xlink:href="file.htm"
xlink:show="new"
xlink:acuate="onLoad"
```

None of this can be done in Illustrator.

SVG Rollovers

What you're doing: Changing the appearance of objects based on the actions of users.

What you should know: You can code rollovers manually in the SVG or in Illustrator by using JavaScript.

In this section, we'll look at the common practice of creating rollover effects. In SVG graphics, you can create rollovers by manually adjusting SVG code or by attaching a JavaScript file and calling commands from it. As noted earlier, a JavaScript file for this purpose is installed with Illustrator. You can also download the file from `Sybex.com`.

SVG Color Rollover

To set up a rollover directly in the SVG code, you'll use the `<set>` tag. This tag switches an attribute when events you specify are met. Here, we'll use it to change the color of a button when the user mouses over. Here's a sample of the code:

```
<a xlink:href="link_page.htm" id="link">
<ellipse style="fill:#B7B7B7;stroke:#000000;" cx="41.4"
 cy="38.4" rx="40.9" ry="37.9">
<set begin="link.mouseover" end="link.mouseout"
 attributeName="fill" to="#FFFF66"/>
</ellipse>
</a>
```

There are a couple things you should notice here. The `<set>` tag is inside both the `<link>` and the `<ellipse>` tags. You could also position the `<set>` tag to apply an attribute (such as the opacity) to an entire group. The `<set>` tag uses `begin` and `end` attributes. The value of each attribute consists of the ID of the link, a dot, and the event, in this example, `mouseover` or `mouseout`.

To create this rollover, you'll need to edit the default SVG out of Illustrator. Follow these steps:

1. In Illustrator, select the object to which you want to apply the rollover effect. Locate the item in the Layers palette, double-click it, and give it a unique name. This will help you locate the object in the SVG code later.

2. Use the Attributes palette to make the item a link. See "SVG Linking" above for details.
3. Save the file in the SVG format. If you're using the Save For Web command, make sure the slice is set to SVG. Do not compress the SVG.
4. Open the SVG in a word processing application. Locate the element you named in step 1. The code should look similar to the following. In all but very simple files, there will be more code within the `<link>` tags.

   ```
   <a xlink:href="link_page.htm">
   <ellipse style="fill:#B7B7B7;stroke:#000000;"
    cx="41.4" cy="38.4" rx="40.9" ry="37.9"/>
   </a>
   ```

5. Add an `id` attribute to the link. This will set the "hot" area that activates the rollover.
6. Illustrator closes the tag of many objects with the forward slash at the end of the tag. Delete that slash to open the element and add the `<set>` code shown at the beginning of this section. You can change the `attributeName` value to adjust stroke width, color, opacity, and so forth.
7. Add the closing tag for the element. Make sure it still appears before the closing tag of the link. In this example, the closing tag for the element is `</ellipse>`.

If you open a manually customized SVG file in Illustrator and then save it, Illustrator may rewrite your code. Typically this means rewriting the `<set>` command slightly and dropping the link `id` attributes. Without the link `id` attributes, the rollover won't work. Reinserting the attributes typically fixes the problem, but that process can be time consuming. Consider the kinds of edits you need to make to the file before editing in Illustrator. You may be able to effect the changes in the SVG with minor code tweaks. For more examples of SVG code rollovers, see `Sybex.com/HiddenPower`.

JavaScript Rollovers

JavaScript rollovers are easier in some ways than manually coding SVG. It also enables you to save SVGZ files directly from Illustrator. The basic process involves linking a JavaScript file to the document, naming the object that gets the rollover in the Layers palette, and then entering a line or two of code in the SVG Interactivity palette. The linked JavaScript file is required in order for the rollovers to function. In these examples, we'll use the `events.js` file included with Illustrator. Follow these steps:

1. Copy the `events.js` file into the local directory of your website or project folder. Place the file in the location you expect it will live in relative to the SVG file you're creating. This is often the same folder, but it need not be.

2. Choose JavaScript files from the SVG Interactivity palette menu. In the resulting dialog box, click Add.

3. Navigate to the events.js file you moved in step 1. Add relative addressing to the location if required. The results will look like Figure 10.4. Close the dialog box.

4. Select or target the item that will change as a result of the rollover. Locate the item in the Layers palette and double-click it to open the Options dialog box. Give the item a unique name. You don't have to use web-safe naming, but if you don't, Illustrator will rewrite the name in the SVG to remove spaces and so forth.

5. Highlight the item that will activate the rollover effect. This is usually the same object, but it doesn't need to be. In the SVG Interactivity palette, select the event onmouseover to start the rollover. Enter the codes listed here (based on the type of rollover you want to create). Substitute the name of the rollover object from step 4 for name but leave the single quotes intact:

   Change Fill Color: elemColor(evt, 'name', '#336699')

   Change Stroke color: elemStrokeColor(evt, 'name', '#000000')

   Change stroke weight: elemStrokeWidth(evt, 'name', '2.5'

   Hide item: elemHide(evt, 'name')

   Reveal item: elemShow(evt, 'name')

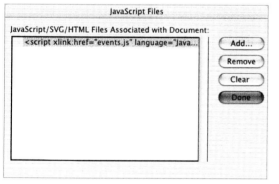

Figure 10.4
A JavaScript file added to the document

6. Press Return (Mac) or Enter (PC) after entering the code. You have to enter the code by hand; you can't paste directly into the field. Be careful as you enter code; it's easy to make mistakes, and there aren't visual cues when you've made an error.

7. To reset the appearance of the objects after the mouse leaves, choose the onmouseout event and enter the code shown in step 5 to restore the object.

8. Save the SVG or SVGZ file in the correct directory relative to the events.js file.

ROLLOVER EXAMPLE

In this example, our goal is to cause the interior shape of a button group to lighten when the mouse hovers over it. The task is mildly complicated by the fact that we want the effect to take place when the mouse enters any portion of the button, not just the interior shape. This means that the painted area of the trigger object must cover the entire button area. The effect will look like Figure 10.5.

To set up the rollover effect:

1. Create the art as shown in Figure 10.5. After building the button shapes, select them all by choosing Object → Group. Grouping the items provides a platform to which you can attach the image map and JavaScript. Without grouping, you'd need to build an invisible object over the button area.

2. Locate the interior path shape in the Layers palette and double-click it. Give the object a custom name; in this example, we'll name it switch. Set the Color palette to Web Safe Color and note the fill value of switch. You may want to jot that down on a handy piece of paper. In our example, it's A2A2A2.

3. Target the group. In the Attributes palette, choose either a rectangle or polygon image map and enter the link URL. The results will look like Figure 10.6.

4. With the group still targeted, open the SVG Interactivity palette. Choose JavaScript files from the SVG Interactivity palette. Navigate to the events.js file as described earlier, and attach the file.

5. With the group still targeted, set the Event menu in the SVG Interactivity palette to onmouseover. In the JavaScript field enter this code: **elemColor(evt, 'switch', '#336699')**. The name of the item being changed is in the single quotes, and the hex value of the color it is being switched to appears in quotes after the pound sign. Press Return (or Enter) once you are done. The full line of code will move into the lower section of the SVG Interactivity palette.

6. Now you need to reset the color when the mouse leaves. Set the event in the SVG Interactivity palette to onmouseout. Repeat the text you entered in step 5, but use the hex code you noted in step 2. It should read elemColor(evt, 'switch', '#A2A2A2').

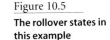

Figure 10.5

The rollover states in this example

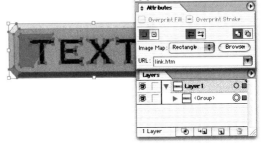

Figure 10.6

Attaching a link to the button group

Applying SVG Filters

The SVG schema features filters. They are akin to Illustrator's effects. Filters change the appearance of objects without permanently changing the underlying shapes. Examples out of the box include blurs and drop shadows. Being able to switch the appearance of graphics with filters enables the user to create rollovers without using multiple graphic files. It also removes the need for hefty pixel-graphics for soft-edge effects, such as drop shadows.

Filters are coded into the SVG as named strings with properties. For example, this is the code for a Gaussian Blur filter:

```
<filter  id="AI_GaussianBlur_4">
       <feGaussianBlur  stdDeviation="4"></feGaussianBlur>
</filter>
```

The code `fe` is a filter element; `stdDeviation` is the standard deviation, or blur amount of the filter. Objects can use the filter by linking to its `id`. Illustrator may write the name of the filter as an entity and refer to it in the style, or point directly to it, as in:

```
<g filter="url(#AI_GaussianBlur_4)">
```

Knowing a little code will make it easier to create and customize SVG filters, but it's not completely required. You can open the default filters and inspect their code in Illustrator. Although this process is somewhat awkward, you should be able to create the most common effects easily enough.

Some SVG filters don't display correctly or completely in Illustrator. You may see hard, pixilated edges. This doesn't translate to the SVG file in a browser. There isn't a way to work around this, other than by testing the file in a browser.

Applying SVG Filters

What you're doing: *Adding effects to SVG objects.*

Why you're doing it: *The goal is to circumvent the need for raster art or multiple graphics.*

This section explains how to apply SVG filters to existing objects. We'll look at the Appearance palette and show you how to apply SVG filters to different classes of objects.

You can apply an existing SVG filter to an object by targeting it and choosing one of the canned filters from the SVG Filter menu in the Effects menu. Be sure that the SVG filter appears last in the Appearance palette. This is usually only an issue when you're attaching effects to layers or objects with complex appearances. Most of the prebuilt effects are good, but you'll typically want to adjust them to suit your needs. Creating a drop shadow is a typical example.

To apply a customized SVG filter:

1. Target the item that you want to receive the effect. In this example, we want the drop shadow to go to the upper left instead of the lower right.

2. Choose Effect → SVG Filter → Apply SVG Filter. In the Apply SVG Filter dialog box, select `AI_Shadow_1` and click the Edit SVG Filter button. The Edit SVG Filter dialog box opens, as shown in Figure 10.7.

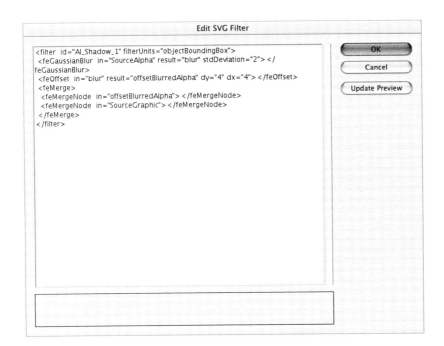

Figure 10.7

Preparing to edit a canned SVG filter

3. In the dialog box, The direction of the shadow is controlled by the dy and dx values in the feOffset line. The units are in pixels; positive numbers put the shadows to the right and down. So, to set the shadow to appear at the upper left of the object, use the code:

    ```
    <feOffset  in="blur" result="offsetBlurredAlpha" dy="-4" dx="-4"></feOffset>
    ```

    As you edit the numbers, click the Update Preview button to inspect the results as you go.

4. The blur distance is found in the feGaussianBlur line; after the stdDeviation attribute. So, a smaller blur might read:

    ```
    <feGaussianBlur  in="SourceAlpha" result="blur" stdDeviation="3"></feGaussianBlur>
    ```

SVG WHIZ

For a deeper look at SVG and SVG developing, consider these resources:

- www.adobe.com/svg: Adobe's official page on the subject, which good links and examples.
- www.svgx.org: A good portal for SVG examples.
- www.w3.org/Graphics/SVG/overview.htm8: The W3C's overview of SVG with links to the official recommendation and resources.
- www.svgnotebook.com: A nice SVG site with a tutorial and links for more details.

Index

Note to the Reader: Throughout this index **boldfaced** page numbers indicate primary discussions of a topic. *Italicized* page numbers indicate illustrations.

A

actions
    batch, **240**
    building, **239–240**
Actions palette, 239
activated layers, 63
ADA (Americans with Disabilities Act), 251
Adaptive option, 85
Add Arrowheads dialog box, 211, *211*
add mode for compound shapes, 61, *61*
Add New Fill command, **173–174**
Add New Stroke command, 174
adjusting
    GIF colors, **234–235**, *234*
    JPEG quality, **237**
Adobe RGB option, **144**
Adobe SVG Viewer, 99
Advanced Mode option, **143**
Align palette, 53
aligning objects, **53**, *53*
Alt field for image slices, **74**, **251**
Americans with Disabilities Act (ADA), 251
anchor points
    for envelope objects, 212, *212*
    for kicking animation, 284, *284*
    for stamp buttons, 214, *214*
animations, **267**
    blending modes for, 269
    creating, **268–269**, *268*
    export for, **285**
        banner ads, **288–290**, *288–290*
        converting layers to frames, **286–288**, *287*
        pasting art, **290–291**
    motion and opacity. *See* motion and opacity animation
    stop-frame, **269–271**, *270–271*
Anti-Alias option, 101
Anti-aliased Artwork option, **133**

anti-aliasing
    for curves, **133**
    with exporting images, 286
    for raster art, 186, *187*
    with small type, 231
    for smoothing, 101
Appearance palette and appearances, 40, **179**
    for animation, 277
    applying, **175–176**, *176*
    auto-expanding buttons, **184–185**, *184–185*
    bounding box for, **174–175**, *174–175*
    for color, **47–49**, *48*
    group outlines for, **179–180**, *179–180*
    group perspective drop shadows, **180–181**, *180–181*
    menu in, **173–174**
    options in, **171–174**, *171*
    outline live type effect, **183–184**, *183–184*
    for rotation, 279
    saving as graphic styles, **176–179**, *176*
    stacking order for, **174–175**, *174–175*
    strokes behind type, **182**, *182*
    strokes for gradient meshes, **182–183**, *182–183*
    in SVG, **301**
Append Extension option, **142**
Apple RGB option, **144**
Apply SVG filter dialog box, 312
applying
    appearance and effects, **175–176**, *176*
    strokes to gradient meshes, **182–183**, *182–183*
    SVG filters, **311–313**, *313*
area type, **54–55**, *55*
arrowheads for buttons, 211, *211*
art
    imported, swatches from, **154–155**
    left-side, 218
        gradient fade effects for, **218**, *218*
        short stripes for, **218**, *219*
        wave patterns for, **219–220**, *219*

pasting into Flash, **290–291**
pre-rasterizing, **231**, *231*
Art Brush Options dialog box, 284
Artboard
    purpose of, **24**, *25*
    settings for, **146–149**, *147–148*
Ask When Opening option, **145**
Ask When Pasting option, **145**
Attribute Appearance section, **172**
Attributes palette and attributes
    for background color, 114
    for layers, 175
    for links, 254–257
    for objects, 47
    of selections, **172**
    for SVG elements, **299–305**, *303*
    for SVG files, **298–299**
    in SWF format, 14
auto-expanding buttons, **184–185**, *184–185*
auto slices, 244
Auto Trace Tolerance option, **136**
automation, **238–239**
    batch actions for, **240**
    building actions in, **239–240**
    resources for, **238**

B

Back buttons, **211**, *211*
background
    color
        in GoLive, **119–123**, *121–123*
        in HTML. *See* HTML background color
    images, **217**, *217*
        left-side art, **218–220**, *218–220*
        previewing HTML results, **221–222**, *221–222*
        seamless patterns, **220–221**, *220–221*
    in output, **82–83**
    for slices, **73**
banner ad animation, **288–290**, *288–290*
banners for HTML pages, 242
Baseline Shift option, **135**
basic bevel buttons, **187–190**, *187–190*
basic links, **254–256**, *255*
basic selecting, **50–51**
batch actions, **240**
bevel buttons, **187–190**, *187–190*
beveled caps and joins, 269
bit channels, 8

bitmapped graphics, **6–7**, *6–7*
blending modes for animations, **269**
blends
    in animation. *See* motion and opacity animation
    purpose of, **38–39**, *39*
    for stamp buttons, 214–215, *214*
Blur option, **91**
bodies of HTML pages, 242, *242*
bounding boxes
    for appearance, **174–175**, *174–175*
    for Artboard, 146, *146*
Break Link to Style button, **177**
broadband, 16
Browser Dither command, **83**, *84*
browser templates, **164–168**, *165–168*
brushes
    for fills and strokes, 176
    for guided movement animation, 283, *283*
Brushes palette, 176
building actions, **239–240**
buttons, **185**
    auto-expanding, **184–185**, *184–185*
    bevel, **187–190**, *187–190*
    domes, **197–198**, *197–198*
    inside shadows, **198–200**, *199–201*
    interface, **196–197**, *196–197*
    pills, **190–194**, *191–194*
    rollover. *See* rollover buttons
    and symbol workflow, **201–202**, *201*
    for symbols and icons, **209**
        E-mail Me, **212–216**, *212–216*
        Forward/Back, **211**, *211*
        Home, **210**, *210*
    tabs, **194–196**, *194–196*
    web issues in, **186–187**, *186–187*

C

cable modems, 17
canvas, 298
caps
    for animation, 269
    for strokes, 45
cardinal focal fills, 172
Cascading Style Sheets (CSSs)
    in Dreamweaver, **124**
    for graphics space, **3**, *3*
    for HTML background color, **115–116**
    settings for, **96**

Cell Alignment options
    for HTML text, 75, **252**
    for image slices, 75
    for no-image slices, **252**
cells
    in Dreamweaver, **111–112**
    in tables, 2
Character palette and characters
    outline live type effect for, **183–184**, *183–184*
    for tracking, 183, *183*
    for type size, 137
<circle> tag, **302**
classes, **25–26**
Clear Appearance option, **173**
Clipboard setting, **143**
clipping groups, 29
clipping masks, **28–29**, *28–29*
CLUTs (color lookup tables), 157–158, *158*
CMYK working spaces, **145**
code in SVG
    requirements for, **296–297**
    reuse of, **305–306**
Coding section, **81**
color
    for domes, 198, *198*
    families of, **156–157**, *157*
    in file formats, **8**
    in GIF
        matte, **87–88**
        reducing and adjusting, **234–235**, *234*
        settings for, **85–86**
    HTML background. *See* HTML background color
    names for, **17**
    for pill buttons, 192–193, *193*
    readouts for, **76–77**
    saving as swatches, **153–154**, *153*
    for SVG rollovers, **308–309**
    swatches for. *See* Swatches palette and swatches
    Tool palette for, **42**
    web preferences for, **143–145**, *144*
    web-safe, **18**, 42, 43, **235**
Color/B&W Setup dialog box, 159, *159*
color controls, **39**
    Appearance palette, **47–49**, *48*
    Color palette, **42–43**, *43*
    fills and strokes, **39–40**, *40*
    libraries, **44–45**
    Stroke palette, **45–46**, *46*

styles, **49**
Swatches palette, **43–44**, *43–44*
Tool palette color controls, **41–42**, *41–42*
Transparency palette, **46–47**, *47*
color lookup tables (CLUTs), 157–158, *158*
color palettes
    for attributes, 47
    for background, 120–123, *120–121*, *123*
    for fill and stroke, 42, *43*, 176
    for GoLive, 120–123, *120–121*, *123*
    reusable. *See* reusable color palettes
    for swatches, 42–44
Color Picker dialog box, 41
color reduction algorithm, **85**
Color tables
    controls for, **99–100**, *100*
    converting to swatches, **157–159**, *158–159*
    in GIF, 9, *9*
ColorMatch RGB option, **144**
combining slices, **248**, *248–249*
common layout
    building, **261**
    L pattern pages, **262–265**, *264*
complex selecting, **51–52**
compound paths
    in Appearance palette, 171
    creating, **32–33**, *33*
compound shapes
    creating, **33–34**, *34*
    for inside shadows, 200, *201*
    in transformations, **60–61**, *60–61*
Compressed option, **97–98**
Compressed SVG (SVGZ), 15
compression, **11–12**
confirming images
    in GIF, **232**
    in JPEG, **236**
Constrain Angle setting, **132**
constraining in transformations, **60**
converting
    buttons to symbols, **201–202**, *201*
    color tables to swatches, **157–159**, *158–159*
    graphics, **21**
    layers to frames, **286–288**, *287*
copying
    art into Flash, **290–291**
    layers for rollover buttons, 204, *204*
    objects, **52**, *52–53*

pages, **107–108**
in seamless patterns, 221, *221*
for transformations, **60**
core transform tools, **55–56**, *57–59*
Corner Radius setting, **132**
cropping, **224–225**, *225*
CSS layers
  exporting to, **101**, *101*
  generating, **253**
CSSs (Cascading Style Sheets)
  in Dreamweaver, **124**
  for graphics space, **3**, *3*
  for HTML background color, **115–116**
  settings for, **96**
current fills and strokes, 40
Curve Quality option, **93**
custom options for color reduction algorithm, **85**
customizing shortcuts, **163–164**, *164*

D

Decimal Places (1–7) option, **98**
<def> tag, **305–306**
Default Language setting, **141**
defaults
  adjusting, **161–162**
  dictionary, **141**
  fill and stroke, **42**, *42*
defined areas, cropping to, **224–225**, *225*
Delete Color control, 100, *100*
Delete Graphic Style button, **177**
Delete Selected Item option, **173**
Delete Settings command, 78
design of graphics, **19**
Design View in Dreamweaver, **125**, *125–126*
Diffusion dithering option, 86
Digital Subscriber Line (DSL), **16**
Direct selection tool, **49–50**
  for aligning, **53**, *53*
  for basic selecting, **50–51**
  for complex selecting, **51–52**
  for duplicating, **52**, *52–53*
Disable Auto Add/Delete option, **133**
Disable Warnings option, **133**
distorted object animation, **283–285**, *283–285*
Dither Amount setting, **87**
dithering
  amount of, **87**
  avoiding, 18

methods for, **86**
in preview, **83**, *84*
Dithering Algorithm setting, **86**
Divide Slice dialog box, 248, *248*
dividing
  areas, 81
  slices, **248**, *248–249*
document features, **24**
  Artboard, **24**, *25*
  Page Tiling, **25**, *25*
  Pasteboard, **24–25**, *25*
Document Setup dialog box, 149
domes, **197–198**, *197–198*
Dreamweaver
  file dimensions in, **110**
    in Layout View, **110–111**, *111*
    table cell size, **111–112**
  HTML background colors in, **123**, *124*
    with CSSs, **124**
    in Design View, **125**, *125–126*
    in layers, **127**, *127*
  rollover buttons in, **207**, *207*
drop-down menus for CSSs, 3, *3*
drop shadows
  group perspective, **180–181**, *180–181*
  layers for, 170, *170*
  for objects, 176, *176*
DSL (Digital Subscriber Line), **16**
Duplicate selected Item option, **173**
duplicating
  art into Flash, **290–291**
  layers for rollover buttons, 204, *204*
  objects, **52**, *52–53*
  pages, **107–108**
  in seamless patterns, 221, *221*
  for transformations, **60**
dynamic options for color reduction algorithm, **85**

E

E-mail Me buttons, **212**, *212*
  envelope objects, **212**, *212*
  postmark, **213**, *213*
  Shopping Cart icons, **215–216**, *216*
  stamp, **214–215**, *214*
Edit Output Settings command, **79–83**
Edit Style Sheets dialog box, 124
Edit SVG filter dialog box, 312–313, *313*
editing views, **151–152**, *151–152*

effects, applying, **175–176**, *176*
element tags, **299–305**, *303*
<ellipse> tag, **302**
embedded font information, 96
Encoding options, **97**
entities for code reuse, **305**
envelopes
    creating, **212**, *212*
    objects in, **36–37**, *37*
exclude mode for compound shapes, 61, *61*
existing files and graphics
    HTML background color of, **114–115**
    size of, **106**
export
    for animation, **285**
        banner ads, **288–290**, *288–290*
        converting layers to frames, **286–288**, *287*
        pasting art, **290–291**
    to CSS layers, **101**, *101*
Export As: AI Layers To SWF Files option, **94**
Export As CSS Layers option, **227**, *227*
Export dialog box, 204, *205*, 286
extrusions for 3D animation, **276–277**, *277*
Eyedropper tool
    in Save for Web, **76**
    for swatches, 154, *154*

F

fade-in animation, **272–274**, *272–274*
families of colors, **156–157**, *157*
file dimensions in Dreamweaver, **110**
    in Layout View, **110–111**, *111*
    table cell size, **111–112**
file formats, **5**
    color in, **8**
    GIF, **8–10**, *9–11*
    JPEG, **11–12**, *11–12*
    lossy and lossless compression, **11–12**
    pixel-based graphics vs. vector, **6–7**, *6–7*
    PNG, **12–13**, *13*
    SVG, **14–15**, *15*
    SWF, **13–14**, *14*
Files & Clipboard preferences, **142–143**, *142*, 291
fills
    brushes and color for, 176
    cardinal focal, 172
    in SVG, **299–300**
    swatches for, **41–42**

    working with, **39–40**, *40*
filters in SVG, **311–313**, *313*
fixed options for color reduction, **85**
Flash, pasting art into, **290–291**
Floating Box palette, 123
floating boxes, 3
Font Location option, **95–96**
Font Subsetting option, **95**
formats
    file. *See* file formats
    for GIFs, **233**
    for JPEGs, **237**
    for SWF, **93–94**, *93*
Formatting section, 80
Forward buttons, **211**, *211*
4-Up tab, **71**
Frame Rate option, **93**
frames
    converting layers to, **286–288**, *287*
    in SWF, **93**
    working with, **3–4**, *4*
Free Distort dialog box, 180–181, *181*

G

<g> tag, **304**
gathering required information, **103**
    HTML background color. *See* HTML background color
    pixel dimensions. *See* pixel dimensions
General web preferences, **131–134**, *131*
Generate HTML option, **94**
generating
    complete pages, **19–20**, *20*
    CSS layers, **253**
GIF (Graphics Interchange Format), **8–10**, *9–11*, **84**, *84*
    color in
        matte, **87–88**
        reducing and adjusting, **234–235**, *234*
        settings for, **85–86**
    Dither Amount setting, **87**
    Dithering Algorithm setting, **86**
    Interlaced option, **88**
    Lossy slider, **84**
    optimizing, **232–236**, *234*
    Transparency setting, **87**
    Web Snap option, **89**
global swatches, **155**, *155–156*
glyphs, 95

Glyphs palette, 211, *211*
goals for graphics
    converting graphics, **21**
    generating complete pages, **19–20**, *20*
    single graphics, **21**
GoLive
    background color in, **119–120**
        in grids, **120–121**, *121*
        in layers, **123**, *123*
        in tables, **122**, *122*
    pixel dimensions in, **107–108**
        graphics in grids, **108–109**, *108*
        graphics in tables, **109–110**, *109*
    rollover buttons in, **205**, *205–206*
gradient meshes, strokes for, **182–183**, *182–183*
Gradient palette and gradients
    in duplicating objects, 52
    for fill and stroke, 42
    in GIF, 9, *9*
    for inside shadows, 199, *199*
    for left-side art, 218, *218*
    for patterns, 40
    for pill buttons, 193, *193*
    for swatches, 43
    Tool palette for, **42**
graphic space in HTML, **2**
    CSSs, **3**, *3*
    frames, **3–4**, *4*
    PDF files, **5**, *5*
    tables, **2**
Graphic Styles palette and graphic styles, 170–171, 176, *176*
    menu on, **177–178**
    saving appearances as, **176–179**, *176*
graphics
    converting, **21**
    goals for
        converting graphics, **21**
        generating complete pages, **19–20**, *20*
        single. *See* buttons; single graphics
    size of
        existing, **106**
        in GoLive, **108–110**, *108–109*
        new, **105–106**
        on websites, **106–107**, *107*
Graphics Interchange Format. *See* GIF (Graphics Interchange Format)
graphs, **38**
Greeking option, **135**

Grid preferences, **138**, *140*
grids in GoLive
    background color in, **120–121**, *121*
    graphics size in, **108–109**, *108*
group outlines, **179–180**, *179–180*
group perspective drop shadows, **180–181**, *180–181*
groups
    clipping, 29
    for objects, **170–171**, *170–171*
    working with, **27–28**, *27*
guided movement animation, **281–283**, *282–283*
guides
    setting for, **138**, *139*
    slices from, **246–247**, *247*
    working with, **35**, *35*
Guides & Grid web preferences, **138–139**, *138–140*

H

Hand tool, **72**
hex color numbers, **127**
hiding
    objects, **65**
    slices, **249**
Home button, **210**, *210*
hot points for text, 54, *55*
HTML
    background color for. *See* HTML background color
    graphic space in, **2**
        CSSs, **3**, *3*
        frames, **3–4**, *4*
        PDF files, **5**, *5*
        tables, **2**
    output options for, **80–82**, *81*
    page layout for, **242–243**, *242–243*
    previewing results, **221–222**, *221–222*
    text slice controls, **75**, *75*, **252**, *252*
HTML background color, **112–113**, *112–113*
    determining, **113–114**
        existing files, **114–115**
        in pages with CSSs, **115–116**
    in Dreamweaver, **123**, *124*
        with CSSs, **124**
        in Design View, **125**, *125–126*
        in layers, **127**, *127*
    in GoLive, **119–120**
        in grids, **120–121**, *121*
        in layers, **123**, *123*
        in tables, **122**, *122*

for layers, **118–119**
pasting hex color numbers for, **127**
for tables, **116–118**, *117*
Hyphenation preferences, **140–141**, *141*

I

ICC Profile option, **91**
icons, **209**
    E-mail Me buttons, **212–216**, *212–216*
    Forward/Back buttons, **211**, *211*
    Home button, **210**, *210*
Image Format options, **94**
Image Location option, **96**
image maps for links, 255, *255*
Image Size controls, **100–101**, 100*ii*
image slice controls, **73**
<image> tag, **303**
ImageReady
    banner ad animation in, **288–290**, *288–290*
    converting layers to frames in, **286–288**, *287*
    rollover buttons in, **207–208**, *208*
images, **29–30**, *30*
    background, 217, *217*
        left-side art, **218–220**, *218–220*
        previewing HTML results, **221–222**, *221–222*
        seamless patterns, **220–221**, *220–221*
implementation of graphics, **19**
imported art, swatches from, **154–155**
Include Extended Syntax For Variable Data option, 99
Include File Info option, 99
Include Slicing Data option, 99
Info palette, 134
Insert Rollover Image dialog box, 207, *207*
inside shadows, **198–200**, *199–201*
Inspector palette
    for background color, 119–122
    for floating boxes, 123
    for graphic size, 109–110, *109*
    interactivity in SVG, **295–296**
        linking in, **306–308**
        rollovers in, **308–311**, *310–311*
interface buttons, **196–197**, *196–197*
interlaced GIFs, 10, *10–11*, **88**
intersect mode for compound shapes, 61, *61*
invisible links, **256–257**, *256*
Item appearance settings, **172**

J

JavaScript, **309–311**, *310–311*
joins
    for animation, 269
    for strokes, 45–46
JPEG (Joint Photographic Experts Group), **11–12**, *11–12*, **89**, *89*
    Blur option, **91**
    ICC Profile option, **91**
    matte color, **91**
    Optimized option, **89**
    optimizing, **236–237**
    Progressive option, **90**
    Quality option, **89–90**, *90*

K

Keyboard Increment setting, **131**
Keyboard Shortcuts dialog box, 163–164, *164*
kicking animation, **283–285**, *283–285*

L

L pattern pages, **262–265**, *264*
large graphics, troubleshooting, **228–229**, *229*
Large List View command, **178**
Layer appearance settings, **172**
layer masks, 29, *29*
Layers palette and layers, **61–62**, *62*
    for animation, 268, *268*
        3D, 278, *278*
        fade-in, 274, *274*
        kicking, 284, *285*
    for attributes, 175
    background color in, **123**, *123*, **127**, *127*
    for clipping masks, 107
    for compound shapes, 34, *34*
    converting to frames, **286–288**, *287*
    CSS, 3
        exporting to, **101**, *101*
        generating, 253
    in Dreamweaver, **127**, *127*
    in GoLive, **123**, *123*
    for gradients, 48
    for groups, 27–28, *27*
    HTML background colors for, **118–119**
    for HTML pages, 243, *243*
    for locking and hiding, **65**

for masks, **65**, *65*
for object classes, 25
for objects, **63**, *63*, **170–171**, *170–171*
for optimizing file sections, **226–227**, *227*
for Release to Layers, **66–67**, *66*
for rollover buttons, **204–205**, *204–205*, **207–208**, *208*
for targets and selection, **63–65**, *63–64*
troubleshooting with, **228–229**, *229*
layout
building, **261**
HTML page, **242–243**, *242–243*
L pattern pages, **262–265**, *264*
Layout View in Dreamweaver, **110–111**, *111*
left-side art, **218**
gradient fade effects for, **218**, *218*
short stripes for, **218**, *219*
wave patterns for, **219–220**, *219*
libraries, **44–45**
lighting
bevel buttons, 188, *188*
pill buttons, **192–194**, *192–194*
<line> tag, **302**
Link Slices command, **79**, *80*
linked font information, 96
links and linking, **253–254**
basic, **254–256**, *255*
images, 30
invisible, **256–257**, *256*
slice, **258–259**, *261*
in SVG, **295–296**, **306–308**
SWF, **257–258**
text, **259–261**, *259–260*
loading swatches, **159–160**, *160*
Lock Color control, 100, *100*
locking
objects, **65**
slices, **249**
lossy and lossless compression, **11–12**
Lossy slider, **84**

M

maps for links, 255, *255*
masks
clipping, **28–29**, *28–29*
Layers palette for, **65**, *65*
for pages, **107**
matte color
in GIF, **87–88**

in HTML background, 112–113, *112–113*
in JPEG, **91**
menus for CSSs, 3, *3*
Merge Graphic Styles command, **178**
meshes
for envelopes, 37
for pill buttons, 192–193, *192–193*
strokes for, **182–183**, *182–183*
working with, **35–36**, *36*
Message field, **74**, **251**
modem transfer times, **16**
Monitor RGB option, **144**
monitor size, **165–168**, *165–168*
motion and opacity animation, **271–272**
2D rotation, **281**, *281*
3D, **275–278**, *275–278*
distorted object, **283–285**, *283–285*
fade-in, **272–274**, *272–274*
guided movement, **281–283**, *282–283*
rotation loops, **278–280**, *278–280*

N

names
for color, **17**
for image slices, **73**, **250–251**
for objects, **138**
Names option, **138**
navigation elements, 242, *242*
New Art Has Basic Appearance option, **173**
New Brush dialog box, 283–284
New Color control, 100, *100*
New Document dialog box, 105–106, 145, *145*, 166
new documents, **145**, *145*
Artboard settings for, **146–149**, *147–148*
setup options for, **149**
New Graphic Style button, **177**
new graphics, size of, **105–106**
New Swatch dialog box, 192, *192*
No Dither option, 86
no-image slices, **74–75**, *75*, **252**, *252*
Noise dithering option, 86
None dithering option, 86
Numbers Without Units Are Points option, **137**
numeric transforming, **56**, *57*

O

object classes, **25–26**
blends, **38–39**, *39*

clipping masks, **28–29**, *28–29*
compound paths, **32–33**, *33*
compound shapes, **33–34**, *34*
envelopes, **36–37**, *37*
graphs, **38**
groups, **27–28**, *27*
guides, **35**, *35*
images, **29–30**, *30*
meshes, **35–36**, *36*
paths, **26**, *26*
slices, **37**, *37*, **244–245**, *245*
symbols, **31–32**, *31–32*
Object Selection by Path Only option, **132**
Objects palette and objects
    for grids, 108–109
    Layers palette for, **63**, *63*
    for layout, 110–111
    styling hierarchy of, **170–171**, *170–171*
Offset Path dialog box, 189
opacity
    in animation. *See* motion and opacity animation
    in GIF, 10
openness in SVG, **295–296**
Optimize For Adobe SVG Viewer option, 99
Optimize menu, **78–83**, *80–81*
Optimize palette, 288
Optimize To File Size dialog box, **78–79**
Optimized option, **89**
Optimized tab, 70
optimizing
    file sections, **224**
        cropping to defined areas, **224–225**, *225*
        layers for, **226–227**, *227*
        slices, **225–226**, *226*
    GIFs, **84–89**, *84*, **232–236**, *234*
    JPEGs, **89–91**, *89*, **236–237**
    output options, **230–231**, *231*
    pre-rasterizing art for, **231**, *231*
    SVG, **95–98**, *95*
    SWF, **92–94**, *93*
orientation, text, **54**
Original tab, 70, *71*
outline live type effect, **183–184**, *183–184*
Output Options dialog box, 253
output options in optimizing, **230–231**, *231*
Output Settings dialog box, **79–80**
    background options, **82–83**
    for HTML, **80–82**, *81*, 222
    saving file options, **83**

Over option, 205, *206*
Override Character Color command, **178**

P

Page Properties for background color
    in Dreamweaver, 123, *124*
    in GoLive, 119, *120*
Page Tiling, **25**, *25*
pages, **241**
    background color. *See* HTML background color
    common layout for, **261–265**
    CSS layers for, **253**
    layout for, **242–243**, *242–243*
    links for. *See* links and linking
    pasting and masking, **107**
    slicing. *See* slices
palettes, color. *See* color palettes; reusable color palettes
Pasteboard, **24–25**, *25*
pasting
    art into Flash, **290–291**
    hex color numbers, **127**
    pages, **107**
path object type, 171
<path> tag, **303**
path type for text, **55**
Pathfinder palette
    for 3D animation, 275
    for compound shapes, 34, *34*, 61
    for inside shadows, 199, *199*
    for stamp buttons, 215
paths
    in Appearance palette, 171
    components of, **26**, *26*
    compound, **32–33**, *33*
    for envelopes, 37
    for tabs, 195–196, *195–196*
Pattern dithering option, 86
patterns
    seamless, **220–221**, *220–221*
    wave, **219–220**, *219*
PDF files, **5**, *5*
Perceptual option, 85
Photoshop Options dialog box
    for exporting files, 286
    for rollover buttons, 204–205, *205*
pill buttons, **190–194**, *191–194*
pixel-based graphics, **6–7**, *6–7*

pixel dimensions, **104**
    of common elements, **104–105**
    in Dreamweaver, **110**
        for graphics, **110–111**, *111*
        for table cells, **111–112**
    in GoLive, **107–108**
        graphics in grids, **108–109**, *108*
        graphics in tables, **109–110**, *109*
    size of graphics
        existing, **106**
        new, **105–106**
        on websites, **106–107**, *107*
Place dialog box
    for graphic size, 106
    for symbols, 30, *31*
plug-in requirements in SVG, **297**
Plug-ins & Scratch Disks preferences, **141–142**, *142*
Plug-ins Folder setting, **141**
PNG (Portable Network Graphics) format
    optimization options, **88**
    working with, **12–13**, *13*
point of transformation, **56**
point type, **54**
points for paths, 26, *26*
<polygon> tag, **302**
polygonal image maps, 255, *255*
<polyline> tag, **302**
Portable Network Graphics (PNG) format
    optimization options, **88**
    working with, **12–13**, *13*
postmark buttons, **213**, *213*
pre-rasterizing art, **231**, *231*
preferences
    for output, **80**, *81*
    web. *See* web
preview bounds for transformations, **59–60**
Preview menu, **83**, *84*
preview models, **149–151**, *151*
previewing
    HTML results, **221–222**, *221–222*
    in Save for Web dialog box, **77**, *77*
Profile Mismatch dialog box, 145
Profile Mismatches settings, **145**
progressive JPEGs, 12, **90**
Properties palette
    for Dreamweaver background, 125, *125–126*
    for graphic size, 111–112

Q

quality in JPEG, **89–90**, *90*, **237**

R

Rasterize dialog box, 231, *231*
Read Only option, **92**
<rect> tag, **301–302**
Rectangle Grid Tool Options dialog box, 216, *216*
rectangular image maps, 255, *255*
Red, Green Blue (RGB) color space
    working space options for, **144**
    working with, 8
Redefine Style command, **174**
Reduce To Basic Appearance option, **173**
reducing
    GIF colors, **234–235**, *234*
    JPEG quality, **237**
reference points for transformations, **59**
Reflect dialog box, 196
reflecting objects, 56, *58*
Release to Layers command, **66–67**, *66*
Repopulate Views command, 79
Reset All Warning Dialogs option, **134**
resolution
    of monitors, **165–168**, *165–168*
    in SWF, **94**
Resolution option, **94**
reusable color palettes, **153**
    for converting color table to swatches, **157–159**, *158–159*
    for creating swatches
        global, **155**, *155–156*
        from imported art, **154–155**
        without selecting, **154**, *154*
    families of colors on, **156–157**, *157*
    for loading swatches, **159–160**, *160*
    for saving swatches, **159–160**, *160*
        color as, **153–154**, *153*
        for everyday use, **161**
        for semi-regular use, **160–161**, *160*
RGB (Red, Green Blue) color space
    working space options for, **144**
    working with, 8
rollover buttons, **202**
    in Dreamweaver, **207**, *207*
    in GoLive, **205**, *205–206*
    in ImageReady, **207–208**, *208*
    setting up, **204–205**, *204–205*

sizing, **203**, *203*
for SVG files, **308–311**, *310–311*
SWF links with, **257–258**
Rotate dialog box, 281
Rotate tool, 281, *281*
rotating objects, 56, *58*
rotation loops, **278–280**, *278–280*
Rounded rectangle tool, 195, *195*

S

Save dialog box
    for extensions, 142
    options in, 98
Save As dialog box, 160, *160*
Save for Web dialog box, **69–70**, *71*, 147, *147–148*
    color readouts in, **76–77**
    Color table controls, **99–100**, *100*
    for exporting to CSS layers, **101**, *101*
    Eyedropper tool in, **76**
    for GIFs, **84–89**, *84*
    Hand tool in, **72**
    Image Size controls, **100–101**, *100ii*
    JPEG optimization controls, **89–91**, *89–90*
    for JPEGs, **236**
    for links, 260, *260*
    Optimize menu in, **78–83**, *80–81*
    Preview menu in, **83**, *84*
    previewing in, **77**, *77*
    Settings menu in, **78**, *78*
    Slice Select tool in, **72–75**
    SVG optimization controls, **95–99**, *95, 99*
    SWF optimization controls, **92–94**, *93*
    Toggle Slices Visibility option in, **76**
    view tabs, **70–72**
    Zoom Level option in, **76**
    Zoom tool in, **75**
Save Optimized As dialog box
    for background images, 221, *221*
    for output settings, 79
    for rollover buttons, 205
    for slices, 226, *226*
    for text links, 261
Save Output As dialog box, 78
Save Settings command, 78
saving
    appearances as graphic styles, **176–179**, *176*
    color as swatches, **153–154**, *153*
    GIF settings, **235–236**

JPEG settings, **237**
    options for, **83**
    swatches, **159–160**, *160*
        for everyday use, **161**
        for semi-regular use, **160–161**, *160*
    views, **151–152**, *151–152*
    to web formats, **230**
scalable art, **295**, *295*
Scalable Vector Graphics. *See* SVG (Scalable Vector Graphics) format
Scale dialog box, 134
Scale Strokes & Effects option, **134**
scaling
    images, 30
    objects, 56, *57*
    in SWF format, 13, *14*
scatter brushes, 283, *283*
Scratch Disks setting, **142**
scripting, **238–239**
    batch actions for, **240**
    building actions in, **239–240**
    resources for, **238**
    for SVG rollovers, **309–311**, *310–311*
seamless patterns, **220–221**, *220–221*
seamless rotation loops, **278–280**, *278–280*
segments for paths, 26, *26*
Select All Unused command, **178**
Select Same Tint Percentage option, **133**
selections
    Direct selection tool for. *See* Direct selection tool
    Layers palette for, **63–65**, *63–64*
    slices from, **246–247**, *247*
Selective option, 85
semi-regular use, saving swatches for, **160–161**, *160*
Settings menu, **78**, *78*
Settings section, **143**
setup options for new documents, **149**
shadows
    for buttons, **198–200**, *199–201*
    group perspective, **180–181**, *180–181*
    layers for, 170, *170*
    for objects, 176, *176*
Shape dialog box, 186–187, *187*
shapes
    compound
        creating, **33–34**, *34*
        for inside shadows, 200, *201*
        in transformations, **60–61**, *60–61*
    for text boxes, 186–187, *187*

shearing objects, 56, *59*
ShockWave Flash format. *See* SWF (ShockWave Flash) format
Shopping Cart icons, **215–216**, *216*
short stripes for left-side art, **218**, *219*
shortcuts, customizing, **163–164**, *164*
Show Font Names in English option, **135**
Show Tool Tips option, **133**
single graphics, **169**
    Appearance palettes. *See* Appearance palette and appearances
    background images, **217–222**, *217–222*
    buttons. *See* buttons
    creating, **21**
    Graphic Styles palette, 170–171, **176**, *176*
        menu on, **177–178**
        saving appearances as, **176–179**, *176*
    symbols and icons, **209–216**
size
    of common elements, **104–105**
    of graphics
        in Dreamweaver, **110–111**, *111*
        existing, **106**
        in GoLive, **108–110**, *108–109*
        new, **105–106**
        on websites, **106–107**, *107*
    of monitors, **165–168**, *165–168*
    of rollover buttons, **203**, *203*
    of table cells, **111–112**
    of type, **137**
Size/Download Time option, **83**
Size/Leading option, **134–135**
Slice Options dialog box, **250–252**, *250*, *252*, 259, 261
Slice Output section, **81–82**
Slice Select tool, **72**
    options for, **73–74**, *73*
        HTML text, **75**, *75*
        No image, **74–75**, *75*
    in Save for Web dialog box, **72–75**
slices, 37, *37*, **243–244**, *243–244*
    displaying, 140
    dividing and combining, **248**, *248–249*
    from guides and selections, **246–247**, *247*
    links to, **258–259**, 261
    locking and hiding, **249**
    optimizing file sections, **225–226**, *226*
    options for, **250–252**, *250*, *252*
    output settings for, **81–82**
    stacking order with, **245–246**, *246*

    standard and object, **244–245**, *245*
    troubleshooting with, **228–229**, *229*
Slices setting, 140
small graphics, troubleshooting, **228**, *229*
Small List View command, **178**
Smart Guides & Slices preferences, **140**, *141*
SmartObjects, 21, 208
smoothing color, 112–113, *112–113*
Snap To Point feature, **53**, *53*
Sort By Name command, **178**
spacer graphics, 8
spines for blends, 273, *273*
spot illustrations, **223**
    automation in, **238–240**
    optimizing
        file sections, **224–229**, *225–227*, *229*
        GIFs, **232–236**, *234*
        JPEGs, **236–237**
        output options, **230–231**, *231*
        pre-rasterizing art, **231**, *231*
    troubleshooting, **228–229**, *229*
square caps and joins, 269
sRGB option, **144**
stacking order
    for appearance, **174–175**, *174–175*
    for slices, **245–246**, *246*
stamp buttons, **214–215**, *214*
standard slices, **244–245**, *245*
stop-frame animation, **269–271**, *270–271*
Stroke palette and strokes, **39–40**, *40*
    for gradient meshes, **182–183**, *182–183*
    in SVG, **300**
    swatches for, **41–42**
    behind type, **182**, *182*
    working with, **45–46**, *46*
Style Options command, 177, **179**
Style palette and styles, **49**
    for fill and stroke, 42
    saving appearances as, **176–179**, *176*
    in SVG, **299–305**, *303*
subtract mode for compound shapes, 61, *61*
SVG (Scalable Vector Graphics) format, **14–15**, *15*, **293**
    attributes for, **298–299**
    basics, **294**
    benefits of, **294–296**, *295*, *297*
    code in
        requirements for, **296–297**
        reuse of, **305–306**
    element tags for, **299–305**, *303*

filters in, **311–313**, *313*
interactivity in, **295–296**
    linking in, **306–308**
    rollovers in, **308–311**, *310–311*
optimization controls, **95**, *95*
    additional options, **98–99**, *99*
    Compressed option, **97–98**
    CSS Properties options, **96**
    Decimal Places (1–7) option, **98**
    Encoding options, **97**
    Font Location option, **95–96**
    Font Subsetting option, **95**
    Image Location option, **96**
pitfalls of, **296–297**
for text, 7, 14, *15*, **295–296**, *297*
SVG Options dialog box, 305
SVGZ (Compressed SVG), 15
swapping fill and stroke, **41**, *41*
Swatch Options dialog box, 44, *44*, 153, **155–156**, *155–156*, 159
Swatches palette and swatches
    for attributes, 47
    for background color, 119–123, *120–121*, *123*
    converting color tables to, **157–159**, *158–159*
    creating without selecting, **154**, *154*
    for domes, 198, *198*
    for fills and strokes, **41–42**, 176
    global, **155**, *155–156*
    in GoLive, 119–123, *120–121*, *123*
    from imported art, **154–155**
    loading, **159–160**, *160*
    saving, **159–160**, *160*
        for everyday use, **161**
        for semi-regular use, **160–161**, *160*
    saving color as, **153–154**, *153*
    working with, **43–44**, *43–44*
SWF (ShockWave Flash) format, 7, **13–14**, *14*
    layers in, 271, 274
    optimization controls, **92**
        Curve Quality option, **93**
        format options, **93–94**, *93*
        Frame Rate option, **93**
        Read Only option, **92**
        Type of Export menu, **92**
    for rollover links, **257–258**
SWF Options dialog box, 271, 274
Symbol Strainer tool, 202, *202*
<symbol> tag, **304–305**

symbols
    E-mail Me buttons, **212–216**, *212–216*
    Forward/Back buttons, **211**, *211*
    Home button, **210**, *210*
    for stop-frame animation, 270, *270*
    for text, **209**
    workflow for, **201–202**, *201*
    working with, **31–32**, *31–32*
Symbols palette, 31, *31*

T

<table> tag, 122, *122*
tables, **2**, *2*
    Color
        controls for, **99–100**, *100*
        converting to swatches, **157–159**, *158–159*
        in GIF, 9, *9*
    in GoLive
        background color in, **122**, *122*
        graphics size in, **109–110**, *109*
        HTML background colors for, **116–118**, *117*
        size of cells in Dreamweaver, **111–112**
tabs, **194–196**, *194–196*
tags in SVG, **299–305**, *303*
targets
    for image slices, **74**, 251
    Layers palette for, **63–65**, *63–64*
    for SVG file linking, **307–308**
<td> tag, 122, *122*
templates, browser, **164–168**, *165–168*
text, **53**
    for animation, **269**
    graphics for, 6–7
    for inside shadows, 200, *201*
    in SVG, 14, *15*, **295–296**, *297*
    type, **54–55**, *55*
Text Displayed In Cell field
    for HTML text, **75**, 252
    for slices
        HTML text, 252
        image, 75
        no-image, 252
Text Is HTML option, 252
text links, **259–261**, *259–260*
3D animation, **275–278**
3D Extrude & Bevel dialog box, 276
3D Mapping dialog box, 276–277, *277*

3D Options dialog box, 188, *188*, 276–277, *277*
Thumbnail View command, **178**
Toggle Slices Visibility option, **76**
Tools palette
   color controls
      Color, Gradient, and None, **42**
      fill and stroke swatches, **41–42**, *41–42*
   for fill and stroke attributes, 39
   for view depth, 106
Top Object envelopes, 37, *37*
<tr> tag, 122, *122*
Tracing Gap option, **136**
Tracking option, **135**
transfer times, **15**
   in cable, **17**
   in DSL, **16**
   in modems, **16**
Transform palette and transformations
   compound shapes, **60–61**, *60–61*
   core transform tools, **55–56**, *57–59*
   for graphic size, 106–107, *107*
   options in, **59–60**, *59*
Transform Pattern Tiles option, **134**
Transparency palette and transparency
   in GIF, 10, *10*, **87**
   in PNG, 13, *13*
   in SVG, **300–301**
   for tabs, 196, *196*
   working with, **46–47**, *47*
troubleshooting with slices and layers, **228–229**, *229*
tweening, 289
Twist dialog box, 220
twist effects, 175, *175*
2-Up tab, **71**
2D rotation animation, **281**, *281*
type, **54–55**. *See also* text
   outline live effects, **183–184**, *183–184*
   size, 137
   strokes behind, **182**, *182*
Type & Auto Tracing preferences, **134–136**, *135*
Type Area Select option, **135**
Type of Export menu, **92**

U

Undo: Minimum Undo Levels setting, **137**
Units & Undo preferences, **136–138**, *137*
Units: General setting, **137**
Units: Stroke setting, **137**
Units: Type setting, **137**
Unlink All Slices command, **79**
Unlink Slices command, **79**
Update Links option, **142**
URLs for image slices, **74**, **251**
Use Area Select option, 50–51
Use Low Resolution Proxy for Linked EPS option, **143**
Use Precise Cursors option, **132**
Use Preview Bounds option, **59–60**, **134**
<use> tag, **304–305**

V

vector graphics, **6–7**, *6–7*
view tabs
   2-Up option, **71**
   4-Up option, **71**
   optimized option, **70**
   original option, **70**
viewBox in SVG, 298
views, saving and editing, **151–152**, *151–152*
visual transforming, 56, *57–59*

W

warp envelopes, 37, *37*
wave patterns, **219–220**, *219*
web
   button issues in, **186–187**, *186–187*
   formats for, **230**
   graphics size on, **106–107**, *107*
   pages on. *See* pages
   preferences for, **130–131**
      Color, **143–145**, *144*
      Files & Clipboard, **142–143**, *142*
      General, **131–134**, *131*
      Guides & Grid, **138–139**, *138–140*
      Hyphenation, **140–141**, *141*
      Plug-ins & Scratch Disks, **141–142**, *142*
      Smart Guides & Slices, **140**, *141*
      Type & Auto Tracing, **134–136**, *135*
      Units & Undo, **136–138**, *137*
   save options for. *See* Save for Web dialog box
   terms and concepts, **2**
      color issues, **17–18**
      file formats. *See* file formats
      graphic space in HTML, **2–5**, *2–5*
      transfer times, **15–17**

workflow, **18–19**
    basic goals, **19–21**, *20*
    design and implementation, **19**
web-safe colors
    for GIFs, **235**
    purpose of, **18**
    RGB, 42, *43*
Web Snap, **89**, 100, *100*
Wingdings typeface, 212, *212*
wipes, 270, *270*
work environment, **129**
    browser templates, **164–168**, *165–168*
    defaults, **161–162**
    new documents, **145–149**, *145–148*
    preview models, **149–151**, *151*
    reusable color palettes. *See* reusable color palettes
    saving and editing views, **151–152**, *151–152*
    shortcuts, **163–164**, *164*
    web preferences. *See* web
Working Spaces: CMYK settings, **145**
Working Spaces: RGB settings, **144**

Z

Zapf Dingbats typeface, 209
Zoom Level option, **76**
Zoom tool, **75**

Get Savvy

Sybex introduces Savvy,™ a new series of in-depth, premium graphics and web books. Savvy books turn beginning and intermediate level graphics professionals into experts, and give advanced users a meaningful edge in this competitive climate.

In-Depth Coverage. Each book contains compelling, professional examples and illustrations to demonstrate the use of the program in a working environment.

Proven Authors. Savvy authors have the first-hand knowledge and experience to deliver useful insights, making even the most advanced discussions accessible.

Sophisticated Package. Savvy titles have a striking interior design, enhanced by high-quality, coated paper for crisp graphic reproduction.

Flash™ MX 2004 Savvy
by Ethan Watrall
and Norbert Herber
ISBN: 0-7821-4284-2
US $44.99

Photoshop® CS Savvy
by Steve Romaniello
ISBN: 0-7821-4280-X
US $44.99

Maya™ 5 Savvy
by John Kundert-Gibbs,
Peter Lee, Darius Derakhshani,
and Eric Kunzendorf
ISBN: 0-7821-4230-3
US $59.99

Dreamweaver® MX 2004 Savvy
by Christian Crumlish and
Lucinda Dykes
ISBN: 0-7821-4306-7
US $44.99

www.sybex.com

Style. Substance. Sybex.

Solutions™ FROM SYBEX®

iMovie 3 Solutions brings high-end visual effects to the iMovie community with easy-to-follow projects, step-by-step instructions, and companion sample videos. Whether you're a hobbyist, a budding producer, or a dedicated video prosumer, *iMovie 3 Solutions* will help you create unique and breathtaking videos on a budget.

The companion CD is packed with project videos, as well as a 30-day fully functional version of Photoshop Elements.

iMovie™ 3 Solutions™: Tips, Tricks, and Special Effects
by Erica Sadun
ISBN: 0-7821-4247-8 • US $40.00

Photoshop® Elements 2 Solutions™
by Mikkel Aaland
ISBN: 0-7821-4140-4
US $40.00   full color throughout

With **Photoshop Elements 2 Solutions**, noted photographer and author Mikkel Aaland has thoroughly updated his best-seller to include all the smart new features in the latest version of the program. Learn everything from how to fix bothersome red eye to how to fuse images to make beautiful panoramic pictures.

The companion CD comes with utilities to make your work easier, plus trial versions of fun and useful plug-ins.

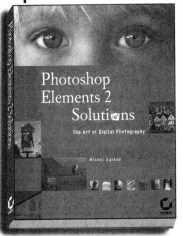

Coming soon:

DVD Studio Pro® 2 Solutions
by Erica Sadun
ISBN 0-7821-4234-6
US $39.99

Acrobat® and PDF Solutions
by Taz Tally
ISBN 0-7821-4273-7
US $34.99

www.sybex.com

Shooting Digital: Pro Tips for Taking Great Pictures with Your Digital Camera

By Mikkel Aaland
ISBN: 0-7821-4104-8
US $35.00

Noted photographer and best-selling author Mikkel Aaland has drawn on his 28 years of experience in the field to bring you *Shooting Digital: Pro Tips for Taking Great Pictures with Your Digital Camera*. Containing wisdom and images from more than 30 contributors, this tutorial covers all the bases to help you get consistently great results. Through simple instruction and illustrative examples you'll learn how to:

- Use digital-specific techniques to take great pictures of virtually everything

- Fully exploit the minimovie capabilities of your digital camera

- Recognize and compensate for the dreaded shutter release lag

- Use the LCD preview to turn portrait subjects into collaborators

- Create stunning panoramas and object movies

- Work with RAW data, the holy grail of digital photography

- Extend the tonal range of digital cameras

- Archive your digital images while on the road. And much more...

"You can't go wrong with Mikkel when it comes to working with digital imagery."

– Russ Walkowich, MyMac.com

Mikkel Aaland is an award-winning photographer and author of eight books, including *Digital Photography*, *Photoshop for the Web*, and *Photoshop Elements 2 Solutions*. His photography has been published in *Wired*, *Newsweek*, and has also been exhibited in major institutions around the world, including the Bibliothèque Nationale in Paris and the former Lenin Museum in Prague.

www.sybex.com

TELL US WHAT YOU THINK!

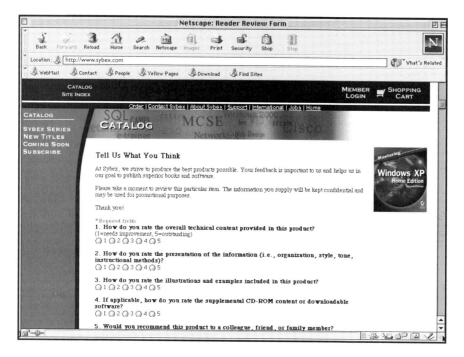

Your feedback is critical to our efforts to provide you with the best books and software on the market. Tell us what you think about the products you've purchased. It's simple:

1. Go to the Sybex website.
2. Find your book by typing the ISBN or title into the Search field.
3. Click on the book title when it appears.
4. Click **Submit a Review.**
5. Fill out the questionnaire and comments.
6. Click **Submit.**

With your feedback, we can continue to publish the highest quality computer books and software products that today's busy IT professionals deserve.

www.sybex.com

SYBEX Inc. • 1151 Marina Village Parkway, Alameda, CA 94501 • 510-523-8233